The Spanish Inquisition, 1478–1614
An Anthology of Sources

The Spanish Inquisition, 1478–1614

An Anthology of Sources

Edited and Translated by
Lu Ann Homza

Hackett Publishing Company, Inc.
Indianapolis/Cambridge

For further information, please address:
Hackett Publishing Company, Inc.
P.O. Box 44937
Indianapolis, IN 46244–0937
www.hackettpublishing.com

Cover design and cross illustration by Abigail Coyle
Text design by Meera Dash
Composition by Agnew's, Inc.
Printed at Versa Press, Inc.

Library of Congress Cataloging-in-Publication Data
The Spanish Inquisition, 1478–1614 : an anthology of sources / edited and
    translated by Lu Ann Homza
        p.   cm.
    Includes bibliographical references and index.
    ISBN 0-87220-795-1 (cloth) — ISBN 0-87220-794-3 (pbk.)
        1. Inquisition—Spain—History—Sources. 2. Spain—Church
    history—Sources. I. Homza, Lu Ann, 1958– .
BX1735.S63   2006
272'.20946—dc22   2005029082

ISBN-13: 978-0-87220-795-0 (cloth)
ISBN-13: 978-0-87220-794-3 (pbk.)

The paper used in this publication meets the minimum standard requirements of
American National Standard for Information Sciences—Permanence of Paper for
Printed Library Materials, ANSI Z39.48–1984.

CONTENTS

ACKNOWLEDGMENTS

This book has been a collaborative endeavor from the start. The idea for the volume came from Alison Weber, of the Department of Spanish, Italian, and Portuguese at the University of Virginia. She originally imagined that we would write it together but, regretfully, her other research obligations forced her to leave the project. I deeply appreciate her support, her astute ideas about potential sources, and her initiative with publishers. I am most grateful to Benjamin Ehlers of the Department of History at the University of Georgia, who vetted all the translations with great linguistic and historical sensitivity, efficiency, and good humor. I happily thank Kimberly Lynn Hossain, doctoral candidate at The Johns Hopkins University, for offering acute suggestions on numerous introductions, sending crucial materials from Madrid's Archivo Histórico Nacional, and helping me keep my audience in sight. My editor at Hackett Publishing Company, Rick Todhunter, has offered enthusiastic and diligent guidance over the last two years.

As usual, Thomas Payne was a constant source of encouragement and cheerfulness, even though the work here coincided with a number of personal and environmental accidents, most of which we can laugh about now. Finally, I dedicate this book with love to my parents, Daniel and Marjorie, who have always valued good teaching and are excellent teachers themselves.

INTRODUCTION

Although the Spanish Inquisition existed from 1478 to 1834, it belongs as much to mythology as to history. In the sixteenth century, Dutch and English Protestants seized upon it as both symbol and proof of the cruelty and fanaticism of their Spanish enemies. Two hundred years later, scholars in the United States found that the Spanish Inquisition could serve as a perfect inversion of American virtues.[1] Meanwhile, modern politicians, regardless of nationality, still tend to invoke the Spanish Inquisition in their denunciations of overly zealous prosecutions or the abuse of prisoners of war. The Spanish Inquisition, in other words, has always been useful for invective, and its very existence has been used to justify Spain's classification as a country estranged from the rest of Western Europe. After all, the methods and effects of the Spanish Inquisition seem obvious: it blended religion and politics in the persecution of difference; it used torture and secrecy to win guilty verdicts; it must have terrified the populace into submission. No wonder the Inquisition's greatest historian, writing in the early twentieth century, asserted that it demonstrates what happens when men attempt to control the consciences of others.[2]

No one would deny the power of the Spanish Inquisition as a metaphor for religious intolerance. But since 1975—when the death of Spanish dictator Francisco Franco liberated scholars to work on controversial topics in Spanish history—an explosion of publications has made it clear that the Inquisition in Spain was a historical phenomenon in the fullest sense of the phrase. It was created at a specific moment to solve a particular problem; its targets and penalties changed over time; its prosecutions could be affected by bribery, enmity, even empathy.[3] Over the last several decades, historians

1. Richard L. Kagan, "Prescott's Paradigm: American Historical Scholarship and the Decline of Spain," *American Historical Review* 101 (1996): 423–46. In *Modern Inquisitions: Peru and the Colonial Origins of the Civilized World* (Durham, NC: Duke University Press, 2004), Irene Silverblatt challenges the extent to which the Spanish Inquisition's values and effects were alien to the West's. Also see note 4 below.

2. "In Spain, under peculiar conditions, this resolve to enforce unity of belief, in the conviction that it was essential to human happiness here and hereafter, led to the framing of a system of so-called justice more iniquitous than has been evolved by the cruellest despotism. . . . [T]he great lesson taught by the history of the Inquisition is that the attempt of man to control the conscience of his fellows reacts upon himself." Henry Charles Lea, *A History of the Inquisition of Spain,* 4 vols. (New York: American Scholar Publications, Inc. 1966; first issued 1906–7), vol. 4, 532–33.

3. As a sample, see Bartolomé Bennassar, ed., *L'Inquisition espagnole, xve–xixe siècle* (Paris: Hachette, 1979); Haim Beinart, *Conversos on Trial: The Inquisition in Ciudad*

have been far more interested in pointing out fluctuations and accidents in Inquisition history than in treating this institution as a moral lesson for the rest of the world.[4] By the same token, few scholars today would seriously argue that the Spanish Inquisition demonstrates eternal truths about the Spanish character. Instead, the best recent work highlights the Inquisition's regional and chronological variation, identifies potential discrepancies between its theory and its practices, and seeks to establish the theological motives, legal discretion, and practical contexts of the inquisitors themselves. We now know that the Inquisition was never a monolithic institution, despite efforts to standardize its procedures. And while its bureaucracy was highly sophisticated, most current work disputes the idea that it functioned like a machine, if only because the officials who worked in its tribunals were all too human.

Roman Antecedents

The Spanish Inquisition was fundamentally indebted to legal developments in the Roman Empire and the Middle Ages. The term "inquisition" comes

---

Real (Jerusalem: Magnes Press, 1981); Jaime Contreras, *El Santo Oficio de la Inquisición en Galicia, 1560–1700* (Madrid: Akal, 1982); Joaquín Pérez Villanueva and Bartolomé Escandell Bonet, eds., *Historia de la Inquisición en España y América*, vols. 1 and 2 (Madrid: BAE, 1984), and *idem,* vol. 3 (Madrid: BAE, 2000); José Martínez Millán, *La hacienda de la Inquisición (1478–1700)* (Madrid: CSIC, 1984); Jean-Pierre Dedieu, *L'Administration de la foi: l'Inquisition de Tolède, XVI–XVIII siècle,* Bibliothèque de la Casa de Velázquez, vol. 7 (Madrid: Casa de Velázquez, 1989); E. William Monter, *Frontiers of Heresy: The Spanish Inquisition from the Basque Lands to Sicily* (Cambridge: Cambridge University Press, 1990); Stephen Haliczer, *The Inquisition in the Kingdom of Valencia (1478–1834)* (Berkeley: University of California Press, 1994); Lu Ann Homza, *Religious Authority in the Spanish Renaissance* (Baltimore: The Johns Hopkins University Press, 2000), chapter 1; Sara T. Nalle, *Mad for God: Bartolomé Sánchez, the Secret Messiah of Cardenete* (Charlottesville, VA: University Press of Virginia, 2001).

4. Recognizing the Spanish Inquisition's deep historical context, in *Modern Inquisitions* Irene Silverblatt nevertheless highlights the Inquisition's contributions to modernity via its contributions to bureaucracy, "race thinking," and the development of the state. Neither Silverblatt's book nor the new survey by Helen Rawlings in *The Spanish Inquisition* (Oxford: Blackwell Publishing, 2006) takes religious beliefs seriously as a motivating factor for inquisitors' actions. Rawlings writes, "[Heresy] was a suitably explosive concept that, given the prevailing religious climate, was deliberately exaggerated to justify the [Inquisition's] ends," *ibid.,* 15. It remains to be seen, of course, how historians could prove that inquisitors were "exaggerating" their perceptions of the heresies they were prosecuting.

from the Latin noun *inquisitio,* or "investigation"; it should be stressed that inquisition is fundamentally a legal procedure that was first codified in ancient Rome. By the third century CE, inquisition signified a trial for a public crime, conducted by a single magistrate whose officials carried out the search for evidence.[5] The magistrate initiated these prosecutions at his own discretion. In such a trial, the accused could be condemned by the testimony of two eyewitnesses who agreed on the details of the same event, or by a confession; either constituted a "complete proof." Yet without those two eyewitnesses or a confession, the magistrate was left with only partial proof, and no number of partial proofs could ever add up to a full one. Because complete proofs were so important, torture was used as an interrogation technique to gain a confession. Romans knew to doubt the reliability of confessions made under torture, and required that confessions obtained in such circumstances be ratified afterward.

Magistrates practicing inquisition gradually monopolized the pursuit of public crime in the Roman Empire. The definition of what constituted a public crime was simultaneously enlarged, with treason becoming the public crime par excellence under Roman emperors. The use of torture for the purpose of interrogation also became more widespread, to the point that free citizens as well as slaves could be tortured, especially in cases of treason. By the time the Roman Empire officially converted to Christianity in the fourth century, Roman criminal law was thoroughly inquisitorial in its principles, and inquisition was applied to opponents of Christian beliefs, namely heretics and pagans. The term "heretic" comes from the Greek noun *haeresis,* meaning "choice" or "thing chosen." In the Latin West, heresy came to denote a theological error; heresy was not doubt, but the formal, public denial of some aspect of orthodox Christian theology or religious practice. Because the *rejection* of Christian doctrine implied that such teaching had been formalized and disseminated in the first place, the formation of orthodoxy and heresy was related; the one couldn't exist without the other, and as Christian orthodoxy changed over time, so did definitions of heretics. When the Roman Empire embraced Christianity, enemies of religion became enemies of the state; heretics were judged guilty of treason and were liable to the same penalties—for example, fines, confiscation of goods, exclusion from inheritance, exile, and death—as other perpetrators of public crimes.

---

5. The material here is indebted to Edward Peters' magisterial account in *Inquisition* (New York: Free Press, 1988), chapter 1. For other relevant developments in medieval law and the classification of heretics, see *idem, The Magician, the Witch, and the Law* (Philadelphia: University of Pennsylvania Press, 1978), and *idem, Torture* (Philadelphia: University of Pennsylvania Press, 1987).

Medieval Inquisitions

Compilations of Roman law, such as the Emperor Justinian's *Corpus iuris civilis* (issued in 534 CE) preserved the inquisition process as well as the condemnation of heretics. Roman law in turn was resuscitated in the eleventh and especially twelfth centuries when kings and popes in Western Europe began to look for tools to help consolidate their rule. Roman law was unified;[6] legal codes in Germany, France, and Italy were not. This resurrection of Roman law in the Middle Ages produced two important effects. First, inquisitorial procedure gradually (and sometimes incompletely) infiltrated secular and ecclesiastical law.[7] Civil and canon law progressively elevated the importance of confession or two eyewitnesses to the same event, and allowed torture for interrogatory purposes, as the Roman model dictated; in the twelfth century, it was common for jurists to state that confession had the highest legal value, and to call it the "queen of proofs" (*regina probationum*).[8] Second, popes and kings gradually worked Roman definitions of heresy and Roman penalties into their own pronouncements. Thus in 1184, Pope Lucius III issued *Ad abolendam* in conjunction with Frederick I, the Holy Roman Emperor: this decretal[9] called heretics insolent and contumacious, commanded bishops and archbishops to solicit information about heretics in their dioceses, and asked secular authorities to fully employ secular law against the culprits. In 1197, King Peter II of Aragón banished all heretics from his domains under threat of confiscation of property and death at the stake. In 1199, Pope Innocent III issued *Vergentis in senium*, which explicitly identified heresy with treason under the Emperor Augustus Caesar, and demanded the confiscation of heretics' goods. Finally, between 1220 and 1232, Holy Roman Emperor Frederick II decreed banishment, confiscation of property, and death to heretics in his realms.

These papal and secular mandates reflected a more severe, centralizing impulse in Western Christianity. Up to this point, archbishops and bishops had

---

6. Roman law's relatively codified state should not imply that it was *not* subject to interpretation.

7. Inquisition replaced the accusatorial model, in which an accuser leveled formal charges against a suspect, the case was proven through oaths rather than evidence, and reprisals could ensue if charges were unsubstantiated.

8. There was still room for oaths, however, namely through the process of compurgation, when a defendant called seven or nine witnesses to swear his innocence. Compurgation was attempted when cases were immovable.

9. A decretal is a papal letter, strictly one in response to a question. It has the force of law within a pope's jurisdiction. Decretals, among other things, are what make up canon or church law.

been responsible for identifying and sentencing heretics in their dioceses, with excommunication being the strongest punishment inflicted, and some variety in process being the norm. But the revival of Roman law, an increasing concern with heretics, the perception that episcopal measures had failed, and an amplified sense of the pope's responsibility for the souls of the faithful produced an innovation. In 1231, Pope Gregory IX asked the prior of the Dominican convent in Regensberg, Germany, to act as an apostolic inquisitor of heretical depravity; the Dominican was to travel, preach, and diligently seek out heretics or those who were reputed as such.[10] Gregory IX made the first inquisitors "judges delegate": they were given a share of papal legal authority— usually for a particular case, region, or period of time—and were answerable only to the pope himself. These papal inquisitions were thus spontaneous creations, designed to take care of specific problems. It was no accident that Gregory IX and his successors chose their inquisitors from the mendicant orders, the Dominicans and Franciscans; these monks were separated from local, secular communities, and enjoyed an ample reputation for holiness.

By 1249, the routines of medieval inquisitors had become somewhat codified. At the start of their inquisition, they preached a sermon and announced a period of grace, during which they heard voluntary confessions without exacting any penalty. They also accepted depositions from sworn witnesses, which led them to suspect particular individuals. Suspects who were arrested were presented with charges which they had to answer orally and immediately, but details in the charges which might allow witnesses to be identified were erased. Defendants were supposed to reveal their own religious errors *and* those of their acquaintances or accomplices. And all inquisitors always aimed at confession as the best possible proof.

Defendants were presumed guilty. If they confessed quickly and completely, they would be ordered to abjure their heresy, the sentence of excommunication they had incurred would be lifted, and they would be received back into the Church with a punishment, which the inquisitors called a penance. Confessed heretics heard their sentences in a public ceremony whose aim was above all didactic; when the assembled audience listened to the details of condemned heresies, the distinctions between orthodoxy and its counterpart were reinforced. The penances that the condemned received also served a pedagogical function for the rest of the community, since most were fulfilled in public. The guilty could be sentenced to carry out a pilgrimage, or to wear yellow crosses on their outer garments. At

---

10. Peters, *Inquisition,* 55. The general narrative here again relies on Peters. For questions as to whether medieval heresy ever existed outside of inquisitors' and theologians' constructions of it, see Christine Caldwell Ames, "Does Inquisition Belong to Religious History?" *American Historical Review* 110 (2005): 11, n. 4.

the next level of severity, houses could be razed, life imprisonment mandated, and property confiscated. Death at the stake—which had to be effected by secular authorities, since ecclesiastics were forbidden to shed blood—was reserved for those who refused to confess despite adverse testimony, and individuals who relapsed into heresy after previously confessing and abjuring. Medieval inquisitions hardly ever found defendants innocent. And medieval inquisitors were just as interested in pursuing the dead as they were the living, for the deceased also could be convicted of heresy via eyewitness testimony, whereby their property could be confiscated and their corpses exhumed and burned.[11]

Numerous principles and practices of medieval inquisitions also governed the Inquisition in Spain. For both, only *baptized* Christians should have been liable to inquisitorial investigation, because it took an implicit or explicit rejection of baptismal vows to make a heretic: thus Muslims and Jews were theoretically off-limits. The same presumption of guilt, elevation of confession, concepts of abjuration and relapse, rule of secrecy, quest for accomplices, torture for interrogatory purposes, confiscation of property, and death penalties carried out by secular authorities all occurred in the Spanish Inquisition. Emphasis on written documentation and record keeping continued as well.[12] Furthermore, two key features of inquisition history—one that bothered the inquisitors themselves, another that bothers us—also remained constant. Medieval inquisitors always had to think about conflicts of jurisdiction with archbishops and bishops, because the latter had been in charge of handling heretics in their dioceses since the primitive Church; even after the first inquisitors were named in 1231, the episcopate's responsibilities for heretics were not redefined. Significantly, three centuries later, jurisdictional disputes between inquisitors and churchmen were also routine in Spain, even though Spanish inquisitors had a special mandate for the prosecution of heretics.[13] Continuous too was the explicit, overarching purpose of Christian inquisition, which was repeatedly stated in both the medieval

11. James B. Given, *Inquisition and Medieval Society: Power, Discipline, and Resistance in Languedoc* (Ithaca, NY: Cornell University Press, 1997), 68–90, explains the medieval inquisitions' system of punishment and hypothesizes as to its purpose. His assertion that inquisitors were attempting to "impose their own moral order" on the Languedoc has recently been refined by Ames in "Does Inquisition Belong to Religious History?"

12. Given, *Inquisition and Medieval Society*, 39–44, explains the power of the inquisition archives and the consequent loathing and fear they generated among the people of the Languedoc.

13. The mandate came via the bull of Sixtus IV, dated November 1, 1478, which gave King Ferdinand and Queen Isabella the power of naming inquisitors for their realms. On the 1478 bull, see below.

and early modern epochs: the aim, quite simply, was "to reconcile heretics to the Church." The pursuit, investigation, and punishment of heretics was supposed to be motivated out of concern for their souls; hence inquisitors in the Middle Ages and in Spain imposed *penances* of fasting and pilgrimage, and even called imprisonment a *penitential exercise*. This mixture of pastoral impulses and legal compulsion has frequently baffled modern commentators, who have often dismissed the inquisitors' vocabulary as a ruse.[14] But part of the historian's task is to wrestle with the values of long-dead subjects. And it seems clear that medieval and early modern inquisitors believed their purpose was to persuade the otherwise damned to return to the Church, via a range of options that ran from fraternal persuasion (*persuasio*) to coercion (*coercio*). We should take their language seriously if we hope to grasp what *they* thought they were doing.[15]

The Creation of the Spanish Inquisition

Recognizing the profound links between medieval inquisitions and the Spanish one of 1478–1834 helps to curb the notion that this legal procedure was invented in Spain. At the same time, the Spanish Inquisition was more than a mirror image of its predecessors, and scholars always treat it as a separate entity while acknowledging its antecedents. It involved a different power dynamic between popes and kings; it pursued different heretics; its officials expounded their procedures to an even greater extent.

The Spanish Inquisition was created in 1478 because of a heresy which Church authorities called "judaizing": judaizers were Christians who allegedly continued to practice Jewish ceremonies and espouse Jewish beliefs. Spain had the largest population of Jews in Western Europe until 1391, when preaching by Dominican friars provoked the forced baptism of Jews and the destruction of their neighborhoods. Almost instantaneously, these "new" Christians, called *conversos,* generated debate within Spanish society; questions arose as to whether they were sincere in their new beliefs, and whether they should be allowed to hold the public and ecclesiastical offices that were now open to them because of their baptism. (The papacy and numerous Spaniards, it should be noted, answered yes to both questions.) Significantly, the identification of *conversos* through blood lineage meant that *descendants* of original converts were also categorized as different from Old Christians, and viewed with suspicion.

14. For an eloquent argument that *persecutio* and *religio* belonged together in the medieval religious world, see Ames, "Does Inquisition Belong to Religious History?"

15. Which is not to deny that inquisitors' actions could have unforeseen effects. See note 4 above.

Antagonism toward the *conversos* was inflamed by their social success, since many *converso* families deftly climbed a social hierarchy that had been off-limits before their baptism. *Conversos* came to occupy 85 percent of the posts on the city council in Cuenca, held prominent positions at the royal court, and could achieve remarkable success in the Church.[16] Historians think the *conversos'* social prominence compounded local, urban rivalries and resulted in controversy throughout the fifteenth century. For example, *conversos* were banned from municipal offices in 1449 in Toledo and 1467 in Ciudad Real; anti-Jewish polemics were composed by both Old and New Christians; interest in genealogy surged, to prove a lack of *converso* bloodlines.[17] Scholars disagree dramatically over the *conversos'* true religious beliefs—alternately claiming that this population was self-consciously Jewish or Christian, or simply heterogeneous—but all tend to point to social conflict as triggering suspicion about the *conversos'* religiosity.

In the winter of 1477, King Ferdinand and Queen Isabella stayed in Seville, where they heard the preaching of Dominican friar Alonso de Hojeda. The king and queen were told that the religious situation was dire: judaizing *conversos* were supposedly practicing Mosaic law, undisturbed by ecclesiastical authorities.[18] The monarchs consequently asked Pope Sixtus IV for a bull that would allow them to name two or three bishops or priests to fulfill the inquisitorial office in the cities and dioceses of their kingdoms. Sixtus responded with the bull *Exigit sincerae devotionis affectus,* dated November 1, 1478, which stated that Ferdinand and Isabella would name two or three inquisitors who were over forty years of age, of respectable customs, and with theological or law degrees. These inquisitors in turn would receive the powers that were customarily exercised, by law or custom, by episcopal representatives and pontifical inquisitors of heretical depravity. The monarchs' privilege of naming inquisitors was granted in perpetuity, and no other constitution or ordinance was allowed to block the validity of Sixtus' bull.[19]

16. For instance, the Rabbi of Burgos, Salomon Halevi, converted to Christianity in 1390, took the name Pablo de Santa María, and ultimately became the bishop of Cartagena and Burgos, as well as a papal legate. For some details on the Santa María family, see Henry Kamen, *The Spanish Inquisition: A Historical Revision* (New Haven: Yale University Press, 1997), 29.

17. David Nirenberg, "Mass Conversion and Genealogical Mentalities: Jews and Christians in Fifteenth-Century Spain," *Past and Present* 174 (2002): 3–41.

18. "Mosaic Law" refers to the Jewish law of the Pentateuch, the first five books of the Torah.

19. Juan Meseguer Fernández, "El período fundacional (1478–1517)," in *Historia de la Inquisición en España y América,* eds. Joaquín Pérez Villanueva and Bartolomé Escandell Bonet (Madrid: BAE, 1984), vol. 1, 281.

Although papal inquisitions had been instituted before in the kingdom of Aragón, no "pontifical inquisitors of heretical depravity" had ever acted in Castile; instead, it had always been presumed that the efforts of bishops and archbishops against heretics would be sufficient there. But bishops were geographically bound to their dioceses, and by 1477 judaizing *conversos* were purportedly moving from place to place. Convinced they had no legal instrument to cope with the problem, Ferdinand and Isabella wrote accordingly to Sixtus IV. These monarchs were accustomed to name bishops and heads of religious orders whom the papacy would subsequently approve, so the sheer process of who-named-which-ecclesiastic was not entirely innovative. But inquisitors were peculiarly powerful, and Sixtus IV's bull gave Ferdinand and Isabella an unprecedented role in deputizing them. After 1478 in Castile, inquisitors would be politically subject—and hence politically loyal—to monarchs, even though the authority and jurisdiction of those inquisitors had to come from the pope himself. Pope Sixtus IV quickly realized the implications of what he had done, and attempted afterward to reassert his own authority and put the Spanish Inquisition back under the control of bishops; Ferdinand, however, won their intense negotiations.[20] From the beginning, then, the Spanish Inquisition differed fundamentally from the medieval, papal inquisitions, because of the prominent role Spanish kings played in its institution.

Ferdinand and Isabella possessed Sixtus' bull for a year and a half, more or less, before naming any inquisitors: that period was filled with efforts to persuade Seville's *conversos* through preaching campaigns and episcopal ordinances; authorities thus began their work with measures that fell on the less-coercive side of the scale.[21] But when those steps did not appear successful, two Dominican theologians, Miguel de Morillo and Juan de San Martín, were invested with inquisitorial powers on September 27, 1480, in the northern Castilian city of Medina del Campo. The Dominicans arrived in Seville in November, and published their edict of grace about December 1. The edict stated that individuals who appeared and confessed within thirty days would be pardoned and their goods untouched, but the *conversos'* first reaction was to flee the city entirely. Ferdinand and Isabella reacted by ordering all inhabitants of Seville and its archdiocese to remain in their customary housing.[22] Suspects were subsequently arrested. Unfortunately, no documentation exists for the trials that ensued, but we know that Seville's

20. *Ibid.,* 300–06.
21. Archbishop of Seville, Pedro González de Mendoza, headed these efforts with the help of his vicar-general and Bishop of Cádiz, Pedro de Solis.
22. Ferdinand and Isabella also threatened any noble who sheltered judaizers with canonical penalties and the release of those nobles' vassals from their oaths of loyalty.

repentant heretics were reconciled to the Church in 1481, while their unrepentant or fugitive brethren were burned at the stake the same year. Chroniclers attested that the penances were harsh, and the social status of the condemned high.

Generally speaking, the first two decades of the Spanish Inquisition reveal the same kind of gaps in evidence that occur for Seville in 1480 and 1481. We lack sure documentation on which inquisitors were named when, where they worked, and even how the Inquisition's hierarchy came into being. At first, the inquisitors deputized by Ferdinand and Isabella were supposed to be completely peripatetic; it soon became clear, however, that they would work more effectively if they operated out of tribunals established in cities. The creation and placement of these tribunals came in response to perceived need; fixing the exact date of their foundation as well as their geographic scope can be difficult, since it is not clear whether the presence of inquisitors in a given locale implies a tribunal or simply an inquisitorial visit. Between 1480 and 1504, tribunals in southern Spain were present in Seville, Córdoba, Jaén, Cádiz-Jerez de la Frontera, and Granada. For the same time period in New Castile, in the center of the country, tribunals were founded in Ciudad Real and Cuenca; the first moved permanently to Toledo in 1485, while the second absorbed the tribunal of Sigüenza between 1495–1499. On the border with Portugal, in Extremadura, there was a tribunal in Llerena, and another in Murcia on the Mediterranean coast. To the north, in Old Castile, tribunals were founded in fewer numbers and with even poorer documentation. They existed in Medina del Campo (1484) and Valladolid (1485), and tribunals, or simply inquisitors, also seem to have been clustered according to bishoprics, as inquisitors showed up in Ávila, Burgos, Calahorra, León, and Palencia in 1488–1503.[23] Over time, as tribunals' work slowed or seemed redundant, they might be suppressed or merged; hence multiple Old Castilian tribunals were incorporated into one at Valladolid in 1503. There could be later changes as well: tribunals were founded at Las Palmas, in the Canary Islands, in 1505; in Santiago de Compostela, in Galicia, in 1574; and a tribunal was reestablished in Granada in 1526, after having become inactive in 1501 and 1502.

Founding the Inquisition in the kingdom of Aragón was more difficult. The Aragonese kingdom in the Spanish peninsula encompassed the states of Aragón, Valencia, and Catalonia; each of these states retained its own privileges (*fueros*) that could block or complicate the importation of a Castilian institution and Castilian officials. Moreover, historical precedent in Aragón

---

23. For the interesting coincidence between the earliest inquisitors and bishoprics in Old Castile, see José Martínez Millán, *La hacienda de la Inquisición (1478–1700)* (Madrid: CSIC, 1984), 12.

dictated that inquisitors were named only by popes or masters-general of the Dominican Order. It ultimately took some armed force and multiple papal bulls before the Inquisition was finally established, in four permanent tribunals, in Zaragoza and Valencia (1484), Barcelona (1487), and Las Palmas on the island of Mallorca (1488).[24] Making the Inquisition function in Aragón's overseas possessions was an even more convoluted process. Though inquisitors were named for Sicily and Sardinia as early as 1487 and 1492, respectively, they were practically inactive until after 1510.[25] And when King Ferdinand attempted to install the Inquisition in Naples in 1509, the Neapolitans rioted and formed a sworn coalition against the Inquisition which extended across all social classes; they behaved in the same fashion when Charles V tried again to institute the Inquisition in 1542. In both instances, the Inquisition was suppressed in Naples almost as quickly as it was established.

In the sixteenth and seventeenth centuries, after all the mergers and suppressions, the *permanent* tribunals of the Spanish Inquisition were located in the following cities:

Kingdom of Castile	*Kingdom of Aragón*[26]
Seville	Zaragoza
Córdoba	Valencia
Toledo	Barcelona
Llerena	Mallorca
Logroño	Sicily
Valladolid	Sardinia
Murcia	
Cuenca	
Las Palmas	
Granada	
Santiago de Compostela	
Madrid	

24. Meseguer Fernández, "El período fundacional," 330–39, and J. Angel Sesma Muñoz, *El establecimiento de la Inquisicíon en Aragón (1484–86): documentos para su estudio* (Zaragoza: Institución Fernando el Católico, 1987). For a general history of the Aragonese Holy Office, see Monter, *Frontiers of Heresy*.

25. For the Inquisition in the Italian possessions of Aragón, see Monter, *Frontiers of Heresy*, 15–18, and Manuel Rivero Rodríguez, "La inquisición española en Sicilia (siglos XVI a XVIII)," in *Historia de la Inquisición en España y América*, eds. Joaquín Pérez Villanueva and Bartolomé Escandell Bonet (Madrid: BAE, 2000), vol. 3, 1031–222.

26. Tribunals in the Americas, which belonged to the Secretariat of Aragón, were founded in 1568 in Mexico City, in Lima in 1570, and in Cartagena de Indias in

The founding of tribunals was accompanied by other bureaucratic developments. In 1483, Pope Sixtus IV named Tomás de Torquemada, the Dominican prior of the convent of Santa Cruz in Segovia, as Spain's first inquisitor-general, and gave him powers over Aragón as well as Castile. Between 1484 and 1488, the inquisitor-general was given counselors who came to form the "Council of the Supreme and General Inquisition," called the *Suprema*.[27] The Suprema, made up of six members in the early seventeenth century, corresponded with tribunals, replied to queries from inquisitors in the field, issued edicts and instructions, and vetted difficult cases—the same activities as performed by the inquisitor-general himself.[28] In fact, the hierarchy between the inquisitor-general and the Suprema was never explicitly established; members of the latter were appointed by the king, and they could issue orders without the inquisitor-general's approval. Meanwhile, the authority of the inquisitor-general depended upon circumstances and his own personality, and this was true throughout the early modern period.

Conversos and the Jewish Expulsion of 1492

The development of tribunals, higher officials, and councils was supposed to help the Inquisition function more effectively; between 1480 and 1521, its targets remained basically the same, namely, *conversos* who might be judaizing heretics. The Inquisition's focus on *conversos* quickly affected the lives of Spain's Jews. The inquisitors believed the task of ferreting out judaizing *conversos* was gargantuan, and between 1480 and 1492, as they arrested baptized men and women[29] for purportedly following the dietary laws and religious rituals of Judaism, it occurred to them that their suspects were being

---

1609–1610. See the essays by Bartolomé Escandell Bonet, Alvaro Huerga, and María de Pilar Pérez Canto in *Historia de la Inquisición en España y América,* vol. 1.

27. Castilian documents indicate that there were multiple inquisitors-general in the first years of the inquisition there, who were probably designated as such by Torquemada himself. See Martínez Millán, *La hacienda de la Inquisición,* 6–12, and José Ramón Rodríguez Besné, *El Consejo de la Suprema Inquisición: Perfil jurídico de una institución* (Madrid: Editorial Complutense, 2000). For the temporary creation of a separate inquisitor-general in Aragón, see the introduction to Document 2.

28. That correspondence was divided between two secretariats, one for Aragón and the other for Castile.

29. On the predominance of women as suspected judaizers, Renée Levine Melammed, *Heretics or Daughters of Israel? The Crypto-Jewish Women of Castile* (New York: Oxford University Press, 1998); and the introduction to Document 3.

"contaminated" by Jews. Upon the urging of inquisitors, Ferdinand and Isabella began a process of expelling Jews from various cities and dioceses, in order to block their contact with the *converso* population. At the end of 1482, Jews were expelled from Jerez de la Frontera. In January 1483, they were expelled from the dioceses of Seville, Córdoba, and Cádiz; in 1486, they were expelled by royal order from the dioceses of Zaragoza, Albarracín, and Teruel.[30]

Despite these partial expulsions, inquisitors continued to find judaizing *conversos* ten years after starting work in Seville. The Inquisition therefore ultimately recommended the ejection of the entire Jewish population. Ferdinand and Isabella finally conquered Granada, the last Islamic kingdom in Spain, in January 1492; that victory seemed to signal the impending triumph of Christianity in the peninsula. Two months later, on March 31, 1492, Ferdinand and Isabella issued an edict of expulsion that covered Jews in both Castile and Aragón, who had to accept Christian baptism or leave the country by July 31. Prominent Jews—led by Rabbis Isaac Abrabanel (chief treasurer of the *Santa Hermandad,* the royal, rural police force) and Abraham Senior (chief rabbi of Castile and principal royal treasurer)—visited the king multiple times and begged him to reconsider. Ferdinand refused, though he ultimately gave Spain's Jews until 1499 to convert and return.[31]

The Jews who fled the country—and who were not allowed to take gold, silver, or valuables with them—went primarily to Portugal, where they would be forced to convert or leave in 1497. Their efforts to go overseas frequently met with disaster: they were murdered in North Africa, or shipwrecked en route to Italy, Greece, and Turkey. The number of Jews who left Spain cannot be calculated with any reliability; the figure 150,000 to 165,000 has been suggested. There are no reliable statistics, either, for the number of Jews who chose to remain and convert, though it seems certain that the 1492 Expulsion created a whole new generation of *conversos.*[32] As for the *conversos* who were arrested, sent to the stake, or penanced by the Inquisition between 1478 and 1521, most of the trial records have been lost

---

30. My material on the partial expulsions comes from Kamen, *The Spanish Inquisition in the Sixteenth and Seventeenth Centuries,* 13–14, who notes that Jews were also expelled from towns on local initiative, despite royal protests.

31. Luis Suárez Fernández, *Documentos acerca de la expulsión de los judíos,* Biblioteca "Reyes Católicos," Documentos y textos, n. XI (Valladolid: CSIC, 1964) is the best place to start for primary sources on Jewish history relating to the Expulsion.

32. Kamen contends that the 1492 generation of *conversos* was much more likely to judaize, in comparison to the more assimilated *conversos* whose ancestors had converted in 1391. In his view, the Expulsion intensified the *converso* problem rather than solving it. See *The Spanish Inquisition,* 27.

for this earliest period in inquisition history. Hence statistical extrapolations from the documents we do possess can be misleading, since they often involve percentages drawn from little data.[33] Still, historians suspect that penalties in this earlier time period, whether for judaizing or other heretical offenses, were more severe than ones exacted later in the next century.

Personnel, Procedures, Punishments

The basic procedures and penances that the Spanish Inquisition applied to its first heretics were carried over to later trials, and the staffing of the tribunals remained relatively consistent as well. In the *Instructions* issued by Inquisitor-General Torquemada in 1498, each tribunal was told to have two inquisitors, either a theologian and a canon law jurist, or two jurists.[34] Those inquisitors were assisted by:

— A prosecutor (the *fiscal*)
— A constable who put suspects into custody and brought them into the tribunal (*alguacil*)
— Theologians who acted as assessors and weighed the evidence for heresy (*calificadores*).[35] They were not in the employ of the tribunal
— The receiver who handled the tribunal's finances (*receptor*)
— A warden who handled residents in the tribunal's prison (*alcaide*)
— The quartermaster who distributed food to the prisoners (*despensero*)
— A notary "of the secret" who wrote down and witnessed testimony (*notario del secreto*)
— A notary "of the sequestration" who registered any sequestered property (*notario del secuestro*)
— A general secretary who registered the sentences, edicts of grace, and *autos de fe*

33. For key bibliography on *converso* religion, see the introduction to Document 3. Formerly, scholars were fond of lifting percentages from only a small quantity of *converso* trials; thus we might read that 90 percent of all *conversos* in a particular time period were sent to the stake, but that figure becomes less meaningful if the number of extant cases is less than twenty, for example.

34. By the end of the sixteenth century, the major tribunals customarily had three inquisitors apiece.

35. The *calificadores* consulted on cases in which the evidence was ambiguous; their opinions were sought before a formal accusation was launched by the prosecutor or *fiscal*. The *calificadores* thus acted before an arrest order was issued.

— various scribes and other subordinate personnel
— legal and theological consultants (*consultadores*), who also included the representative (*ordinario*) of the relevant bishop. The *consultadores* conferred with inquisitors at the end of a trial and voted upon the sentence; they were not in the employ of the tribunal[36]

Though Dominican friars acted as the first inquisitors in Spain (as they had in the Middle Ages), canon lawyers rapidly replaced them; still, inquisitor-jurists were frequently in holy orders and held church offices. It was also typical for inquisitors-general in the sixteenth century to have previously been archbishops or bishops, a coincidence that demonstrates once again this institution's nexus between legal and religious responsibilities.

Trials in the Spanish Inquisition were instigated by depositions that witnesses made under oath, which had to be ratified at a later date in order to be entered into evidence. Witnesses could depose before the prosecutor or *fiscal* of a given tribunal, or, if they lived too far away, they could give their statements to a *comisario,* who was usually a parish priest and represented the tribunal in the countryside.[37] After an initial denunciation was made, inquisitors could actively seek to interview additional witnesses, or wait for more deponents to appear. If there were some question as to whether the allegations involved heresy—and again, conceptions of heresy evolved with notions of orthodoxy—inquisitors could call in the *calificadores* (theological assessors) who would evaluate the evidence and pronounce on its gravity. When the depositions against a suspect reached a critical weight—and only the inquisitors' discretion dictated when that point occurred—the prosecutor requested the capture of the suspect, and the constable accordingly seized the individual and placed him in a holding cell inside the tribunal. After a defendant arrived, inquisitors would arrange three separate meetings with him, during which they would admonish him to state why he had been arrested and to disclose what he knew about other heretics or persons suspect in the Faith; the inquisitors would repeatedly tell the defendant that his soul

36. The *consultadores'* vote was not binding on the inquisitors; for details, see Document 20.

37. For excellent descriptions and analyses of the *comisarios* in English, see Sara T. Nalle, *God in La Mancha* (Baltimore: The Johns Hopkins University Press, 1992), 58–59, and *idem,* "Inquisitors, Priests, and the People during the Catholic Reformation in Spain," *Sixteenth Century Journal* 18 (1987): 557–87. *Comisarios* should not be confused with "familiars"—*familiares*—who were lay servants of the Inquisition and were attached to individual tribunals. Familiars ran errands for inquisitors and were not supposed to receive witness testimony.

INTRODUCTION

was endangered. Through these admonitions, the inquisitors were hoping to elicit a confession. If their strategy failed, they proceeded to trial.

The trial process began when the prosecutor drew up a list of charges and formally, orally accused the suspect, in his or her presence, of heresy. The charges omitted any identifying details about witnesses for the prosecution; the prisoner was supposed to answer the charges orally and immediately. After this interchange, both sides were received for proof. The prosecutor's accusation would be transcribed, again with specifics about witnesses erased, and a copy would be given to the defendant, who was expected to answer the charges in writing. A defense lawyer—who was attached to the tribunal—would usually be assigned to the case, but private communication between that lawyer and the defendant was prohibited, and the defense was supposed to notify inquisitors if the case "lacked justice."[38]

Because the prisoner was not told who had testified against him, he had only a few defense strategies within his reach. He could try to demonstrate his Christian beliefs and behavior with character witnesses, which was called, in legal shorthand, *abonos.* He could call witnesses who might cast doubt on specific accusations, a tactic called *indirectas.* And he could try to invalidate the prosecution witnesses—whose identity he had to guess—by naming individuals who were his capital enemies or had reason to wish him ill; this strategy was called *tachas.*[39] In all three schemes, the defendant provided questions which were put to his witnesses, to either prove his Christianity, mitigate the prosecution's evidence, or verify other witnesses' hostility against him. Finally, a defendant might try to recuse an inquisitor or a prosecutor for personal enmity, or simply refuse to mount a defense at all and appeal his case to the Suprema.[40] The defendant could ask the inquisitors for a hearing and confess at any point during the trial.

Once the defense's testimony and the prosecutor's ratified depositions had been entered into evidence, inquisitors called in *consultadores*—theologians

38. According to the first instructions issued to inquisitors in 1484, defense lawyers were supposed to be given to prisoners if prisoners requested them; see their responsibilities, and their limitations, under "Publication of witness testimony and defense lawyers" in Document 7.

39. Heresy trials allowed witnesses to testify who otherwise would not have carried any weight, such as the underaged, women, and even other suspected or convicted heretics. Nonetheless, Roman law and inquisitorial procedure vetoed a witness who deposed out of capital (meaning "murderous") enmity, and if a defendant could prove such antagonism, he might undermine a deposition.

40. Henry Charles Lea believed that recusation was no defense at all, since it rarely worked; see *A History of the Inquisition in Spain,* vol. 3, 68–69. For an episode in

or legal experts, as well as the *ordinario* or representative of the local bishop
—to confer over the verdict and the sentence.[41] *If* the evidence was ambiguous, and the defendant declined to confess, the *consultadores* and inquisitors might decide to mandate a session of torture in the hope of gaining
a confession. Torture was conducted in a separate room in the tribunal by a
trained professional; at least one inquisitor and a scribe were supposed to be
present, and whatever the defendant said during torture was written down.
The forms of torture in the Spanish Inquisition—and there is no evidence
they ever changed—were the *toca,* wherein large quantities of water were
poured down the defendant's nose and mouth to simulate drowning; the
potro or rack, on which the prisoner was bound with cords that could be
tightened; and the *garrucha,* in which the prisoner was hung by his wrists
tied from behind.[42] Inquisitors explicitly warned defendants that any injuries they suffered during torture would be their own fault. They also repeatedly asked the defendant to confess from the moment they all entered
the torture room. If the defendant did confess during torture, whatever he
said had to be ratified on a subsequent day; if he later revoked what he had
confessed, he could be tortured again for the same purposes. Though torture remains one of the most lurid features of the Spanish Inquisition, scholars now believe it was applied rarely.

Prisoners in the Spanish Inquisition were presumed guilty and almost
never acquitted outright. When proof remained ambiguous—whether because defendants withstood torture and denied the charges, or witnesses
were unique, suspect, or disqualified, or a combination of such scenarios—
the inquisitors had two alternatives. They could call for compurgation,
whereby a certain number of witnesses would swear to the defendant's Christianity; after such oaths, the prisoner would be absolved and released.[43] The

---

which it did, see the Carranza case in this volume. María de Cazalla, whose trial is
also excerpted here, used appeals to her advantage. And for examples of a deliberate
nondefense, see the cases of Juan de Vergara and Francisco Ortiz, in, respectively,
Homza, *Religious Authority,* chapter 1; and *idem,* "How to Harass an Inquisitor-General: The Polyphonic Law of Friar Francisco Ortiz," in *A Renaissance of Conflicts: Visions and Revisions of Law and Society in Early Modern Italy and Spain,* eds. John A.
Marino and Thomas Kuehn, Centre for Reformation and Renaissance Studies, *Essays and Studies* 3 (Toronto: CRRS Publications, 2004), 299–336.

41. See Document 20 for the voting procedure during such consultations, explained
in the Instructions of 1561.

42. For a torture sequence, see Document 5.

43. If all the witnesses so swore, the defendant was acquitted and freed. The difficulty

inquisitors also could decide to suspend the case pending further developments, whereby old and new charges (and depositions) could be reinstated.
When proof was verifiable—ideally through a full confession offered before
the conclusion of the trial—the wording of the verdict turned on the sort of
heresy involved. Suspects who fully admitted their offenses and named accomplices—and who were charged with major heresies such as judaizing,
the practice of Islam, Protestantism, and so forth—were absolved of excommunication and were said to be "reconciled" (*reconciliados*) to the
Church. Suspects who confessed, identified accessories, and repented *lesser*
heresies—such as blasphemy, bigamy, and so forth—were also reconciled to
the Church, but in such instances they forswore a light (*de levi*) or grave (*de
vehementi*) *suspicion* of heresy, and inquisitors called them "penanced" (*pen-
itenciados*).[44] The "penanced" were just as convicted as their "reconciled"
counterparts and just as vulnerable to charges of relapse.[45]

Meanwhile, death at the stake was reserved for people who had been convicted of heresy once and then relapsed, or had refused to confess despite
explicit evidence. The sentence of death at the stake was called "relaxation
to the secular arm" because such persons were handed over ("relaxed") to
secular authorities for execution. Burning heretics was always done outside
of cities. If someone confessed while on the way to the execution ground,
inquisitors were supposed to evaluate that confession for signs of sincerity;
they could decide to take the culprit back to the tribunal for further interrogation. At the same time, though, the inquisitors' discretion dictated
whether to act benevolently or not. In cases involving the stake, it was customary before lighting the fire to strangle any heretic who confessed and
repented en route.

Aside from the acquitted, the suspended, and the relaxed—and the first
two groups could be ordered to pay court costs—reconciled and penanced
heretics in the Spanish Inquisition were subject to a wide range of punishments, which inquisitors called penances. Penances usually featured an
element of public humiliation. Most defendants were condemned in
public "acts of the faith," or *autos de fe,* which could draw huge crowds.
Their sentences would be read aloud and they would wear symbols of their
penalties, such as a rope whose knots signified the number of lashes to be

---

lay in knowing *which* witnesses to call, given that friends and relatives could have
acted as witnesses for the prosecution, and the defendant would never know it.

44. Historians have argued that the Inquisition's punishments differed depending upon
whether the guilty were "reconciled" or "penanced," but the fact is that the inquisitors'
discretion was always in play to some degree in the mandating of punishments.

45. See note 13 in Document 20 for the concept of "ostensible" relapse.

administered.[46] Individuals frequently were sentenced to wear *sanbenitos*[47] —yellow smocks with red crosses—for a specific length of time in public, after which the robes would be hung in their parish churches, with their names and heresies inscribed below. They could be enclosed in a monastery or convent for several years to be educated in the faith, or sent to "perpetual prison," a sentence that was always commuted. They could be ordered to sponsor and attend a certain number of masses, or to pay monetary fines. The worst penalties in the repertory of punishments were galley service in the king's fleet, which was first exacted by Aragonese inquisitors in the 1540s, and often amounted to a death sentence;[48] and (of course) burning at the stake. Finally, reflecting the medieval belief that heresy ran in families, and the Spanish identification of *conversos* through lineage, the Inquisition could classify the heirs of the relapsed or convicted as "infamous," a legal category that prevented those descendants from holding public office, carrying arms, riding horses, possessing luxury items, or entering clerical orders.

No matter what the outcome, all defendants before the Inquisition were ordered, under oath, to preserve as secret everything they had seen or heard while in the tribunal. Secrecy, in fact, was the rule during every stage of the process, from being held incommunicado in a tribunal, to not knowing the identity of prosecution witnesses, to not being able to divulge events afterward—though whether the principle worked as well in practice as in theory is open to question.[49]

Another element that accompanied every sentence for serious heresy was the confiscation of the heretic's goods.[50] The suspect's possessions would have been inventoried and sequestered almost at the moment of the arrest,[51] and a "sequestrator" remained in charge of them during the trial. From the sequestered goods, the sequestrator paid all the prisoner's debts and any taxes owed to the royal treasury or any other authorities; sequestered goods also supported the prisoner in terms of food and clothing. (If prisoners were so

46. The Spanish inquisitors' *autos de fe* had the same didactic purpose as their medieval predecessors' *sermones generales*.

47. The term comes from *saco bendito,* or "blessed smock."

48. Secular officials began to employ galley service as a punishment much earlier; see Monter, *Frontiers of Heresy,* 32–38.

49. See the episode involving inquisition prisoners and secret correspondence at the end of Document 12.

50. "Serious heresy" was defined by the Spanish Inquisition as cases of relaxation to the secular arm, relapse, reconciliation, and abjuration of grave (*de vehementi*) suspicion of heresy.

51. That inventory took place through questions pitched to the defendant; for an example, see Martínez Millán, *La hacienda de la Inquisición,* 64.

poor that their households could not support them, the tribunal itself provided food and clothing.) Throughout the potentially long trial, the sequestrator was supposed to treat the defendant's property as his own, and to provide an account of income and expenses every six months to the receiver of goods attached to the tribunal.[52] The prisoner's goods were not formally confiscated until he was convicted of grave heresy, at which point the sequestrator turned the movable and immovable goods over to the Inquisition, and they were sold at public auction.[53] If a prisoner was released with only a light suspicion (*de levi*) of heresy, or his case was suspended, his goods were returned to him intact. Though historians used to believe that inquisitors supported themselves purely through the confiscation of prisoners' property, we now know that the financing of the Inquisition was far more complex. While confiscations were a primary source of income, albeit a most inconsistent one, tribunals also bought government annuities (*juros*), enjoyed quit-rents (*censos*), and controlled ecclesiastical offices.[54] Spanish inquisitors constantly complained about their insufficient salaries and their inability to pay their officials.[55]

Targets

Although the procedures, staffing, and financing of the Inquisition's tribunals remained fairly consistent between 1478 and 1609, its victims did not.[56] Trials for judaizing slowed after about 1510, and there were substantial rumblings about reforming the Inquisition's jurisdiction and legal procedures.[57] Still, the Inquisition survived the attacks, and the writings of

52. The receiver (*receptor*) administered the finances of a tribunal and handled the income and expenses therein.

53. Martínez Millán, *La hacienda de la Inquisición*, 59–73, lays out the process of sequestration, confiscation, and sale. Penitential fines should not be confused with the confiscation of goods.

54. Especially in the wake of reforms carried out by Inquisitor-General Fernando de Valdés after 1559. For Valdés' energetic direction of the Holy Office, José Luis González Novalín, *El inquisidor general Fernando de Valdés (1483–1568): su vida y obra*, 2 vols. (Oviedo: Universidad de Oviedo, 1968 and 1971).

55. The most authoritative source on Inquisition finances is Martínez Millán, *La hacienda de la Inquisición*.

56. While the basic elements of procedure, staff, and finance were in place within the first decade or so of the Inquisition's existence, later inquisitors-general such as Fernando de Valdés clarified features of all three. See below, and the introduction to Document 20.

57. Kamen, *The Spanish Inquisition*, 74–80.

Martin Luther gave the inquisitors ample justification for their office.[58] Luther was excommunicated by Pope Leo X in 1521 and put under the ban of empire by Charles V, king of Spain and Holy Roman Emperor, the same year. Simultaneously, the Spanish Inquisition ordered its officials to confiscate Lutheran books, and prohibited Castilians from selling, reading, or preaching Lutheran works and ideas. Inquisitors in Aragón, Valencia, and Navarre found Lutheran contraband as soon as they began to look for it.

From 1521 to 1535, this search for *luteranismo* led inquisitors to investigate a variety of spiritual leaders, preachers, and intellectuals, most of whom happened to be *conversos,* but none of whom was specifically charged with judaizing. Inquisitors in the field had little idea what Luther specifically promoted, but Spain in the 1520s was full of religious experimentation, much of it directed by women. Moreover, Spanish printing presses were producing translations of Latin works by Desiderius Erasmus,[59] the most famous intellectual of the epoch, who explicitly criticized Church ceremonies and trumpeted a Christianity that was closer to the New Testament. Erasmus' critical remarks about monks, as well as his emendations of the Greek and Latin New Testament, provoked numerous clerics in Spain to attack him publicly. The environment was consequently replete with debate about the proper techniques of prayer and contemplation, the primacy of Scripture, and the worth of monasticism and scholasticism. Thus, when inquisitors shifted their gaze from judaizing, they consequently had a wide if ill-defined range of potential suspects. Beginning in 1524, the Toledo tribunal prosecuted the *alumbrados* ("the illuminated ones"), who rejected priestly intermediaries between God and human beings, and disowned the external

58. Martin Luther (1483–1546) founded the German Reformation. A member of the monastic order of Augustinian Hermits, he was a doctor of theology at the University of Wittenberg who had a revelation between 1512 and 1515 that faith alone saves mankind without external works. Luther formally broke from the Catholic Church in 1520 with the publication of three decisive treatises; the linchpins of his Protestant theology were "scripture alone," "grace alone," and "faith alone," and he drew the inspiration for his insights from the evangelist Paul. For Luther, the only source of religious truth was the Word of God as revealed in Scripture, and people were saved through an infusion of faith that was the gift of divine grace.

59. Desiderius Erasmus (c. 1469–1536) was a Renaissance humanist who used philological and historical insights to correct the texts of the Greek and Latin New Testament—and to edit works by the Greek and Latin Church Fathers. Erasmus also wrote satirical dialogues and earnest treatises that argued for Church reform. His critiques of papal excommunication, external works and ceremonies, and the monastic orders led Spaniards to say that "Erasmus laid the egg that Luther hatched," though Erasmus and Luther formally and publicly disagreed over the existence of free will, among other things.

rituals of Catholicism, such as meditation on Christ's Passion; key arrests involved Isabel de la Cruz, Pedro Ruiz de Alcaraz, and Francisca Hernández.[60] In 1525, Inquisitor-General Alonso Manrique called a conference of theologians to peruse the alleged statements of the *alumbrados*, which resulted in their formal condemnation; two years later, the same inquisitor-general called another meeting of theologians to vet the writings of Erasmus for heresy, though this group never issued a formal conclusion.[61] The web of arrests eventually caught Juan de Vergara, secretary to the Archbishop of Toledo, and María de Cazalla, leader of the *alumbrados* since 1524, for a mélange of *alumbradismo*, Lutheranism, and Erasmianism.[62]

Thus between 1521and 1535, inquisitors broadened their prosecutorial efforts to include more ambiguous deviations from Catholic faith and practice. This widening of the field of investigation continued throughout the sixteenth century. Historians generally agree that Fernando de Valdés, Inquisitor-General from 1547 to 1566,[63] inaugurated a new stage in inquisition history through the infractions his inquisitors pursued, the cultural measures he sponsored, and the reforms his tribunals implemented. During Valdés' tenure, blasphemy, scandalous statements, fornication, bigamy, sodomy, and the solicitation of sexual favors by priests—what we might call

60. For the *alumbrados*, see Antonio Márquez, *Los alumbrados: orígenes y filosofía, 1525–1559* (Madrid: Taurus, 1972) and Stefania Pastore, *Un'eresia spagnola: spiritualità conversa, alumbradismo e inquisizione (1449–1559)* (Florence: Leo S. Olschki, 2004). For categorization of the *alumbrados'* theology, see Melquiades Andrés Martín, *La teología española en el siglo XVI,* (Madrid: Editorial Católica, 1976): vol. 2, 198–259. For Erasmus in Spain, see Marcel Bataillon, *Erasmo y España: estudios sobre la historia espiritual del siglo XVI,* trans. A. Alatorre, 2nd Spanish ed., rev. (Mexico City: Fondo de Cultúra Económica, 1966); Lu Ann Homza, "Erasmus as Hero or Heretic? Spanish Humanism and the Valladolid Conference of 1527," *Renaissance Quarterly* 50 (1997): 78–118; and Homza, *Religious Authority,* chapters 1–2. For Luther in Spain, see Augustín Redondo, "Luther et l'Espagne de 1520–1536," *Mélanges de la Casa de Velázquez* 1 (1965): 109–65; and Werner Thomas, *La represión del protestantismo en España, 1517–1648* (Leuven: Leuven University Press, 2001).

61. Márquez, *Los alumbrados* transcribes the 1525 edict against the *alumbrados* in an appendix. On the Valladolid conference on Erasmus, see Homza, "Erasmus as Hero or Heretic?"

62. Groups of *alumbrados* resurfaced at the end of the sixteenth century in Extremadura and Andalucia. See the works of Alvaro Huerga, such as *Los alumbrados de Extremadura (1570–1582)* (Madrid: FUE, 1978), and Alison Weber, "Demonizing Ecstasy: Alonso de la Fuente and the *alumbrados* of Extremadura," in *The Mystical Gesture: Essays on Medieval and Early Modern Spiritual Culture in Honor of Mary E. Giles,* ed. Robert Boenig (Aldershot, Hampshire: Ashgate, 2000), 147–65.

63. For Valdés' work as inquisitor-general, see Documents 17–20.

"moral offenses"—were liable to prosecution by the Inquisition: the reasoning was that no true Christian would blaspheme, fornicate, and so forth.
Once these new offenses fell under the Inquisition's purview, inquisitors began to prosecute Old Christians, or Spaniards without any *conversos* in their
backgrounds. As the range of potential heresies became more extensive, so
did the crop of suspects.[64] In addition to deliberately expanding the inquisitors' gaze, Valdés could also diminish the chances of leniency; when cells
of Protestants were discovered in 1557–1558 in Seville and Valladolid, suspects were treated with the utmost severity, even when they confessed and
asked for reconciliation to the Church.[65] In fact, the fear of Protestantism
was so paramount for Valdés and his Suprema that the Inquisition issued an
enlarged Index of prohibited books in 1559, which included fourteen works
of Erasmus in Spanish translation, multiple vernacular treatises on popular
piety, and nineteen purely literary compositions.[66]

If scholars think of the Inquisition under Valdés as a newly energized institution, they also believe it was a highly codified one, not least because of
the measures that this inquisitor-general implemented with his officials. He
limited the number of *familiars,* or auxiliary lay officials, whom tribunals
could commission, and set behavioral standards for the same. He asked one
inquisitor from each tribunal to go on a four-month visitation every year;
the number of visitations went up accordingly. Finally, Valdés' experience
with the Protestants of Valladolid and Seville—as well as Toledo Archbishop
Bartolomé de Carranza—apparently convinced him to issue a more replete
and mandatory set of instructions for inquisitors in 1561. The Valdés *Instructions* dictated inquisitorial practice until the Inquisition ended in 1834.

64. Interest in the morality of Old Christians continued under Gaspar de Quiroga,
appointed inquisitor-general in 1573. For a classic study of the Inquisition and Old
Christians, see Nalle, *God in La Mancha.*

65. On those Protestant cells, see Document 17. For bibliography on Spanish
Protestants in the middle of the sixteenth century, see Gordon Kinder, *Spanish Protestants and Reformers in the Sixteenth Century: A Bibliography* (London: Grant & Cutler, 1983); *idem, Casiodoro de Reina: Spanish Reformer of the Sixteenth Century*
(London: Tamesis, 1975); Casiodoro de Reina, *The Spanish Confession of Faith: London, 1560/61,* trans. Gordon Kinder (Exeter: University of Exeter, 1988); and
Thomas, *La represión del protestantismo.*

66. See Document 19, as well as Virgilio Pinto Crespo, *Inquisición y control ideológico en la España del siglo XVI* (Madrid: Taurus, 1983), and Jesús Martínez Bujanda, "Índices de libros prohibidos del siglo XVI," *Historia de la Inquisición,* vol. 3,
773–828. There was ample precedent for the 1559 Index in Spain. Books were prohibited by the University of Paris in 1542, and in Louvain in 1546 and 1551; the
Catholic Council of Trent also issued an Index of Prohibited Books in 1564. The Index, in other words, was not a Spanish invention.

Modern historians have noted the extent to which inquisitors focused on the Old Christian population in the middle of the sixteenth century. But that finding should not blind us to the fact that the Inquisition also continued to prosecute converts from religious minorities. Substantial numbers of Portuguese *conversos* began to appear in Spanish *autos de fe* after 1570, and their numbers only increased after Spain conquered Portugal ten years later.[67] Significantly, though Spanish Jews had fled *to* Portugal after the 1492 Expulsion, and Jews *in* Portugal were told to convert or leave five years later, the final version of the 1497 order to convert noted that Portuguese *conversos* should not be persecuted for twenty years after their baptisms. Eventually, the Portuguese king announced the foundation of an inquisition in 1532, the first Portuguese *auto de fe* occurred in 1540, and the papal bull that determined the structure of the Portuguese Inquisition was issued in 1547. But in contrast to the newly baptized Jews in Spain in 1492, *conversos* in Portugal had about four extra decades—from 1497 to the 1540s—to practice their Judaism without fear of efficient, official persecution. Small wonder that certain Portuguese *conversos* were often much more sophisticated about their Judaism than their Spanish counterparts, and acted as mentors to the latter in the Jewish faith.[68]

Under the reign of Philip II, Portuguese *conversos*—who excelled as bankers, merchants, and traders—began to enter Spain because it was their homeland, or because it lay in between business routes to France and the Netherlands. The dire financial situation of later Spanish kings often led them and their ministers to try to take advantage of these Portuguese *conversos'* wealth in exchange for temporary respites in persecution.[69] For example, in 1602 Philip III accepted an offer of more than one million ducats from the Portuguese in exchange for a pardon for judaizers; the papal decree was published in 1605, whereupon three tribunals in Portugal released 410

67. For important general treatments of the *converso* problem in the later early modern period, see Michele Escamilla Colin, *Crimes et chatiments dans l'Espagne inquisitorial: Essai de typlogie délictive et punitive sous le dernier Habsbourg et le premier Bourbon* (Paris: Bey International, 1992), vol. 1, and Pilar Huerga Criado, "El problema de la comunidad judeoconversa," in *Historia de la Inquisición*, vol. 3, 441–98.

68. Kamen argues that the influx of Portuguese *conversos* after 1570 was related to inquisition activity in Portugal itself, and he could well be correct; see *The Spanish Inquisition*, 287–88. Portuguese *conversos* began to appear in Spanish *autos de fe* before the union of the two countries in 1580. For the religiosity of the Portuguese *conversos*, see Miriam Bodian, *Hebrews of the Portuguese Nation: Conversos and Community in Early Modern Amsterdam* (Bloomington, IN: Indiana University Press, 1997).

69. James C. Boyajian, *Portuguese Bankers at the Court of Spain, 1626–1650* (New Brunswick, NJ: Rutgers University Press, 1983).

prisoners.[70] When emigration of Portuguese Jews to France, Italy, and England in the 1620s threatened loss of a precious financial commodity for Spain, the prime minister of Philip IV, the Count-Duke of Olivares, decided to try to stop the flow of *conversos* and money outside the peninsula.[71] In 1623, Olivares spearheaded the modification of *limpieza de sangre* (purity of blood) statutes, which had prevented *conversos* from holding public and ecclesiastical offices since the fifteenth and sixteenth centuries; in 1628, he gave Portuguese financiers the liberty to settle and trade without restriction. These pro-*converso* measures did not help Olivares' popularity among Castilians, and after the revolt of Catalonia and Portugal in 1640, and Olivares' own fall in 1643, Portuguese *conversos* at the royal court and its environs were picked off by a wave of inquisition trials that lasted through the 1650s.[72] Those who were able fled the country, but *conversos* continued to make up the majority of the Inquisition's business until approximately 1730.

The other religious minority that made a substantial appearance before the Inquisition in the second half of the sixteenth century consisted of Muslims who had converted to Christianity, called *moriscos*.[73] When the Islamic kingdom of Granada capitulated to Ferdinand and Isabella in 1492, Muslims were assured that they could retain their property, customs, laws, and religion; they were also told that anyone who wanted to emigrate was free to do so. In turn, Christian religious authorities—headed by the first Archbishop of Granada, Hernando de Talavera—hoped to persuade Muslims to convert

70. Lea, *A History of the Inquisition in Spain*, vol. 3, 267–70. When the archbishops of Portugal announced new initiatives against judaizers in 1628, *conversos* paid Philip IV more than eighty thousand ducats to be allowed to leave Portugal itself.

71. Bernardo J. López Belinchón, "Olivares contra los portugueses. Inquisición, conversos, y guerra económica," in *Historia de la Inquisicion*, vol. 3, 499–530.

72. The wealth confiscated from the Portuguese *conversos* in Madrid was staggering. For figures and a succinct narrative, see Kamen, *The Spanish Inquisition*, 291–94.

73. For broad treatments of the Spanish *moriscos*, see Mercedes García Arenal, *Los moriscos* (Madrid: Editora Nacional, 1975); Anwar Chejne, *Islam and the West: The Moriscos, a Cultural and Social History* (Albany, NY: SUNY Press, 1983); and Antonio Domínguez Ortiz and Bernard Vincent, *Historia de los moriscos: vida y tragedia de una minoría,* 2nd ed. (Madrid: Alianza Universidad, 1993). Also consult Louis Cardaillac, ed., *Les morisques et l'Inquisition* (Paris: Publisud, 1990); Rafael Benítez Sánchez-Blanco, "La Inquisición ante los moriscos," and Mikel de Epalza, "Los moriscos frente a la Inquisición, en su visión islámica del cristianismo," both in *Historia de la Inquisición*, vol. 3, 695–736, and 737–72, respectively; Mark Meyerson, *The Muslims of Valencia in the Age of Fernando and Isabel: Between Coexistence and Crusade* (Berkeley: University of California Press, 1991); Benjamin Ehlers, *Between Christians and Moriscos: Juan de Ribera and Religious Reform in Valencia, 1568–1614,* forthcoming, The Johns Hopkins University Press, 2006.

through patience, preaching in Arabic, and the composition of Spanish religious treatises aimed at an Islamic audience.[74] Soon, though, coercion won out over persuasion. In 1499, royal confessor and Franciscan friar Francisco Ximénez de Cisneros—soon to become the archbishop of Toledo and inquisitor-general—argued that stricter measures should be employed, including mass baptisms and the conversion of mosques into churches.

Three years later, in 1502, all Muslims in Castile were ordered to convert or emigrate. The same mandate was applied to Muslims in Valencia in 1525, and Muslims in Aragón in 1526.[75] After 1526, then, all Muslims in Spain were formally and officially Christians, except that the baptized *moriscos* steadfastly refused to be assimilated into Christianity and fiercely tried to preserve their customs, laws, and religion. Throughout the sixteenth century, ecclesiastical authorities alternated between arguing for rigorous measures against the *moriscos,* and noticing that no one had bothered to catechize them; policy wavered accordingly.[76] To complicate matters further, *moriscos* might feel more or less protected in their practice of Islam depending upon where they lived; in Valencia, noble lords consistently blocked any interference with their *morisco* vassals, and the Inquisition itself cut a deal in 1526 not to prosecute the *moriscos* there for forty years. In contrast, *moriscos* in Granada were a majority of the population and enjoyed a full-blown civilization of their own, but lacked a substantial counterweight to either the Inquisition or the king.

Though *moriscos* were occasionally prosecuted by the Inquisition before the 1560s, a confluence of events in that decade dramatically heightened the frequency of *morisco* trials for heresy. (By practicing Islam after baptism, *moriscos,* like judaizing *conversos,* were heretics by definition of Christian religious authorities.) First, the Council of Trent ended in 1564, after having spent seven years over three decades defining the Catholic process of justification, the canon of sacred texts, the sacraments, and proper ordering of the

74. On that process of religious acculturation, see David Coleman, *Creating Christian Granada: Society and Religious Culture in an Old-World Frontier City, 1492–1600* (Ithaca, NY: Cornell University Press, 2003).

75. The forced conversion of Muslims in Valencia had already mostly occurred; in 1520–1521, groups of brotherhoods (*germanías*) rebelled against the local aristocracy and attempted to break the nobles' power over the countryside by baptizing their Muslim vassals. After much discussion, the authorities decided that the Muslims' baptism, however coerced, was valid. It then appeared unreasonable to tolerate unbaptized Muslims in Aragón, and the decrees of Charles V followed.

76. To see this dynamic in action with Juan de Ribera, the Archbishop of Valencia, consult Ehlers, *Between Christians and Moriscos.*

Church hierarchy.[77] Spain was one of the first countries to promulgate the decrees from Trent; diocesan synods were called accordingly, and questions about proper Christian behavior consequently arose. Next, in the Revolt of the Alpujarras (1568–1570), the *moriscos* of Granada rebelled against Philip II's orders to abandon their dress, customs, religious practices and language. The revolt ended with the *moriscos'* surrender and their forced redistribution throughout Castile, whereby the center of *morisco* culture moved to Valencia. Scholars believe that newfound proximity to *morisco* communities, memory of the *moriscos'* rebellion, and Philip II's ongoing war against the Islamic Ottoman Empire engendered religious hostility that played into the hands of Spanish inquisitors. *Moriscos* were the defendants in most inquisition trials for Aragón, Valencia, and Granada between 1560 and 1614, though attempts at palliation still took place; in 1571, Valencian *moriscos* agreed to pay 2,500 ducats per year to the inquisition tribunal there in return for the nonconfiscation of their property. The deal was intended to guard the workers and lands of Christian lords.

Over the last two decades of the sixteenth century, Philip II repeatedly heard proposals to expel the *moriscos;* he refused. His heir, Philip III, who became king in 1598, heard similar propositions debated, but the nobility of Aragón and Valencia, royal confessors and advisors, and numerous public intellectuals (*arbitristas*) opposed expulsion through 1607. Two years later, though, the "favorite" of Philip III, the Duke of Lerma—a Valencian noble in his own right, with *morisco* vassals of his own—presented a memo to the Council of State which argued that Valencian lords should be compensated with the lands of their *moriscos* if the latter were ejected. Those Valencian seigneurs ultimately put financial gain ahead of protecting their vassals.[78] The attractiveness of their expulsion proposal to Philip III may have had something to do with the twelve-year truce he had just been forced to sign with the Dutch. The *moriscos* were officially expelled on April 4, 1609, and the process took place in stages through 1614; unlike the Jewish Expulsion of 1492, the Inquisition played no role here. Approximately 300,000 *moriscos* were forced to leave Spain, and their departure was highly controversial both then and now.[79] Historians strongly contend that the

---

77. Called originally by Pope Paul III, the Council of Trent was in session in 1545–1547, 1551–1552, and 1562–1563. *The Canons and Decrees of the Council of Trent,* trans. Rev. H. J. Schroeder, O.P. (Rockford, IL: Tan Books, 1978).

78. They also could have been provoked by a certain sense of demographic pressure. See Kamen, *The Spanish Inquisition,* 227, for details on the relative proportion of *moriscos* to Old Christians in Valencia, Granada, and Aragón.

79. The idea of a *morisco* expulsion was rejected by numerous public commentators

expulsion of the *moriscos* between 1609 and 1614 was an agricultural and financial disaster, coming as it did after severe bouts of plague: the productivity of the land declined, as did the amount of taxes collected. The Inquisition lost business too. In 1611, the tribunals of Zaragoza and Valencia told the Suprema they were bankrupt, since so much of their financing had come from the *morisco* population.[80]

The Spanish Inquisition did not disappear with the *moriscos;* its officials simply focused on *conversos* for the rest of the seventeenth century, including a wave of persecutions on the island of Mallorca between 1675 and 1691.[81] Business generally waned in the eighteenth century, though there were a few bursts of activity: judaizers preoccupied inquisitors for the first several decades, then gave way to foreign Protestants and Freemasons.[82] The end of the Inquisition came in fits and starts, and it was finally undone by monarchs, just as kings originally created it. When Ferdinand VII and his father Charles IV handed Spain to Napoleon Bonaparte in 1808, one of Napoleon's first actions was to extinguish the Inquisition. During Spain's ensuing War of Independence against Napoleon, Spanish parliamentarians abolished the Inquisition themselves in 1813. Once back on the throne, King Ferdinand VII restored it in 1814, but was forced to suppress it again in 1820. The Spanish Inquisition was finally and forever eliminated by Queen Isabella II of Spain on July 15, 1834.[83]

The Inquisition lasted 356 years, and it was not unopposed. New research has demonstrated substantial elite resistance to it—on theological, pastoral, and legal grounds—in the sixteenth century.[84] Such findings imply that the Spanish Inquisition might still surprise us, and suggest that we should continue to ask subtle questions about this institution even as we debate its backwardness or modernity, its objectives or effectiveness. The point of this collection is to introduce students and general readers to the earliest and

---

and ecclesiastical leaders; it was by no means acceptable to a significant proportion of the learned population.

80. Kamen, *The Spanish Inquisition,* 228.

81. Angela Selke, *Los chuetas y la Inquisición: vida y muerte en el ghetto de Mallorca* (Madrid: Taurus, 1971).

82. For *converso* prosecutions in the eighteenth century in Llerena and Logroño, see essays by José Martínez Millán and M. Torres Arce, in *Historia de la Inquisición,* vol. 3, 557–695. On Freemasons, see J. Ferrer Benimelli, "Inquisición y masonería," in *Historia de la Inquisición,* vol. 1, 1286–304.

83. For details, see M. Jiménez Montserín, "La abolición del Tribunal (1808–1834)," in *Historia de la Inquisición,* vol. 1, 1424–86.

84. Stefania Pastore, *Il vangelo e la spada: l'inquisizione di Castiglia e i suoi critici (1460–1598)* (Rome: Edizione di storia e letteratura, 2003).

most active period in Spanish Inquisition history, the era between 1478 and 1600. I make no claims whatsoever to completeness, whether geographical, chronological, or thematic. Nearly all the documents translated here pertain to tribunals and inquisitors in Castile; their end date is 1593; texts I had wanted to include had to be cut in the interests of space and time. Primary sources from the Spanish Inquisition are peculiarly useful for teaching historical method, since they force us to contemplate gaps in the evidence, the challenges of legal records, and the difficulties of uncovering religious beliefs and cultural practices in earlier centuries. Above all, these texts exhibit alterity: they demonstrate the foreignness of the past, and in the process reveal that Spain and the Inquisition were far more complex than mythical stereotypes allow.

NOTE ON TRANSLATIONS

All translations are my own. In translating from original, hitherto untranscribed sources, I have resolved abbreviations and allotted punctuation; I have also added diacritics in the interests of clarity. Spelling has been standardized when it could lead to confusion. Any errors or infelicities that remain are my sole responsibility.

SELECTED BIBLIOGRAPHY

Ahlgren, Gillian T. W. *The Inquisition of Francisca: A Sixteenth-Century Visionary on Trial.* The Other Voice in Early Modern Europe. Chicago: The University of Chicago Press, 2005.

Ames, Christine Caldwell. "Does Inquisition Belong to Religious History?" *American Historical Review* 110 (2005): 11–37.

Bataillon, Marcel. *Erasmo y España: estudios sobre la historia espiritual del siglo XVI.* Trans. A. Alatorre. 2nd Spanish ed., revised. Mexico City: Fondo de Cultúra Económica. 1966.

Beinart, Haim. *Records of the Trials of the Spanish Inquisition in Ciudad Real 1483–1527.* 4 vols. Jerusalem: Israel National Academy of Sciences and Humanities, 1974–1985.

———. *Conversos on Trial: The Inquisition in Ciudad Real.* Jerusalem: Magnes Press, 1981.

Benítez Sánchez-Blanco, Rafael. "La Inquisición ante los moriscos." In *Historia de la Inquisición en España y América,* vol. 3, 695–736. Eds. Joaquín Pérez Villanueva and Bartolomé Escandell Bonet. Madrid: BAE, 2000.

Bennassar, Bartolomé, ed. *L'Inquisition espagnole, xve–xixe siècle.* Paris: Hachette, 1979.

Bethencourt, Francisco. *La Inquisición en la época moderna: España, Portugal, Italia, siglos XV–XIX.* Madrid: Akal, 1995.

Bilinkoff, Jodi. *Related Lives: Confessors and Their Female Penitents, 1450–1750.* Ithaca, NY: Cornell University Press, 2005.

———. "A Spanish Prophetess and Her Patrons: The Case of María de Santo Domingo." *Sixteenth Century Journal* 23 (1992): 21–35.

Bodian, Miriam. *Hebrews of the Portuguese Nation: Conversos and Community in Early Modern Amsterdam.* Bloomington, IN: Indiana University Press, 1997.

Boyajian, James C. *Portuguese Bankers at the Court of Spain, 1626–1650.* New Brunswick, NJ: Rutgers University Press, 1983.

Cardaillac, Louis, ed. *Les morisques et l'Inquisition.* Paris: Publisud, 1990.

Chejne, Anwar. *Islam and the West: The Moriscos, a Cultural and Social History.* Albany, NY: SUNY Press, 1983.

Cohen, Jeremy. *Living Letters of the Law: Ideas of the Jew in Medieval Christianity.* Berkeley: University of California Press, 1999.

———. *The Friars and the Jews: The Evolution of Medieval Anti-Judaism.* Ithaca, NY: Cornell University Press, 1982.

Coleman, David. *Creating Christian Granada: Society and Religious Culture in an Old-World Frontier City, 1492–1600.* Ithaca, NY: Cornell University Press, 2003.

Contreras, Jaime. *El Santo Oficio de la Inquisición en Galicia, 1560–1700.* Madrid: Akal, 1982.

Contreras, Jaime, and Gustav Henningsen. "Forty-four Thousand Cases of the Spanish Inquisition (1540–1700): Analysis of a Historical Data Bank." In *The Inquisition in Early Modern Europe*, 100–29. Eds. Gustav Henningsen and John
Tedeschi. DeKalb, IL: Northern Illinois University Press, 1986.

Dedieu, Jean-Pierre. *L'Administration de la foi: l'Inquisition de Tolède, XVI–XVIII siècle*. Bibliothèque de la Casa de Velázquez. Vol. 7. Madrid: Casa de Velázquez,
1989.

Díaz-Mas, Paloma. *Sephardim: The Jews from Spain*. Trans. George K. Zucker. Chicago:
The University of Chicago Press, 1992.

Domínguez Ortiz, Antonio, and Bernard Vincent. *Historia de los moriscos: vida y
tragedía de una minoría*. 2nd ed. Madrid: Alianza Universidad, 1993.

Eire, Carlos M. N. *From Madrid to Purgatory*. Cambridge: Cambridge University
Press, 1995.

Ehlers, Benjamin. *Between Christians and Moriscos: Juan de Ribera and Religious Reform in Valencia, 1568–1614*. Baltimore: The Johns Hopkins University Press,
2006.

———. "La esclava y el patriarca: las visiones de Catalina Muñoz en la Valencia de
Juan de Ribera." *Estudis* 23 (1997): 101–16.

Epalza, Mikel de. "Los moriscos frente a la Inquisición, en su visión islámica del cristianismo." In *Historia de la Inquisición en España y América*, vol. 3, 737–72. Eds.
Joaquín Pérez Villanueva and Bartolomé Escandell Bonet. Madrid: BAE, 2000.

Escamilla Colin, Michele. *Crimes et chatiments dans l'Espagne inquisitorial: essai de
typlogie délictive et punitive sous le dernier Habsbourg et le premier Bourbon*. 2 vols.
Paris: Bey International, 1992.

Ferrer Benimelli, J. A. "Inquisición y masonería." In *Historia de la Inquisición en
España y América*, vol. 1, 1286–304. Eds. Joaquín Pérez Villanueva and Bartolomé
Escandell Bonet. Madrid: BAE, 1984.

García Arenal, Mercedes. *Inquisición y moriscos: los procesos del tribunal de Cuenca*.
Madrid: Siglo Veintiuno, 1987.

———. *Los moriscos*. Madrid: Editora Nacional, 1975.

García Fuentes, José María. *La Inquisición de Granada en el sigo XVI: fuentes para su
estudio*. Granada: Universidad de Granada, 1981.

Giles, Mary E. "Francisca Hernández and the Sexuality of Religious Dissent." In
Women in the Inquisition: Spain and the New World, 75–97. Ed. Mary E. Giles.
Baltimore: The Johns Hopkins University Press, 1999.

Given, James B. *Inquisition and Medieval Society: Power, Discipline, and Resistance in
Languedoc*. Ithaca, NY: Cornell University Press, 1997.

González Novalín, José Luis. "Las instrucciones de Valdés." In *Historia de la Inquisición en España y América*, vol. 1, 637–47. Eds. Joaquín Pérez Villanueva and
Bartolomé Escandell Bonet. Madrid: BAE. 1984.

———. *El inquisidor general Fernando de Valdés (1483–1568): su vida y obra*. 2 vols.
Oviedo: Universidad de Oviedo, 1968 and 1971.

Gracia Boix, Rafael. *Autos de fe y causas de la inquisición de Córdoba*. Colección de textos para la historia de Córdoba. Córdoba: Publicaciones de la Excma. Diputación Provincial, 1983.

——. *Colección de documentos para la historia de la inquisición de Córdoba*. Córdoba: Publicaciones del Monte de Piedad y Caja de Ahorros de Córdoba, 1982.

Haliczer, Stephen. *The Inquisition in the Kingdom of Valencia (1478–1834)*. Berkeley: University of California Press, 1994.

Henningsen, Gustav. *The Witches' Advocate*. Reno, NV: University of Nevada Press, 1980.

——. *The Salazar Documents*. Leiden: Brill, 2004.

Homza, Lu Ann. "How to Harass an Inquisitor-General: The Polyphonic Law of Friar Francisco Ortiz." In *A Renaissance of Conflicts: Visions and Revisions of Law and Society in Early Modern Italy and Spain*. Eds. John A. Marino and Thomas Kuehn. Centre for Reformation and Renaissance Studies. *Essays and Studies* 3, 299–336. Toronto: CRRS Publications, 2004.

——. *Religious Authority in the Spanish Renaissance*. The Johns Hopkins University Studies in Historical and Political Science. 118th Series. No. 1. Baltimore: The Johns Hopkins University Press, 2000.

——. "Erasmus as Hero or Heretic? Spanish Humanism and the Valladolid Conference of 1527." *Renaissance Quarterly* 50 (1997): 78–118.

Huerga Criado, Pilar. "El problema de la comunidad judeoconversa." In *Historia de la Inquisición en España y América*, vol. 3, 441–98. Eds. Joaquín Pérez Villanueva and Bartolomé Escandell Bonet. Madrid: BAE. 2000.

Jiménez Montserín, Miguel. *Introdución a la inquisición española: documentos básicos para el estudio del Santo Oficio*. Madrid: Editora Nacional, 1980.

Kagan, Richard L. "Prescott's Paradigm: American Historical Scholarship and the Decline of Spain." *American Historical Review* 101 (1996): 423–46.

Kagan, Richard L., and Abigail Dyer, eds. and trans. *Inquisitorial Inquiries: Brief Lives of Secret Jews and Other Heretics*. Baltimore: The Johns Hopkins University Press, 2004.

Kamen, Henry. *The Spanish Inquisition: A Historical Revision*. New Haven, CT: Yale University Press, 1997.

Kinder, Gordon. *Spanish Protestants and Reformers in the Sixteenth Century: A Bibliography*. London: Grant & Cutler, 1983.

——. *Casiodoro de Reina: Spanish Reformer of the Sixteenth Century*. London: Tamesis, 1975.

Lea, Henry Charles. *A History of the Inquisition of Spain*. New York: American Scholar Publications, Inc. Reprint edition. 4 vols. 1966.

Llorca, Bernardino. *La inquisición española y los alumbrados (1509–1667), según las actas originales de Madrid y de otros archivos*. Salamanca: Universidad Pontificia, 1980.

López Belinchón, Bernardo J. "Olivares contra los portugueses. Inquisición, conversos, y guerra económica." In *Historia de la Inquisición en España y América,* vol. 3, 499–530. Eds. Joaquín Pérez Villanueva and Bartolomé Escandell Bonet. Madrid: BAE, 2000.

Márquez, Antonio. *Literatura e Inquisición en España (1478–1834).* Madrid: Taurus, 1980.

————. *Los alumbrados: orígenes y filosofía, 1525–1559.* Madrid: Taurus, 1972.

Martínez Bujanda, Jesús. "Índices de libros prohibidos del siglo XVI." In *Historia de la Inquisición en España y América* vol. 3, 773–828. Eds. Joaquín Pérez Villanueva and Bartolomé Escandell Bonet. Madrid: BAE, 2000.

————. *Index de l'Inquisition espagnole: 1583, 1584.* Sherbrooke: Centre d'études de la Renaissance, Université de Sherbrooke, 1993.

————. *Index de l'Inquisition espagnole, 1551, 1554, 1559.* Geneva: Librarie Droz, 1984.

Martínez Millán, José. "La persecución inquisitorial contra los criptojudíos en el siglo XVIII: El Tribunal de Llerena (1700–1730)." In *Historia de la Inquisición en España y América,* vol. 3, 557–656. Eds. Joaquín Pérez Villanueva and Bartolomé Escandell Bonet. Madrid: BAE. 2000.

————. *La hacienda de la Inquisición (1478–1700).* Madrid: CSIC, 1984.

Melammed, Renée Levine. *Heretics or Daughters of Israel? The Crypto-Jewish Women of Castile.* New York: Oxford University Press, 1998.

Meseguer Fernández, J. "El periodo fundacional (1478–1517)." In *Historia de la Inquisición en España y América,* vol. 1, 281–370. Eds. Joaquín Pérez Villanueva and Bartolomé Escandell Bonet. Madrid: BAE. 1984.

Meyerson, Mark. *The Muslims of Valencia in the Age of Fernando and Isabel: Between Coexistence and Crusade.* Berkeley: University of California Press. 1991.

Monter, E. William. *Frontiers of Heresy: The Spanish Inquisition from the Basque Lands to Sicily.* Cambridge: Cambridge University Press. 1990.

Muñoz Fernández, Ángela. "Madre e maestra, autora de doctrina: Isabel de la Cruz y el alumbradismo toledana del primer tercio del siglo xvi." In *De leer a escribir, I: La educación de las mujeres: ¿libertad o subordinación?,* 99–122. Ed. Cristina Segura Graiño. Madrid: Asociación Cultural AL-MUDAYNA, 1996.

————. *Beatas y santas neocastellanas: ambivalencia de la religión, correctoras del poder (ss. XIV–XVII).* Madrid: Comunidad de Madrid, 1994.

Nalle, Sara T. *Mad for God: Bartolomé Sánchez, the Secret Messiah of Cardenete.* Charlottesville, VA: University Press of Virginia, 2001.

————. *God in La Mancha: Religious Reform and the People of Cuenca, 1500–1650.* The Johns Hopkins University Studies in Historical and Political Science, 2. Baltimore: The Johns Hopkins University Press, 1992.

————. "Literacy and Culture in Early Modern Castile." *Past and Present* 125 (1989): 65–96.

————. "Inquisitors, Priests, and the People during the Catholic Reformation in Spain." *Sixteenth Century Journal* 18 (1987): 557–87.

Netanyahu, Benzion. *The Origins of the Inquisition in Fifteenth-Century Spain.* New York: Random House, 1995.

Nirenberg, David. "Mass Conversion and Genealogical Mentalities: Jews and Christians in Fifteenth-Century Spain." *Past and Present* 174 (2002): 3–41.

Ortega-Costa, Milagros. *Proceso de la Inquisición contra María de Cazalla.* Madrid: Fundación Universitaria Española, 1978.

Pastore, Stefania. *Un'eresia spagnola: spiritualità conversa, alumbradismo e inquisizione (1449–1559).* Florence: Leo S. Olschki, 2004.

———. *Il vangelo e la spada: l'inquisizione di Castiglia e i suoi critici (1460–1598).* Rome: Edizione di storia e letteratura, 2003.

Pérez Escohotado, Javier. *Antonio Medrano, alumbrado epicúreo: proceso inquisitorial, Toledo 1530.* Madrid: Editorial Verbum, 2003.

———. *Proceso inquisitorial contra el Bachiller Antonio de Medrano (Logroño 1526–Calahorra 1527).* Logroño: Gobierno de La Rioja, 1988.

Perry, Mary Elizabeth. "Contested Identities: the Moriscan Visionary, Beatriz de Robles." In *Women in the Inquisition: Spain and the New World,* 171–88. Ed. Mary E. Giles. Baltimore: The Johns Hopkins University Press, 1999.

Peters, Edward. *Inquisition.* New York: Free Press, 1988.

———. *Torture.* Philadelphia: University of Pennsylvania Press, 1987.

———. *The Magician, the Witch, and the Law.* Philadelphia: University of Pennsylvania Press, 1978.

Pinto Crespo, Virgilio. *Inquisición y control ideológico en la España del siglo XVI.* Madrid: Taurus, 1983.

Poska, Allyson. "When Bigamy Is the Charge: Gallegan Women and the Holy Office." In *Women in the Inquisition: Spain and the New World,* 189–208. Ed. Mary E. Giles. Baltimore: The Johns Hopkins University Press. 1999.

Redondo, Augustín. "Luther et l'Espagne de 1520–1536." *Mélanges de la Casa de Velázquez* 1 (1965): 109–65.

Rivero Rodríguez, Manuel. "La inquisición española en Sicilia (siglos XVI a XVIII)." In *Historia de la Inquisición en España y América,* vol. 3, 1031–222. Eds. Joaquín Pérez Villanueva and Bartolomé Escandell Bonet. Madrid: BAE. 2000.

Rodríguez Besné, José Ramón. *El Consejo de la Suprema Inquisición: Perfil jurídico de una institución.* Madrid: Editorial Complutense, 2000.

Sarrión Mora, Adelina. *Beatas y endemoniadas: mujeres heterodoxas ante la inquisición, siglos xvi a xix.* Madrid: Alianza Editorial, 2003.

Schutte, Anne. *Aspiring Saints: Pretense of holiness, Inquisition, and Gender in the Republic of Venice, 1618–1750.* Baltimore: The Johns Hopkins University Press, 2001.

Selke, Angela. *Los chuetas y la Inquisición: vida y muerte en el ghetto de Mallorca.* Madrid: Taurus, 1971.

———. *El Santo Oficio de la Inquisición: Proceso de Dr. Francisco Ortiz (1529–32).* Madrid: Ediciones Guadarrama, 1968.

Selke, Angela. "El caso del Bachiller Antonio de Medrano: iluminado epicúreo del siglo xvi." *Bulletin hispanique* 58 (1956): 393–420.

Sesma Muñoz, J. Angel. *El establecimiento de la Inquisición en Aragón (1484–86): documentos para su estudio.* Zaragoza: Institución Fernando el Católico, 1987.

Silverblatt, Irene. *Modern Inquisitions: Peru and the Colonial Origins of the Civilized World.* Durham, NC: Duke University Press, 2004.

Tausiet, María. *Ponzoña en los ojos: brujería y superstición en Aragón en el siglo XVI.* Zaragoza: Instituto Fernando el Católico, 2000.

Tellechea Idígoras, José Ignacio. *Fray Bartolomé Carranza: documentos historicós.* Archivo documental espanol, vol. XIX, 1. 2 vols. Madrid: Real Academia de la Historia, 1962.

Thomas, Werner. *La represión del protestantismo en España, 1517–1648.* Leuven: Leuven University Press, 2001.

Torres Arce, M. "Los judaizantes y el Santo Oficio de Logroño en el reinado de Felipe V." In *Historia de la Inquisición en España y América,* vol. 3, 557–695. Eds. Joaquín Pérez Villanueva and Bartolomé Escandell Bonet. Madrid: BAE, 2000.

Vincent, Bernard. "Un espacio de exclusión: la cárcel inquisitorial en el siglo XVI." In *Minorías y marginados en la España del siglo XVI.* Ed. Bernard Vincent. Granada: Diputación provincial de Granada, 1987.

Weber, Alison. "Demonizing Ecstasy: Alonso de la Fuente and the *alumbrados* of Extremadura." In *The Mystical Gesture: Essays on Medieval and Early Modern Spiritual Culture in Honor of Mary E. Giles,* 147–65. Ed. Robert Boenig. Aldershot, Hampshire: Ashgate, 2000.

Zarri, Gabrielle. *Finzione e santità tra medioevo ed età moderna.* Torino: Rosenberg & Sellier, 1991.

Map of Spain during the Inquisition

THE FIRST YEARS OF THE INQUISITION

DOCUMENT 1

Recollections of the Reign of the Catholic Kings, Written by *Bachiller* Andrés Bernáldez[1]

[Andrés Bernáldez, a chronicler and parish priest in Los Palacios, near Seville, apparently observed the first actions of the first inquisitors under Catholic Kings Ferdinand and Isabella, though he wrote his account in the early sixteenth century. His narrative owes as much to religious fervor as to any eyewitness reporting. Bernáldez filtered his chronicle through Western European, Christian clichés about Jews, from blindness and dissipation to the Jews' alleged preference for the Talmud over the Torah; and his account is also problematic when it comes to causation and statistics. Historians recognize that the pogroms and forced baptisms of 1391 created a Spanish population of converts from Judaism to Christianity; they also know that Ferdinand and Isabella spent the second half of 1477 in Seville where they heard the preaching of Friar Alonso de Hojeda. But it is not known who suggested that the monarchs write to Pope Sixtus IV and request the privilege of naming inquisitors, and it is impossible to document the activities of the first inquisitors themselves, since the records of their cases have disappeared.]

Chapter 43: On the beginning of the heresy and the beginning of the Inquisition, and when Mosaic depravity and the punishment of Jewish ceremonies had its climax

Heretical Mosaic depravity reigned for a long time, hidden away in corners, not daring to show itself; and it was allowed to exist through the negligence of the prelates—namely, the archbishops and bishops of Spain—who never acknowledged or denounced it to the kings or the popes as they were obliged to do.

This Mosaic heresy had its start in the year of Our Lord 1390, at the beginning of the reign of King Henry III of Castile, when the plundering of

---

1. *Memorias del reinado de los Reyes Católicos, que escriba el bachiller Andrés Bernáldez,* edition and study by Manuel Gómez-Moreno and Juan de M. Carriazo (Madrid: Real Academia de la Historia, 1962): 94–103. A *bachiller* signifies a man with a basic university education.

the Jewish quarter occurred as a result of the preaching of Friar Vincent Ferrer, a holy, Catholic, and learned man, of the Order of St. Dominic. At that
time, Ferrer wanted to convert all the Jews of Spain through preaching and
proofs from the Holy Law and Scripture, and to put an end to that obstinate, stinking synagogue.[2] He and other preachers preached a great deal to
the Jews in the synagogues, churches, and fields; the Jewish rabbis, completely convinced by the Scripture of the Law and its prophecies, did not
know how to reply.[3] But they were deceived and misled by that gloss called
the Talmud . . . made after the birth of Our Lord, in the year 400.[4] [The
Jews have] ten times as many copies of the Talmud as they do the Bible, and
they sent it throughout the world, wherever there were Jews, to strengthen
them. . . . There were very great lies and intricate arguments in that Talmud. . . . The Jews deny the truth and are ignorant of it; thus it is said, "There
is no argument against those who deny the truth." [*Contra negante veritatem
nulla est disputatio.*]

As a result, Friar Vincent Ferrer could convert only a few Jews, and the
people spitefully put the Jews in Castile to the sword and killed many, and this
occurred all over Castile in a single day, Tuesday. Then the Jews themselves
came to the churches to be baptized, and so they were; and very many in Castile
were made into Christians. After their baptism, some went to Portugal and
to other kingdoms to be Jews; others, after some time had passed, returned
to being Jews in places where they were not known. Many unbaptized

2. St. Vincent Ferrer (c. 1350–1419) was canonized in 1455. His preaching helped
to provoke the pogroms that swept through Spain in 1391. He also helped to inspire
anti-Jewish legislation in Castile in 1412.

3. Judaism shares with Christianity and Islam the belief in one universal God, conceived as personal, who is the Creator of the universe and the highest source of values. Judaism's most sacred, scriptural source is the Torah, which corresponds to the
Christian Old Testament, and which is made up of the Law, the Prophets, and Writings. The first five books of the Torah are called the Pentateuch and contain, among
other things, the laws that Moses received from God and disseminated to the Jewish
people. For more information on Judaic rituals, see the introduction to Document 3.

4. The Talmud encompasses the oral, rabbinical teachings of the Jews (the Mishnah) and the collection of discussions on the Mishnah (the Gemara). The Talmud
exists in two main forms, the Babylonian and the Palestinian, which are not identical; both were formed during the fifth century. In twelfth-century Europe, Christian
theologians began to believe that the Jewish population's reliance on such rabbinical
teachings over the Old Testament betrayed its divinely sanctioned role as first witness to God. The Talmud accordingly became a symbol of Jewish falsity. See Jeremy
Cohen, *The Friars and the Jews: The Evolution of Medieval Anti-Judaism* (Ithaca, NY:
Cornell University Press, 1982), and *idem, Living Letters of the Law: Ideas of the Jew
in Medieval Christianity* (Berkeley: University of California Press, 1999).

Jews and synagogues still remained in Castile, and the lords and kings always protected them because of their great utility.[5]

The baptized Jews who stayed were called *conversos;* this is the origin of the name "*converso,*" which means those converted to the Holy Catholic Faith. The *conversos* observed the Faith very badly . . . for the most part they were secret Jews. In fact, they were neither Jews nor Christians, since they were baptized, but were heretics, and [yet] without the Law [of Moses]. Thus this heresy was born, as you have heard. . . .

In the first years of the reign of the very Catholic and Christian Kings Ferdinand and Queen Isabel,[6] this heresy was so bold that its learned men were on the verge of preaching the Law of Moses, and its simple men could not disguise the fact that they were Jews. When the King and Queen went to Seville for the first time, the Archbishop of Seville, Pedro González de Mendoza, was there as well; and Friar Alonso [de Hojeda], a holy and Catholic Dominican from the monastery of San Pablo, who always preached and fought against this heresy, was there too. He and other religious and Catholic men told the King and Queen about the great evil and heresy in Seville. They in turn committed the matter to the Archbishop, so that he could punish the guilty and remedy the matter.[7] He issued certain orders about it, and promulgated them in the city and the entire archbishopric, and put deputies in place. And two years passed, and his measures were worthless.

According to what we saw at that time, this horrible beast[8] walked around very freely, and the ill-fated, heretical Jews fled from ecclesiastical doctrine

5. An implicit reference to the employment of Jews as tax collectors.

6. Ferdinand was king of Aragón from 1479 to 1516, and sovereign of Castile from 1474 to 1504; Isabella was queen of Castile from 1474 to 1504. By the terms of their marriage agreement in 1469, Ferdinand's personal authority in Castile was sharply restricted; though their correspondence styled them "sovereigns" of both Castile and Aragón, there was neither fusion of the two kingdoms, nor was one subordinated to the other. By the terms of Isabella's will in 1504, the crown of Castile would pass to her daughter Juana as her chosen successor, and Ferdinand would be king of Aragón only. This arrangement did not quite work out as Isabella had imagined; see Bethany Aram, *Juana the Mad* (Baltimore: The Johns Hopkins University Press, 2004).

7. Bernáldez' remarks illustrate that Ferdinand and Isabella first treated the problem of heresy as a matter for archbishops. Up to now, heresy had been an episcopal matter in Castile, since the medieval, papal inquisition had been introduced only in Aragón. Thus Archbishop Pedro González de Mendoza and his vicar-general, Pedro Fernández de Solís, authorized preaching campaigns and promulgated ordinances to vivify Seville's religious life, and Ferdinand and Isabella waited to deploy the papal bull of 1478 to see if such tactics would work.

8. By "horrible beast," Bernaldez means the heresy of judaizing, which he is tying, metaphorically, to the Antichrist in the book of Revelation.

[sic] and Christian customs. Those who could avoid baptizing their children, did so; and those who did baptize them, washed them in their houses as soon as they brought them home. . . . You also have to know that before the Inquisition arrived, the customs of ordinary *conversos* were the same as the same stinking Jews', which was why they continually talked to each other. Thus they were gluttons and comrades, and they never stopped the Jewish customs of eating little dishes and stews cooked overnight with coals, little dishes of onions and garlic fried with oil, and meat cooked with oil, and they used that meat instead of pork and fat, in order to avoid the pork. The oil with the meat and the other things that they stewed smelled very bad on the breath, so their houses and doors smelled very bad from that food. Thus they themselves had the smell of the Jews, on account of the food they ate. . . . They did not eat pork except by force. They secretly ate meat during Catholic feast days, vigils, and the four ember weeks.[9] They observed Passover and Saturdays as best they could: they sent oil to the synagogues for the lamps; they had Jews who preached to them in their houses, in secret, especially to the women.[10] They had Jewish rabbis who strangled sheep and birds for their gatherings. They ate unleavened bread during the three-day feast of the Jews, and secretly performed all the Jewish ceremonies as best they could, the men as well as the women. They always avoided receiving the Sacraments of the Holy Church, except when they were constrained by the Church's constitutions. They never confessed the truth. . . .

They did not believe that God rewarded virginity and chastity; their whole aim was to increase and multiply. At the time that this heretical depravity arose, many monasteries founded by Gentiles and merchants were violated, and many professed nuns were corrupted and mocked, some of them by gifts, others by trickery . . . and the *conversos* did it to injure Jesus Christ and the Church.[11] Most of them were usurers who had many artful ways and tricks, because they all supported themselves from leisurely sorts

9. The four ember weeks are four groups of three days in the church year—the Wednesday, Friday, and Saturday after the feasts of St. Lucy (December 13), Ash Wednesday, Pentecost, and the Holy Cross (September 14)—which were observed as days of fasting and abstinence in the Western Church.

10. It is interesting that Bernáldez highlights women as more likely to fall into judaizing than men, since the extant trials for the period from 1480 to 1520—when judaizing was the inquisitors' primary target—do reveal a preponderance of female defendants. It's likely that Bernáldez' remarks reflect a sex disparity that became apparent only after the prosecutions began.

11. Charges of sexual lasciviousness are routine in antiheretical literature, dating back to ancient Romans' calumny against Christians. See Peters, *The Magician, the Witch, and the Law.*

of work, and in buying and selling they had no conscience where Christians were concerned. They never wanted to take jobs that involved plowing or digging, or walking through the fields guarding flocks, nor did they teach their children; rather, they took work in town, which involved sitting down and earning something to eat with little effort. . . .

The King and Queen were assured of all the above when they were in Seville. When they left that city, they gave the job of seeking out and punishing the guilty to the vicar-general of Seville, who was the Bishop of Cádiz, Pedro Fernández de Solís; and Diego de Merlo, who was the Chief Officer of Justice who remained in Seville at that time . . . and Friar Alonso [de Hojeda], imitating Friar Vincent Ferrer, remained as well to look into the matter along with other clerics and friars. And seeing that the situation could not be tolerated or fixed in any other way except by an inquisition, they clearly and distinctly proclaimed the matter in detail to their Highnesses, and made them understand how, where, and by whom these Jewish ceremonies were performed, and how powerful people in much of the city were involved.[12] The King and Queen were simultaneously informed that this monstrous affliction ran through all of Castile. They obtained a bull from Pope Sixtus IV to proceed against this heresy and to punish it with fire. The papal bull was conceded and the inquisition ordered in 1480.

Chapter 44. How they began to seize, burn, and reconcile Jewish heretics in Seville. And the great pestilence of 1481

Their Highnesses having obtained the bull for the Inquisition . . . the first inquisitors came to Seville: two Dominican monks, a provincial and a vicar, one named Friar Miguel [de Morillo] and the other Friar Juan [de San Martín]. Accompanying them was Dr. Medina, a cleric of San Pedro. The three, working as one, began their inquisition with great diligence, at the start of 1481.[13]

In a very few days, through various ways and means, these three men knew

12. What Bernáldez does not mention is that Seville was a hotbed of noble, Old Christian factionalism, involving the Marquis of Cádiz and the Duke of Medina Sidonia. It is possible to view Ferdinand and Isabella's measures against Seville's *conversos* as part of a larger plan to quell civil unrest. See Meseguer Fernández, "El periodo fundacional (1478–1517)," in *Historia de la Inquisición,* vol. 1, 290–96.

13. Morillo and San Martín were named as inquisitors on September 27, 1480 in Medina del Campo. They arrived in Seville in November and issued an edict of grace a month later, which gave Sevillans thirty days in which to spontaneously confess or depose. Those who spontaneously confessed would be pardoned and not have their goods confiscated.

the truth of this wicked heretical depravity, and began to seize the guiltiest men and women and put them into the monastery of San Pablo.[14] Then they seized some of the most honorable and wealthiest aldermen and town councilors, bachelors of arts, scholars, and men of much favor; Diego de Merlo, Chief Justice, seized these men.

Afterward, many men and women fled Seville . . . and the inquisitors demanded the castle of Triana, where they put the prisoners.[15] There they held their hearings. They had a prosecutor, a constable, and scribes, and everything else that was necessary; and they carried out the trial according to the guilt of each. And they called upon secular learned men from the city and the Chief Justice to see the trials and enact the sentences, so they might see how justice was done.

They began to sentence people to death by fire. The first time, they took out six men and women to the Plaza La Tablada to be burned, and so they were burned; and Friar Alonso [de Hojeda] from San Pablo (who was zealous for the faith of Jesus Christ, and the one who tried the hardest to get this inquisition in Seville) preached. He saw no more than the first burnings, though, for within a few days he died of the plague that had started to make the rounds in the city. Within a few days three of the most prominent people in the city, and the richest, were burned, who were Diego de Susán, whom they said was worth ten million and a great rabbi, and it seemed he died like a Christian; and the other was Manuel Sauli, and the other Bartolomé de Torralva. They seized Pedro Fernández Benadeba, who was majordomo of the cathedral . . . and one of the most prominent men in the cathedral chapter, and he had in his house enough arms to equip one hundred men; and they also seized Juan Fernández Abolasia, who was for a long time justice of the peace, and very learned; and many other very rich and prominent people were seized. They too were burned. Favors and riches never helped them.

After this burning, all the *conversos* who had confessed were terrified . . . and they fled the city and the archbishopric. A penalty was imposed upon them, that they could not flee the city under pain of death, and guards were put at the city gates; so many were seized that there was no place to put them.

14. The first inquisitors in Seville consequently did not have a tribunal or a prison of their own but initially used the monastery of San Pablo for suspects' internment.

15. Numerous people did flee to the lands of the Marquis of Cádiz and the Duke of Medina Sidonia, expecting noble immunity would save them. Isabella subsequently ordered all inhabitants of Seville and its archdiocese to remain in their customary residence; she also threatened the marquis and duke with canonical penalties for having sheltered heretics and told them she would absolve their subjects of oaths of loyalty.

Still, many fled to the lands of nobles, to Portugal, and to the land of the Moors. . . .[16]

From the great and general plague, people everywhere died in extraordinary numbers, whether in cities, villages, or rural areas. In Seville, more than fifteen thousand died, with just as many dead in Córdoba. In Jerez and Ecija, eight or nine thousand people died apiece; and so it was in all the other villages and places. . . .

When the inquisitors saw that the plague was increasing in Seville, they fled to Aracena, where they found they could work. There they seized and burned twenty-three people, men and women, all of whom were miserable heretics. They also burned the bones of many people whom they discovered had died in the Mosaic heresy, who were calling themselves Christians but were Jews, and so as Jews they died.

That year, after the plague ended, the inquisitors returned to Seville and continued their inquisition. And over the next eight years, until 1488, they burned more than six hundred people and reconciled more than five thousand, whom they put into perpetual prisons. Some people were in those prisons for four or five years or more. And the inquisitors would take people out of prison and put *sanbenitos*[17] on them—with red crosses in front and behind—and they had to walk around in those *sanbenitos* for a long time. Afterward the *sanbenito*s were removed.

Among those burned in those eight years were three ordained clerics and three or four monks, all of *converso* lineage. The inquisitors also burned a doctor, a monk of the Trinitarian order called Savariego, who was a great preacher and a great liar, a trickster heretic. . . . They burned an infinite number of bones from the yards of the Trinity, San Agustín, and San Bernardo neighborhoods, where the *conversos* were buried one on top of another, in Jewish fashion. They publicly proclaimed and burned in effigy many fugitives who were found to be condemned. . . .

It was a courageous thing to reconcile this people,[18] since it was known through their confessions that they were all Jews. It was known in Seville that the heretics of Córdoba, Toledo, Burgos, Valencia, Segovia, and all of Spain were all Jews. They lived with that hope that the people of Israel had in Egypt, that [though] the Israelites had many bruises from the Egyptians, they hoped that God would deliver them, as He did afterward with a strong hand and an extended arm. And so the heretics in Spain held that the

16. I have chosen to translate *moro* as "Moor" throughout this volume, to capture the Spanish sense that Muslims came primarily from Africa, and the racial implications therein. To use the term "Muslim" would imply a respect that was not there.

17. For a definition of *sanbenito,* see the Introduction.

18. Perhaps because Bernáldez thought they were so persistent in their Judaism.

Christians were the Egyptians and worse; they believed that God would miraculously sustain and defend them, and held that they would be removed from the Christians through the hand of God, and taken to the Holy Promised Land. They confessed that they had lived among Christians with these crazy beliefs, in such a way that the whole lineage remained defamed and touched by this sickness. There was a reconciliation in Seville on a Friday, in which more than five hundred people, men and women, went through the streets in procession, with their faces uncovered.

This holy inquisition had its start in Seville; afterward, it was in Córdoba, where there was another enormous synagogue of bad Christians. Then inquisitors were placed throughout Castile and Aragón, and an infinite number of *conversos* were burned, condemned, reconciled, and imprisoned in all the archbishoprics and bishoprics of Castile and Aragón. Many of the heretics who were reconciled to the Church returned afterward to judaizing, and they were burned through the same sort of prosecution in Seville and in parts of Castile.[19]

Now I do not wish to write more about this, because it's not possible to describe the evils of this heretical depravity . . . it will be necessary for this fire to burn until all those who judaize are consumed by it, so that not one remains, not even their children, those who are twenty years and older. It should burn even the younger ones, if they are touched by the same leprosy.[20]

It was at the start of this year, 1481, that many floods occurred after Christmas. The Guadalquivir river rose and ruined the Copero, which had more than eighty residents . . . and the swell rose through the Almenilla of Seville and through the ravine of Coria to the highest level ever, and so it remained for three days without descending, and the city greatly feared it would be washed away by water.

19. These *conversos*—convicted of heresy once—would have been guilty of relapse if convicted a second time. The penalty for a relapse into heresy was "relaxation to the secular arm," meaning death at the stake.
20. Despite Bernáldez' attitude, the Inquisition was officially instructed to be merciful toward the children of condemned heretics and to take special care of orphans. See Document 7.

DOCUMENT 2

Establishing the Inquisition
in the Kingdom of Aragón

[Though King Ferdinand II may have intended from the outset to establish the new inquisition in Aragón, three major obstacles stood in his way. First, a pontifical inquisition—wherein popes named inquisitors—had existed in Aragón from the Middle Ages. Second, papally sanctioned precedents allowed the master-general of the Dominican Order in Aragón to name inquisitors. And finally, the kingdom of Aragón encompassed the states of Catalonia, Valencia, and Aragón proper, each with its own privileges (fueros) that could prohibit the imposition of Castilian officers or require the explicit recognition of its own prerogatives. Ferdinand thus negotiated with Sixtus IV for three years—from 1481 to 1483—before that pope heeded royal petitions and stipulated that Castilian Tomás de Torquemada, Inquisitor-General of Castile, should act in the same capacity for Aragón, with identical powers.

Aragonese resistance to the new, royally driven inquisition, was marked: the city of Teruel refused to let inquisitors enter the city from 1484 to 1485, and relented only when Ferdinand massed troops against it; inquisitor Pedro Arbués was murdered in the Zaragoza cathedral in September 1485; Barcelona refused to accept Ferdinand's inquisition until a papal bull of 1487 reiterated the powers of Castilian Inquisitor-General Tomás de Torquemada over the Kingdom of Aragón. After Queen Isabella's death in 1504, when Ferdinand became only governor of Castile, the Aragonese inquisition would receive its own inquisitor-general in 1507 from Pope Julius II. But the practice of having two inquisitors-general ended forever in 1518, after Charles I, grandson of Ferdinand and Isabella, began to rule both Castile and Aragón; and Pope Leo X made the Inquisitor-General of Aragón, Adrian of Utrecht, Inquisitor-General of Castile as well. Aragón's combination of fueros, small population, and generally rural character has led certain historians to speculate that the Inquisition never had much of an impact on most of that kingdom's inhabitants.[1]]

---

1. See, for instance, Kamen, *The Spanish Inquisition,* and *idem, The Phoenix and the Flame: Catalonia and the Counter Reformation* (New Haven: Yale University Press, 1993). For a contrary view of the Aragonese Inquisition as busy, effective, and generally well-tolerated, especially within the peninsula, see Monter, *Frontiers of Heresy,* especially 321–25.

Tarazona, May 7, 1484[2]

By his own authority, Don Ferrando, etc.

To the distinguished, respectable, noble, magnificent councilors and all our beloved; and to any deputies, generals, viceroys, spokesmen of our central government, general justices, royal officials, bailiffs, justices, judges, municipal councilors, town magistrates, justices of the peace, prison wardens, and any other of our officials and subjects who exercise any office and jurisdiction, presently and henceforth, in any of our kingdoms and lands now and henceforth so constituted, and the deputies of those officials, and any other person to whom these letters shall come: greetings and affection.

Inasmuch as the Holy Father has been informed that there are many people in our kingdoms who have forgotten the proper health of their souls and follow Jewish and Muslim rituals and other actions deviating from the Faith, our Holy Father has ordered, with our consent and volition, that an inquisition be carried out in all our kingdoms to correct and regulate those who have committed the crime of heretical depravity.[3]

Therefore we say, charge, and order you—under the risk of incurring our anger, indignation, a penalty of 10,000 gold florins, and the deprivation of your office if the contrary is done by you or any of your retinue—that you honor and recognize each one of the inquisitors and other inquisitorial officials and agents, according to their rank, estate, and condition. We further order you to give them all the help and assistance they need and request whenever they require it, when their need relates to the conduct of their office and to the carrying out of all the business that has to be done in that inquisition. Refrain from doing the opposite in any way, and do not consent or allow the opposite to be done, to the extent that my favor is dear to you, and that you do not wish to incur my anger, indignation, and the aforesaid penalty.

> Given in Tarazona, May 7, in the Year of Our Lord 1484.
> I the King.
> The Lord King so ordered me, Petro Cananyas.
> Another similar letter was provided for the Principate of Catalonia.

---

2. J. Angel Sesma Muñoz, *El establecimiento de la Inquisición en Aragón (1484–86): documentos para su estudio* (Zaragoza: Institución Fernando el Católico, 1987), 41–42.

3. Note who seems to be the "prime mover" of the Inquisition in Ferdinand's account of it.

Córdoba, August 3, 1484[4]

The King.
Judge, justices of the peace, and town magistrates of our city of Teruel.

We saw your letter that Joan de la Mata and Sir Jayme Mora brought us, and we heard what they told us for your side. The effect was to increase the anger and displeasure that we have toward you for having so dishonestly and so without cause prohibited the inquisitors of heretical depravity from entering your city to carry out the inquisition. We know that this could not have happened without the intervention of certain malignant people who, caring for their own interest— [but] little for our Holy Catholic Faith and the well-being of our city—have spoken complete lies, for which you can be sure they will be suitably punished.

Our unchangeable will is that the inquisitors shall enter that city and be received peacefully along with their agents. We now explicitly order you to go out personally into the road and to peacefully bring that inquisitor and his agents into your city.[5] Not only shall you allow him to freely carry out his office, but you shall also give him all the favor and help that he may need and ask of you, since it is certain that the inquisitor and his agents in no way violate established practice in canon law nor do they do anything against the legal privileges and liberty of that city in carrying out that inquisition. They shall exercise all the mercy and piety that the law and good conscience allow when people who know their error come to reconcile themselves as they ought to do.

We have ordered your messengers to communicate our fixed will to you. They shall not leave here until it is known that you have completed our orders. If those orders are not completed, the disobedient shall receive such a punishment as to forever remain an eternal memory and example.

Thus, ceasing all delay, consultation, or any other excuse, let what is said here be completed. If the city receives that inquisitor and his agents, and afterward the city finds itself wronged,[6] we shall instantly take steps to restore justice, out of regard for the privileges and liberties of that city, since we desire the observation of that city's privileges and liberties more than you do. And be mindful and diligent that neither the persons nor the goods of that inquisitor and his agents are injured or bothered in any way, because it is certain that if such occurs, it will not pass without severe punishment.

So that we may know more quickly and certainly how this letter's orders are completed and put into effect, we have ordered Joan Ferrandez de Heredia

4. Sesma Muñoz, *El establecimiento*, 75–76.
5. Not being able to enter Teruel itself, the inquisitor had set up operations in Cella.
6. Meaning, if Teruel's privileges (*fueros*) were violated.

to go in person to give you the letter. He shall write to us how you have completed it.

Given in the city of Córdoba, August 3, 1484.

Seville, February 6, 1485[7]

I the King.
Our magnificent and beloved subjects:

You already know the disobedience that the officials, townspeople, and residents of Teruel have committed against apostolic orders and our own. . . . Because our will is to complete the provisioning of the military in every way, and to favor and help the inquisitors of heretical depravity (as we have written to you many times), we thus affectionately charge you to complete the provisioning for us and the inquisitors. You shall be required to favor and help them as if my own person were involved, with the largest number of foot soldiers and horsemen that you can muster. In such a way God's service and ours shall be done well and completely, assuring you that in this, you do us the greatest and most agreeable service.

> I the King.
> Secretary Camanyas.
> Directed to the judges, cathedral chapter, and city council of
> Zaragoza.
> Under the same form, signature, and order, it was written to the
> following:
> First, to the justices, municipal councilors, officials, and city council
> of Calatayud and Daroca.
> To the judges, justices of the peace, officials, and the council of the
> city and community of Santa Maria de Albarrazino . . .
> To the governor, magistrates, and council of the community of
> villages of Calatayud; and to the scribe, governor, magistrate, and
> council of the community of villages of Daroca.

---

7. Sesma Muñoz, *El establecimiento*, 126.

THE INQUISITION'S FIRST TARGETS: JUDAIZING *CONVERSOS* IN CASTILE, 1484–1513

DOCUMENT 3

Inquisition Proceedings against Isabel, Wife of *Bachiller* Lope de la Higuera, 1484[1]

[Fourteenth-century Spain had the largest population of Jews in Western Europe. But in 1391, that situation came to end when urban mobs throughout the peninsula destroyed Spain's major Jewish quarters and massacred or forcibly baptized their cities' Jews. The result was a body of coerced Christians called conversos; *the sincerity of their Christianity, and their descendants', became a matter of debate for the next several centuries. The subject of the* conversos *and their religiosity remains one of the most hotly contested issues in modern scholarship on early modern Spain, and the historians who focus on it can be divided into three general groups. The first maintains that the* conversos *thought of themselves as Jews and practiced a surreptitious Judaism that had to be modified in the wake of organized oppression and the absence of rabbinical guidance.[2] The second group uses contemporary rabbinical writings to insist that the* conversos' *conversion was sincere, and that the Inquisition's persecution of that population was racial, not religious, in intent.[3] The third stresses the lack of homogeneity among the* conversos *and allows them to have held a range of religious convictions.*

The Spanish Inquisition was founded to investigate, punish, and reconcile conversos *who continued to practice Judaism, and inquisitors quickly codified the external behaviors they thought signified internal conviction—a connection between the external and the internal that they took for granted. The reader will notice that three out of the four documents in this section involve women. This disparity reflects the sex ratio of* converso *defendants during the first forty years of the Inquisition's existence, when female defendants apparently*

1. Haim Beinart, *Records of the Trials of the Spanish Inquisition in Ciudad Real* (Jerusalem: The Israel National Academy of Sciences and Humanities, 1974), vol. l, 360–61.

2. Haim Beinart is the best-known proponent of this approach. See his *Conversos on Trial: The Inquisition in Ciudad Real* (Jerusalem: Magnes Press, 1981).

3. Benzion Netanyahu, *The Origins of the Inquisition in Fifteenth-Century Spain* (New York: Random House, 1995).

outnumbered male ones by a large proportion.⁴ The reason for the inequality lies in the signs of Judaism that the inquisitors found meaningful, most of which revolved around the household. Within the Law of Moses, especially the books of Deuteronomy and Leviticus, strict, detailed dietary laws are set forth which distinguish between clean and unclean foods, and the proper or kosher method of butchering. For the purposes of the documents here, it is crucial to understand that Jews are prohibited from consuming animals with hoofs which are not cloven-footed and do not chew their cud, such as pigs, as well as anything that swarms, crawls on its belly, goes on its paws on all fours, or goes in the water but lacks fins and scales.

As for worship, Jews in Spain possessed an annual liturgical cycle that was apportioned into solemn holidays, major holidays, minor or commemorative holidays, and fasts.⁵ Jews observed the weekly Sabbath, which begins at sundown on Friday and lasts through Saturday. Such observation involves daily sacrifices (Num. 28:9), special gatherings for worship (Lev. 23:2), and complete abstinence from work (Exod. 20:10), including food preparation. The Sabbath represents the rest God took on the seventh day from His work of Creation; it was a day set apart for the worship of Him. Ritual bathing, clean clothing, new candles or oil wicks, and the lighting of lights with oral prayers marked the beginning of the Sabbath each Friday. The principal Jewish festival of the year was Passover, celebrated over a three-day period each spring. According to Passover's institution in Exodus 12, a lamb should be killed in each household and its blood sprinkled on the lintel and doorposts of the house in commemoration of the fact that the Lord "passed over" such marked houses when the firstborn in Egypt were slain. The eating of this Paschal lamb was always associated with unleavened bread.]

February 24, 1484. Case of Isabel, wife of *bachiller* Lope de la Higuera⁶

We—Pedro Díaz de la Costaña, licentiate in holy theology; and Francisco Sánchez de la Fuente, doctor in canon law, inquisitorial judges by apostolic

4. On this disparity, see Melammed, *Heretics or Daughters of Israel?* The reader should again note that we have very incomplete records for the Inquisition's earliest history.

5. For the rituals and rites of Sephardic Judaism—*Sepharad* being the Hebrew term for Spain, and *Sephardim* meaning the "people from *Sepharad*"—see Paloma Díaz-Mas, *Sephardim: The Jews from Spain*, trans. George K. Zucker (Chicago: The University of Chicago Press, 1992).

6. The term *bachiller*, which translates as the English "bachelor," signified a man with a basic university education.

authority—and I, Pedro Díaz, licentiate, as an officer and general vicar [*or-dinario*] for the most reverend lord, Pedro González de Mendoza, cardinal of Spain, archbishop of Toledo,[7] have witnessed a trial that occurred as a result of a denunciation brought by the honorable Fernando Rodríguez del Barco,[8] chaplain of the King, against Isabel, wife of the *bachiller* de la Higuera.

In the denunciation, Rodríguez del Barco said that Isabel is a resident of this place, Ciudad Real, and lives with the reputation of a Christian, but in offense to our Lord and contempt for His Holy Faith, she heretically and apostatically follows the Law of Moses and practices its ceremonies. She lights new candles early on Friday evenings, out of ritual and reverence for the Sabbath. She cooks her meals for Saturday on Friday, and eats on Saturday what she had thus cooked on Friday. She does not do any sort of work on Saturday, but instead puts on clean undergarments and clothing, and shaves [sic] and dresses up on those days.

On those Saturdays she would withdraw to pray, sometimes alone and sometimes with other women; they would shut themselves up in a common room and would read and pray through Jewish books. She kept the Jewish feast days with the solemnities and ceremonies that they observe, especially that of the Lamb [i.e., Passover]. She kneaded and ate unleavened bread, and ate from new plates, casks, and bowls on those feast days. She kept those fasts that the Jews usually keep, not eating until nightfall; and she breakfasted by eating meat. The meat she ate had to be killed according to Jewish ceremony; it had to be purged, removing the fat. She ate nothing that was forbidden in the Law of Moses, and she did not make the sign of the Cross upon herself, nor the [other] signs of a Christian woman; nor did she go to Mass or hear the other divine offices. And when she had to swear an oath, she said He-brew words. She did everything in the style of a Jewish woman and as the Jews do them.

Because of these things—which she did in this city; and afterward left so that she could do these things at will, and remain in her damned opinion—Rodríguez del Barco asked that she be declared a heretic and condemned as such. And we have given our summons in the form of an edict against Is-abel, with a time limit of thirty days for her to come to respond and defend herself over this charge of having judaized and apostasized. This summons

7. The earliest instructions for the Inquisition stipulated that a representative of the relevant bishop had to be present during deliberations over torture and sentencing. This representative, called the *ordinario,* was deputized to supervise legal proceed-ings on the bishop's behalf. The fact that inquisitors and *ordinarios* deliberated to-gether reflects the theoretically and historically shared jurisdiction over heresy between inquisitors and bishops that existed from the thirteenth century on.

8. Rodríguez del Barco was the *fiscal* or chief prosecutor of the Ciudad Real tribunal.

was read and made known before the doors of the houses where Isabel used to live, and it was distributed and proclaimed in the city plaza, and read at St. Peter's Church on a feast day (the inhabitants being there to hear the divine offices). And the summons was affixed to the door of that church, where it remained for the entire thirty-day period. Isabel's failure to appear[9] before the inquisitors was cited by the prosecutor within the proper time limits; she was held in default, and the prosecutor was received for proof of what his denunciation contained. He proved everything contained in his denunciation through a sufficient number of witnesses, and performed all the acts required for the trial.

As the trial was seen by us and shared with learned men and religious people of learning and good conscience,[10] following their common opinion and advice,

HOLDING GOD BEFORE OUR EYES:

We find that we must declare Isabel, wife of *bachiller* Lope de la Higuera, to be a heretic and apostate. She has incurred a sentence of greater excommunication, and all the other spiritual and temporal punishments contained in the laws against heretics, as well as the loss and confiscation of her goods. We relax her[11] to the virtuous gentleman Juan Pérez de Barradas, knight of Cieca, royal magistrate in this city and its territory; and we also relax her to this territory's governors and magistrates, and to any other judges of any other cities, villages and places within these kingdoms and outside of them, wherever the aforesaid Isabel might be found, so that they may do with her what they can and should do by law. We thus pronounce judgment through this sentence.

---

9. The original term for Isabel's nonappearances—*rebeldías*—is multivalent. It signifies "default" in a legal setting but clearly also implies rebelliousness, disobedience, and stubbornness.

10. Meaning the inquisitors called in *consultadores*—possibly lawyers as well as theologians, in addition to the *ordinario* or representative of the bishop—to confer over the verdict. For the voting procedure and the process by which a verdict was reached, see Document 20 and the Introduction to this volume.

11. The inquisitors were "relaxing" Isabel "to the secular arm"; she was subject to the death penalty, as carried out by secular officials.

DOCUMENT 4

Inquisition Trial of Pedro de Villegas, 1483–1484[1]

Nine o'clock in the morning on December 19, 1483, in the houses where the reverend lord inquisitors reside and hold their court. The reverend lords were seated, and in our presence—we being the secretaries and witnesses written below—the honorable Fernando Rodríguez de Barco, who is a cleric, a chaplain of the King, and a chief prosecutor of the Holy Inquisition, appeared. He said that he intended to accuse Pedro de Villegas, a resident of this city, who is being held in the Holy Inquisition's prison, and he asked the inquisitors to order Villegas taken out and brought before them. Seeing his petition, the inquisitors ordered the constable, who was present, to remove Villegas and bring him to the court. With Villegas present, the chief prosecutor then submitted a writ of accusation against him, the content of which follows.

Reverend and Virtuous Lord Judges, Inquisitors of heretical iniquity:

I, Fernando Rodríguez de Barco, chaplain of the King, chief prosecutor of the Holy Inquisition, appear before your lordships and accuse Pedro de Villegas, resident of this city. I say that Pedro de Villegas lives with the reputation of a Christian, is called a Christian, and exercises and enjoys the privileges of a Christian. Yet with calumny against our Lord and His Holy Catholic Faith, and in violation of the censures and penalties for heresy and judaizing, Pedro de Villegas has observed the Law of Moses and its ceremonies and rituals, and apostatized in this way:

First, Pedro de Villegas ate meat during Lent without a need or a reason for it, on account of Jewish ceremony and in contempt of our Holy Catholic Faith.

Next, he ate unleavened bread on the Jewish Passover.

Next, he willingly observed the Sabbath on Saturdays in his house, on account of reverence [for] Jewish ceremony. He ordered his household adorned as if it were a feast day.

Next, Pedro de Villegas is a judaizer and a heretic and observed Mosaic Law in other matters and instances that I will make known in this brief trial, as they come to my attention.[2]

1. Beinart, *Records of the Trials of the Spanish Inquisition*, vol. 1, 212–23. Villegas' wife, Catalina, was tried and relaxed to the secular arm at some unknown date; 212 n. 1.

2. Prosecutors could add new charges with new depositions or information against a defendant.

On account of which behaviors—and for not presenting himself before
your Lordships during the Edict of Grace to confess lovingly and willingly
his heretical errors—Pedro de Villegas must be considered a heretic and
apostate, and should receive a sentence of greater excommunication, along
with other civil and criminal penalties established in the law.[3] Virtuous
Lords, I ask and implore that you find him a heretic and an apostate, and
that justice be done.

Answering the accusation by himself in court, Pedro de Villegas said it
was true that he ate meat during Lent, but that he did so out of necessity,
not for another reason. He denied everything else contained in the accusation, and thus he concluded. Witnesses: Alvaro Fernández, Ruíz Daza, Francisco de Hozes.

Then the chief prosecutor said that since Villegas had responded to the
accusation and concluded, that he would conclude as well. The inquisitors
said that since both parties had finished and offered themselves for proof,
they would consider as finished the first stage of the trial and would receive
both parties for proof. They then assigned a legal period for the presentation
of proof, to begin the third day from now, and to encompass the next nine
days in which the inquisition tribunal was not closed, etc. [sic] Witnesses:
Juan Gómez and Juan de Hozes, clerics.

Afterward, on January 2, 1484, in the houses where the reverend lords reside and hold their court, the honorable master Juan Ruíz de Córdoba and
Juan de Hozes were present; both are clerics and hold benefices in this city;
they were empowered by the inquisitors to receive and examine witnesses.[4]
There appeared _____ [sic][5] in the name of Pedro de Villegas, as his attorney and defender. Villegas presented a written interrogatory
to the court; he likewise said that he would bring forward the following residents of this city as witnesses for himself and his wife: Fernando de Hozes,
city magistrate; Diego Philipe; Juan Bastante; Antonio, the stitcher; Friar
Juan de Ribarredondo;[6] and Friar Francisco de Trujillo.[7]

3. On the centrality of confession in the inquisitorial process, see the Introduction.

4. Here it looks as if *comisarios* are deposing witnesses in the tribunal itself—perhaps an indication of procedures not quite codified? For *comisarios,* see the Introduction, note 37.

5. Haim Beinart notes that the blank space was left so that the name of the defense
solicitor could be entered; in Villegas' case, he conducted his own defense. Beinart,
Records of the Trials of the Spanish Inquisition, vol. 1, 215 n. 3.

6. Though named, this witness' testimony does not appear in the trial record.

7. These are character witnesses whom Villegas hoped would verify his reputation
as a good Christian. This defense strategy of calling character witnesses is called
abonos. Villegas' defense witnesses had certain elements in common which tended to
heighten their trustworthiness in the inquisitors' eyes.

The deputies received an oath from each witness in isolation from the others, as stipulated by the law. In the oath, the witnesses said they swore by God, Holy Mary, and the Words of the Holy Gospels (on which they placed their hands) and by the sign of the Cross (which each of them touched with their right hands), that they would speak the truth about everything they knew and everything they were asked. The deputies told the witnesses that if they swore and spoke the truth, God might help their bodies in this world and their souls in the next; but if they said and swore anything falsely, God might demand evil for their bodies in this world and for their souls in the next, where they had to stay even longer. The witnesses responded to the imprecation of the oath and said they so swore. Amen. What each one testified is what follows, as they were questioned by the deputies secretly and separately.

January 2, 1484. Interrogatory of Pedro de Villegas for his defense witnesses[8]

Reverend and Virtuous Lords, Inquisitorial Judges:

I, Pedro de Villegas, appear before your Lordships and affirm my denial of the prosecutor's accusation. If I ate meat during certain Lenten seasons, on a day when the Church had forbidden it, it was because of an illness I have, which recurred at that time. I caught this illness in this way: my hand was hurt while I was stretching a cloth over a frame, and the frame ripped the cloth in half; the spring came loose and carried me the length of three or four men from where I'd been standing, and it "broke and wounded me," as the saying goes. As a matter of fact, I am debilitated. If I rested on certain Saturdays, it was not because of a ceremony of Mosaic Law; I have never, God forbid, intended to follow Mosaic Law, for I come from an Old Christian lineage on both my father and mother's side. And I never talk with Jews, nor was I raised to have such an inclination. If I rested on some Saturdays, it would have been at a time when my job of cloth making wasn't flourishing; there happened to be a month or two during which I did not work at all. This happened two or three times over the year, or on feast days, or days the Church ordered us to observe, or when I was sick.

And unleavened bread is such a foreign thing to me, it's as likely I ate it as it is that Muhammed ate pork.[9] I am a man brought up in a home with a common room and a generous atmosphere.[10] I do not remember having eaten unleavened bread, as I have no intention of judaizing, nor am I of such

8. These headings have been added for the ease of the reader.

9. Islamic as well as Jewish dietary laws prohibited the consumption of pork.

10. The term Villegas uses is *palacio,* which in the Toledo region in this time period signifies a room devoid of purpose, a leisure area.

a lineage. But though I have no intention of judaizing, and am not of that lineage, it is possible that I would eat it if I were hungry and if people offered it to me repeatedly, especially if I had no other bread and if it were good; still, I do not remember having seen it [i.e., the unleavened bread]. Therefore I ask your Lordships that the witnesses presented on my behalf answer the following questions:

First, if they know me, Pedro de Villegas.

Next, if they know, saw, or heard it said, or if they believe, that I am reputed to be a Old Christian in this city and territory, on both my father and mother's sides, and I was brought up with gentlemen in a house with a common room until I was thirteen or fourteen, and that I married, and took this job of cloth maker.

Next, if they know, etc., whether all the time that I have lived in this city and have been married, that whenever the occasion arose to do my work or any other work on a Saturday, that I performed that work in the same way as I would have on any other day of the week. Unless it was a feast day, or there was no work and I had nothing to do.

Next, if they know, etc., that about ten or eleven years ago, more or less, as I was stretching a cloth on the frames of _____ [sic] that are in the city, that the cloth tore in half and the spring came loose and I was carried the length of three or four men from where I was, and that I tore my skin and hurt my hand.

Next, if they know, etc., that I am a loyal and Catholic Christian and have such a reputation. And that I do the works of such a man: I have gone to churches and heard Masses and divine sacrifices; I have confessed and received the Eucharist in times of affliction and at the times so commanded by the Church; I have held, believed, and confessed all that the Holy Church commands us to hold and believe, and commands us to perform and observe.

May your Lordships make these questions pertinent to the case. I beg your noble office to do what is required and request that justice be done. Thus I ask for testimony.

And given, Virtuous Lords, that the aforesaid frame broke and wounded me, for which reason I ate the meat at that time, and I would now be able to eat it if my defense were successful, I ask you in the best way I can, by law, that you investigate the accident and seek evidence of it.

What the witnesses testified as they were secretly, separately, and individually asked the interrogatory, is what follows.

Statement of Diego Philipe

Diego Philipe, a witness presented by Pedro de Villegas, being legally sworn and then asked the questions of the interrogatory, said to the first question that he had known Villegas for twelve years, a little more or less.

Asked the second question, he replied he didn't know, but he'd heard it said of Pedro de Villegas.

To the third question, he replied he had seen Pedro de Villegas working as a cloth maker, and that Villegas worked as much on Saturday as on any other day in the week. And he saw this because he lodged with Villegas, and the door to his room opened on the inside of the house.

To the fourth question, he replied he did not know.

To the fifth question, he replied that he had sometimes seen Villegas in St. Peter's Church, hearing Mass like a Christian, and that he didn't know about the rest of the question.

For the other questions pertaining to the case, he said that he'd heard Villegas himself say that he was hurt. And he reaffirmed his testimony.

Statement of Antonio, the cloth maker

Antonio, a witness presented by Pedro de Villegas for his defense, being legally sworn and then asked the questions of the interrogatory, said to the first question that he had known Pedro de Villegas over the last five years, and that he'd had business dealings with him in stitching cloth.

To the second question, he said Villegas told him that his mother was a *conversa* and his father an Old Christian, and he'd seen [sic] him say that he had lived with Fernando de Villegas, and this is what he knows concerning the question.

To the third question, he said that he worked with Villegas in cloth making. In that job he had seen Villegas work on Saturday as if it were any other day.

To the fourth question, he said that he knew nothing more than what he had heard from Villegas' wife.

To the fifth question, he said he had seen Villegas in church many times with Pedro Alegre, in order to hear masses and sermons. He knows that four or five years ago, Villegas was seized by illness, and he personally carried Villegas, who was very exhausted, to his house. He knew that Villegas confessed to a Dominican friar in the house, and afterward the friar gave him the Eucharist near St. Peter's [feast day].[11] That is all he knows.

To the sixth question, he said that he once saw Villegas eat meat on a Friday (he does not remember what day it was), and Antonio then told his friends about having seen it. And he reaffirmed his testimony.

---

11. St. Peter's feast day is June 29.

Statement of Friar Francisco de Trujillo

Friar Francisco, a witness presented by Pedro de Villegas for his defense, being legally sworn and asked the questions of the interrogatory, said to the first question that he has known Villegas for three and a half years, more or less.

To the second question, he said he does not know.

To the third and fourth questions, he said he does not know.

To the fifth question, he said that he sometimes saw Villegas in the church of St. Francis, hearing Mass and the Divine Offices like a Christian, and this witness said that he has heard Villegas' confession two or three times over the past three years.[12] As to the other parts of the question, he has neither seen it nor does he know about it.

Asked the other questions pertinent to the case, Friar Francisco said that he knows Villegas is a sick man, according to what he has heard people say who know it for certain; so, if Villegas ate some meat during Lent, he believes it would be due to his illness and not for any other reason. He said he would stick by what he had said regarding everything else, and reaffirmed his testimony.

Statement of Fernando de Hozes, alderman

Fernando de Hozes, a witness presented by Pedro de Villegas for his defense, being legally sworn and then asked the questions of the interrogatory, said that he had known Pedro de Villegas for twenty years, more or less.[13]

To the second question, this witness said he considered Villegas to be an Old Christian, but whether he was an Old Christian on both his father and mother's sides he didn't know. He had not known them.

To the third question, he said that he knows Villegas worked at cloth making on Saturday like any other day of the week. He said that he knows this because he has frequently seen him do it, as he is his neighbor.

To the fourth question, he said he does not know.

To the fifth question, he replied that he has seen Villegas often enough at the churches of this city, hearing Mass and the Divine Offices like a Catholic Christian, but whether Villegas does it or believes in it sincerely, that he does not know.[14] He knows nothing more concerning the question, and reaffirms his testimony.

---

12. Villegas undoubtedly boosted his defense by calling members of the clergy as character witnesses.

13. The duration of some of these friendships helped Villegas' case as well.

14. This sort of ambiguity surfaced repeatedly in *converso* trials. When suspects ob-

Statement of Juan Bastante, dyer

Juan Bastante, a witness presented by Pedro de Villegas for his defense, being legally sworn and then asked the questions of the interrogatory, said to the first question that he had known Villegas for thirteen years, a little more or less, and said he had business dealings with him.

To the second question, he said that insofar as he knew him, he considered Villegas a good Christian. He had heard it said that Villegas is the child of a *conversa* and an Old Christian, a gentleman. And he said that insofar as he knew Villegas, he thought he was truly a good Christian.

To the third question, he said that it was true, because he frequently joined Villegas in his work, and he saw Villegas work on a Saturday just like any other day of the week.

To the fourth question, he said that he neither saw it nor knew it, except insofar as he had seen Villegas suffering in pain. People said he was injured from a certain failure of the frame.

To the fifth question, he said that he frequently saw Villegas in church, hearing masses like a good Christian, and this witness considered him as such. But he never saw Villegas confess or receive the Eucharist (though he had heard it said that he had), because most of the time he worked with him in the cloth making business. And he had heard it said by other people that Villegas had confessed and received the Eucharist, but they did not say how many times, or on what dates.[15] And he reaffirmed his testimony.

Witnesses for the Prosecution

Afterward, on January 2, 1484, in the houses where the inquisitors resided, in the lower room where they held their hearings, the honorable Fernando Rodríguez del Barco, cleric and chaplain of the King, and chief prosecutor of the Office of the Holy Inquisition, appeared there before lord Francisco Sánchez de la Fuente, inquisitor. To prove his accusation against Pedro de Villegas, Rodríguez del Barco presented as witnesses Catalina de Zebrón, daughter of Juan Alonso de Zebrón [sic]; and Leonor, wife of Benito Sánchez, a farmer. The inquisitor received legally sworn oaths from both women. They swore by God, Holy Mary, the four Holy Gospels, and the sign of the Cross (upon which each one put her right hand) that they would

---

served Christian rituals or voiced Christian prayers, were they acting out of religious belief or dissimulating?

15. The deputies probably attempted to solicit information on time and dates through direct questions.

tell the truth about what they knew in this case. The inquisitor told them that if they testified truthfully, God would help their bodies in this world and their souls in the next, where they had to stay even longer. If they did not testify truthfully, God would demand great evil to fall upon them, as happens to those who swear His Holy Name in vain. To the imprecation of the oath, each one of the women said: yes, I swear, etc., Amen.

What follows is what Catalina de Zebrón and Leonor, wife of Benito Sánchez, said in the judicial process and general inquisition when they were received as witnesses by the honorable Juan Ruíz de Córdoba, master in holy theology, and Juan Martínez, parish priest of Yevenes, who were empowered by the inquisitors to examine witnesses.

Having been legally sworn, Catalina de Zebrón, an aforesaid witness presented by the prosecutor, said that she was a neighbor of Pedro de Villegas. She saw that his wife observed Saturdays, and walked around very made-up, clean, and adorned on that day. She saw this because she lived next door to her, and many times she saw it through a hole in the wall of her house. She ratified her statement.[16]

Having been legally sworn, Leonor, wife of Benito Sánchez, an aforesaid witness presented by the prosecutor, said that fifteen years ago, more or less, she lived with Pedro de Villegas, cloth maker, who then resided at Santiago and now lives in Puerta de Arcos. At that time, she observed that Villegas and his wife ate meat during Lent, and she saw them eat unleavened bread. This is what she knows, and no more. She ratified her statement.

Sentence

We—Pedro Díaz de la Costaña, licentiate in holy theology, and Francisco Sánchez de la Fuente, doctor in canon law, acting as inquisitorial judges of heretical iniquity by apostolic authority—and I, Pedro Díaz, licentiate, officer and general vicar for the most reverend lord Pedro González de Mendoza, Cardinal of Spain, Archbishop of Toledo, have witnessed a trial now pending before us, between two parties. On the one hand, the honorable Fernando Rodríguez del Barco, cleric, chaplain of the King, our chief prosecutor; on the other, Pedro de Villegas, a resident of Ciudad Real, concerning an accusation that the prosecutor presented against him. In his accusation, the prosecutor said that though Villegas has the reputation and name of a Christian, he in fact is a heretic and apostate, for he follows

16. Per standard procedure, witnesses' statements could not be entered into evidence, or given in publication to the defendant (albeit with identifying details erased) until they were ratified. In the Villegas trial, the prosecutor observed this rule.

Mosaic Law and performs its ceremonies; specifically, that Villegas ate unleavened bread in the Passover of the Jews, and agreed to clean and decorate
his house in honor of Saturday, and to observe Saturday as the Sabbath. He
ate meat during Lent without a need to do so, in contempt of our Holy Faith
and in order to honor and follow Mosaic Law. The prosecutor says Villegas
performed other ceremonies and Jewish rituals to honor and follow that Mosaic Law, and accordingly asks that Villegas be declared a heretic and that he
incur the legal punishments against heretics, and that justice be served. And
seeing how Villegas denied the accusation, saying he had been a good and
faithful Christian and never had done the things of which he was accused,
Pedro de Villegas and the chief prosecutor were together received for proof.[17]
Each party presented the witnesses that he wanted, and their statements and
depositions were written down, and each party was provided with a copy of
that material.[18] And each party was given a time limit to allege whatever they
wished in the defense and prosecution of their rights. Once this was done,
we decided this trial was concluded.[19] Having [shared] our opinion and
counsel with learned men and religious people of good and sound conscience, and having imparted to them this entire trial, following their advice,
common opinion, and deliberation[20]

HOLDING GOD BEFORE OUR EYES:

We find the chief prosecutor did not prove the accusation against Pedro de
Villegas, according to what he had to prove by law; and conversely, Pedro de
Villegas proved himself to have lived as a good and faithful Christian. If certain ceremonies of Mosaic Law were performed in his house, he contradicted
them, and neither consented to nor permitted them when they came to his
attention or when he was informed about them. Whereby we absolve Pedro
de Villegas;[21] he shall be freed and released from the accusation, and we order that he may receive as penance the time he has been a prisoner in our
jail, because he did not know and inquire with greater diligence as to what

---

17. If Villegas had confessed during the admonitory phase of the trial—during the
first days of his confinement in the inquisition prison—or in the wake of the accusation, the trial would have ended forthwith and the period of proof would never
have been stipulated.

18. Providing a copy of witness testimony to the defense—with all identifying details erased—was called the *publicación de testigos,* "publication of witnesses" or "publication of testimony."

19. In other words, none of these crucial steps was omitted.

20. Another reference to the *consultadores.* See the Introduction and Document 20.

21. To be completely absolved of suspicion was very rare.

things were done in his house against the Holy Faith, so that such things could have been fought against and punished, as they must be by law. We reserve the right to impose additional penances upon Pedro de Villegas beyond what is imposed upon him in this sentence. He must perform and complete those penances when he is commanded to do so by us, in satisfaction and emendation of his negligence and remission. Thus we declare our sentence through these writings.

In Ciudad Real, February 13, 1484, Juan Sánchez de Tablada and Juan de Segovia, cleric and chaplain of the Queen, apostolic and public notaries of the Office of this Holy Inquisition; and before the witnesses, the reverend lord inquisitors Pedro Díaz de la Costaña and Francisco Sánchez de la Fuente, being in the lower room where they usually hold their hearing, gave this sentence in the presence of Pedro de Villegas. After the sentence was read by one of us, the notaries ordered Juan de Alfaro, the warden of the Inquisition, to release Villegas from the chains and shackles on his feet.[22] They sent him away in peace to his house. Witnesses who were present, who saw and heard the sentence read: Licentiate Jufre de Loaysa; *bachiller* Gonzalo Muñoz, his brother; the prior of Santo Domingo; the *bachiller* called Camargo.

22. The first formal instructions for the Inquisition, dated 1484, stipulated the circumstances in which someone could be sentenced outside a public ceremony or *auto de fe*. The fact that the tribunal absolved Villegas may have had something to do with the sentence being rendered in private.

DOCUMENT 5

Inquisition Trial of Marina González, 1494[1]

In the very noble city of Toledo, January 9, 1494, the reverend lords licentiate Fernando de Mazuecos and canon of Granada, Fernando Rodríguez del Barco,[2] inquisitorial judges of heretical iniquity in the city and the entire archbishopric by apostolic and ordinary authority, held their general hearing as they usually do, in my presence, Diego de San Martín, public scribe of Toledo and the Holy Office. Then honorable *bachiller*[3] Diego Martínez de Ortega, chief prosecutor of the Holy Office, appeared in person, and announced that he intended to place an accusation against Marina González— wife of Francisco de Toledo, spice merchant and resident of Ciudad Real—for the crime of heresy and apostasy. He therefore asked the inquisitors to order her brought into the hearing, as she is a prisoner in the tribunal's prison. Then the lord inquisitors ordered Pedro González, the Flat-Nosed, warden of the Holy Office, to bring Marina González to the hearing. He brought her before the lords. Then the chief prosecutor presented a writ of accusation that he made me, the notary, read, as follows:

Marina's Confession from 1484[4]

Most Reverend and Devout Fathers,

I, Marina González, am the wife of Francisco de Toledo, a spice merchant, who is a resident of this village of Almagro. I present myself before Your

---

1. Beinart, *Records of the Trials of the Spanish Inquisition,* vol. 2, 8–41. Marina was married to Francisco de Toledo, whose mother was a *conversa.* After Marina was relaxed to the secular arm, Francisco remarried; his second wife, Juana de Chinchilla, was condemned for judaizing in 1504, and his third wife was named as a practicing Jew in the trial of María González in 1511.

2. By 1494, Rodríguez del Barco had been promoted from chief prosecutor to inquisitor in the tribunal, which now was located in Toledo; compare to Documents 3 and 4.

3. The term *bachiller,* which translates as the English "bachelor," signified a man with a basic university education.

4. In 1484, Marina confessed during an Edict of Grace, when people who found themselves guilty of heresy were invited to declare their sins to the Inquisition, receive a penance, and be reconciled to the Church. The problem was that the original confessions were preserved, and could be used as evidence of relapse if the

Lordships to declare my faults and the sins I have committed, in offense against our Redeemer and Master Jesus Christ and against our Holy Catholic Faith. I shall declare all the sins that are in my memory at the moment with great shame, contrition, and heartfelt repentance; and I intend to complete the penance that your lordships may impose. Thus I declare my guilt:

First, Reverend Fathers, I state that I sinned by observing the Sabbaths and certain Passovers that I can remember. I put on clean clothes out of ceremony, cooked on Fridays for the Sabbath, ate the food on the Sabbath, and lit an oil lamp on Friday night out of ceremony.

I sinned in that I fasted sometimes out of ceremony . . . and asked forgiveness from others, and others asked it of me.

I sinned because I sometimes made unleavened bread and ate it.

I sinned because I ate animals that had been ritually decapitated, and I removed the fat from the meat because of Jewish ceremony.

I sinned in hearing prayers read, and in going to hear them said. I especially remember having sometimes heard them in Alvar López de Córdoba's house; he lives in Ciudad Real.

I sinned because I gave up eating pork and meat stew and things that were prohibited.

I sinned because I broke certain feast days that the Holy Mother Church ordered us to observe; I did not keep them as I ought.

I sinned through having eaten certain foods on days on which those foods were prohibited by the Holy Mother Church; I ate some things forbidden by the Church.

I sinned because on the seventh night after I had a child, some people came to my house and ate, and rested, and said it was the night of the fairies [sic].[5]

I sinned because I ate dishes of fish at a low table during a funeral.

I state, Reverend Fathers, that I was compelled to do all the things I have just reported by two men who are married to my sisters. One is called García Molina, the other Lope Rodríguez, and they reside in Ciudad Real. I was a girl at the time, and they told me I would be saved by such things.

I state, Reverend Fathers, that once on a Friday—it happened to me innocently—without thinking that it was Friday, I told my girl to cook a piece of meat that was left over. After I had arranged everything, my husband sent the same girl out to buy fish, and he ordered me to cook it. I said to him, "Why do we need fish on a meat day?" And he answered, "How can you say

---

penanced individual reappeared before the tribunal, which is exactly what happened here; the prosecutor's accusation in 1494 reproduced Marina's earlier confession and treated it as evidence against her.

5. The night of *las fadas* or "fairies" was the naming ceremony for Jewish girls in Spain. See Díaz-Mas, *Sephardim: The Jews from Spain,* chapter 1.

this is a meat day when it is Friday?" Then he saw the pot with the meat on the fire, and took it off and threw it all out. He was very irritable about it. I told him I had done it innocently, without thinking what day it was.

I lay this before Your Reverences and ask for penance because I offended Our Redeemer and Master Jesus Christ, going against our Holy Catholic Faith in certain necessary things. Though I cannot remember all of these things at the moment, I assure you I will declare them when they come to me. And from today onward I will live and die and finish up in the Holy Catholic Faith, which I embrace in her defense all the days of my life. For all the things I've confessed, I beg pardon and the redemption of our Lord Jesus Christ. May your reverences give me a penance that is healthful for my soul, which I am ready to complete.

January 15, 1484   Marina González, who was ill in bed in her house, made this confession before me, Juan de Segovia, notary of the Holy Inquisition. She swore that the content of her confession was true; and said that she had wanted to perform this confession ever since she can remember . . . she is thirty-two years old. She was taught by her two brothers-in-law, one García Molina and one Lope Rodríguez, residents of Ciudad Real.

Arraignment, January 15, 1494   Very Reverend Lords, I, *bachiller* Diego Martínez Ortega, chief prosecutor of the Holy Inquisition in the very noble city of Toledo and its diocese, appear before your reverences to accuse Marina González, wife of Francisco de Toledo, spice merchant, of Ciudad Real. She has received the holy sacrament of baptism, lives with the name and reputation of a Christian woman and calls herself such, and enjoys the privileges and liberties that Christians enjoy. But with contempt for the Holy Mother Church, with disdain for the Christian religion, and in great offense toward Our Redeemer Jesus and condemnation of her soul, she has heretically and apostatically followed the Law of Moses and its rites and ceremonies. Once before she pretended to confess some things to your lordships and was reconciled to the Church; she publicly abjured those errors and heresy, especially the observance of Mosaic Law. Then, postponing the fear of God, in condemnation of her soul, she returned, like a dog to its vomit,[6] to commit the very errors she abjured.

Following her reconciliation to the Church, she rested on Saturdays; she does no work or household chores as she does on other days of the week. She ritually purged the meat she had to eat in order to observe Jewish ceremony. Likewise, she did not eat pork, nor any food from a pig, nor did she want to

---

6. This particular metaphor was a cliché in medieval theologians' writings about heretics, and it became formulaic as well in statements produced by medieval and early modern inquisitors.

eat at a table when pork is placed there. When certain people ate pork, she did not want to drink out of the glass he [sic] had used, because he had eaten pork. She did not eat partridges or strangled birds. What proves her heresy even more is that she had no picture or figure of any male or female saint in her house, nor the sign of the Cross, nor any other sign of a Christian, because she did not consider herself as such.[7] She is impenitent because she has not fulfilled the penance imposed upon her by your Reverences; she has worn things that were forbidden at the time she was reconciled. She does not believe that the Church's orders restrain her from sin.

She is a heretic and an apostate in other instances and things, rites and ceremonies, which I assure you I will make known in this trial. Hence Marina González was and is a heretic, an apostate, relapsed and impenitent, and she should incur a sentence of major excommunication and the confiscation and loss of all her possessions, as well as the other legal penalties against similar relapsed heretics.[8]

Thus I beg and request, very reverend lords, that you pronounce Marina González such a heretic . . . and relax her to justice and the secular arm. Above all, I ask that justice be done, and ask your noble office to do what is necessary. And I swear by God, Holy Mary, and the sign of the Cross that I do not place this accusation maliciously, but only because I am so informed and advised. . . .

And so the accusation was read by me, the notary.

Marina González responded by saying that she had done none of the things contained in the accusation, and asked that it be transcribed so that she could respond to it.[9]

Their reverences ordered a period of three days for her reply.

Then, before their reverences, Marina González gave complete power to defend this case to Diego Tellez, notary and resident of Toledo, etc. [sic].[10] Witnesses: Pedro González the Flat-Nosed and Juan de Castro.

7. Throughout Marina's trial, the significance of visual signs and outward behavior is highlighted again and again. When it came to religious identity, Marina's contemporaries drew a direct line from external action to internal belief.

8. Relapse into heresy provoked the harshest possible penalty, death at the stake, called "relaxation to the secular arm."

9. Defendants were required to respond immediately and orally to the prosecutor's charges; those charges were then "given in publication," meaning put into writing, for the defendant. In both the oral and written transmissions of the accusation, all identifying details about the prosecution witnesses were erased.

10. Chronologically, Diego Tellez is the first defense attorney readers will encounter in this volume. The ambiguities of Tellez' position become clear in this trial: employed and paid by the inquisition tribunal itself, the defense lawyer's *theoretical* duty

Subsequently, on January 17, 1494, Diego Tellez appeared before the lord inquisitors in God's name, and presented a writ of reply, the content of which follows:

January 17, 1494   Very Reverend Lords. As the attorney for Marina González, wife of Francisco de Toledo, spice merchant, resident of Ciudad Real, I, Diego Tellez, respond to the accusation brought against my party by Diego Martínez de Ortega, chief prosecutor of the Inquisition. . . . I state that my party is not a criminal, nor is she guilty of anything contained in the accusation, because of the following. First, the accusation was not begun at the time and in the way it should have been. Secondly, it contains no details about place or time that I could contemplate and respond to. . . . And, responding to each of its points, I state:

That after she was reconciled, my party never rested on Saturdays, but rather worked on them as much or more than other days of the week (except for Church feast days). She never rested out of honor for the Sabbath. Instead she cooked, kneaded bread, and did all the washing on those Saturdays, like a Christian woman.

As for purging the meat, she never did it, but ate what was in the pot, with pork, strangled birds, partridges, and all kinds of game when she had it. Even further from the truth is the idea that she would not drink from the glass of someone who had been eating pork. She ate pork herself. And she ate all the other foods of a Christian woman, without any distinction whatsoever. If she ever stopped eating pork on occasion, it would have been on account of her heart pains, and the other ills she suffered from giving birth.

As for the pictures and statues, she did not forsake them, but rather owned some of them, namely one of St. Catherine, and a Cross of St. Anthony that she'd had since she was a girl. They were placed where she prayed, on a piece of silk opposite the common room; she prayed even more in church. And she completed her penance, and lived, dressed, and spoke like a good Christian woman after she was reconciled, hearing masses, confessing, receiving the Eucharist, and fasting the fasts of the Church, like a good penitent. She never wore things that were forbidden at her reconciliation; and even though she wears . . . some little red skirts made of fine cloth, such was not prohibited by Your Reverences in Almagro. Your Reverences only decreed that her clothing could not be fine *scarlet* cloth.[11] Therefore, I say that since the

was to help persuade suspects to confess if he believed them to be guilty; still, in this instance, Tellez appears to have worked diligently for his client. For restrictions on defense attorneys, see Document 7.

11. Marina confessed in the village of Almagro, perhaps during the inquisitors' visitation of the district of Toledo. Penances could stipulate that women could not wear

accusation is worthless, may your Lords absolve, free, and release my party,
promising to return her goods to her, and ordering her released from this
prison. I implore your noble office for all this and everything else necessary,
ceasing innovation, and setting aside what is prejudicial. I thus conclude.
The writ being thus presented before the lord inquisitors, Diego Tellez, in
Marina González' name, said he concluded. Then the chief prosecutor said
he likewise would conclude, and requested judgment.

Then the lord inquisitors said that since both parties had concluded . . .
they must receive both parties for proof . . . and they assigned a period of
the nine subsequent days on which the tribunal was not closed, etc.

And after the above, on February 1, 1494, Diego Tellez appeared and
submitted a list of questions in Marina's name, which he wanted his witnesses to be asked as they appeared at the trial. The list is as follows:

Interrogatory for the defense witnesses. February 1, 1494

I, Diego Tellez, in the name of Marina González, the wife of Francisco de
Toledo, spice merchant, resident of Ciudad Real, ask that the witnesses for
my party, presented for Marina's defense . . . shall be asked the following:[12]

1. First, if they know Marina González, wife of Francisco de Toledo, spice
merchant, resident of Ciudad Real, and for how long they have known her.

2. If they know, have seen, or heard it said that Marina González reconciled herself, of her spontaneous will, during the Edict of Grace, and received
and completed her penance.[13]

3. Next, if they know, etc., that after her reconciliation, Marina González
lived, dressed, and talked like a good Christian woman, hearing masses and
sermons, observing Sundays and feast days of the Church, confessing and receiving the Eucharist very devotedly, and doing all the works of a Christian.

4. Next, if they know, etc., that after her reconciliation, Marina González
worked on Saturdays, spinning, sewing, or washing as much and more than
on other days of the week, if it were not a feast day of the Church, or unless
she was so ill that she could not work.

---

cloth of a certain quality—quality being gauged according to number of threads per
warp—nor the color red. See Document 7.

12. Here the defense used a strategy called *abonos,* when character witnesses were
called to substantiate a suspect's Christianity—or so Marina hoped.

13. Throughout the early modern period, Spanish suspects who came freely to inquisition tribunals and confessed quickly and openly were treated more leniently
than those who did not.

5. Next, if they know, etc., that after her reconciliation, Marina González never purged the fat from the meat; and that she threw pork into the pot as well as partridges, pigeons, hares, rabbits, and all the foods of a Christian. If occasionally she stopped eating pork, it would be because she was severely ill, but she always ate the meat cooked with the pork, despite all her pain.

6. Next, if they know, etc., that after her reconciliation Marina González prayed with great devotion to the Cross of St. Anthony and to the pictures of St. Catherine and the other saints that she had.

7. Next, if they know, etc., that Marina González never wore prohibited things, nor anything scarlet (except a little skirt that was red, with 2,400 threads per warp), because in Ciudad Real and Almagro she was not forbidden any color except for scarlet, not any other red cloth.

8. Next, if they know, etc., that after her reconciliation Marina González never did or said anything against our Holy Faith. And, given the lengthy conversation that the witnesses had with her, if Marina had done anything against the Faith, would they have seen or known about it.[14] And whether they never saw or knew anything of the sort, but only that Marina lived and acted like a good Christian.

Next, if they know that all the above is a matter of public opinion and reputation.

Presentation of defense witnesses for
Marina González, wife of Francisco de Toledo

February 6, 1494

Alfonso de Zarza, resident of Ciudad Real,[15] presented as a witness and legally sworn, etc., was asked the first question of the interrogatory.

To the first question, he said that he has known Marina González for two years, a little more or less, by sight, but had no other acquaintance with her.

To the second question, he said that he had heard it said that she was reconciled, and he knew nothing about the rest.

To the third question, he said that he knew nothing about it except that he had seen her sometimes at masses.

To the fourth, fifth, sixth, and seventh questions, he said he did not know, except that she did have a red skirt, but he did not know in what year.

14. This question's stress on possibilities would be fatal for Marina's defense.

15. Beinart notes that Zarza was on the town council. Nevertheless, the status of Marina's defense witnesses was consistently lower than that of witnesses for Pedro de Villegas in his trial. Compare Document 5 to Document 4. A discrepancy in the witnesses' confidence may be detectable as well.

To the eighth question, he did not know.

To the other questions pertaining to the case, he said he meant what he said, and ratified his testimony.

Marina Ruíz, wife of Bartolomé de Badajoz, resident of Ciudad Real, sworn and presented as a witness, etc., was asked the questions of the interrogatory.

To the first question, she said she knows Marina González by sight, conversation, and friendship, because she lived opposite her for more than two years.

To the second question, she said she did not know.

To the third question, she said that she saw Marina go to Mass on Sundays, and last Easter, she heard her say that she had confessed and received the Eucharist. And to the rest, she did not know.

To the fourth question, she said that on Saturdays she saw her working very continually, doing her household jobs, working just as on other days of the week.

To the fifth question, she said that she knew nothing else about it, except that she saw her carry partridges into the house, and for the rest, she does not know.

To the sixth question, she said she does not know, except that she saw some pictures in her house, crosses, and the Cross of St. Anthony.

To the seventh question, she said she does not know anything except that she saw Marina wear the red skirt, and for the rest, she does not know.

To the eighth question, she said she has not seen Marina do or say anything against the Catholic Faith. But if Marina had wanted to do or say something, she could have done it without this witness seeing it.

To the other questions pertinent to the case, she said she meant what she had said, and ratified her testimony.

• • • •

Leonor Fernández, former wife of Lope de Villareal, who resided in Ciudad Real, a witness sworn and presented, etc., was asked the questions of the interrogatory.

To the first question, she said she has known Marina González for thirty years or more, because she is her cousin.

To the second question, she said that she does not know, except that she heard that Marina was reconciled.

To the third question, she said that she saw Marina at Mass and sermons, and she saw her observe Sundays and feast days of the Church. As for the rest, she does not know.

To the fourth question, she said that she saw Marina on Saturday, doing her household duties just as on the other days of the week, especially last year from St. John's day to Carnival, when Marina and her husband lived in her neighborhood.[16]

To the fifth question, she said she did not see Marina purge the meat. She saw Marina eat the foods listed in the question, except she did not see her eat hare and rabbit. Sometimes Marina told this witness that she did not eat pork because it made her sick, and other times Marina ate it.

To the sixth question, she said she used to see Marina praying in Church, but she did not know what she was praying. As for the rest, she does not know.

To the seventh question, she said that she did not see Marina wear anything forbidden, except that she saw the red skirt.

To the eighth, she said that she did not see Marina do or say anything against the Catholic Faith, but if Marina had wanted to do so, she easily could have done it so that this witness would not have seen it.

To the other questions pertinent to the case, she said she meant what she said, and ratified her testimony.

Fernando de Madrid, resident of Ciudad Real, a witness sworn and presented, etc., asked the questions of the interrogatory [his testimony is missing from the record.]

In Ciudad Real, February 7, 1494

Catalina López, wife of Diego de la Membrilla, resident of Ciudad Real, a witness sworn and presented, etc., asked the questions of the interrogatory.

To the first question, she said she has known Marina González for one or two years, since they came from Almagro to live here. Marina lived a wall and a half away from this witness, and went in and out of her house; likewise the witness went in and out of hers, especially on feast days.

To the second question, she said she does not know.

To the third question, she said she considered Marina a Christian, because she saw her go to Mass and saw her rest on Sundays and Church feast days. Last Easter she saw Marina walking around looking for a confessor, saying it was for her daughter, as she had already confessed. As for the rest, she does not know.

To the fourth question, she said she saw Marina on certain Saturdays turning things upside down by doing her household chores, just as on other weekdays.

To the fifth question, she said she does not know.

16. The time frame here would be from June 23 to the beginning of Lent the following winter.

To the sixth question, she said she does not know.

To the seventh question, she said she saw the skirt mentioned in the question; for the rest, she does not know.

To the eighth question, she said she never saw Marina do or say anything against our Holy Catholic Faith. But if Marina had wanted to do it, she easily could have done so without this witness seeing it.

To the other questions pertinent to the case, she said that she meant what she had said, and ratified her testimony.

Bartolomé de Badajoz, resident of Ciudad Real, a witness sworn and asked the questions of the interrogatory.

To the first question. He has known Marina González for a little more than one year, by sight and to speak to, because they are neighbors. He sometimes went into her house, and she frequently went into his.

To the second question, he does not know.

To the third question, he said he considered her an Old Christian, and saw her at Mass sometimes. As for the rest, he does not know.

To the fourth question, he does not know.

To the fifth question, he does not know, except that he had heard that she did not eat pork, cuttlefish, or rabbit. He believed he had heard Marina herself say she did not eat rabbit.

To the sixth question, he does not know.

To the seventh question, he saw her in the red skirt, and touched it [sic]; as for the rest, he said he had not seen it, nor does he know about it.

To the eighth question, he has not seen Marina do or say anything about the Faith, and she could have easily done so without this witness seeing it.

Asked by the party of the chief prosecutor, this witness said he did not consider her a Christian.[17] Asked why, he said because she was raised among the *conversos* of Córdoba, and it seemed to him that she had the signs of not being a good Christian woman.

After the above, January 8, 1494, the chief prosecutor presented as witnesses Pedro de Teva, resident of Almagro; and on February 5, Fernand Falcon, resident of Ciudad Real; and on February 8, Juana de Cadena, the wife of Diego Falcon, resident of Caracuel. And on February 11, he presented Gracia, daughter of Juan de Espina, resident of Almagro. All the witnesses were legally sworn according to the law, etc.[18]

17. Here Bartolomé reverses himself abruptly. It is not clear from the trial record why the prosecutor spontaneously queried him, but the prosecutor was allowed access to defense testimony, as well as any confessions made by the defendant.

18. Based on the trial transcript, it looks as if the prosecutor had one deposition

These upright and religious people were present for the examination of the witnesses: Fray Pedro de Toledo; Friar Fernando de Suaso, OP; Pedro Pablo de Varco, cleric; and Juan de Castro.

Pedro de Teva, resident of Almagro, sworn witness, etc., said, under the charge of the oath he just swore, that last year, 1492 [sic], while living in Ciudad Real, he was good friends with Francisco de Toledo and knew him well.[19] Many times he ate with him in his house, consuming pork, strangled partridges, and other things, and Francisco's wife Marina did not eat any of it. One day, when he was eating a piece of wild pig with her husband, this witness said to her, "Lady, aren't you coming to eat?" and she said, "I cannot eat now." Her husband said to her, "I swear to God, woman, you are tempting fate." And she said to him, "Leave it alone, afflictions may come." From this point on, this witness watched her carefully, and though he saw her many times, she never ate pork or strangled partridges. If they ate pork, she did not eat at the table, nor [when] they brought the pork would she eat anything that was cooked with it. If her husband ate pork, she did not want to drink out of the same glass as he did.

Many times this witness watched her carefully on Saturdays. She never spun thread, though she used to do light chores about the house in front of him, as if she were pretending to do something. And on account of it, the witness said to her, "Well then, cousin!" and she replied, "Well, yourself!" In his opinion, this woman is a Jewess, even though he could not say more about her than what he suspects from the above. He heard that Marina and Flor González, wife of Alvaro de Madrid, made unleavened bread last year. And he heard Gracia del Espina say that she had seen Marina remove the fat from the meat.

Francisco de Toledo,[20] spice merchant, resident of Ciudad Real, sworn witness, under charge of the oath he had sworn, said that after her reconciliation, Marina González, his wife, sometimes refused to eat pork when they had it. And because this witness scolded her for not eating it, she certainly only stopped eating it out of concern for her health, not on account of any

---

on which to base his original accusation—other prosecution witnesses testified after the trial had officially opened—and none of his witnesses explicitly ratified their statements. If true, both lacunae violated proper procedure; see Documents 7 and 20.

19. Our Spanish subjects, like their European counterparts, dated the start of a New Year from Easter.

20. Though Francisco de Toledo's name was not among the prosecutor's witnesses as transcribed by the notary, he was called to depose, as husbands and wives could be forced to testify against each other in inquisition trials. Readers might consider whether he attempted to deflect suspicion from his wife.

religious ceremony. She ate everything that was cooked in the house, and even ate pork sometimes. Then he said likewise that some Saturdays she left the house to do some business, and this witness said something about it, and scolded her for it, telling her that she not only had to answer to God for her action, but also to the world. Asked why he scolded her if she simply left to do her errands, he said it was because she was thumbing her nose at God and the world, and on that day he had to do everything he should, so that no one would have anything to say about her.

Ferrand Falcon, resident of Ciudad Real, a sworn and questioned witness, etc., under charge of the oath he had sworn, said that he was in Francisco de Toledo's house, the spice merchant, resident of that city, when they seized his wife and sequestered her goods. Entering the house, he saw no pictures of male or female saints, nor a cross, nor any sign of a Christian. Adding to his statement, he then said that on certain Saturdays he saw Marina, the prisoner, in the city, dressed up in fine clothes, as if she were dressed for a feast day. He then said that he had heard Francisco de Toledo say, when he was talking about his wife's imprisonment, that she neither wanted to eat pork nor throw it in the pot. Francisco de Toledo quarreled with her so that she would not leave their house on Saturday, but after she had done some housework, she left. Adding to his statement, Falcon then said that fifteen days ago, more or less, when he was in Caracuel, at the house of his brother, Diego Falcon, they ended up talking about the imprisonment of Francisco de Toledo's wife. Then Juana de la Cadena, Diego Falcon's wife, said, "Is it really true that they seized Francisco de Toledo's wife?" And this witness said, "Yes." And she replied, "May my father's soul prosper, she is a Jewess, and I will tell you what I saw while living in Almagro, a little while before she came to live in Ciudad Real. Diego Falcon and I were in her house; we went there to negotiate over a grapevine, and we were staying there, in Francisco's house. While there, I followed her one Saturday, and saw how she got up and rested all day. I also saw how, after eating, she took her veil and left the house to walk outside, and did not return until nightfall. Then, the following Sunday, I saw her working flax in her house, and said to her, 'This, cousin?' And she replied, 'I owe my husband nothing except to feed him and his mule.' A saint's day fell that week, which we were supposed to observe, and I saw her do household tasks and spin the entire day."[21]

When Ferrand Falcon was asked how long ago Francisco, the spice merchant, and his wife came to live in the city, he said it could be twenty months, more or less.

---

21. This is a remarkably verbatim account of a conversation conducted by third parties.

Juana de la Cadena, wife of Diego Falcon, a resident of Caracuel, a witness sworn and questioned, etc., said under charge of the oath she had sworn, that two years ago, more or less, she and her husband went to the village of Almagro to lodge at the house of Francisco de Toledo, the spice merchant, who now lives in Ciudad Real. While there, this witness saw how one Friday, in Almagro, Francisco de Toledo's wife washed some linen cloths and put them out to dry, and cleaned a veil and a silk shirt. Then the next day, Saturday, she saw Marina take her veil and leave the house after eating, and before Marina ate, the witness saw her do nothing except walk about the house. Then on Sunday, after her siesta, this witness got up and found Marina working linen. Juana looked at her and stopped speaking. And then she said, "Lady, you're doing that on this day?" And Marina said, "Yes, cousin, and were it not for my work, I'd be worth nothing, nor have a dowry for my daughter, as Francisco is lazy and doesn't know how to earn."

While the witness was there, another obligatory feast day occurred; she thinks it was for an apostle, but does not remember very well. After eating, she found Marina again working linen and scolded her, and Marina said, "If I did not work the linen, I would not have this." And she showed the witness a mountain of linen pieces that she had inside a chest. Asked if Marina rested that Saturday, the witness said yes, she did not see her do anything. She has seen other *conversas* rest on Saturday, and they walk around to observe the Sabbath, thus revealing their evil lineage. Because of this suspicion, she watched Marina and saw her, as is stated.

Gracia, daughter of Juan de Espina, a sworn witness, etc., under charge of the oath she had sworn, said that three years ago, during Carnival, while living in Almagro . . . she made pastries with pork fat, and Marina did not want to eat them. Marina was even more adamant against eating pork, and would try to give it back to this witness, if this witness gave it to her; nor did Marina cook pork in the pot. One day, when the witness was in Marina's house, they brought meat, and Marina took it and moved away from this witness, and looked at Gracia to see if she were watching. Then Marina cut up a piece of meat into little pieces, and threw it out, so that Gracia would not know what she threw out. And a hen ate what she threw away.

Afterward, on February 26, 1494, the reverend lord inquisitor Fernando Rodríguez del Barco was in the hearing, and defense lawyer Diego Tellez appeared before him and requested the publication of the proof offered in this trial. His reverence ordered the publication of the witnesses' statements that were presented by both parties, and ordered that both parties be given a copy and transcript, with a limit of nine days in which to respond, etc.

March 15, 1494   Diego Tellez appeared in God's name before the lord judge and submitted a writ of reply and contradiction, which is as follows:

Very Reverend Lords. I, Francisco de Toledo, suspect that the witnesses named below could have spoken against Marina González, my wife, with hatred, ill will, and enmity. I hold them as doubtful and hateful:[22]

The first witness whom I suspect is Juana de la Cadena, the wife of Diego Falcon. She was a sinful person before she married Diego Falcon. She hated my wife, because once she and her husband, who is my wife's cousin, came to stay at my house in Almagro, and my wife said to him, "Congratulations, cousin, that you agree to such a thing! People tell me that your wife gives herself to as many gentlemen as pass your house, and if it is true, it looks horrible to God and the world." He said it was not true, and told his wife what my wife said; for that reason, Juana continued to feel great hatred toward my wife. Whereby, lords, she might avenge herself by giving false testimony, all of which Diego Falcon knows.

Likewise, lords, I suspect Juana, the wife of Martin the butcher, and the daughter of Carrillo, the town crier of Almagro. She was my servant; I had her for eight years and advanced her money. She left without serving me for the stipulated time because of the many injuries my wife inflicted on her. Because of which, and because I pressed her earnestly to repay the money I had advanced her, she hated my wife and me, so much so that she said publicly that she would make sure my wife would not come back from Toledo, but would die in the process. Don Enrique's concubine knows this, as does Juana's sister who lives in Almagro, as well as the daughter of Gonzalo de Chinchilla, and other people. Juana lives in Almagro; she is a whore, a drunk, a pimp, and most days is worse than addle-headed. A short time ago, in Almagro, they whipped her through the plaza and the streets for being a public pimp. Witnesses to this are Alvaro de Oviedo, and his wife and mother-in-law; and Sancho de Alvarez, and his wife and his sister-in-law, Beatriz.

I suspect Mayor, the . . . wife of Juan de Villarreal, wool carder, who lives in Ciudad Real and was my servant. . . .Your Lordships will find that when this servant Mayor was in my house, my wife became very jealous of her, and thought I committed adultery with her. For this reason, my wife made Mayor's life miserable until finally she forced her from the house, dragging her by the hair, calling her a public whore and the concubine not only of her

---

22. At this point, Marina's defense strategy changed to one of *tachas,* whereby she and her relations attempted to disqualify prosecution witnesses—whose identity they did not know—for capital enmity, scandalous reputation, or some other quality that would erase or lessen the impact of the depositions. Because the prosecution witnesses' names were not included in the publication of witnesses, attempting to disqualify (*tachar*) them amounted to a guessing game of who was most hostile to whom within a given community. Not all the prosecution witnesses impugned by Francisco de Toledo actually testified against his wife.

own husband but the entire village. Mayor went away and threatened my wife, calling her a Jewish whore and saying she would make her burn; she said this to many people, who from hearsay will be able to depose against my wife. This is known by García de Alvarez; his wife; García Rodríguez, son of Bartolomé Rodríguez; Pedro Díaz, son of Menzia Rodríguez; and Alvaro de Oviedo, all residents of Almagro.

I suspect Catalina, wife of this Bartolomé [Rodríguez], who resides in Ciudad Real. She is a very poor woman, and one of little honor and understanding who has no common sense. Many times she entered my house under the pretext of doing some favor for us, and my wife good-heartedly gave her things. As Catalina became accustomed to this, every day she wanted more, so that if my wife did not give her what she wanted, she left the house cursing that my wife was a Jewish heretic, and swearing that she would pay her twice over. . . .

I suspect Mari Ruiz, daughter of Miguel Ruiz, chaplain, who lives in Almagro. She could speak against my wife because when we left to lodge at _____ [sic] we left our house closed up. It was near hers, and Mari made a hole in the wall so that she could get into my house and use everything in it. When we returned to Almagro, my wife quarreled badly with her, and during the fight she threatened my wife. Witnesses to this are Hernando, the silversmith, and his wife. . . .

I suspect the wife of Hernando de Segovia, a resident of Almagro, who could speak against my wife because Marina said she was partly a *conversa.* She resented this very much, because she did not have the reputation of a *conversa,* and she threatened my wife, saying that she would say something about her that would be even more damaging.

I suspect Catalina la Toledena, wife of Domingo, the wool carder, who could speak against my wife because Catalina was a sinful woman. My wife said that Catalina still persisted in her evil ways even though she was married. After Catalina heard this, she said, with great anger, that it was even more certain my wife persisted in heresy. . . .

I suspect Gracia de Espina,[23] who could say something about my wife because she is her relative. Marina chastised her not to be an evil woman, because Gracia is sinful, something her own mother and brothers know. . . .

March 15, 1494 Very Reverend Lords. I, Diego Tellez, in the name of Marina González, wife of Francisco de Toledo, spice merchant, resident of Ciudad Real, say that your reverences have seen the statements and

23. A marginal note in the manuscript says "[She has] spoken; it isn't sufficient"; what wasn't sufficient was Francisco de Toledo's objection to her. The inquisitors found no manifest enmity in Gracia's own statement, and not enough evidence in Francisco's challenge to her testimony.

depositions of our witnesses to her good character, and thus will find very complete proof of my party's intention, to wit:

After Marina was reconciled, she always lived, dressed, and spoke like a good and faithful Christian woman, hearing Mass on Sundays and Church feast days, and confessing and receiving the Eucharist. She worked continuously on Saturdays just as on other days of the week. Out of devotion, she had pictures of saints and the Cross of St. Anthony in her house. Likewise, she spun on Saturday and ate pork, except when she was ill with some pain and stopped eating it. She never did or said anything against our Holy Faith.

The proof that the venerable prosecutor adduced against her has not impeded our case. First, his witnesses are changeable, and they deposed from hearsay and about frivolous incidents, while for serious events, they give neither motives nor reasons. Their statements contradict each other, and then they contradict themselves, and they do not prove that for which they were produced. Secondly, they did not testify or ratify their statements during the period of proof,[24] and gave false testimony with a great deal of hatred, frivolity, and capital enmity. Regarding the first witness, who wanted to say that there was no picture of a male or female saint in her house, nor any other sign of Christians, the witness clearly gave false testimony; consequently, all the others did too, because it is very clearly proven that Marina had pictures of the saints and the Cross of St. Anthony. Therefore the witness who asserted that Marina did not have these things when he was asked, is clearly a liar. Nor is his testimony worth anything when he said Marina observed the Sabbath because she left the house dressed up, because leaving the house does not have to mean anything; she did not stay at home every day. Her clothing was not very festive, in fact she never wore festive clothing, except a little red skirt that she has in prison; only scarlet was prohibited by the reverend fathers [i.e., inquisitors] in Ciudad Real. Again, this first witness does not say she rested on Saturdays, but simply heard it said by someone, and therefore he does not hurt our case.[25]

Nor did the other witness—who says that Marina left the house often on Saturdays, and her husband quarreled with her over it—damage our case. This quarrel seems to have occurred because her husband forbade her to leave the house and walk outside; it looks like it happened out of jealousy, rather than because it happened on Saturday, since it is not more forbidden to walk around on Saturday than on other days. The other witnesses hurt the case even less, since it is proven that Marina continuously worked on Saturdays. And the other witness, who said Marina pretended to do certain

24. There was no explicit ratification of any of the prosecution witnesses' statements, in violation of procedure.
25. Tellez knew that eyewitness testimony was worth more than hearsay.

tasks, seems to testify out of hatred; he declares things not on the basis of human understanding, but from a knowledge of the heart and interior motive that God alone has. Thus his statement is worthless. And as to his saying that she didn't want to eat pork, this was because she was sick, and she left it alone out of illness, since on other occasions she is proven to have eaten it. Still less does the last witness hurt the case, who says he watched her carefully, and she did not seem like a good Christian to him because she was raised among *conversos* who were not good Christians, and she had the same teachers that they had. Logically this argument is not admissible, but rather demonstrates his hatred and rudeness toward my party's family and against whoever raised her. It seems clear that he is hateful and even frivolous, and his statement is worth nothing.

The witnesses for my party should be believed rather than such false ones, who testified with hatred and enmity. I suspect the prosecution witnesses because of the suspicions that Marina González has; the people whom she suspects, and whom she remembers, are the following:[26]

First, I suspect[27] Torres, Mari Godias' husband, because he sold wine and was my neighbor. When I began to sell wine, he became so angry that he threatened me, saying that if we did not stop selling it, it would cost us dearly. Witnesses: Badajoz' wife and daughters, and others whom Francisco de Toledo would know.

Next, I suspect this Torres' wife. We quarreled over some cloths that my daughter embroidered and did not wish to sell, and also over an anklebone that I did not want to give her. On another occasion, we quarreled over some bread that I did not want to lend her. We quarreled all these times, and she flared up against me and said: "By this cross, after this time another will come," implying that she marked me for a bad end. Witnesses: the wife of _____ [sic], the wife of Bartolomé de Badajoz, and others from the neighborhood.

Next, I suspect a brother of this Torres because of a quarrel he had with my son, Diego, over a bridle that my husband sold. He remained so angry against me and my son that he would give false testimony. Witnesses: Diego, a silk weaver, and others who saw them quarrel.

I suspect Mayor, my servant girl, whom the wool carder Juan de Villareal took as a wife. She came up to me as I was walking and said, very aggressively: "What did you say about me to my parents?" I did not answer her and left, knowing I had done nothing whatever that she could report. Moreover, before this, when she was a servant in my house, I used to see how she

---

26. What follows is Marina's own list of *tachas,* or objections against the prosecution witnesses whom she guessed had testified.

27. The trial record shifts to Marina's voice.

went around like a prostitute with certain men, and I punished her, until I finally had to throw her out. Therefore she retained a lot of hatred for me, and could be easily induced to give false testimony, because she is imprudent and has wicked ways. Witnesses: Juan Rodríguez, son of Benito Rodríguez; and Mayor's son by Mencio Rodríguez. . . .

I, Diego Tellez, remit these objections for your diligent appraisal, since I cannot know or guess if they are relevant.[28] I ask that you free Marina, annul the contents of the accusation, order her released from this prison and return her possessions, given that my party's intention has been well proven, and the venerable prosecutor's has not. I implore your noble office to do all that is necessary.

With the writ so presented to the lord inquisitor, Diego Tellez, in God's name, said that he concluded, etc.

Then the chief prosecutor said his reverence would find his own intention well and completely proven by trustworthy witnesses who were above objection and who practice the Faith. The objections alleged by Marina González should not be admitted, because they are not such that the law recognizes. She names untrustworthy witnesses in the proofs: they are her relatives and intimate friends, or relatives by marriage; they are beneficiaries, children, or grandchildren of condemned heretics, so their statements and depositions must not be trusted.[29] Therefore, the prosecutor asked their reverences not to admit the objections, but rather to throw them out. He said that if they did this, they would do what was just. . . .

Then Inquisitor Fernando Rodríguez said that since the parties had concluded, and did not wish to say or advance anything else, that he likewise was finished with them. He said he held this trial as concluded, and assigned a period in which to give the sentence, etc.

Vote of the *consultadores*. Toledo, April 18, 1494

This case was voted on by:

> *Bachiller* Juan Alvarez Guerrero, chief governor of Toledo. He voted that Marina be declared a relapsed heretic. Because she is suspected of knowing others, they should give her the water torture.
>
> The prior of St. Peter Martyr, Friar Juan de Aca, the same.

28. Not even the defense attorney was given the identities of the witnesses against his client; he could not know in advance whether the *tachas* would succeed, either.

29. The prosecutor means that Marina's witnesses are tainted because they are either close relatives of hers, or because they are related to *conversos* condemned for judaizing. Contrary to the prosecutor's statement, people suspected of heresy were taken seriously as witnesses all the time—at least, when they were testifying for the *prosecution*.

Master Friar Fernando de Espina de Córdoba, of St. Francis, the same.

Master Friar Juan del Puerto, head of the Trinitarian monastic order in Toledo, the same.

Licentiate Fernando de Mazuecos, inquisitor, voted that she be tortured; if she did not confess, he said her innocence should be proven with eight witnesses [via compurgation].[30]

Fernando Rodríguez del Barco, inquisitor, the same.

April 29, 1494   After the above, when the lord inquisitors were in their customary hearing, they ordered Marina González brought before them. When she appeared, they requested and admonished her to confess the truth. If she did, said, or committed the things contained in her confession, or some of them, or some other heretical crime, then she should state it and confess it, and their reverences would receive her with all clemency.

Marina González said that after she confessed [in 1484] before their reverences, she never did nor committed any great heresy, etc. [sic], nor did she observe the Sabbath, or observe any other things whatsoever, except sometimes she ate pork, and other times she did not, etc. [sic]

Their reverences said that having seen the decrees and records of the trial, they found they must put her to torture, and ordered that she be given the water torture. By their sentence they so pronounced, declared, and ordered, etc. [sic]

She then was transported to the place of torture, where their reverences requested and admonished her to tell the truth. They said that if during the torture some evil, damage, wound, or death occurred to her, it would be her fault and not theirs. They asked her again for testimony, etc. [sic][31]

She was stripped of her old skirts and put on the rack, and her arms and legs were tied tightly with cords. She also had a cord tied tightly around her head. They put a hood in front of her face, and with a jar that held three pints, more or less, they started to pour water down her nose and throat. Having poured up to a pint, lord inquisitor Mazuecos asked her if she had done anything; she said no.

They continued to give her water, and told her to speak the truth; she said nothing. They gave her more water and said if she would speak the truth, they would not give her any more; she said nothing. His reverence ordered her to be given water until the three-pint jar ran out; she never said a word. He said that they should take the cord off her head, and she would speak the truth; the cord was taken off, but she said nothing. They tied her up again

30. See note 32 below.

31. The inquisitors' explicit denial of responsibility for any injury suffered by a defendant during torture was standard practice.

and began to give her more water from the jar, which they had refilled. He said that they should raise her head so she would speak the truth; they raised her, and she said nothing.

When they put her back down again, she asked that she might be raised up, and for Holy Mary's sake, she would tell everything. . . . They gave her more water, and she said she would tell everything, for Holy Mary's sake. She said that a neighbor woman fasted during some fasts, and [she knew this] because she was her neighbor. She said that if they would take her from that place she would tell them about it, and if they would raise her head she would speak the truth. But when she was raised up, she refused to say anything at all. They again put the cord on her head, very tightly, and told her to say everything. They gave her more water, until the jar was empty, and she never said anything at all. Their reverences ordered her removed from the torture, as they did not hold her to torment her, etc. [sic]

When she was removed from the torture, she said that her neighbor, the wife of Gómez de Chinchilla, resident of Ciudad Real, fasted. Asked which fasts, those of Jews or of Christians, she said those of Jews. Asked why she believed this, she said because the neighbor observed Saturdays. Witness: Pedro Pucherón. Asked if the neighbor said anything to her, she said no. Asked how long ago this happened, she said a little while, perhaps a year ago, more or less. . . .

May 5, 1494 After the above, when the lord inquisitors were in their customary hearing, they pronounced sentence in the presence of Marina González:

Having seen and diligently examined this case pending before us, between the chief prosecutor, who is the accuser, and Marina González, a reconciled *conversa*, we must declare that the chief prosecutor has not completely proven his intention. But inasmuch as the chief prosecutor's proof results in a vehement suspicion against Marina González, we must invoke canonical compurgation.[32] We order that her case be proven canonically with eight witnesses who are trustworthy and zealous in the faith. Which we order within the next nine days. And thus we pronounce our sentence, etc. Witnesses: Pedro González the Flat-Nosed and Juan de Castro, notary.

May 22, 1494 After the above, Marina González was brought to the lord inquisitors in their hearing. Their reverences asked if she had decided

32. In cases in which proof was ambiguous, inquisitors might call for compurgation, whereby a set number of witnesses, named by the defendant, swore that the defendant was a good Christian and was innocent of heresy. If all the witnesses so swore, the prisoner would be acquitted and released. Compurgation was used in the Middle Ages in both canon and secular law. The term comes from the Latin *purgere,* or "to clear of a charge." "Compurgation" thus means to clear of a charge with or through others.

upon her compurgatory witnesses. Through a memorandum written in prison, she said she named as her witness and guardian Bartolomé de Badajoz, resident of Ciudad Real; she also named the son of Antonio de Caracuel, resident of Almagro. [But] as the rest of the names were read, she [suddenly] said that they were nothing, that she did not want to name them as witnesses, nor others in their place. Then their reverences ordered that her witnesses should be brought and should declare the evidence against her as false within the next fifteen days. Otherwise, their reverences would order her to remain in their judgment. If the witnesses were produced, their reverences were ready to receive the compurgation; but if the time limit passed without the witnesses coming forward, then they would hold Marina González as having failed that requirement, etc. [sic]

May 30, 1494   After the above, the chief prosecutor appeared before their reverences and said that since Marina González, wife of Francisco de Toledo, refused to accept the canonical compurgation, and hence implied that she knew she was guilty of the crime of which she was accused, she should be held as having failed it. [In prison] she despaired of life and was killing herself by not eating, without any excuse of real illness, but voluntarily, so she would be left to die without receiving the punishment that she deserves. Accordingly, she should be held as convicted. Therefore, he asked their reverences to pronounce and declare her a heretic and relax her to justice and the secular arm, and he asked that justice be done. He begged their lordships to request testimony [on these matters]. Their lordships told him to present the information, and said they were ready to do justice.

Then the chief prosecutor presented as a witness Pedro González the Flat-Nosed, warden of their lordships' prison, from whom they received a legal oath on the sign of the Cross and the words of the Holy Gospels, etc., under charge of which he was asked if he knows Marina González, wife of Francisco, spice merchant, resident of Ciudad Real. He said he has known her since they brought her to the prison. Asked if he has seen her say and do anything against Our Holy Catholic Faith since she became a prisoner, he said that he has seen her since she was imprisoned and the accusation placed, and she does not want to eat, though she was not sick. By order of their reverences, this witness brought a doctor to see if she were sick; this doctor saw her and took her pulse, and told the witness she had no illness at all, and ordered him to bring herbal water to induce her to eat.

Asked why she stopped eating, the witness said she told him that since they intended to kill her, why bother to eat. This witness knows that she has stopped eating in such a way that she would eat only by pure force. They have forced her to eat in that way, against her will. He said that she has done this more fixedly since she was entrapped by the compurgation. He said that

while speaking with her over the last two days, he asked if she wanted to confess, because it seemed to him that she needed it, since she was so weak and
thin from not wanting to eat. It seemed to him that she was dying. She
replied that she did not want to confess. Asked if she had confessed later in
prison, he said no. Since he saw that she did not want to confess, this witness asked her, among other things, if she was a Christian; she said no. This
witness asked her likewise if she believed what the Holy Mother Church
holds and believes, and she said, "If I believed it, I would not be here," or "I
would not have come here"; he cannot remember which. She said this in
front of six or seven women prisoners and Rodrigo de Valdelecha, this witness' servant.

This same day, May 30, 1494, the chief prosecutor presented Rodrigo de
Valdelecha, who is a jailer and the servant of Pedro González the Flat-Nosed,
as a witness. Their Reverences received his legal oath, etc. He was asked if he
knows Marina González, wife of Francisco, spice merchant, resident of Ciudad Real. He said that he has known her for three months, more or less.
Asked if she stopped eating after she was seized, he said for the past ten or
eleven days he has seen that she does not want to eat, if not forced to do so.
She says she does not want to eat since this witness has to rip her to shreds;
she begs this witness to kill her and rip her to pieces; she asks this of him sincerely, not as a joke, or so it seems to him.[33] This witness has told her to confess and has offered to bring her a confessor. She tells him she does not want
to confess, since they have to do what they have to do. This witness asked
her if she wanted to believe in God, or if she believed in God and in what
the Holy Mother Church orders; she answered that if she believed it, she
would not be there. Asked if he thinks she is a Christian, he said that according to what he had seen her do and say, he does not take her for a Christian. And he affirmed his testimony, etc.

June 9, 1494   After the above, the reverend lord Fernando Rodríguez
del Barco, inquisitor, received a legal oath from Mayor del Castillo, wife of
Juan Mendez, who is a prisoner in the Holy Inquisition's jail. By virtue of
which they asked her to say what she knows about Marina González, wife
of Francisco de Toledo, spice merchant, resident of Ciudad Real, who also
is a prisoner in the jail, and why Marina González does not want to eat. The
witness has heard Marina say many times she does not want to eat because
they have to kill her and rip her to shreds. The witness has seen her eat sometimes and she is well; and other times the witness has heard Marina say that

33. For the possible emotional identification between jailer and defendant, or tor-
turer and defendant, see Lyndal Roper, *Witch-Craze* (New Haven, CT: Yale University Press, 2004), 44–66.

she does not want to eat since they have to rip her to shreds. Sometimes the witness has heard from other prisoners that when they tell Marina to commend herself to God and His Blessed Mother, she becomes silent and will not answer them at all. And this witness believes that Marina does not want to eat, that she has no fever, and that she is deliberately killing herself. Asked if she has seen Marina in her right mind, she said that sometimes she has seen her sane and sometimes not. Asked if Marina was well and without fever when she stopped eating, she said yes, she was well, except that Marina said she thought a great deal about how the witnesses against her had testified.[34] From that point on she stopped eating, and at that time she had no fever nor any other illness. This is what she knows and has seen and heard since she was imprisoned, according to the oath she swore.

Sentence. June 30, 1494   [Verbatim repetition of the chief prosecutor's accusation]. . . . Likewise having seen how Marina, being a prisoner, tried to kill herself in prison to avoid confessing her errors, and having deliberated over all the other events and records of the trial, and above all having had our consensus and vote, [after] counsel with the learned men who were present for the viewing and examination of this trial:

HOLDING GOD BEFORE OUR EYES:

We find that we must pronounce and declare that the chief prosecutor's intention has been well proven, while the party of Marina González has not proven anything useful. Therefore, we must declare her a relapsed heretic and an apostate. She has incurred a sentence of major excommunication, and the confiscation and loss of all her possessions. We must relax her to justice and the secular arm, and we declare our judgment through these writings.

This judgment was given in Toledo, June 30, 1494, by the lord inquisitors in the Plaza de Zocodover in that city, acting as the tribunal, while standing on a wooden scaffold; this judgment was read in a loud voice in the presence of Marina González. Juan de Sepúlveda and Nicolas Fernández, canons of Toledo, were witnesses, as were the doctor of Canisales, and the magistrate Francisco de Vargas (treasurer of their Highnesses), and many other noblemen.

34. Again, Marina would not have been told the identity of witnesses who testified against her, and she obviously tormented herself with thinking about who they might have been. Doubt over the loyalty of her acquaintances—would they have testified against her, or not?—was what led her to stop in despair while naming her compurgatory witnesses.

Document 6

Inquisition Trial of María González, Wife of Pedro de Villarreal. Ciudad Real, 1511–1513[1]

December 30, 1511   Before the Reverend Lord Inquisitors, Alonso de Vaena presented this document:

Very Reverend Lords,

I, Alonso de Vaena, appear before your Reverend Fathers as the defense lawyer for María González, wife of Pedro de Villarreal, merchant, resident of Ciudad Real. I say that my party has confessed all the offenses she remembers having committed against our Holy Catholic Faith, and asks for penance for them. The chief prosecutor insists that my party, María González, is being silent and hiding other people who committed the crimes with her. This assertion is not believable. But because the naming of others is usually included in these matters and is natural, and is even more natural in women, I ask your Reverend Fathers to order her to name such people as the law allows, secretly or publicly, not out of rigor, but equity. On account of which I beg for testimony, [and ask] that justice be done and consciences charged.[2]

February 19, 1512   After the aforesaid, on February 19, 1512, in Toledo, the reverend lords licentiate Alonso de Mariana and licentiate Villanueva, inquisitors, were in the hearing of the Holy Office of the Inquisition; they ordered María González brought before them. When María González was present, their reverences said that it was already known that she had confessed the heretical crimes of which the prosecutor accused her, and that she had been required and admonished many times to confess the truth about

---

1. Beinart, *Records of the Trials of the Spanish Inquisition*, vol. 2, 270–76; Beinart's complete transcription of this trial is on pp. 240–319. María's prosecution by the Inquisition occurred in two parts. She was first arrested in 1511 after Lucía Fernández denounced her as a judaizer; María confessed, deposed against dozens of allegedly judaizing *conversos*, and was sentenced to perpetual prison in 1512. Her trial was reopened in July 1513 when the prosecutor set out to prove that she had perjured herself through false testimony. Lying under oath was an act of heresy.

2. For details on the defense lawyer in the inquisitorial system, see the Introduction and Document 7. Here is an instance in which the defense lawyer put his loyalty to the tribunal first.

the other people who had committed the crimes with or without her; and she had always refused to do so. Now, they once more required and admonished her to tell the truth about these other people, because information existed that she had committed her crimes with others, and had seen people commit other heresies. And by telling the truth, she would do what she ought, and would unburden her conscience. Otherwise, the Inquisition would proceed against her according to what it discovers by law.

María González said she had confessed everything she knew about the charges, about herself as well as others, and had no more to say.

Then their reverences told her that since she persisted in her denial, and they had information to the contrary, that if she thought that some people wished her ill she might think about whether she wanted to object to them, or to defend her case in other ways. If she wanted to do so, she should tell them, because their reverences were ready to hear her and do justice in her case.

María González said she wanted to object to no one and had no more to say or confess, whether about herself or other people, besides what she had already stated and confessed before the lord inquisitors. She begged their reverences to treat her mercifully.

After the aforesaid, on March 26, 1512, the reverend lord inquisitors, licentiates Alonso de Mariana and Francisco de Herrera, who were in the hearing, ordered María González brought before them. When María González was present, they asked her if she remembered mentioning certain people in her confession. María González said yes, she remembered mentioning Juana Nuñez, Juan de Teva's wife, and other people contained in her confession. The inquisitors ordered me, the notary, to read her confessions; I, Cristóbal de Prado, notary, [then] read, word by word, all the confessions that María González had made up to the present day. After hearing me read them, María González said that everything in her confessions was true; she ratified her confessions, and said they contained the truth, and everything had happened as she had stated and confessed many times, and she swore in the necessary way, etc. [sic].

Afterward, March 30, 1512, the reverend lord inquisitors—the licentiate Alonso de Mariana, and Francisco de Herrera, apostolic and ordinary inquisitor—were in the hearing of the Holy Office of the Inquisition, in my presence, Cristóbal de Prado, notary. They ordered Melchor de Sayavedra, the prison warden, to bring María González to the hearing. When María González was present, the lord inquisitors told her that she had been admonished many times to declare the truth about what she knew, about herself as well as other people, and to declare her accomplices, and still she has not wanted to speak the truth. Thus it was necessary to treat her with all the severity of the law. They ordered me, the said notary, to read the following sentence in María González' presence:

Sentence of torture[3]

Having seen, etc.

Given the circumstantial evidence and suspicions that result from the trial against María González, and the fact that she has been silent about the people who participated with her in the crimes of heresy which she has confessed, we find that we must order her put to the question of torture. The torture shall be given according to our will until such time as she declares the truth about accomplices and participants in the said crimes. And so we pronounce and order by these writings.

This sentence was given and pronounced by the lord inquisitors on the aforesaid day, month, and year, María González being there and in my presence, the notary.

Afterward, on the same day and year [March 30, 1512], the lord inquisitors were in the place of torture with María González, and ordered her to undress. Then María González said that she wanted to declare the truth about everything she knew, about herself as well as others. She begged the lord inquisitors not to torture her, saying she wanted to declare the truth about what she knew, and to unburden her conscience. What she said, declared, and confessed is what follows:

Confession. March 30, 1512   She said the truth is, that when she performed the heretical crimes which she has confessed, María López, her aunt and the wife of Hernando de Villarreal (a painter, resident of La Membrilla), acted with her. Hernando de Villarreal is the brother of the accused's father, whose name is Hernando de Merida.[4] The crimes that the accused committed with María López occurred in the accused's house over the last three years, [with] María López very frequently coming from La Membrilla to her house in Ciudad Real, to do the said things at different times of the year. She was asked if María López lodged in her house; she said no, but in the house of Beatriz Alonso, wife of Hernando de Merida, the father and mother of the accused. María López came to the accused's house to perform Jewish ceremonies, just as the accused performed them, and with the same belief in the law of the Jews. The accused and María López, her aunt, also went to the house of Diego de Teva, who is dead, and a resident of Ciudad Real; and there they met with María González,[5] his wife, in his house. There they also met Blanca Ximénez, Juan Ximénez' wife (a merchant, dead, resident of La

---

3. Headings have been added for the benefit of the reader.

4. These identifying details appear to have come from direct questions that are not recorded in the transcript.

5. María González, wife of Diego de Teva, was also the defendant's aunt.

Solana), whom the accused believes is a prisoner of the Inquisition in Jaén. Blanca is her father's sister.

They also assembled with Gracia de Teva, wife of Diego Alvarez (spice merchant, resident of Ciudad Real); Juana Nuñez, wife of Juan de Teva (merchant, resident of Ciudad Real); María González, wife of Rodrigo de Chillon (landlord, has charge of meat market, resident of Ciudad Real) and a cousin of the accused; as well as the mother of [her aunt] María González, named Inés de Merida, wife of Diego de Huelva (dead, resident of Yepes). Inés de Merida now lives in Ciudad Real. The accused and all of the above women met in the house of her aunt, María González, wife of Diego de Teva (cloth maker, dead), on certain Friday nights to rest and observe those nights. They ate pancakes and other things, according to the season and what was available. On those Friday nights, María González, Diego de Teva's wife, lit two clean oil lamps with new wicks two hours before it was dark. She adorned and cleaned her house, and adorned it on those Friday nights out of esteem for the Law of Moses.

And on those Friday nights, all the aforesaid and the accused bathed from a large jar with water heated with herbs, chamomile and such, for the sake of Jewish ceremony. María González, Diego de Teva's wife, prepared that water and sent the accused to call all the aforementioned women when it was ready, so that they might come and bathe. And the younger ones bathed before the older, and the old women bathed the bodies of the younger. Diego de Teva's wife sent two of her own daughters to call the aforesaid and the accused; one is named Catalinica, aged eleven, and the other Juanica, aged eight. At that time, María González had a stepchild in her house named María López, who is now married to Pedro de Dueñas, a wool carder, resident of Ciudad Real. That girl was there, and saw the things that they did in Diego de Teva's house, and she too bathed with the aforesaid and the accused. . . .

And sometimes they talked about matters of the Church and the Christian Faith, and ridiculed the Mass. She knows that the aforesaid women did not believe in the Mass, nor did they want to go to hear it; on those occasions when they did go to Mass, it was only to keep up appearances, not for the Mass [itself]. And the accused did the same, because the women said something to her about it, and vice versa, and they talked about it with each other, holding the Mass and the Christian Faith as a joke. She knows that many times they made themselves sick to get out of going to Mass. Asked how she knows this, she said because they told her, she saw it, and she did the same thing. She knows that all of them observed some fasts of the Jews two days a week, she believes on Mondays and Fridays, or Thursdays;[6] she does not

6. Bodian, *Hebrews of the Portuguese Nation,* explores the ways in which *conversos* creatively altered Jewish rituals in the absence of rabbis. *Weekly* fasts were not part of orthodox Judaism.

recall very well if it was Friday or Thursday. Each woman fasted in her own house and then ate dinner, and after they had eaten, they came to the house of Diego de Teva's wife, and there, being together, they chatted and told each other how they had fasted and what they had eaten for dinner.

On the days they fasted, they did not eat all day until nightfall. The accused knows this because she did it herself, and they told her about it, and some performed more fasts than others. The accused fasted fewer times, because she always was either pregnant or had just delivered. . . .

July 15, 1513[7]   The lord inquisitors were in the hearing of the Holy Office of the Inquisition; they ordered María González, who is in the perpetual prison,[8] brought before them. When she was present in the court, their reverences told her that it was well known that she had spoken against many people in her confessions and depositions since being imprisoned, whether spontaneously or under torture. Their reverences doubt whether her comments about certain people, whom she named as accomplices, are true. They therefore admonished her by God our Lord and His Blessed Mother the Virgin Mary to speak the entire truth, and if through fear or confusion or enmity, or some other reason, she had said something against someone that was not true, then she should say so. If she did this, she would unburden her conscience as a good Christian should, because their reverences' intention was only to do justice and to protect the parties' rights.

[María González confirmed the truth of her previous confessions and depositions.]

• • • •

Sentence of torture, July 19, 1513[9]

It has been seen how María González deposed and testified against many other people, with whom she said she had committed the heretical crimes, after she was imprisoned in the Holy Office's prison and had confessed her own crimes. She [also] spoke against other people with whom she did *not* commit said crimes, according to what is contained at greater length in her confessions, statements, and depositions. Some of the people against whom she testified have been prisoners in the inquisition prison, and some of them

---

7. Beinart, *Records of the Trials of the Spanish Inquisition,* vol. 2, 292–93.

8. In the Spanish Inquisition, a sentence to "perpetual" prison—which was not located in a tribunal—almost never signified imprisonment until death; after some years, the sentence would be commuted. The creation of perpetual prisons was a matter of some concern for inquisition tribunals; see Documents 7 and 20.

9. Beinart, *Records of the Trials of the Spanish Inquisition,* vol. 2, 297–302.

have confessed to crimes of heresy committed with other people, but they have not confessed anything at all about being an accomplice of María González'. It should be noted that some of the prisoners, who revealed that they committed heretical crimes with certain people, with whom they were very much allied, confessed nothing at all like what María González says they did with her, even though some of them have been put to the question of torture over it. And the character of María González has been taken into account, as well as what is proven against her in various trials; her style of deposition, as well as her vacillation and hesitation in her statements and depositions, has been noted. She has said some things that do not seem reasonable; and though investigations were carried out, no eyewitness testimony supports what María González herself declared in her depositions and statements.[10]

And because of other reasons that move us to ascertain the truth, as we are obliged to do for God and our consciences, we find that we must order María González put to the question of torture, which may be given and continued at our will until she speaks the truth and perseveres in it, according to the law.[11] Thus we order it through these writings, by the sitting tribunal.

This sentence was pronounced on July 19, 1513 by the reverend lord inquisitors in front of María González. She said she had told the truth in everything she confessed, and her confession is true, and she will not say more except that it is true, even if they kill her over it, that what she has said is true, and if she recanted during torture and they killed her, it should be on their consciences.[12] She has said the truth and she affirmed it.

Then their reverences ordered Melchor de Sayavedra, warden of the Holy Office's prison, who was present, to take María González to the torture room. He took her with him. Then their reverences went to the torture room and admonished María González to declare the truth about what she had said against the people and accomplices with whom she says she committed the crimes. For it was imperative for their reverences to know the entire truth, and they assured her that if she should receive death, a wound, or the loss of some limb during the torture, it would be her own fault, because their

---

10. Here the inquisitors' discretion led them to doubt the linchpin of the inquisitorial process, namely the confession.

11. Suspects who confessed under torture were required to ratify their confessions the next day; ergo, the requirement that María "persevere" in the truth she was expected to utter.

12. Contrary to María's statement, before torture sessions inquisitors explicitly stated that any bodily or mental injuries that prisoners might incur were the *prisoners'* fault, since the suspects had the ability to confess and prevent the torture from occurring in the first place. See next paragraph.

intention was nothing more than to know the entire truth about what she had said in her confessions and the depositions she had made, whether those statements were made when she was incarcerated in the prison for suspects, or where she is now, in the perpetual prison.[13]

María González said that she has spoken the truth in her confessions and depositions, and she affirmed it; their reverences could do what they liked, what she had said is true. Their reverences ordered her to undress, and again they admonished her in the following manner. Their reverences told her to speak the entire truth of what she had stated and testified against the people she had named, and if she had told the truth to say so, and if not, to say so. She said that she had already spoken the truth, and even if they tore her into a thousand pieces in the torture and in the cart [on the way to the stake], she would say nothing else but the truth she has already told. God would help her, as she has spoken truthfully. Their reverences ordered her undressed, and admonished her again. She said she had spoken the truth and had not lied in anything she had said. She was ordered onto the rack and was tied with cords; once on the rack, she said, "Tighten them and kill me, I will say no more than what I have already said," and may an evil pestilence befall the person who put her there, that she has spoken the truth, and what more did Our Lord Jesus Christ suffer. She asked it to be held as evidence that if she recanted and was burned because of the injuries of torture, it would be on their reverences' consciences, and she left it to God that she spoke the truth.

She commended herself to God and the Virgin Mary that she had spoken the truth. And being tied up, she said that she made it all up, she made it all up because she detested them. She couldn't stand those wives of Rodrigo de Chillon and Fernando de Córdoba; they treated her badly and wrecked her marriage. Their reverences warned her that if she has spoken the truth about something, not to recant it; and if she has said something false about someone, to say so. She asked them to untie her, that she would speak the truth.

She was asked if it is true what she said against Francisco Ruiz, the spice merchant; she said it was true, she heard him say that there was nothing else except birth and death.[14] She was asked if what she said against Alonso Ruiz, his brother, is true; she said that Alonso Ruiz was there, and said: "By God I believe it."

She was asked if what she said against Juana Nuñez, wife of Juan de Teva, is true; she said it is. They snacked one day and observed two Saturdays, and

---

13. A clear statement of difference between the prison in the tribunal, and the one in which convicted heretics served their sentences. See Documents 7 and 20.

14. See Nalle, *God in La Mancha,* 61 for other stock phrases that inquisitors could read as heretical or blasphemous. This particular formula seemed to reflect the *conversos'* disbelief in Christian salvation.

Juana Nuñez' mother was there, and they observed the two Saturdays in Juan de Teva's house, and another in her house, and they fasted one Friday until nightfall, and at night they ate eggs for dinner, and it was a Jewish fast. Lucia, Juana Nuñez' servant, knows that her mistress observed the Sabbaths; this witness did not see them observe it. She was asked how she knows that Juana Nuñez observes Saturdays with the intention of judaizing; she said that Nuñez never told her the intention, but only the act, and as the accused intended to judaize, so she thought that Juana Nuñez did it for the same reason. When they fasted they did not tell each other the reason, only the act.

Asked if what she said against Inés López is true, she said that it is, and that she saw her make some cakes and stews on Friday, which she and the accused ate on Saturday.

Their reverences ordered a jar of water poured into her nose and mouth, which was started, and she said she affirmed everything she had said. Their reverences admonished her to tell the truth. She said she would tell the truth. As the jar of water was emptied, she said she would speak the truth. She said everything she had said in her confessions before their reverences is completely true; they can put her into a fire, and still everything she said is true. Their reverences asked her the details of what she had said, and she replied that everything she had said is true. Their reverences ordered the water torture continued. As she was given the water, she said she had told the truth, and that everything she has said and confessed is true, and they could put her into a fire over it, because everything she said and confessed is true.

She was asked if what she said against Gracia de Teva, married to Diego Alvarez, is true; she said it is. They bathed out of ceremony, and ate things cooked in earthenware dishes. Gracia rested on Saturdays, and one day she bathed at the accused's house, and another day at Diego de Teva's house. And given what the accused did, and saw the aforesaid do, the accused believed that they [sic] did it for the same reason that she did. And because Gracia de Teva made fun of the accused for going to Mass, the accused believed she was a heretic, and since both of them ridiculed the Mass, the accused thought Gracia did so with the same wicked intention as herself. . . .

The order was given to pour another jar of water. She said, "I speak the truth, I have spoken the truth, I have already spoken the truth, I speak the truth, what I have said is true, I am telling the truth, I do not tell any lies, I have not lied, I have spoken the truth, I have spoken the truth." The jar of water was finished. She said she had spoken the truth. Their lordships admonished her in the same style as above. She said, "Sirs, I have already told the truth. Why do you conclude that I have not spoken truthfully?" She said that what she had declared was true, and she would agree to their throwing her into the fire. And what she said about the book, which Fernando de Córdoba read, it was about medicine and belonged to the accused's mother. At

the beginning, she claimed it belonged to Diego de Madrid, thinking her
mother was at risk if she said it belonged to her. They had found the book
in her mother's house; she knows it was about medicine, she heard people
read from it, and they took recipes from it for medicines.[15] She saw Fernando
de Córdoba, who was sick with kidney trouble, read from it. And she has
spoken the truth about everything except this book, [but] everything else
about herself and the others is true, and she affirms it.

Their reverences ordered the water continued, and the cloth placed [over
her face]. She said, "Leave me alone. I will speak the truth." She said she
could not stand Lorenzo Franco's wife; she wanted to see her ground into
dust. Asked if what she had said against her is true, she said she spoke against
her because of the great hatred she has for her. One Saturday, at Rodrigo de
Chillon's house, they rested and ate beans, but she said all those other things
because she hated her, she is a very wicked woman, and vain. . . . As for the
wives of Rodrigo de Chillon and Lorenzo Franco and Fernando de Córdoba
. . . she wanted to see them burned. . . .She was asked if the meetings in the
houses of Rodrigo de Chillon and Diego de Teva and Fernando de Córdoba
really happened; she said she hated those women, and wished they might
come here with her . . . and everything she said about Fernando de Córdoba's
wife was a lie. She attributed it falsely so that that woman would come here
with this witness, because she is her capital enemy; Fernando de Córdoba's
wife persecuted her and caused trouble many times with her husband and
deliberately wrecked her marriage. . . .

August 22, 1513[16]   In the afternoon hearing, the reverend lords, Licentiate Alonso de Mariana and Francisco de Herrera, inquisitors, said that they
had seen the new petition drawn up by the prosecutor of this Holy Office
against María González, and that everything contained in the petition appears to be notorious and true, given the proceedings and María González'
own confessions. María González is [now] known to be someone who confessed falsely and is impenitent, from having said many things about herself
and others, that afterward she said were false. She has revoked her statements
and persevered in her revocation. Thus, according to the law, they could treat
her as a notorious case, a distinction that would conform to the vote of the
learned men who had conferred on the case.[17]

15. Books in Hebrew were suspicious by default, irrespective of subject. In this instance, María attempted to deflect evidence that could have been used against her
mother—a Hebrew book about medicine, found in her mother's house—by claiming that it was owned by someone else (Diego de Madrid), and then *read* by someone else (Fernando de Córdoba).

16. Beinart, *Records of the Trials of the Spanish Inquisition,* vol. 2, 313.

17. A reference to a session with the *consultadores.*

But the aforesaid notwithstanding, the inquisitors still wished, for greater conformity with justice, to give a written copy of the prosecutor's new petition to María González, so that she might respond to it with the advice and counsel of her defense lawyer.[18] They did not do so, however, because they speculated that if María González were given the copy, she would fall into a desperate state and could lose her soul. They conjectured in this way; since her last imprisonment in the tribunal,[19] she has said on many different occasions that she feared they had to kill her, since she had retracted what she had first reported.[20] She has said many times in the hearings that she greatly deserves death, begging their reverences to let her go raise her children, even though she knew she deserved to die.

And so they did not order a transcript given to her beforehand, in agreement with the vote and the opinion of the [*consultadores*], out of fear of the aforesaid, and because it is notoriously clear as well that María González can summon no defense that will nullify and exclude her false confessions and impenitence and her various perjuries in a matter of the Faith. For greater conformity with justice, they ordered María González to appear in the hearing. Once she was present, their reverences said that . . . she had testified against many different people, and now . . . she had revoked what she had said against those people who purportedly committed crimes of heresy; and she had ratified her revocation. Again the inquisitors admonished her, since she had been able to deliberate for many days, to tell the truth about what she had confessed and later revoked, and to affirm the truth, and if something had occurred to her recently, to declare it and make it known, and in everything to speak entirely the pure truth.

María González said that she had spoken the truth in the revocations she had made, and she had imputed falsely what she had first said she had seen, and that was the truth, and they well knew that she deserved death on account of all those people. For which reason she begged their reverences that

---

18. In other words, after María's revocation, the prosecutor created new charges that the inquisitors wished to present to her in publication.

19. María was first held in the tribunal prison during her trial. She then was sent to the "perpetual prison" after her sentence. When her case was reopened on suspicion of perjury, she was again remitted to the prison in the Toledo tribunal. The phrase here refers to the last stage of her imprisonment, before she was relaxed to the secular arm.

20. In later commentaries on inquisitorial practice, revocations were viewed with suspicion; inquisitors were told that people who revoked their confessions were likely suborned perjurers. See Diego de Simancas, "De retractione testium," *Enchiridion iudicum violatae religionis*, Venice 1573, tit. 36, ff. 51v–52r. Thanks to Kimberly Lynn Hossain for this reference.

they let her go raise her children who walked astray. She asked for mercy, begging their reverences to spare her life so she might go and raise her children.[21]

Their reverences ordered her returned to the prison, and said that in conformity with the *consultadores'* vote, María González must be relaxed to justice and the secular arm for having falsely confessed and being impenitent. . . .

September 7, 1513[22]   This sentence was read in a loud, intelligible voice on Wednesday, September 7, 1513, in Toledo. The lord inquisitors, acting for the tribunal, were in the Plaza de Zocodover, on top of a wooden scaffold; and María González was on top of a different wooden scaffold. Witnesses present: Rodrigo Thenorio, Pedro de Yepes, and Luis Dávalos, canons of the cathedral in Toledo; Lord Fernando de Sylva and his brother, Francisco de Sylva; Diego Ferrandes de Oseguera, and licentiate Alonso Nuñes Arnalte, with many other people from the city as well as many other places and venues.[23]

---

21. See Document 7 for the Inquisition's attempts to handle the problem of orphans.
22. Beinart, *Records of the Trials of the Spanish Inquisition,* vol. 2, 316–17.
23. Compare this rudimentary *auto de fe* to the one in 1593, Document 26.

CODIFICATION

Gaspar Isidro de Argüello. *Instructions of the Holy Office of the Inquisition, Handled Summarily, Both Old and New.* Part I

[In 1627, Gaspar Isidro de Argüello, a member of the Suprema, published an excerpted collection of inquisitorial instructions that had been issued originally between 1484 and 1561. He called his book Instructions of the Holy Office of the Inquisition, Handled Summarily, Both Old and New, *and its title clarifies its scope: the mandates were selected with no pretense of completeness, and the excerpts came from both the "old instructions," composed before 1503, and the "new instructions" promulgated afterward. (In Argüello's opinion, his original contribution to the book lay in its table of contents, which he had broken into topics arranged alphabetically, or* por abecedario.) *It should be stressed, then, that readers are perusing a sample of inquisitorial instructions and not a complete corpus of them.[1] Because Argüello's collection—printed in 1627 and 1630—is both more accessible and chronologically broader than other editions of the Inquisition's instructions, it seems appropriate to translate portions of it here.*

Instructions for inquisitors were composed as early as the fourteenth century by Bernardo Gui and Nicolau Eymeric. The first formal instructions of the Spanish Inquisition were issued in 1484 by Inquisitor-General Tomás de Torquemada, who added to them in 1485, 1488, and 1498; Torquemada's mandates were then amplified by Inquisitor-General Diego Deza in 1500 and 1503. Together, their precepts are known as the "old instructions." The "new instructions" refer to precepts issued between the tenures of Inquisitors-General Alonso Manrique (1523–1539) and Fernando de Valdés (1547–1566).[2] The passages that follow are mostly from the pre-1503 mandates collected by Argüello. Paragraph titles have been provided to assist the reader, though they

1. Inquisitor-General Fernando de Valdés' complete instructions of 1561 have been transcribed in Jiménez Montserín, *Introdución a la inquisición española*, 198–240.
2. Thus instructions that fall between 1503 and 1523 are in a sort of classificatory limbo, being designated as neither "old" nor "new."

do not occur in the original. The reader should note that legal theory does not always dictate legal practice, in any epoch.³]

Compilation of Instructions of the Office of the Holy Inquisition, produced by the very reverend lord Friar Tomás de Torquemada, Prior of the Monastery of Santa Cruz of Segovia, first inquisitor-general of the kingdoms and lordships of Spain; and by the other most reverend lord inquisitors who succeeded him, concerning the order that must be observed in the exercise of the Holy Office. These instructions were compiled . . . by order of the most illustrious reverend lord Alonso Manrique, Cardinal of the Twelve Apostles, Archbishop of Spain, Inquisitor-General of Spain⁴

The first instructions for inquisitors are composed, 1484   In the name of God, our very Holy Father Innocent VIII, residing in the Holy Church of Rome. And reigning in Castile and Aragón, the most high and powerful princes, most noble and excellent lords Fernando and Isabel, most Christian King and Queen of Castile, León, Aragón, Sicily, Toledo, Valencia, Galicia, Mallorcas, Seville, Cerdeña, Córdoba, Corcega, Murcia, Jaén, the Algarves, Algecira, Gibraltar; Counts of Barcelona; Lords of Vizcaya and Molina; Dukes of Atenas and Neopatria; Counts of Rosellon and Cerdania; Marquises of Oristan and Gociano. Being called by order of their Highnesses and by the Reverend Father Friar Tomás de Torquemada, Prior of the Monastery of Santa Cruz in the city of Segovia, the royal confessor and in-quisitor-general, in their name; the devout fathers, inquisitors of the city of Seville, Córdoba, Ciudad Real, and Jaén; together with other learned

3. It is worth mentioning that inquisitors were also interested in the theoretical and historical aspects of their office. Throughout the early modern period, they wrote commentaries and histories on the procedures and evolution of the Holy Office. As examples, see Francisco de la Peña's *Directorium inquisitorum* (1585), which is a commentary on Nicolau Eymeric; Diego de Simancas' *Theorice et praxis haereseos, sive Enchiridion judicum violatae religionis* (1568); and Luis de Páramo's *De origine et progressu Officii Sanctae Inquisitionis* (1598).

4. Gaspar Isidro de Argüello, *Instruciones del santo oficio de la inquisición, sumariamente, antiguas y nuevas.* (Madrid: Imprenta Real), 1630. I have used the edition from 1630. In 1537, Inquisitor-General Alonso Manrique collected and printed instructions dated before 1507; they were published at least once more in 1576. The question of whether and when inquisitorial instructions were published in early modern Spain—and the degree to which they circulated—deserves further investigation.

gentlemen of good conscience from the Royal Council. All the aforesaid were gathered in the noble and very loyal city of Seville on November 29, year of the birth of our Savior Jesus Christ, 1484, in the first year of the pontificate of our very Holy Father the Pope. . . .

And then the lord inquisitors and learned gentlemen said that through the order of the said Kings, our lords, they were experienced in certain matters pertaining to the Holy Inquisition of heretical depravity, such as the form of proceeding, and other relevant actions. And in conformity with the law and equity, they had given their opinion on certain chapters, which they all agreed upon, revering the service of God . . . and [those opinions were] contained in a notebook that they presented before us, the notaries and aforesaid witnesses. They solemnly declared that they intended to submit anything they decided to the determination of the Holy Mother Church and to our very Holy Father the Pope, and they had no intention of contravening that authority in any way. All the conclusions and determinations that they had given, and might give in the future concerning the business of the Faith, were offered with the same healthy intention. It seemed to them that the conclusions and decisions should be preserved in this form of a notebook, in conformity with the law and good equity; they consequently asked us, the notaries, to present it as testimony marked with the Cross; and they asked those present to act as witnesses. The contents of the said writing, and the chapters contained in it, are as follows, word for word. . . .

The inquisitors arrive in their districts First, the lord inquisitors and learned gentlemen said that each time inquisitors are newly placed in some diocese, city, or village, or in any such territory that up to that time has not had an inquisition over the crime of heretical depravity and apostasy, that the inquisitors, once installed, must afterward present their license and proof of their authority to the prelate and governing chapter of the principal church, or to its judge; likewise to the chief magistrate and aldermen of that city or village, and to the lord of the territory, if the place is not royal patrimony. Then, through public announcement, the inquisitors shall call the whole population and the clergy together on a feast day, and order everyone to gather in the cathedral church (or in the most principal church the place has) to hear a sermon on the Faith, which should be pronounced by some good preacher, or by one of the inquisitors, whichever is best. The inquisitors shall explain their license, authority, and intention in such a way that the population becomes calm and edified. At the end of the sermon, all faithful Christians must be ordered to raise their hands; a cross and the Gospels should be put before them, so that they may swear to favor the Holy Inquisition and its ministers, and not impede them directly or indirectly, nor solicit any such impediment on account of an extraordinary pretext. The inquisitors must receive this oath especially from the chief magistrates and other justices of that city, village, or place, and they must have proof of that oath before their notaries.

The edict of grace Moreover, at the end of the sermon, the inquisitors shall read and proclaim a clear warning, with censures, which speaks generally against those who are rebels and contrarians. Next, at the end of the sermon, the inquisitors shall proclaim a period of grace of thirty or forty days, whichever is more suitable, so that all people, men as well as women, who find themselves guilty of any sin of heresy or apostasy, or of keeping and performing the rituals and ceremonies of the Jews,[5] or any [rituals] which may be contrary to the Christian religion, may come to disclose their errors before the inquisitors during the said period of grace and up to the end of it. The inquisitors shall assure the audience that all those who come with good contrition and repentance to disclose their errors and everything they know, and who remember things about the said crime (as much about themselves as any others who may have fallen into the said error) shall be received charitably if they wish to abjure the said errors. Those who come to confess shall be given penances that are healthful for their souls; they shall not receive a penalty of death or perpetual prison, and their goods shall not be taken or disturbed for the crimes they confess, inasmuch as it pleases their Highnesses to treat mercifully those who come to truly reconcile themselves during the edict of grace. Those who seek such reconciliation shall be received into union with the Holy Mother Church. It is ordered to leave them alone so that they lose none of their goods, nor shall they have to give any (unless the inquisitors, at their discretion, note the quality of persons and the crimes confessed and decide to impose certain pecuniary penances on the reconciled). . . .

Moreover, people who appear during the said edict of grace (or afterward, or at any time) and say they wish to be reconciled to the Church, must present their confessions in writing before the inquisitors and a notary in their hearing room, with two or three witnesses chosen from among the inquisitors' officials, or other honest people. When the confessions have been presented, a legal oath shall be received from each penitent as to what was contained in the confession, and about other things the penitents knew or were asked. They shall be asked how long they judaized and erred in the Christian Faith, how much time has passed since they separated themselves from false beliefs and repented of them, and how much time has passed since they kept those ceremonies. And they shall be asked about the circumstances surrounding the content of their confession, so that the inquisitors shall know if the confessions are truthful. Especially they shall be asked about the

---

5. Note the presumption that judaizing was the main target.

prayers they said, and where and with whom they gathered to hear preaching on the Law of Moses.

Public or private penance   Next, the inquisitors decided that those who confessed their errors and wished to be reconciled to the Holy Mother Church should abjure their errors publicly when they were reconciled. The inquisitors, at their discretion, should impose public penances on them and treat them with mercy and kindness as far as good conscience allows. The inquisitors must not receive anyone for secret abjuration and penance unless the sin was so hidden that no one else knew or could know about it other than the person who confessed it. In such a case, one of the inquisitors could secretly reconcile and absolve that person, whose error and crime was and is hidden, not revealed and not able to be revealed, because that is the law.

Restrictions on the reconciled   Next, the inquisitors determined that heretics and apostates are legally infamous, even if they return to the Catholic Faith and are reconciled to the Church. And because those reconciled individuals must perform and complete their penances with humility, and feel the pain of their errors, the inquisitors must order them not to possess public offices or benefices; nor may they be advocates, landlords, apothecaries, spice dealers, physicians or surgeons, or bleeders or public criers. They may not carry gold, silver, coral, pearls, or other things, nor precious stones; they may not wear any sort of silk or camlet,[6] nor carry it on their clothes or belongings. They may not ride horses or carry arms their entire lives, under penalty of falling into relapse. They shall fall into relapse if they do the opposite, just like those who do not wish to complete and do not complete the penances imposed upon them after reconciliation.

Pecuniary penance   Moreover, the inquisitors decided that though the crimes of heresy and apostasy are very much prohibited (as indeed they are), and though the reconciled should know, through the penalties given to them, how seriously they have transgressed against our Lord Jesus Christ—even so, reconciled heretics and apostates should be treated with much mercy and kindness. They should be pardoned from fire and perpetual prison and left with all their goods if, as noted, they come and confess their errors within the time period established by the edict of grace. Still, if it seems appropriate to the inquisitors—given the quality of the reconciled person, the crimes confessed, and the duration and seriousness of those crimes—then they must order the reconciled to give a certain part of their goods as an offering in addition to any other penalties. Such pecuniary penances must be applied to the holy war that the most Serene King and

---

6. Camlet was a lustrous wool fabric, usually dyed bright red.

Queen are fighting against the Moors of Granada—enemies of our Holy Catholic Faith—or for some other pious cause that may come up.[7] Just as heretics and apostates offended Our Lord and His Holy Faith, so afterward they shall defend the Holy Faith through pecuniary penances when they are reincorporated and united to the Church. The matter shall depend upon the inquisitors' discretion, according to the order given to them by the Reverend Father Prior of Santa Cruz. . . .

Heretics who are minors   If some minor sons or daughters of heretics, under the age of twenty, have fallen into error through the doctrine and teaching of their parents; and if such people come to reconcile themselves and confess errors about themselves, their parents, and any other people, the inquisitors must receive them kindly and with light penances, even if they come after the period of grace. Such penances shall be less serious than the ones imposed on older people. The inquisitors must see to it that such minors are informed about the Faith and the Sacraments of the Holy Mother Church, because they are excused by virtue of their age and their upbringing by their parents. . . .

Reconciliation of prisoners[8]   Moreover, they decided that if a heretic or apostate has been seized and imprisoned in the inquisitors' jail on legitimate information, and that heretic says he wishes to be reconciled to the Church and confess all his errors, including the Jewish ceremonies he performed, and what he knows about others, without covering anything up—and if he says this in such a way that the inquisitors must presume that he truly wishes to return to the Faith—then the inquisitors must receive him to reconciliation, with penalty of perpetual prison, as the law orders. If, in consultation with the *ordinario*,[9] the inquisitors especially note the deep contrition of the

---

7. Ferdinand and Isabella fought to conquer the last Islamic stronghold in the peninsula—the kingdom of Granada—from 1482 to 1492.

8. The instruction here pertains to individuals who confessed only after they had been arrested. Tougher penalties were advised for those who delayed confessing, were insincere, or persistently denied the accusation, as the next paragraph makes clear.

9. The *ordinario* was the designated judge of matters that pertained to a bishop. The *ordinario* represented the bishop or archbishop in his dealings with inquisitors; his presence in consultations was a living reminder that bishops had responsibility for investigating and punishing suspected heretics in their dioceses before the medieval inquisition was created in the thirteenth century. Although this instruction implies that the *ordinario* was always present in deliberations, such was not the case. On the other hand, though it sometimes appears as if inquisitors trumped bishops when it came to the prosecution of heresy in the sixteenth century, jurisdictional conflicts between the two parties were routine in early modern Spain.

penitent and the quality of his confession, they may grant him a dispensation and commute perpetual prison into another penance as appropriate. Such commutation may take place especially when an apostate heretic says that he wishes to confess and abjure in his first appearance in the hearing, without waiting for the inquisitors' reply; or if he confesses his errors before the publication of the prosecution witnesses against him, or before he knows what those witnesses said against him.

Next, after the criminal has been denounced or accused of the crime of heresy and apostasy and a trial has legitimately been undertaken against him, and the statements and depositions of witnesses against him have been published, there is still an opportunity for him to confess his errors, if he wishes to abjure them and asks for reconciliation, up until the definitive sentence. In such a case, the inquisitors must receive him to reconciliation with penalty of perpetual prison. Still, the inquisitors may come to believe the heretic's reconciliation is feigned and not entertain a good hope of his conversion, after noting the form of his confession and other circumstances. In such a case, the inquisitors must declare him an impenitent heretic and relax him to the secular arm. All of which is remitted to the conscience of the inquisitors.

Denial In cases in which a defendant continues to deny the accusation even after the crime has been investigated and the charges completely proven, the inquisitors can and must condemn him as a heretic; for the crime is legally evident even if the accused confesses the Catholic Faith and says he is and always was a Christian. By refusing to confess his error, the defendant fails to satisfy the Church in all respects and prevents the Church from absolving him and treating him mercifully. But inquisitors must thoroughly investigate such cases, and examine the witnesses and endeavor to know what kind of persons they are, and whether they deposed out of hatred, ill will, or some other depravity. The inquisitors shall diligently interrogate the witnesses again. The inquisitors shall also collect information from other witnesses about the conversation, reputation, and conscience of the witnesses who deposed against the accused. All this is remitted to the inquisitors' consciences.

Half-proofs and torture Next, if the crime appears half proven, the inquisitors, in consultation with the *ordinario,* shall consider putting the accused to the question of torture.[10] If the accused confesses the crime under torture, and afterward ratifies or confirms his confession on the next or third day, he shall be punished as convicted. If, after torture, he revokes the

---

10. The inquisitors and the *ordinario* considered whether torture was warranted; usually, other theological and legal consultants (*consultadores*) weighed the matter with them as well.

confession and retracts it (and if the crime is still not completely proven), the inquisitors must order him to publicly abjure the error of which he is defamed and suspected, on account of infamy and the presumption that results against him. The inquisitors shall give him some arbitrary penance and treat him mildly. They must follow this process whenever a crime is half proven. The aforesaid does not deny that the inquisitors can repeat the question of torture in a case where they must and can do so by law.[11]

Publication of witness testimony and defense lawyers The inquisitors decided, moreover, that . . . by publishing the names and identities of the deposing witnesses, those witnesses may incur great danger and damage to their persons and goods, as experience has shown; some are dead, hurt, and maltreated by heretics for having deposed. And considering in particular that the kingdoms of Castile and Aragón contain a great number of heretics, the inquisitors may not publish the names or identities of witnesses who depose against heretics on account of that great harm and danger. But when proof is obtained, and the witnesses have ratified their depositions, the inquisitors must publish those statements and depositions, hiding the names and circumstances by which the accused could come to know the identities of the witnesses. A copy of the publication, in the form already stated, shall be given to the accused if he asks for it. If the accused asks for a lawyer, the inquisitors shall give him one to assist him, receiving a proper oath from that lawyer that he shall faithfully help the accused, alleging legitimate defenses and all that might be appropriate by law, according to the quality of the crime, without raising quibbles or malicious delays. If, in any part of the case, the lawyer for the defense comes to know that his party has no justice, he may not help him further, and he shall tell the inquisitors. The accused's goods, if he has any, shall be used to pay the salary of the defense lawyer. If the accused is poor, the defense lawyer shall be paid out of other confiscated goods; the mercy of Their Highnesses so orders that it be done. . . .

Being present at torture Moreover, they decided that when torture is given, the inquisitors and *ordinario* must be present, or [at least] one of them. If it seems appropriate, the inquisitors could commit this responsibility to someone else, if perhaps it does not suit them to attend, or if they are impeded from doing so. They must observe that the attending person is a wise, faithful man, of good reputation and conscience; a man who would not be expected to do something he shouldn't out of hatred, affection, or self-interest. . . .

11. The rules prohibited anyone from being tortured more than once. The inquisitors found a way around this legal nicety by declaring torture sessions *suspended* rather than ended.

Prosecution of the dead   Likewise whenever the inquisitors find in their registers and trials that they have sufficient evidence of heresy against a dead person (and notwithstanding that thirty or forty years have passed since that person's death), they must order the prosecutor to denounce and accuse the dead, so that the dead may be declared and anathematized as heretics and apostates under the form of law. Their bodies and bones shall be exhumed and taken from churches, monasteries, and cemeteries; the goods of those heretics shall be confiscated and applied to the Treasury and Exchequer of the King and Queen, our Lords. Their children, any other heirs, and all others whom the case could touch in some way must be called. That summons must be delivered in person before the heirs and successors, and they shall be present in the place where the inquisitors are acting, if they can be found, and so shall others stipulated in the edict. If a copy of the accusation has been given to the children or heirs, and the trial is held in their absence and rebellion, without one of them appearing, the inquisitors shall find the crime proven, and shall condemn the dead. . . . It seems to the lords that the Exchequer of their Highnesses can demand and take the goods, with their fruits[12] that the condemned left to any heirs and successors in whose power those goods may be found.

Orphans   Likewise the inquisitors decided that if people relaxed to the secular arm or condemned to perpetual prison had unmarried sons or daughters of minor age, the inquisitors should provide and order that the said orphans be commended to honest, Christian, Catholic persons, or to members of religious orders, who would bring them up and sustain them. These orphans shall be informed about our Holy Faith. The inquisitors should make a list of such orphans and their individual condition, for their Highnesses, in their mercy, intend to give alms to each one who has need of it in order to [help them to be] good Christians, especially the orphaned girls, who could marry or enter a religious order with those alms. . . .

Gifts   The inquisitors decided that inquisitors, advisors, and other officials —such as lawyers, prosecutors, wardens, notaries, and quartermasters— must not accept donations or presents from anyone, including intermediaries, whom the Inquisition touches or could touch. The lord Prior of Santa Cruz has ordered them not to receive such things under pain of excommunication and loss of office. Offenders shall return what was received and double it.

Cordiality   Next, inquisitors must work a great deal and endeavor to be in harmony and conformity with each other, because the honesty of their

12. "Goods with their fruits" means the profits of a property or a business.

office requires it. Many inconveniences could befall the office as the result of discord between them. Though one of the inquisitors may have the commission and powers of the *ordinario,* he should not wish or presume to wish to have more preeminence in his inquisitorial office than his colleague, even if the colleague does not have the *ordinario*'s powers. Instead, the one shall get along equally with the other so that there is no difference between them, though the honor of their rank and dignities shall be preserved. If some difference between the inquisitors should arise and they cannot reach an agreement, they shall keep the matter secret and immediately inform the Reverend Father Prior of Santa Cruz, who, as their superior [i.e., Inquisitor-General], shall take care of it as he sees fit. . . .

The inquisitors' discretion   A style of proceeding has been given in the preceding chapters for those reconciled for the crime of heretical depravity, such as how and when the reconciliation should be done. Nevertheless, all the cases and their circumstances cannot be declared, and so everything must be left to the will and discretion of the inquisitors. In conformity with the law . . . the inquisitors shall act according to their consciences, so that they fulfill the service of God and their Highnesses.

The lord inquisitors and learned men presented this writing and its chapters to us, the notaries, according to the proper form and with the solemn declarations that have been uttered. Witnesses who were present: the discreet and honorable gentlemen, Juan López del Barco, chaplain of the Queen, prosecutor of the Holy Inquisition in the city of Seville, and Anton de Córdoba and Macias de Cuba, notaries of the Holy Inquisition of the city of Córdoba.

These instructions are signed by Anton Nuñez, cleric of the diocese of Badajoz, and signed also by Diego López de Cortegana, apostolic notaries. These instructions are originally in the Inquisition of Barcelona, where I, Lope Díaz, secretary, saw them.

**1488. Instructions given in Valladolid
by the Prior of Santa Cruz** [marginal notation]

Uniformity of proceedings   After a long quarrel among the lord inquisitors, it was agreed that all the inquisitors of the kingdoms and lordships shall conduct trials, *autos de fe,* and other matters in the same way . . . because variance in procedure and in *autos de fe* has caused some slander and other inconveniences.

Delays   Next, the inquisitors ordered that prisoners should not be worn out in prisons from delay; their trials should be performed immediately, so that there are no grounds for complaint. Nor should prisoners be held for trials in which there is not complete proof, since when proof surfaces, a new trial can be undertaken, notwithstanding the sentence that was given in the previous one.

Lack of learned men   Next, the lords discussed the difficulties that happen every day in concluding trials in the inquisitions of these kingdoms. In some places, learned men[13] cannot be had either at all or in such numbers as the inquisitors desire; this is relevant because inquisitors have to consult with learned men over the cases. And even if the learned men are available, or can be had, they are not of such trustworthiness or confidence as is necessary. As a result, some of the inquisitors do not feel secure or satisfied in their consciences, and for this reason the determination of the trials is delayed, which is against the disposition of the law. The inquisitors wish to remedy this difficulty for all the trials that are ongoing or shall be conducted henceforth in any inquisition in the kingdoms and lordships of Castile or Aragón. They consequently agreed that after the trials have been concluded, they shall have the trials transcribed by their public notaries and, leaving the originals concealed, they shall send the transcripts, authenticated by their prosecutor, to the reverend Lord Prior of Santa Cruz. The Prior of Santa Cruz shall have the transcripts reviewed by the learned men of the Suprema or other suitable ones.[14] The prosecutor of the cases shall come and be present at their consultation and determination in order to provide information on the circumstances, qualities, and other matters that affected the understanding of the cases while the inquisitors were prosecuting them, if the circumstances are such that they may move the hearts of those who have to consult and vote on them. The inquisitors will designate and name a replacement for the prosecutor so that his absence will not block pending business. . . . This process shall be followed in doubtful trials when the learned men who consult on them [or] the inquisitors do not agree in their decision, or when learned men cannot be found to consult on the cases, or when there is an insufficient number of learned men in the city, village, or place where the case is occurring.

Isolation and visitation of the prisoners[15]   Next, it seemed to the inquisitors that given the intention of the law, and the inconveniences and bad experiences that have occurred in the past as a result of allowing visitors to see and speak to the prisoners, henceforth inquisitors, wardens or jailers, or any other persons shall not allow people from outside to see and speak to the

13. The term here is *letrado;* the instruction is raising the scarcity of learned men who can act as *consultadores.* For the role of the *consultador,* see the Introduction.

14. There is no evidence that this very early attempt at centralization was successful.

15. For details on the problems that could arise in Inquisition prisons, see Documents 12 and 21.

prisoners. The inquisitors shall take great care to know if the contrary is done, and they shall punish whoever allowed it, unless those in question were members of religious orders or clerics, who by order of the inquisitors can visit the prisoners to console them and discharge their consciences. The inquisitors are obliged to visit the jails in person every fifteen days, there being no impediment. If there is an impediment, the visitation shall be undertaken by others whom they trust, and they shall provide the prisoners with what is needed. . . .

Protection of documents   Likewise the inquisitors agreed that all the writings of the Inquisition, regardless of condition, shall be collected in chests in a public place where the inquisitors are accustomed to act, so that any writing that may be needed can easily be at hand. Taking the writings outside [the tribunal] is forbidden. The keys of the chests shall pass from the hand of the inquisitors into the power of the notaries of the said office, who witness the acts and writings. They order that this be done under penalty of deprivation of office for doing the opposite.

Communication among tribunals   Next, it frequently happens that though heretics and apostates are natives of one diocese, they have also lived and lodged in other places. As a result, their cases could belong to inquisitors of various places; and it could be that some inquisitors would absolve them, and others condemn them, from which difference would spring inconvenience and discord among the inquisitors. It was agreed that when any such defendant is called, cited, or imprisoned by inquisitors in one place, that other inquisitors henceforth may not pursue that case since the first inquisitors had first jurisdiction. [But] as soon as the other inquisitors know about the case, they shall send in a secure way all the information against the defendant that they can find in their inquisitions. Besides being a matter of law, this procedure helps our holy business, and pacifies the inquisitors and their ministers.

Lack of perpetual prisons   Next, the sentence of perpetual prison has been given to many and even most heretics in our time, who—after having gravely offended the divine Majesty by their crime, and returning to better remembrance and our Holy Catholic Faith—are reincorporated into the body of the Church and union with Catholics, and are absolved from the excommunication they incurred. Though the sentence of perpetual prison was done for most of them, there is a lack of jails and places to put them, and so it seems that the inquisitors may treat the heretics mildly and fix the heretics' houses as prisons after condemning them to perpetual prison, unless the matter is solved in a different way. The heretics may then reside in their houses, and the inquisitors will order them to observe and complete the sentence under penalties that the law provides in such cases. . . .

Salaries   Next, in the past inquisitors and their officials have not been paid their salaries on time as ordered by their Highnesses, because the receivers of confiscated goods were also ordered by their Highnesses to perform certain disbursements. If no remedy is found in this matter, many inconveniences will result and this holy business will be harmed. So that the Inquisition shall even better fulfill its service to God and to their Highnesses—and so that the complaints that are continually sent to the Prior of Santa Cruz shall cease—it was agreed, after a long quarrel, to beg their Highnesses to order that inquisitors and their officials shall be paid before any gift or disbursement is acted upon. The receivers will be so instructed in the letters and decrees they receive, and so shall the receivers swear at the time they are given their office. If there is no other way to pay the inquisitors, the receivers can sell possessions and other things in enough quantity to suffice for the inquisitors' salaries; and if the receivers do the opposite, the inquisitors can remove them and then beg their Highnesses to provide other receivers who shall better perform their duties.

New perpetual prisons   In the chapter above, on the matter of perpetual prison, it was stipulated as expedient that the imprisoned be put into their own houses unless imprisonment could be otherwise provided. It seems necessary to beg their Highnesses to order the receivers to designate, in each place where the Inquisition is carried out, a squared perimeter with little houses in a suitable place, where each of the imprisoned may reside. A small chapel shall be constructed where the prisoners may hear Mass on certain days. Each prisoner shall perform his occupation to earn what is needed for his maintenance and necessities, thereby ending the great financial expenditure that the Inquisition makes on his behalf. The shape, quantity, and place of the prisons shall be at the discretion of the inquisitors and those who undertake the matter. . . .

These orders and chapters were read and published on October 27, year of the birth of Our Savior Jesus Christ, 1488, in the village of Valladolid. The reverend lord Prior of Santa Cruz, Inquisitor-General, was present, as were all the other inquisitors of Castile and Aragón, in the hall of the lodging of their Reverend Father. . . .

Instructions of Ávila, made in 1498, by the Prior of Santa Cruz [marginal notation]

The inquisitors should act in tandem   . . . . First, in each inquisition there shall be two inquisitors: a jurist and a theologian, or two jurists. They shall be good people of knowledge and conscience, who together—not one without the other—shall authorize the capture and torture of defendants and canonical purgation.[16] Together, they shall sign and hand over a copy of the witnesses' statements for the trial record, which also shall include the definitive sentence, because these are serious matters of the greatest import. In all other matters one inquisitor can proceed without the other for the quicker expedition of the cases, because one inquisitor may need to go through the bishopric on matters of the office [i.e., conduct a visitation]. . . .

Proof and imprisonment Next, inquisitors should be cautious in the imprisonment of suspects, and should imprison no one without sufficient proof. Once the suspect is imprisoned, the accusation shall be placed within ten days; the required admonitions shall be made within this time period. Inquisitors shall proceed with all diligence and brevity in the cases and trials, without waiting for more proof to show up . . . and delays shall not be allowed, because inconveniences to people and property result. . . .

Penances Moreover, in the imposition of pecuniary and bodily penances, the inquisitors shall principally consider the quality of the crime; depending upon whether it was serious or light, they shall thus impose the penance, considering likewise the other qualities and circumstances that the law requires. They may not impose greater penalties or unjust penances in order to have their salaries paid.

Commuted sentences Likewise, inquisitors may not without cause commute perpetual prison, a penalty, or a penance for anyone on account of money or a request. When a sentence is commuted, it shall be converted into fasts, alms, and other pious works. . . . And inquisitors cannot remove any *sanbenito*. As for the children and grandchildren of the convicted, their rehabilitation shall be reserved to the inquisitors-general, so that they can provide what seems appropriate according to justice. . . .

False witnesses Next, the inquisitors shall impose punishment and public penance on false witnesses in conformity with the law.

Protection of documents Next, in each inquisition there shall be a chest or room with three locks and three keys, for the tribunal's books, registers, and writings. Two of these keys shall be held by the two notaries, and the third by the prosecutor, so that no one can remove any writing without everyone being present. If a notary does something he shouldn't in his office, he shall be condemned for perjury and as a falsifier, and deprived of his

16. When confessions and witnesses failed to establish guilt, the inquisitors could turn to compurgation or purgation, a process laid out in canon law whereby defendants produced a number of witnesses who swore to their fidelity as Christians. Defendants might hesitate to name such witnesses, however, if they began to wonder whether the people they were thinking of nominating might also have testified against them. Such was the case with Marina González; see Document 5.

office forever; if he is convicted, he may be given a greater penalty of money or exile, according to what the inquisitor-general thinks appropriate. Only the inquisitors, notaries, and prosecutor shall enter into that room [where the chests are kept]. . . .

Consultation with the Suprema   Likewise, when difficult or ambiguous business occurs in the inquisitions, the inquisitors shall consult with members of the Suprema about it, and shall bring or send the trials when they are ordered to do so.

Female prisoners   Likewise, women shall have a separate prison from men.

Work schedules   Next, all the officials of each inquisition shall meet in the hearing room. They shall work six hours—three before eating, and three after—in summer as well as winter. The inquisitors shall fix the work hours when they are to fast.[17] . . .

Lightweight crimes [Seville, 1500]   Next, sometimes inquisitors imprison people for lightweight things that are not legally conclusive of heresy, such as words that are more blasphemous than heretical, pronounced out of peevishness or anger. Henceforth no one of this sort shall be imprisoned.[18]

• • • •

Malfeasance of notaries [Segovia, 1503]   . . . . We of the Suprema of the King and Queen, who are employed in the goods and matters of the Holy Inquisition, are informed that you, the scribes and notaries of the Inquisition in the cities and bishoprics of Burgos and Palencia, etc., have been receiving and examining witnesses without one of the reverend father inquisitors being present, in great injury and detriment to the Holy Office, danger to your consciences, and in deprecation of our ordinances and instructions. Therefore, wanting to provide in the matter (as appropriate to the service of God our Lord, the well-being of the Holy Office, and the discharge of our consciences), for the present we exhort and order you, the notaries—all and any one of you who now hold or may hold that position in that Holy Office, by virtue of holy obedience, under pain of excommunication and deprivation of your offices, and ten thousand *maravedís* for the Treasury and Exchequer of their Highnesses each time you do the contrary—that you shall not examine a witness or receive a witness' statement or deposition, whether in the general inquisition or in the trials undertaken,

---

17. That is, when the inquisitors and their staff observed feast days of the Church.

18. This cautionary distinction between blasphemy and heresy was diminished in the Instructions of Inquisitor-General Fernando de Valdés; see Document 20.

now and henceforth, about the crime of heresy, whether those witnesses are presented by the prosecutor, or by the defendants, whether about objections [*tachas*] or good faith [*abonos*], without at least one of the said inquisitors being present. That inquisitor shall see and hear what the witness says, or what the witnesses say and depose; and in the inquisitor's presence these statements will be affirmed by you or one of you in the books, registers, and trials of the Holy Office. You shall do nothing else in any way, under said penalties. Given in the city of Segovia, November 13, 1503.

Instructions for the prison warden [and constable] [1498]

Instructions that pertain to the jailer are as follows.[19] First, no warden or jailer who has charge of the inquisitorial prison and its prisoners shall consent or allow his wife, or anyone else from inside or outside his household, to speak with any of the prisoners. The person in charge of giving the prisoners their food, who shall be a person of truthworthiness and fidelity, and has been sworn to preserve secrecy, is an exception. And the warden or jailer shall look into what that person takes the prisoners, so that no letters or news are carried in the food.

Next, the constables [*alguaciles*][20] are obliged to exercise their office, and to go seize a defendant in any place so ordered by the inquisitors; and to do all the things their office requires on their salary of sixty thousand *maravedís* without receiving more money. If they should have to transport certain people named by the inquisitors, and place such people in prison, the costs of that transportation shall be estimated, and that amount shall be paid out by the receiver at the inquisitors' order. When the constable must go away, he shall leave in the prison, at his own expense, a person of good conduct and confidence, of whom the inquisitors approve. Surrogate constables shall not take charge of feeding the prisoners, but another person shall do so,[21] who is faithful and of good conduct, and who is put in place by the inquisitors.

Instructions that pertain to the receiver of confiscated goods, and to the scribe [of sequestration] are as follows [1485]

Next, regarding the sequestered goods, if some things under guard are lost and injured (such as bread and wine, or other similar things), the receiver

19. The instructions compiled by Argüello are not always in chronological order, though they generally conform to an "old" and "new" sequence. Argüello isolated specific instructions for specific personnel, as the following mandates illustrate.
20. These 1498 instructions treat the constable (*alguacil*) and the prison warden (*carcelero* here) as if they were interchangeable, which by the 1520s, they were not.
21. The office of quartermaster is clearly under development.

shall arrange with the inquisitors for the damaged goods to be sold at public auction, and the price paid for such things shall be placed in the said sequestration, in the power of the said sequestrators, or in a bill of exchange, as the inquisitors and receiver think best. Likewise if some landed property must be leased, the inquisitors shall tell the sequestrator that together with the receiver, they shall lease that landed property in a public auction.[22]

Likewise, their Highnesses command that each one of the receivers shall gather and receive the goods that come from heretics who are residents and lodgers in the receivers' territory; and the receivers shall not meddle with the goods of any heretic who belongs to another inquisition. As soon as a receiver hears news about some confiscated goods belonging to another receiver, he shall inform him of it immediately, in order for that receiver to recover them. Any receiver who hides such goods shall lose his office and be obliged for the damages and loss. For his negligence, those monies shall revert to the royal patrimony of their Highnesses.

Likewise, no receiver may sequester goods of any heretic or apostate without a special command in writing from the inquisitors. Such goods shall not be put into the hands of the receiver, but rather into the hands of a trustworthy person [i.e., a sequestrator], and the sequestration shall be carried out by the receiver and the constable of the inquisition before the scribe, who shall write down completely what was sequestered, declaring the qualities of each thing. . . .

If, after the declaration and confiscation of the condemned's goods,[23] some debts or goods should be legally disputed . . . the receiver shall not dispose of them by selling them until the designated judge has determined to whom they belong, and whether the goods can be divided properly without prejudice to the Treasury. And the goods shall be divided and each part given to the person who should have it. If things are sold without division, then as soon as they are sold the receiver shall deliver the amount to whom it was owed without spending any bit of it. At the petition of the receiver, the judge shall then publicly proclaim that the goods are confiscated, and if someone hopes to have a right to them or to take action, he should appear within a time period assigned by that judge. Next, if some goods are found in the power of third parties, the receiver shall not possess or sell them until the judge determines if they belong to the Treasury or not. The receiver may place a demand about the matter, and it shall be determined by law. . . .

Likewise, it is avowed to all receivers that if they are negligent in their

22. For the process of sequestration and confiscation of prisoners' property, see the Introduction.

23. Property of a defendant was only formally confiscated after a conviction for serious heresy; see the Introduction.

office, whether in demanding the goods that belong to the Treasury and Exchequer, or in recovering and defending such goods, that all the damage that accrues from their actions shall revert to the Treasury of their Highnesses; and the receivers shall pay that damage, doubled, from their salary; and if that is not sufficient, then from their own goods and properties. . . .

Instructions that pertain to the receiver of confiscated goods and to the scribe [of sequestration] are as follows [1516]

Next, henceforth all salaries paid to agents of receivers are revoked, and the receivers shall content themselves with the salary of sixty thousand *maravedís* which is given to them. If they hire some additional agents, it shall be at their cost, not the Treasury's. . . .

Next, the receiver is obliged to give an account of all the goods of his receivership, with expenditures, and without leaving anything out. If he does not provide such an account of a particular item, he shall be obliged to relay the efforts made with the item over the year; and if he does not do so, he shall not be paid, and he shall pay the interest on the damage that he has made the Exchequer accrue.

1503[24]   We of the Suprema of the King and Queen, who are employed in confiscated goods and matters pertaining to the Holy Inquisition, hereby make known to you, Martín Martínez de Uzquiano—receiver of confiscated goods that are applied to the Treasury and Exchequer of their Highnesses, for the crime of heresy and apostasy in the cities and bishoprics of Burgos, Palencia, Ávila, Segovia, etc.—that we have been informed that you, the receiver, sell many goods, furniture, landed property, and semimovable things (the items having been confiscated, as noted, for that said crime in the said district) when the necessary people are not present at the sale, as declared in our instructions. The result is much damage and prejudice to the Royal Exchequer, and danger to your conscience. Because it falls to us to resolve the matter . . . we admonish and order you by the power of holy obedience, under pain of excommunication, and fifty thousand *maravedís* for the Treasury and Exchequer of His Highness every time you do the opposite; that henceforth you, the receiver, shall not dare to sell, nor shall you sell, at public auction or outside of it, any goods, whether furniture, landed property, or semimovable things of any sort or kind they may be . . . in the cities and bishoprics, and all the other cities, villages, and places that are under the jurisdiction of the inquisitors for whom you are the receiver, without the

24. Here, a specific order from the Suprema to a particular receiver of confiscated property has been incorporated into the collection of instructions, no doubt for its didactic purposes.

notary of those inquisitors being present at the sale. And so that the afore-said may be better effected . . . under the same penalties, we admonish and order Francisco García de Almenara, notary of those cities and bishoprics, and anyone who shall succeed him in that office, that each and every time he shall be called by you, the receiver, he shall go with you to the said cities, villages, and places where the confiscated goods have to be sold. He shall be present and shall act together with you in the sale of such goods; and you two shall be responsible for it all, and neither the one nor the other shall do the contrary in any way. We certify that if such is not done and completed, we shall execute the said penalties upon each of you. Given in the city of Segovia, November 14, 1503.

THE *ALUMBRADOS* IN CASTILE, 1525–1532

DOCUMENT 8

1525 Inquisition Edict on the *Alumbrados*[1]

[The five sources relayed here illustrate the intricacies, both spiritual and practical, of alumbradismo, *an amorphous spiritual movement that became one of the Inquisition's key targets in the 1520s. The term* alumbrado *comes from the verb* alumbrar, *"to illuminate." The* alumbrados, *who were endemic to Castile, believed they possessed an illuminated spirituality because they had abandoned themselves to the love of God; their elevated status was frequently endorsed by people around them. The* alumbrados, *or "illuminated ones," rejected the external rituals of Catholicism, such as meditating on Christ's Passion, bowing before the Eucharist, and praying to saints as intercessors. They also spurned priests as mediators between the human and the divine. The four individuals who appear in the following sources were all confirmed or reported to be* conversos, *as the inquisitors well knew. But the charges against them ranged from* alumbradismo, Lutheranism, and Erasmianism *to false sanctity and deprecation of the Inquisition itself, rather than judaizing.[2]*

Between 1512 and 1532, the alumbrados *in Castile were led by women: Isabel de la Cruz, Francisca Hernández, and María de Cazalla. Isabel and Francisca were* beatas[3]—*unmarried women who were not nuns, but who quested after holiness by taking vows of chastity and often of poverty—while María was married. Unfortunately, Isabel's and Francisca's trial records have been lost, and we can only recover information about them from the prosecutions*

1. Antonio Márquez, *Los alumbrados: orígenes y filosofía, 1525–1559* (Madrid: Taurus, 1972), 273–83.

2. Inquisitors in the mid-1520s had only a vague notion of what Lutheranism connoted, but they believed that doctrine was highly dangerous; still, Luther's teaching was more of a phantom than a real threat in this time period. See Redondo, "Luther et l'Espagne de 1520–1536." The fundamental study of Erasmus' impact on Spain is Bataillon, *Erasmo y España.*

3. For insights into *beatas* in the sixteenth century, see Jodi Bilinkoff, "A Spanish Prophetess and Her Patrons: The Case of María de Santo Domingo," *Sixteenth Century Journal* 23 (1992): 21–35, and Ángela Muñoz Fernández, *Beatas y santas neocastellanas: ambivalencia de la religión, correctoras del poder (s. XIV–XVII)* (Madrid: Comunidad de Madrid, 1994).

of their followers and associates. It is clear from the extant evidence that Isabel, Francisca, and María knew each other and frequently shared disciples; their followers usually included both males and females (except in Francisca's case) and came from both monastic and secular environments, with a significant number belonging to the Franciscans. The Inquisition's prosecution of the alumbrados *was episodic. Isabel de la Cruz and her spiritual co-actor, Pedro Ruiz de Alcaraz, were arrested in 1524; Francisca Hernández was apprehended in 1529, and two of her primary disciples, Francisco Ortiz and Antonio de Medrano, were seized quickly thereafter; María de Cazalla was collared in 1532. The surviving trial records demonstrate the vivacity of Spanish religious culture in the 1520s, the construction of female spiritual authority, and the inquisitors' struggles to fix the boundaries of orthodoxy.*

The 1525 Edict on the alumbrados *resulted from a conference of theological consultants called by Holy Roman Emperor and Spanish King Charles V and Inquisitor-General Alonso Manrique.[4] In the edict, Manrique explains how this new heresy of* alumbradismo *was discovered and investigated; the text then relays particular heretical propositions and the* consultadores' *reaction to them. The edict was composed after the arrests of Isabel de la Cruz and Pedro Ruiz de Alcaraz, and the errors it enumerates stem from Isabel's and Pedro's trials.]*

WE, LORD ALONSO MANRIQUE—BY DIVINE PROVIDENCE ARCHBISHOP OF SEVILLE, APOSTOLIC INQUISITOR AGAINST HERETICAL DEPRAVITY AND APOSTASY IN ALL THE KINGDOMS OF HIS MAJESTY AND OF HIS COUNCIL—MAKE IT KNOWN TO THE MOST REVEREND ARCHBISHOPS, BISHOPS, AND ANY OTHER PRELATES AND PEOPLE APPOINTED TO ECCLESIASTICAL OFFICE; TO THE DEANS AND CHAPTERS OF METROPOLITAN, CATHEDRAL, AND COLLEGIAL CHURCHES;[5] TO THE REVEREND AND DEVOUT PROVINCIALS, PRIORS, GUARDIANS, MINISTERS, AND COMMANDERS[6] OF ALL THE RELIGIOUS ORDERS AND COMMUNITIES; AND TO ALL FAITHFUL CHRISTIANS, MEN AS WELL AS WOMEN, OF WHATEVER RANK, CONDITION, AND PREEMINENCE AND DIGNITY THEY MAY BE, INHABITANTS AND RESIDENTS OF THE SAID DOMINIONS AND TERRITORIES, ESPECIALLY IN THIS ARCHBISHOPRIC OF TOLEDO:

4. Manrique was Inquisitor-General from 1523 to 1539.

5. A metropolitan church belongs to a senior bishop of a province who possesses rights over his comprovincial bishops; the holder of a metropolitan see (such as Toledo) commonly has the titles of archbishop and primate. A cathedral church is the official seat of a bishop of a diocese. A collegiate church is endowed to support a body of canons but is not a bishop's see.

6. These personnel belong to the hierarchy of monastic orders.

That after our very Holy Father entrusted us with the Holy Office of the General Inquisition, we were informed by various people (who were fearful of God and zealous for our Catholic faith)[7] that in certain places in this archbishopric of Toledo, many people spoke and proclaimed certain words that appeared to deviate from our Holy Catholic Faith, and from the common observance of faithful Christians and our Holy Mother Church. [Such people] gathered together, secretly and publicly, in special secret assemblies, and some called them *alumbrados* [the illuminated], *dejados* [the abandoned], and *perfectos* [the perfect]. The matter having come to our attention, and being absent from this archbishopric, we wanted to come personally to investigate it with the care, vigilance, and diligence to which we are obliged. But being occupied in many other difficult concerns of the Holy Office, we could not come personally to investigate it; and therefore we called upon the reverend father in Christ, Gaspar de Avalos, master in holy theology and bishop of Guadix; and the reverend licentiate Alonso de Mariana, abbot of San Vincent, canon of the holy church of Toledo, and inquisitor in the said archbishopric.[8] These are men of education, conscience, experience, and confidence, to whom we committed our powers so that they might go to places in the archbishopric where the errors were spoken and proclaimed, and might know the truth and work to extirpate the said errors, and dissuade the people who held the errors and were deceived, and bring such people back to the union of our Holy Mother Catholic Church.

These men [Avalos and Mariana], tempering rigor . . . and using all kindness and clemency, gave a period of grace to such people, during which they might come to declare their faults and errors about this matter. These men assured their audience that if they came within the specified time, no punishment, public penance, or confiscation of goods would be imposed upon them, but rather they would receive secret spiritual penances, which were beneficial for their souls, according to what was contained at greater length in those edicts of grace. These edicts were proclaimed and many people came before the inquisitors to declare what they knew and had heard, and the faults in which they found themselves, in order to discharge their consciences and their souls, by their own free will, some in writing and others orally. Likewise, many witnesses were received who testified about the propositions and errors contained in the confessions, and the other things that they knew about this matter. All of which [having been] handled in a public and legitimate manner before us, we and the men of the Suprema [then] deliberated upon this

---

7. By this point in time—1525—there was a distinction between the *Catholic* faith and the one espoused by Martin Luther. Luther was excommunicated by Pope Leo X in 1521.

8. Thus an inquisitor and a bishop acted together to investigate this potential heresy.

matter with the Emperor, our lord King [Charles V]. His Majesty [Charles V], with his holy zeal, as a most Christian prince, ordered that many other men be assembled and brought together, in addition to the men of the Suprema, in order to examine the aforesaid testimony.[9] These were religious men of much gravity, belief, conscience, and authority, who were doctors and masters in holy theology and the sacred canons.[10] All of them met with us for many days in various meetings, during which they heard and read the confessions and proofs received by the inquisitors.[11] And after hearing it [all], they conferred and voted separately in other sessions, each one according his order and expertise. They were unanimous in their evaluation of the propositions on account of scriptural and canonical authorities, as follows:[12]

1. There is no Hell, and if they say there is, it is to frighten us, just as they tell children, "Watch out for the bogeyman."
This proposition is heretical, erroneous, and false, contradictory to the Gospel and the order of divine justice, which arranges for the eternal punishment of mortal sins through penance when those sins are not removed from us in this life.

2. That the Father was made flesh like the Son, alleging the authority, *Qui videt me* ["He who sees Me"], etc.
This proposition is heretical.

3. That God could not make a person more perfect or more humble than he already was.
This proposition is heretical because it denies the omnipotence of God.

4. That God would enter a man's soul more entirely than He did the Host if man did what he should; because the Host was a little piece of dough, whereas man was made in God's image.
This proposition is erroneous, false, and heretical. First, because God and man [are both] in the Sacrament of the Altar through hypostatic union; next, because the statement seems to contend that after consecration, the bread's substance remains.

9. In the mid-1520s, Inquisitor-General Manrique became fond of calling conferences to consult on difficult matters of heresy; hence the *alumbrado* conference of 1525, the witchcraft conference of 1526 (see Document 13), and the Valladolid conference on Erasmus' writings in 1527. For the last, see Homza, "Erasmus as Hero or Heretic?"

10. The "sacred canons" refer to canon or Church law; the term "canon" was gradually used exclusively for ecclesiastical rules or laws. Roman Emperor Justinian distinguished between civil and canon laws in the sixth century.

11. This conference, then, was akin to a giant consultation. See the Introduction for details on *calificadores* and *consultadores*.

12. In the list that follows, the numbered statements were either lifted from suspects' confessions, or from the depositions of witnesses. The verdicts in italics below the numbered items reflect the judgment of the *calificadores*, the theologians who conferred on the matter.

5. Although the words of consecration of the Eucharist were not spoken with the mouth, it was enough to utter them internally.
This proposition is false and erroneous.

6. That he was sorry he had not sinned more; and knowing what God's mercy was, he wished he had sinned more in order to enjoy that mercy more. Because the greater the sinner, the more God loves him.
This proposition is morally heretical, scandalous, and contrary to the act of penance, because it induces men to violate God's commandments and implies that any sinner should wish he had committed his sins to a greater extent.

7. They call those people who lament their sins "penance-addicts," "proprietors of themselves," and "weepers."
This proposition is crazy and contemptuous toward the sacrament of penance.

8. Confession is not divine but positive[13] law.
This proposition is Lutheran and has the taste of heresy.

9. The love of God in man is God. And they could abandon themselves to this love of God, which directs people in such a way that they cannot sin mortally or venially. And there are no venial sins; if something appears to be a light sin, it will be a fault without fault [sic]. And once someone reaches this state, there is nothing more to merit.
The first part is false and against the common opinion of Church doctors, inasmuch as it denies the habit of infused charity. The second part is erroneous, heretical, presumptuous, and damned by the Church. The third part is erroneous and heretical. The fourth part is erroneous and damned by the Church.

10. That just as the subject below the prelate does not have to account to God or anyone else for his soul, neither more nor less does a person in this abandonment have to account for his soul to God or anyone else. They should do nothing, but leave it all to God, because by the sheer desire to perform works, they make themselves incapable of the works of this love, to which they are subject. And he who is in this state of abandonment to God has no need of prayer or recollection [*recogimiento*], or a fixed place to pray, or any thing else.[14]
This proposition appears to presuppose that all acts that proceed from free will are mortal sins. It is heretical, and a blasphemy before the tribunal of the Divine Majesty, before which we all must give an account [of ourselves].

13. "Positive" here means man-made or human. Thus the *alumbrados* denied that confession and the sacrament of penance were mandated in Scripture and were divine precepts, a position they shared with Martin Luther.

14. *Recogimiento* was a method of interiorized prayer that was followed by some of the *alumbrados*. The most famous exposition of it is the *Third Spiritual Alphabet* by Franciscan friar Francisco de Osuna (d. 1540); see the translation by Mary E. Giles (New York: Paulist Press, 1981). This method of prayer was also endorsed by Teresa de Jesús, commonly known as St. Theresa of Ávila.

11. After someone abandoned himself to God, this abandonment alone was enough to save his soul, and he had no need to fast or perform works of mercy. And if someone sinned who had already abandoned himself in God, he did not lose his soul, nor must he account to God for the sin. And it would please God if he died for this truth.

This proposition is false and heretical because it advises that charity ought to be idle. As for the second part, it is against Holy Scripture, as are the third and first parts.

12. Having abandoned themselves to God, such people did not have to work, in order not to block whatever God wished to accomplish. They could withdraw themselves from all created things.[15] Even to meditate upon the humanity of Christ[16] hindered abandonment to God. And such people could refuse all thoughts that occurred to them, even if the thoughts were good, because they should look to God alone. They thought refusing such thoughts was virtuous. Being in that spiritual state of quietude, they even thought it was a temptation to remember God, in order not to be distracted.

This proposition is false, erroneous, scandalous, and heretical.

13. External acts of prayer are irrelevant and unnecessary, and to perform them is imperfection. The *alumbrados* do not humble themselves at the name of Jesus, for humility has to be in the heart. A certain person was reprimanded because he knelt at a cross. And as the same person was recommending external works, a certain person said that someone given to saying Mass should not say it; someone given to prayer should abandon it; and someone given to offerings should not offer. And as the Most Holy Sacrament [the Eucharist] was passing through the street, he said to certain people, "What do you want to bet that even if the Most Holy Sacrament passes through the street, I don't get up to see it?" And he did not. [When] a certain person bowed his head at Jesus' name, another certain person smiled and said that the person who thus bowed his head was trying to own his salvation, because that person said that pardons were won by performing such humiliations. He told him not to do it, or that it was unnecessary.

This proposition is erroneous, blasphemous, and heretical because it separates men from the devout and holy customs of the Holy Mother Church.

14. To stand up at the Gospel reading, and perform similar signs and acts of humility, was nothing more than playing with the body in church.

This proposition is erroneous and against the sacred canons.

15. Meaning that the *alumbrados* seemed to be above the emotions of love, anger, lust, and so forth, even when it came to family members. For specifics on the way this detachment might play out in the minds of listeners and accusers, see excerpts from the trial of María de Cazalla (Document 12).

16. As in, to meditate upon Jesus' suffering during His crucifixion. For the *alumbrados'* stand on the Passion of Christ, see number 22 with note 18 below.

15. It was wicked to adorn the statue of our Lady, the Virgin Mary, and take her in a procession through the street; it was idolatry. Speaking about the statue of our Lady, he said they should remove that idol.
This proposition is rash and errs against the praiseworthy customs of the Church.

16. [They said] that people were not healed by venerating the statues of our Lord and our Lady, which were simply sticks; they laughed when men did revere them, saying that the statues, being sticks, took no notice of them.
This proposition is heretical and at another time was condemned by the Church.

17. Upon being asked why he had no statue of our Lady, the Virgin Mary, he replied he would recall the Virgin Mary by looking at a woman.
This proposition is madness and wrong and heretical in origin, because it presupposes that the statues of the saints do not have to be honored.

18. While preaching, a certain person said that the Cross does not have to be adored, because it was a piece of wood; instead, they [should] adore Jesus Christ crucified.
This proposition is pagan, heretical, and cruel.

19. They should abandon themselves to the love of God and not pray, and what was prayer for? He could see the heart of a certain person like he saw his own hand. And what was the point of taking holy water? He never took it. And what was the point of striking oneself on the chest? And why kiss the earth at the *Incarnatus est* ["and was made man"],[17] saying what was the point of it; people who did so were full of self-will and earthly shackles. He reprimanded a certain person who moved from one place to another in order to see the Most Holy Sacrament. [And he said that] upon entering the church, one should not try to heal oneself by making the sign of the Cross or taking holy water, but by holding [God] in the heart.
The things in this article have the taste of heresy; they are erroneous and scandalous because they destroy the holy ceremonies of the Church and the external acts by which faithful Christians are known and distinguished from infidels.

20. Prayer had to be mental, not oral. To pray in church was an earthly shackle. God was not served by oral prayer, and they do not have to pray with the mouth.
This proposition is erroneous and heretical.

21. That one does not have to ask God for something in particular; it was like property to say, "Pray to God for me," [since] God took care of everyone. And [when] a confessor told a certain person that it was good to be specific in petitions, they [sic] said they believed it was better *not* to be so.
The first part of this proposition is erroneous and heretical, [and] against the doctrine of Our Lord Jesus Christ and of the Church; and the second part is crazy.

17. The phrase occurs in the Creed.

22. It was not good for a man to favor particular prayers, because men came to depend upon them out of sentiment, and wicked things were engendered as a result. It was a flaw to think about Jesus' Passion[18] and to console oneself with it; and it bothered him because a woman cried over a certain image of the Passion. One woman whipped her servant because she cried over the Passion. On Holy Thursday he had as much joy and pleasure, as if it were Easter Sunday.[19]

This proposition is heretical in the first and second parts. And to affirm that on Good Friday a person does not have to cry over the Passion of our Lord Jesus Christ, but laugh and enjoy oneself, is a crazy, scandalous, and audacious thing, and against the common custom of the Holy Church.

23. That the priest did not have to ask for anything during the sacrifice of the Mass, but instead should remain suspended [in the love of God].

This proposition is erroneous and against the holy canon of the Mass.

24. That a preacher reprimanded those who prayed to the saints and adored their statues. Why did they adore the Cross, when it was a piece of wood that they could burn?

This proposition is heretical, crazy, and scandalous in all its parts.

25. That married people were more united to God while making love than if they had been praying.

This proposition is false and erroneous, has the taste of heresy, and must be judged heretical, because it is against the apostle St. Paul and the common spiritual counsel of the Holy Church, which advises that at certain times married people should abstain from sexual intercourse in order to more freely and piously devote themselves to prayer.

26. That he had the sort of gift that the saints mentioned. Speaking of the saints' teaching, he waved it off, saying, "This doctrine of the saints! I have to judge and act according to Holy Scripture." And [while] speaking about the insights that God gave the saints and other prodigious spirits, he said, "What was the point of these wonders in the soul? He said that the sacred canons of the Church are good and holy, but whoever wished might observe them; what he wanted instead was to observe the Law of our Lord.

18. "Passion" in the context—from the Latin verb *patior,* meaning "to suffer"— means the suffering and death of Jesus during the Crucifixion. Meditation on the Passion of Christ was a venerated spiritual exercise, enshrined in Thomas à Kempis' *Imitation of Christ* from the late fourteenth century.

19. Thursday was the first day in the *Triduum sacrum* or three-day period during which Christians believe Jesus journeyed to crucifixion, death, and finally resurrection. Catholics were expected to fast, pray, and avoid all festive behavior during the three days before Easter Sunday.

They should not submit to learned men, because learned men did not preach the love of God, but only what He said.

This proposition is pagan, heretical, and a Lutheran error, because to reject the doctrine of the saints is Lutheran madness and a very arrogant error, contrary to the doctrine of the saints. And to say that the holy canons don't have to be observed is a heretical, impious, and Lutheran error because it separates the faithful from the observance of the Church's commandments.

27. What was the point of the excommunications, fasts, and abstinences of the Church? These were shackles, and the soul had to be free.

This proposition is false and erroneous, scandalous, and heretical because it dissuades men from obeying the Holy Mother Church.

28. There was no need for papal bulls. A person could not even begin to say how unnecessary they were. And [when] a certain person wanted to walk the Stations of the Cross to remove a soul from Purgatory, he told him to leave it alone.

To say that papal indulgences are worthless is a Lutheran error and an injurious heresy to the power of the highest pontiff, which was conceded by God.

29. They interpreted the Gospel with the explanation that he [sic] wanted, so that the passage, "He who lost his soul in this world, will find it in eternal life," was understood literally. He understood it to say that a man could save his soul only by loving and serving God. Though this goal might put a man in some danger of conscience, it was better to be very abstemious and very much in God's peace.

This proposition is false and erroneous, and the way these men understand that interpretation of Scripture may be heretical.

30. That it was not good for men to become monks.

To say that men should not observe the counsel of the Holy Gospel, and are not obliged to observe it, is an error, heresy, and a contemptuous blasphemy.

31. That he held it as a mortal sin if he read some book to console his soul.

This proposition, which says it is a sin to read some book to console the soul, is crazy, erroneous, and even heretical.

32. Interpreting that quote of St. John, "God is greater than our heart" [*Major est Deus corde nostro*],[20] they said, "Greater is God, our heart."[21] And

---

20. See 1 John 3:20: "For if our heart should reprehend us, God is greater than our heart, and knoweth all things."

21. While there is evidence that some *alumbrados* and members of their entourage—such as María de Cazalla and Francisco Ortiz—were versed in Latin, here Pedro Ruiz de Alcaraz and Isabel de la Cruz may have not understood that Latin is an inflected language, in which the endings of words signify their grammatical function in the sentence. Pedro and Isabel allegedly read the scriptural verse literally and straight

they contended that the verse had to be understood as they said, namely, that an internal perception of God or His nature, which they found in themselves, was completely from God and sent from the same. From here he came to believe that he did not sin, especially when he held God in his heart. And then they inferred that it could be known if one were in a state of grace or not.

The first part of the proposition, which states that God is our heart, is heretical, and if one understands [the Gospel] according to the interpretation of the witness who declared it under oath, [that interpretation] likewise is heretical, as the corollary that follows it is also heretical to the same degree.

33. That whoever loves his soul or does something for its salvation, loses it; and he won more who lost [his soul] in God and His love. He stopped doing good works to a great extent, since he was involved in a more important exercise.

The first part of this proposition is heretical, because it destroys all the works of virtue.

34. . . . and they had the love of God in them on account of the same God. They mocked anyone who walked around looking for merits, or who said, "I do this or that in order to merit more," holding it as certain that whoever was in their state [of grace] had all the merit. And when a person said there was more merit in some people than in others, he said, "Oh, might I not hear this 'more or less' business!"

To state that there is no inequality of merit is a heresy; to deny the habit of infused charity is against the common teaching of the theologians; similarly, to say that someone can reach such great perfection that he might not be capable of meriting more is a proposition condemned by the Church against the Beghards.[22]

35. That in no way should someone swear an oath.

This proposition is erroneous and heretical.

36. That a man sinned mortally every time he loved a son, daughter, or other person, and did not love that person through God.

---

across, and through linguistic cognates; they purportedly ignored the fact that *corde nostro* is an ablative of comparison.

22. The *Beguines* (female) and *Beghards* (male) were laypeople who attempted to live a holy life in private communities, without taking vows, during the twelfth and thirteenth centuries, especially in the Low Countries; they were attracted to poverty, mysticism, and the Spiritual Franciscans (the Franciscans who attempted to preserve Francis' simplistic, original rule). The fact that the theological *calificadores* in 1525 connected the *alumbrados* to a heretical sect from three centuries earlier demonstrates a common presupposition among religious elites, namely that heresies repeated themselves throughout time. Certain Spaniards would also accuse Erasmus, for instance, of Arianism, a heresy from the fourth century.

This proposition is erroneous and false, and against the common teaching of the saints.

37. By words and gesture, he denied [that] works done out of charity were performed for the love of God, but [rather] for one's own interest.
This proposition is crazy, false, erroneous, and self-contradictory.

38. He did not have to be charitable toward his neighbor except when he could help the neighbor.
This proposition is false, erroneous, and heretical.

39. That he had faith in blessedness.
This proposition is against the common resolution of the saints and even seems heretical.

40. Because a girl crossed the street, he said she had sinned, because in that action she had fulfilled her will.
The foundation of this proposition is heretical, because it seems to state that all action that proceeds from our will is sin.

41. That one might deny one's will even if it were good, and might not fulfill it, in order to do something that was not as good. [He] gave an example of forsaking Mass or a sermon, or neglecting to accompany the Most Holy Sacrament, even if his will was to go, in order to do something for his own household.
This proposition is erroneous and in its foundation heretical, because it presupposes that all good works that spring from free will are mortal sins.

42. One person said that he did not want to have intermediaries between God and himself, because Father Olmillos had advised him that he might hold a cross in his heart. When a certain person said that it was necessary to come to God through the humanity of Jesus Christ, the other said, "You know a great deal; I would prefer you not to know so much." When this certain person said more, namely, that he had certain devotions to the Passion, the other told him to relinquish those little pieties and not read about Christ's Passion, but meditate on the gifts of God instead.
To affirm that our Lord Jesus Christ crucified is not a means for the faithful soul to unite with God is an erroneous and heretical proposition, because it seems to deny the Son of God was made flesh and became the mediator between God and men. And the last part of this proposition is disdainful toward the mystery of our redemption, because it dissuades men from very salutary meditation on the Passion of our Lord Jesus Christ. It is erroneous and has the taste of heresy, and it is against the common custom of the Holy Church.

43. Upon hearing a certain person say that his intention was to serve God and do penance and observe His commandments, the other person said that the highest perfection lay elsewhere.

This proposition is erroneous and heretical, and was condemned in another epoch of the Church against the Beghards.

44. They did not have to renounce temptations and evil thoughts, but rather should embrace them and take them as a burden, and walk onward with this cross. And they give as authorities [sic] for it, "Take up your bed and walk" [*Tolle grabatum tuum et ambula*],[23] and God would remove the temptations and evil thoughts from them when He wished.

This proposition is false and very dangerous morally, and consequently is heretical.

45. That they did not have to be curious to know the metaphors [*figuras*] of Holy Scripture; if they understood something, fine, and if not, they might proceed anyway. If God did not give that understanding to him, it was prideful to want to understand more of Scripture than what its language literally said.

This proposition is heretical.

46. That the end of the world had to occur in twelve years.

This proposition is crazy.

47. That even if Adam had not sinned, he would not have entered Heaven without the death of the Son of God.

This proposition is false and erroneous.

48. The *Soliloquies* of St. Augustine were made up.[24]

Because we believe that we Christians are sown from tares and scandals, and know that the devil feels pain at the unity and peace of Christianity, and thus tries to infuse errors into the souls of some of the faithful, blinding their judgment and sowing his abominations so that they might be attracted to these errors and novelties (and those who consented to such diabolical cogitations are not without fault); and because we wish Christians to flee and withdraw from those errors and deceptions, we order that our letter be sent along with these condemned propositions . . . with learned preachers of authority and good example, whom we send to read the propositions and their condemnation, and to make them known to you on Sundays and obligatory feast days, from the church pulpits where you are parishioners, when you are together in church to hear the divine offices. [These preachers] shall teach you the Catholic things that you must believe in order to save your souls, and the things you must avoid in order not to lose the glory for which you were created.

At present, we order you to withdraw from all the said errors and novelties, not to believe or uphold them, and not to be swayed into them by other people, whether publicly or secretly, in your houses or outside of them, alone

---

23. See Mark 2:9: "Which is easier to say to a paralyzed man? 'Your sins are forgiven,' or 'Arise, take up your bed, and walk'?"

24. There is no censure recorded against this proposition.

or assembled. [If you] do the opposite, which is not what God desires or permits, then we state that we will proceed against each and every one of you, through imprisonment, the confiscation of property, and other lawfully established penalties, just as we proceed against heretics and transgressors of things that are divinely ordained and taught by our Holy Mother Church; as against people who do not believe, and who deviate and withdraw from the common doctrine and instruction of our Holy Catholic Faith and of the Universal Church. As proof we give the signature of our name, marked with our seal and countersigned by our secretary of the general Inquisition.

Given in the city of Toledo, on the 23rd day of September, the year of our Lord Jesus Christ's birth 1525. Alonso [Manrique], Archbishop of Spain. By order of his most reverend lordship, Lope Díaz, secretary.

Document 9

Letter from Friar Francisco Ortiz to Inquisitor-General Alonso Manrique, April 9, 1529, Composed inside the Toledo Tribunal of the Inquisition[1]

[A Franciscan friar, Francisco Ortiz had friends in high places and a successful preaching career before inquisitors seized Francisca Hernández on charges of alumbradismo *on March 31, 1529. One week later, Ortiz went into the pulpit of the monastery of San Juan de los Reyes in Toledo and gave a sermon that publicly chastised Inquisitor-General Alonso Manrique for prosecuting her. Ortiz was tried for abetting heretics, slandering the Inquisition, and scandalizing the residents of Toledo; fifty-two of the fifty-six charges against him highlighted his rebelliousness in giving the sermon in San Juan de los Reyes, defending it afterward, and believing in Francisca Hernández' spiritual gifts. Charges of* alumbradismo *played only a small role in the formal accusation against him. Ortiz' trial lasted from 1529 to 1532. He was made to retract his praise for Francisca, suspended for five years from preaching and hearing confessions, and enclosed for two years in a Franciscan monastery in Torrelaguna, where he chose to remain until his death in 1545. His trial was notorious in the first half of the sixteenth century.*

Immediately after his arrest, in the spring of 1529, Ortiz wrote four long letters to Inquisitor-General Manrique in his own hand, wherein he railed against the injustice of his and Francisca's arrests and set out what the Inquisitor-General should have done instead. The first of these letters is translated below.]

Holy Jeremiah—whom the King Sedecias ordered to be unjustly imprisoned, as it says in chapter 28 [38]—says in chapter 20 that the Word of God

---

1. *Proceso contra Fray Francisco Ortiz, de la orden del San Francisco, 1529–1532.* Sign. Yc 2° 20 (2). Collections [*Sondersammlungen*], Martin-Luther-Universität, Halle, Germany, ff. 34r–39r. For a study of Ortiz' holograph statements, see Homza, "How to Harass an Inquisitor-General." The major study of Ortiz is Angela Selke, *El Santo Oficio de la Inquisición: Proceso de Dr. Francisco Ortiz (1529–32)* (Madrid: Ediciones Guadarrama, 1968). Ortiz' comments on Francisca Hernández' sanctity could be fruitfully combined with Hernández' own depositions, trial documents on Antonio de Medrano, Magdalena de la Cruz, and Catalina Muñoz—see Documents 10, 11, 16, and 25—and Gillian Ahlgren's transcription of Francisca de los Apostoles' case before the Inquisition of Toledo. See Gillian T. W. Ahlgren, ed., *The Inquisition of Francisca: A Sixteenth-Century Visionary on Trial,* The Other Voice in Early Modern Europe (Chicago: The University of Chicago Press, 2005).

became a reproach to him, and for this reason he wished to cease speaking the Word, because apparently it would cost him dearly. But though he resolved to be silent, he says he felt a fire within that roasted him, and he swooned, not being able to bear it, even though he knew that people who had been his peaceful friends would become his enemies [for speaking the Word of God].

This happened to me in the same way, even though I'm a sinner and do not merit the gifts that I have received from God; I have even received such gifts here in this [inquisition] cell (which is precious to me), by means of His most faithful and beloved bride, the blessed Francisca Hernández. Unable to bear the fire that roasted my heart from seeing such an enormous offense to God [in Hernández' arrest], I resolved to speak, even though it would cost me dearly in the eyes of the blind. . . . It is reasonable that Your Reverend Lordship should know through this confession what I began to preach [in San Juan de los Reyes of Toledo], when I was constrained by the testimony of my conscience; namely, that whenever a public and scandalous sin is committed, after two secret warnings *not* to commit that sin, a preacher of truth, who holds God's honor more dearly than his own life, must and can publicly oppose that sin without being hindered by highness of rank. And the blessed St. John the Baptist demonstrates this for us in the rebuke he gave King Herod, and St. John alone is witness enough.[2] Thus if I were to make this universal rule specific in the present case, I would say that the imprisonment of Francisca Hernández, this servant of God, can be proven to be a very serious sin in three ways: first, through external evidence; second, through the internal evidence of conscience; and third, through the superior evidence of God Himself.

As to the first level of evidence (which would be enough for the blind that we so long to be), I ask your Reverend Lordship, what reason did you have to seize the blessed bride of Jesus right now, since in the seven years since her [previous] trial, neither your predecessor in office, Pope Adrian of blessed memory, nor even you yourself, ever demanded that she be placed in a public prison?[3] The first time I spoke to Your Reverence—[when] I felt compelled to keep you from falling into such an enormous sin, when you were being influenced by monks—you well remember that you answered me with these words: "Father, I have taken satisfaction in everything you have told me, and I shall take your opinion because I hold you in very high esteem, and I publicly say that if someone could hear you and your sermons for a

---

2. From the moment Ortiz entered prison, he began to play John the Baptist to Manrique's Herod; see Homza, "How to Harass an Inquisitor-General," 315.

3. For Francisca Hernández' encounters with the Inquisition up to 1529, see Documents 10 and 11.

year, it would be of great value." Then I told Your Lordship that through the same sermons I had acquired great favor [with] this blessed bride of Jesus Christ, Francisca Hernández . . . and you ended that conversation by telling me how much pleasure you took in my positive testimony about her, because others had shown up with different stories; and you would commend the matter to God and return later to hear my opinion. Then you wondered whether it would be good to bring Francisca Hernández here, and I said that the scandal involved must be greatly feared, and your Lordship replied, "May God preserve us, that it be done not with scandal but with great peace."

In this first conversation, your Reverend Lordship voiced no crime against the bride of the Most High God, for which she could be imprisoned; [but] you told me about it when I returned the second time, as your Lordship commanded. I told you that in no way should your Lordship order her brought here, because it could not be done without scandal, and as far as the sanctity of her person was concerned, I wished to do your Lordship a great service, which was to recommend that you write to her with the honor and reverence owed to such servants of God; and commend your person and matters of pastoral care to her. Then your Lordship would feel within the power of her prayers; and this would be better testimony than anything I could say. Your Lordship replied [_____] [gap in the manuscript], completely changed, "Ah, father, you are deceived," and when I demanded the cause of the deception, your Lordship replied that the guardian of my monastery had said how I used to be an angel and a good monk, but after I had spoken with this servant of God [Hernández] . . . I was lost. And the guardian told you that [after I knew her], I preached no one knew what sort of doctrine. . . . As far as this is concerned, I wish to say something that is enough to make one laugh and cry all at once, to see the blindness that passes for truth. I swear before the living God, Who with mercy awaits our penance, that once I was speaking with the same guardian in my cell, and I read him the letter that I had written about Francisca Hernández to the Vicar-General of the Franciscan order, in which I relayed many good things about this bride of the All-Powerful, and warned him not to enter into the dance of the persecutors, because it would cost him dearly. And my guardian said, among other things, "If she said these good things about you, they would be well said; but for you to say them about her is unreasonable." Now, Your Lordship, you shall see how "lost" I am, when they attribute to *me* the good things that I said about the bride of Christ.[4]

I also want to ask *when* I was deceived, and if I've been lost the whole time

4. Ortiz asserted throughout his ordeal that he was held in high esteem by nearly everyone for his preaching and morality, so how could Francisca Hernández have simultaneously made him corrupt? See below.

I've known her. It has been six years since I received such magnificent gifts from God with her holy communication, and your Lordship never knew me before I knew her, and if I was "lost" after communicating with her, then why did your Lordship hold me in esteem, and why was I praised? I want to know why you would give more credit to my guardian, who hopes to lessen my reputation with you . . . given that his heart is so imprudent that he maligns the worth of my teaching against the law of God and against all truth, saying that he doesn't know what I preached. If I were not preaching Catholic doctrine, why did he have me preach for five Easters here in Toledo, as is well known?. . . . I have said all this against the false testimony that the guardian gave against my teaching, in great offense to God, Whose teaching it is. I told your Lordship to investigate my life among the monks, and you will see what my life was. The Franciscans had no novice more obedient, or one who conversed with greater silence and peace among them; I knew nothing more than to be in my cell and to preach according to my strengths, where and when I was so ordered.

Still, your Lordship insisted that you would rather believe the guardian than me. At that point in our conversation—moved by compassion that your Lordship not blind yourself, as I always have desired everything good for you, with a special affection as if toward a father and lord—I wished to tell you about certain marvels which could only have been carried out by the hand of God. (And I know this as a theologian; and God showed me the marvels in his servant [Hernández]). I disclosed the marvels to you under the seal of confession . . . and afterward, your Lordship told me they were demonic illusions . . . and at this reply I could not help being terrified at the boldness with which your Lordship attributed the works of God to the Demon. You did not consider that I had studied and practiced the spiritual road since my childhood, and that it would be more appropriate for me to examine such things rather than someone who did not even know what they were. . . . Here I shall say no more, except that the Demon never performs marvels so that those who are separated from God are converted to serve and love Him with their entire heart; and on this, see John 8 [:]. . . ."[5]

Oh your Reverence, how many witnesses I could produce to confess the great mercies that they received from God with the words of this greatly beloved servant [Hernández]; these witnesses to her gifts left behind many sins and varieties of blindness (even though the monks continually persecuted her, and not all but very many have experienced what I say about her). . . . Though some of those who have spoken with her have turned back [to their sins] and have become her chief persecutors, remember, your Lordship, that

5. The mangled line that follows is not in John 8. That chapter does contain an exchange between Jesus and the Jews as to whether the former is possessed by a demon.

the one who sold Christ, my God and my All-Being, was of Jesus' company. For the glory of His great majesty and the honor of His very holy bride, swearing by the One who is the universal judge of the living and the dead, I say that one of her greatest persecutors, the one who has warred against me the most with your Lordship, told me simultaneously that in his eyes there was no other St. Catherine of Siena or Angela of Foligno.[6] . . . And this persecutor is the one, out of all the monks, who afterward maligned me the most, the very same one who [originally] praised her to me and roused me to venerate her, telling me the marvelous things that God had manifested in her, His servant. . . . Again I beg your Reverend Lordship to pay attention to this contradiction, because there's a great deal to it, and through it you could escape from the blindness into which you've fallen.

In the second conversation, where your Lordship had already completely altered and refused to give me any credit, the thing that made the greatest impression on me was when you said, "If I were to see Francisca Hernández in a monastery, walking in obedience and following its choir and bell, I would believe everything that people say; I am very devoted to people who are in religious orders." Oh your Lordship, I beg God will make you reverse yourself, so you may save your soul. May God make your Lordship consult learned men to see if someone can reach such high perfection without being a monk or a nun; why should the beloved bride of Jesus lose credit because she is not a nun? I do not say this to malign the religious state, to which God, through his mercy, called me. It is public knowledge how often I have preached—against Erasmus—that the religious state should not be held in low esteem. But I maintain that it is heresy, already condemned in many church councils, to maintain that a state of spiritual perfection cannot be reached except by members of religious orders; may your Lordship see what a weak foundation you have for depriving her of credit. [In that

6. Catherine of Siena (1347?–1380) and Angela of Foligno (1248–1309) were paragons of female sanctity in the medieval and early modern periods. Catherine and Angela were members of the Dominican and Franciscan Tertiaries, respectively; these "third orders" [whence, "tertiary"] allowed lay people to live according to a modified monastic rule in the world. Catherine was canonized in 1461; Angela was beatified in 1693. Both women had visions, practiced ecstatic prayer, and were devoted to aspects of the Passion of Christ. Accounts of Angela's visions were written down by her confessor and subsequently circulated; writings about her were translated into Spanish. Catherine left behind letters and a dialogue, and an account of her life was also circulated and translated into Spanish in the early sixteenth century. Both women served as exemplars for women seeking holiness, and they were deliberately imitated and invoked in Spain and Italy. See Jodi Bilinkoff, *Related Lives: Confessors and Their Female Penitents, 1450–1750* (Ithaca, NY: Cornell University Press, 2005) and the bibliography listed in Document 16, note 3.

second conversation], your Lordship answered, "Well then, here we know
very well that Francisca Hernández is a lascivious woman." Oh your Lordship, my heart trembles just from hearing such ugly words. I state the following truths so that no one who reads this shall have an excuse to say otherwise
before the terrifying and rigorous judgment of God:

First, Your Reverend Lordship does not know the very illustrious bride of
Jesus Christ . . . nor do her persecutors. She has walked in a hidden and reserved way through this blind world because she has never, since childhood,
been a friend of great external appearances; rather, she has always abided in
the dress of an honest virgin.

Since the case compels me to it, the second thing I want to say is that I
maintain and swear before the terrible judge God . . . that though I am a
great sinner and a thankless wretch before God, my body has never been pol-
luted with a woman, nor have I ever known one carnally. Everyone knows
that God has given me this gift, since I have said that God has given me ver-
bal abundance in Holy Scripture because of my chastity.

Third, this matter does not belong to your jurisdiction; these disputes do
not come before the Holy Inquisition unless someone dogmatizes that a sin is
not a sin, and then it is a case for your office, for the punishment of that heresy.
And this very clean virgin of Jesus Christ will never say that a sin is not a sin.

Fourth—trusting in Him who, through Daniel, liberated holy Susanna
from the lying elders[7]—bring me all those accusers who attribute indecency
to this shining virgin, and I, with the grace of God and my All-Being Jesus
Christ crucified, will confound them, performing the work of holy Daniel,
that is, "Not I, but the grace of God with me." Thus it shall be known that
this holy virgin Francisca has been another holy Susanna in our times, and
this truth shall be much noted and recognized, because I offer to explain it
with the grace of God. I know that the filth [against her] which filthy hearts
have raised shall not survive in the face of the purity that God has shown me
and worked in me through the means and intercession of his holy bride. I

---

7. In his diatribes against Inquisitor-General Manrique, Ortiz was exceptionally
fond of the apocryphal, Old Testament story of Susanna, which is found in the book
of Daniel. Susanna was a beautiful and holy woman who was married; she was stalked
by two tribal elders who told her she could either have sex with them or they would
accuse her of committing adultery with someone else. When she refused their sexual
advances, the elders went before the community and charged her with adultery; Susanna cried out for justice, God heard her supplication, and Daniel appeared to help
her. Daniel then took the two elders aside, interrogated them, and caught them in a
contradiction that proved Susanna's innocence. For the ways in which Ortiz fit the
Susanna story to his situation with Francisca Hernández, see Homza, "How to Harass an Inquisitor-General," 313–15.

know her so well, and have been so austere in all communication and conversation with women (as can be found through my five years of conversation in Toledo), that I used to call this dove and clean virgin (who had the simplicity and innocence of a child, as I saw) . . . my love, my heart, my guts, my eyes. . . .

Would to God that your Lordship had done what was appropriate in this case and diligently investigated what you did not know. If you had diligently investigated, you would not have committed such a huge offense against God, nor would you have hidden the candle that God lit for the illumination of many. They did not give you power for this, but for edification; . . . no one supposes that I hold this bride of Christ as impeccable, but the wicked nevertheless jump out, [accusing me] of the condemned heresy of the Beghards.[8] I know well that there is no one here who would not fall if the grace of God deserted him. Still, I maintain, with complete truthfulness, that those who accuse and condemn and imprison in this dispute are awash in guilt; and [conversely] the servant of the very high God is far too elevated for this unjustifiable penalty [of imprisonment]. With great happiness and rejoicing in her holy soul, she suffers in order to augment her crown. What her accusers falsely charge will never be discovered. . . .

It is a comic thing, Lord Reverence, for them to make such a fuss over my sermons on the one hand, and to sell me to your Lordship as deceived on the other. In many places they destroy what God has edified with my words. These are not small offenses against God. This is as much as I have to say about external testimony, though other things of some importance have been mixed in as well.

As for the second sort of testimony, which comes from the internal conscience, wherein lies our glory, I say in all truthfulness that the first time I saw this illustrious bride of Jesus Christ (which occurred after the general chapter meeting of the Franciscans that was held in Burgos), it was not without many prayers and tears, because I came and went from her door for seven days, and I never was admitted until God heard my lamentations. Up to now that internal testimony has never failed, but rather has grown, as I believe that this blessed servant of God was the means by which God carried out great gifts for me. And I know well that God could have carried out these gifts through a thousand other means; but I also know that He wanted to use this means [in particular], and it's not necessary to ask now why it was done in this way. . . . And although it is true that from the day God moved me through her doors, I have never lacked for persecutors over this matter, I also confess truthfully that not only have the persecutors not weakened me, but my heart remains even stronger; this is the habit of truth, to be attacked but never

8. See note 22 in Document 8.

vanquished. Even if there were no other testimony except persecution (which has been leveled so continuously against this servant of Christ), it is not wrong to conjecture that there is a great treasure in such persecution.

This same argument can be taken to demonstrate the truth of our Holy Faith in comparison to others; the lies of the holy [sic] philosophers, which were contradictory, were not persecuted, and since they were not perfect, they disappeared like smoke. Only our Holy Catholic Faith was persecuted with great cruelty by the powerful and wise men of the world in the time of the martyrs, and only that faith alone has remained invincible. In the same way I hope in my God and my All-Being that I will be His faithful servant in this; there is very little to fear from persecutors who can kill no more than the body.[9] This is as much as I have to say about the testimony of conscience.

As far as the superior testimony which God gives, with the marvels that He alone performs, I said something to your Reverend Lordship [before] when, without reason, you deprecated it; and I have a great deal more to say, but I shall limit myself to one thing only, which should be enough for anyone. . . . I could have desisted from preaching the truth [about the Inquisition and Hernández], and gained great favors and the estimation of men, [but] I have scorned it all. These heroic shackles on my feet are more precious than a hundred thousand crowns of rich jewels. With the grace of Jesus Christ, I, a sick and weak worm, am ready to suffer for this truth all the torments and types of death that my persecutors can think to inflict upon me. I feel all this with great joy and rejoicing in my soul, which I could not feel unless I received it from God; I even dare to say the clearest truth to your Reverend Lordship, which is a marvel from God. I have been given such a strong heart to fight for God's honor, that the prison of the Holy Inquisition seems most sweet, though it so frightens everyone else. I would not exchange this prison for any royal palace, given the desire that God has given me of leaving this prison of this body and this blind and miserable world, and soon he will dry that world like hay [sic].

It's for this reason, Your Lordship, that I know that what you did so publicly is a sin. The sin is so scandalous that its fame will endure for the next two hundred years. It shall become known through a great part of Christianity, where there are many ready supporters who have received gifts from God through his faithful servant Francisca Hernández. She is not going to stop being revered by many because she is persecuted by monks who have only a name and a habit.

---

9. Ortiz is invoking a well-known trope in Christian history, that the forces of evil are allowed to persecute Christianity and Christians as a test. See Brad S. Gregory, *Salvation at Stake: Christian Martyrdom in Early Modern Europe* (Cambridge, MA: Harvard University Press, 1999).

The sin [of her arrest] is also scandalous against everything I have worked for my whole life, that is, trying to educate [the people] with such continuous sermons. Everyone knows that I am such a child of [Hernández'] heart, that by imprisoning her with such dishonor, you have made all my teaching suspect, and you have robbed me of the authority to preach from this day forward. The exception is the sermon I preached [in San Juan de los Reyes], which had authority, majesty, and truth to it, since the sin of her imprisonment was so public and so scandalous; and it was preceded by two warnings to you not to do it. And since I had no credit left with you, nor a council to which I could appeal, the servants of God and the wise men shall see if I should have been silent, when the holiness of this new Susanna was clear to me. Since the shepherds sleep, the preachers [must] howl.

Oh your Lordship, not without reason did Christ say to St. Peter, "You sleep"; it is fitting that he who has the greater authority should be more vigilant. Only one thing—the fear of death—could have blocked me from preaching that truth which was so necessary for the confirmation of my healthful and Catholic teaching, which I have sowed for so long. But because the great mercy of God has so extended itself toward me—I who am unworthy of all good things, accustomed to drink the blood which my God and All-Being spilled on His holy altar for me—I do not fear to spill my blood for His love, which is sovereign truth; for this reason I said what I did. And I say here that there are not enough torments to make me recant one word of it.

What I recommend to your Reverend Lordship—so that you may reach eternal salvation and pardon for this sin that you have committed, and so that you don't find yourself tricked at the hour of death, which is close, given your age—is that very quickly, without delay, postponing all other business and trials, you get involved in this case . . . and may worldly shame not prevent you from quickly undoing what you so rapidly did, for that shame is the snare of Hell. May saving a soul come as naturally to you as offering counsel does to a wise and prudent man. I will help your Lordship to cry over this sin (which has not been small), though the greater sin belongs to my guardian, who pushed you into it . . . and I know well that if you do not hear me, this piece of writing will call to you on the Day of Judgment. I give inestimable thanks to my God and All-Being, Jesus Christ crucified, because in a time of peace He has given me the opportunity to give my life for Him.

In the meantime, I greatly charge your Lordship's conscience, and through the blood of Jesus Christ I beg you not to add one sin on top of the other. Immediately order the servant Rios to go to serve the bride [Hernández] of the King of Kings, because besides the injustice of her imprisonment, it is a tremendous cruelty to a person as delicate as Francisca Hernández [to be imprisoned]. . . . I know that if Your Lordship knew how delicate and sick my blessed mother [Hernández] is, out of natural kindness you would not consent to leave her alone. Order that doctors of bodies enter her cell to ascertain the disposition of her flesh, and doctors of souls to see the greatness that God has placed in His servant, and how happily she suffers all these things; [note] how the ones shall say how thin and sick she is, and the others how strong and endowed. Note, Sir, that I was informed that she has not been able to eat five eggs in twelve days, thanks to the penitential road you've ordered her to walk; note how enormous are the swoons she suffers in seeing how much God is offended. I beg your Reverend Lordship one hundred-thousand times to hear my petition and my lamentations, and show now all the affection you used to have for me, before the guardian took it away. Oh Sir, do it, so that God may save your soul. All justice remains in your hands. With all my heart I beg my Lord Jesus Christ to put His grace into your heart to carry out His holy will, because you deserve to be among the blessed. From my beloved prison cell of the Holy Inquisition, April 9, 1529.

Document 10
Testimony by Francisca Hernández, June 2, 1531

*[Most unfortunately, our only source of information about Francisca Hernán-
dez comes from the inquisition trials of others; her own prosecution has been
lost.[1] Arrested for* alumbradismo *in 1529, Hernández had already tussled
with inquisitors in Salamanca and Valladolid between 1519 and 1524. She
was a controversial religious figure throughout the decade of the 1520s because
of her devoted circle of male disciples and her alleged spiritual gifts. Her most
ardent followers were Bernardino de Tovar, Antonio de Medrano, and Francisco Ortiz,[2] all of whom appeared before the Inquisition—sometimes multiple
times[3]—for being entangled in* alumbradismo *and Hernández' religious en-
terprises. Deponents against Hernández constantly implied that she had sexual
relationships with her entourage, though Medrano and Ortiz insisted she was
chaste. Witnesses also steadily insisted that Hernández and Medrano were spiritual con artists who promoted her gifts for financial gain, such as telling an
audience that Hernández could report on souls in Purgatory in return for cash.
Though we cannot tell whether Hernández was ever formally charged with
"pretense of sanctity," the inquisitors were at least working toward that concept
as they questioned her.[4] While her reputation for fakery and sexual impropri-
ety damaged her character in the eyes of witnesses, it did not usually diminish
the legal weight of her depositions, and her statements provoked the arrest
and investigation of numerous individuals. Hernández amply fulfilled the
inquisitors' requirement that defendants relay everything they knew about
accomplices. She excelled at pleasing authority figures and anticipating argu-
mentative turns.]*

1. See Mary E. Giles, "Francisca Hernández and the Sexuality of Religious Dissent,"
in *Women in the Inquisition: Spain and the New World* (Baltimore: The Johns Hopkins University Press, 1999), 75–97.

2. For Ortiz and Medrano, see Documents 9 and 11. Tovar's trial has been lost. He
was loyal to Hernández until approximately 1523, when he transferred his affections
to María de Cazalla; see Document 12. For Hernández' authority over Tovar and her
alleged penchant for revenge, see Homza, *Religious Authority,* chapter 1.

3. See the introduction to Document 11.

4. The Inquisition's interest in pretense of sanctity can be traced in this volume
through Documents 10, 11, 16, and 25. The bibliography in Document 16, note 3
is essential.

Witnesses in May and June, 1531[5]

. . . . Another witness, legally sworn, who deposed in the current month of May, 1531, said that the Valladolid inquisitors banned a certain person [Antonio de Medrano] from within five leagues of Francisca Hernández, and from communicating with her, under pain of major excommunication and other punishments.[6] But notwithstanding the prohibition, the certain person [Medrano] communicated with Francisca Hernández, and all the communication was evil and of the flesh. And that person [Medrano] praised Francisca Hernández so people would hold her as a saint. And this witness knew and saw that [Medrano] and Francisca Hernández hid themselves and avoided other people in order to communicate and arrange their business. The whole intention behind it was carnal, so that people would hold both of them as saints; this witness knows that in communicating with Francisca Hernández, the intention of that person [Medrano] was to acquire fame for being holy.

Next, this witness said he knows and saw that person [Medrano] and Francisca Hernández repeatedly touching and kissing, and they did this in Salamanca just as they had in Valladolid; and that person [Medrano] was in Francisca Hernández' bed some nights, and there he touched her and kissed her and touched her lasciviously [sic], and this witness knows Francisca Hernández enjoyed it.

Next, this witness heard that person and Francisca Hernández say that it was not a sin to break fasts. . . .

On June 2, 1531, in the hearing room of the Holy Office, Inquisitor Alonso Mexia ordered Francisca Hernández brought before him. He told her that she [already] knew how many times she had been admonished to tell the truth, and she hadn't done it; and she knew likewise how testimony was again given in publication, and she has denied what it contains. Thus, notwithstanding the many admonitions that she has been given to tell the truth and not hide anything for any reason, Inquisitor Mexia now returned again to admonish her—with God Our Lord, and with His blessed mother, Our Lady the Virgin Mary—to confess the truth and not to hide anything. . . .

Francisca Hernández said it is true that after contact with Antonio Medrano was prohibited, and he was not to come within five leagues of her, that she afterward went to Salamanca, where he remained a long time. This

---

5. Bernardino Llorca, *La inquisición española y los alumbrados (1509–1667), según las actas originales de Madrid y de otros archivos* (Salamanca: Universidad Pontificia, 1980), 289–93. The material translated here appears in the trial of Antonio de Medrano, but Francisca Hernández' statements were first given in her own trial and then copied into Medrano's trial record.

6. See the introduction to Document 11.

defendant was in Valla Vaquerín, and Medrano passed through there, and he asked this defendant if she would give him permission to see her. He sent the request through Pedro de Cazalla. This defendant told Pedro de Cazalla to tell Medrano that she did not wish to see him. But Cazalla came back with a letter, she believes, and in the letter Medrano again requested that she see him. With the incessant urging of the two men, and the fact that they told her Medrano wanted nothing more than to see her, she consented. . . . And so Medrano came and spoke to her, and this defendant said nothing to him except that he would not be able to speak to her or see her anymore. . . .

She was asked why she had said nothing about this up to now, and why she denied seeing Medrano. She said she kept quiet because she believed that she hadn't willingly spoken to Medrano, and hence wasn't obliged to say so, because she had spoken no more extensively to him than if he had been excommunicated, and she just told him that he should not speak to her or see her anymore. . . .

Next she said that what the witness reports about the embraces, kisses, and touches is true; such occurred between her and Medrano. But what the witness says about intent and carnal contact is not true.

Asked if this defendant enjoyed the fact that Medrano kissed, touched, and groped her lasciviously. This defendant said she thought that he had the same love for her as she had for him through God, and for this reason, she consented.

Asked if it is true that someone else slept some nights with her in her bed. She said that sometimes, when she was ill, Bernardino Tovar, M. [sic] Cabrera and Villareal came to where she slept, and sometimes Medrano lay on top of her bed, on top of the covers, to sleep a little. . . .

After the aforesaid, on the next day, in the cell where Francisca Hernández was imprisoned, Inquisitor Mexia asked her if she remembered anything more. On what pertains to the first chapter of the witness testimony, she said no.

Asked if she had any further communication with Medrano after the prohibition and after seeing him in Villa Vaquerín. She said that before Medrano went to Salamanca (which occurred after the last prohibition), Medrano, Tovar, and Villareal went sometimes to the house of Pedro de Cazalla [in Valladolid], and stayed to sleep in the apartment for guests, which was next to this defendant's room. Sometimes Tovar went with Medrano, and other times with M. Villareal. Asked where the aforesaid men slept, she said she never saw any bed.

Asked where her lodging was in the house, she said that next to her bedroom there was a room with an altar, and there one man slept on a chest and another on a platform.

Asked if there was a door in between where this defendant and the men slept, she said yes.

Asked if they closed that door at night, she said she did not remember; sometimes it stayed closed, other times open. Asked if Medrano or one of the other men came at night to this defendant's bed, she said that such a thing never occurred in Valladolid; but in Salamanca she has already said that sometimes Medrano rested in her bed.

Asked who opened the door to those men in Valladolid when this defendant was in the house of Pedro de Cazalla; she said Leonor, his wife, sometimes let them in, and so did Inés López, this defendant's maid.

Asked how the men entered the lodging of this defendant, she said that most times they entered through a door . . . and other times through a little door from the hall.

Asked at what hour of the night the men entered her lodging, she said sometimes they entered early, and other nights well after nightfall; and some nights they ate with Leonor, and on some nights they came to her apartment after eating, and other nights they stayed in their own room.

Asked if some of the men stayed some nights in the apartment of Leonor; she said she did not know. But they spent a lot of time with Leonor while her husband was not there. And Tovar and Medrano continually ate dinner with Leonor; and sometimes she saw Leonor embrace Medrano and call him "my father." One time, she saw Leonor kiss Medrano on the neck. And when Medrano was in Montifer, Leonor and Francisca de Amigán, wife of Antonio de Baeza, and Inés López, her maid, went to see him there, and they tried hard to go wherever he was. . . .

Asked if the contact she witnessed between Medrano and others had evil motives, she said she would not know what to say, except that she was pained over the form of their conversation, and she saw that these women ran after Medrano. As far as Inés López was concerned, she would not trust her for anything.

Asked if she knows that a certain person praised her so that people would hold her as a saint, she said she knows well that Tovar, Medrano, Villareal, and Friar Francisco Ortiz praised her, but she doesn't know the intention behind the praise.[7]

Asked if she herself praised Medrano so that people would think he was a saint, she said she praised him as a good person, and she well believes she would say he was a saint. . . .

Asked if she praised Medrano because she knew he praised *her* as a saint, she said she was never moved to praise him with this intent.

Asked if she and Medrano hid from others in order to communicate in secret, she said the truth was that Medrano never kissed her in the presence of another person, unless perhaps in front of Tovar or Villareal.

Asked if the way she and Medrano lived, and [the reason for] their mutual

7. See the letter by Francisco Ortiz, Document 9.

praise, was to acquire temporal things or honor, or to hide the vice of the flesh; she was asked why they did it. She said they had neither of these motives, and she praised him thinking he was a servant of God. . . .

Asked which people have tempted her with carnal vices, and have attempted, by deeds, to carry out their desires, she said one of them is a man named Cabrera, who came one morning to her house when she was in Salamanca; this defendant was in bed, and Cabrera went to kiss her hand, and she went to kiss his hand, and then Cabrera seized her hands in a very roguish way, and as this defendant felt [sic] his evil intention, she answered him very harshly, and he told her he would give his soul to the devil to have a child by her. He tried to touch her breasts and kiss her, and this defendant resisted him and pushed him away.

The other person who had wicked thoughts and tried to have evil conversation with her was Friar Pedro de Segura, of the Order of St. Jerome, who was in a state of sin.[8] He followed her for a long time and tried to touch her breasts. He tried to kiss her and take her hands, and he attacked her, saying he would die. When he found no corresponding disposition in this defendant, he said, "How is this, lady, that your kindness could not stop my wickedness?" . . .

She felt the same way about Tovar, who had a wicked intention where this defendant was concerned, and his conversation was not on account of God, because sometimes he shaved in order to kiss her. Asked if he did kiss her, she said yes, and he was traitorous. She knew that he had an evil intention in his touches, and she knew the same intention was shared by [Cristóbal de] Gumiel, and at the moment she did not recall anyone else.[9]

Asked why she did not stop conversing with these men, since she knew they did not deal honestly with her, she said that she had immediately put Cabrero away from her, had told Tovar he could go to the devil, and had said the same to Gumiel.

Asked if she knew that Friar Francisco Ortiz' conversation with her was also carnal, she said she never had such a thought.

Asked if Friar Francisco Ortiz kissed her hands, she said yes, and he did it in this way: every time he entered the room, he prostrated himself and kissed the ground near her feet, and then he took her hand and kissed it; but he never clutched her hand, nor did she ever see any evil sign in him.

---

8. Francisca Hernández and Antonio de Medrano could allegedly deduce whether individuals were living in a state of sinfulness or not.

9. Cristóbal de Gumiel was a poor cleric attached to Bernardino de Tovar. After Tovar's arrest, when his half-brother, Juan de Vergara, wrote secret letters to him in the Toledo tribunal's prison, Gumiel acted as a go-between. See Homza, *Religious Authority*, chapter 1.

DOCUMENT 11

Summary of the Prosecutor's Accusation against Antonio de Medrano. Toledo Tribunal[1]

[Antonio de Medrano was born in 1486 in the Rioja region of northern Spain. He studied canon law at the University of Salamanca, became a priest, and encountered Francisca Hernández about 1517.[2] What is both comic and significant is the number of times Medrano got into trouble with religious authorities without serious penalty. In 1519, inquisitors in Valladolid told him to cease communication with Hernández because of reports of scandalous remarks and lascivious acts; the order was ignored. In 1522 and 1523, inquisitors banished Medrano from Valladolid and its environs in ever-greater distances, but he managed to see Francisca anyway and failed to reform his habits. In Salamanca in 1524, an episcopal vicar-general prosecuted Medrano for more lascivious acts and more scandalous statements, and exiled him again. That vicar-general even remitted the case to the Valladolid tribunal, but the inquisitors did not act.

Medrano then returned to La Rioja and occupied a church office in Navarrete. A new inquisition case was launched against him in December 1526; he allegedly had laid hands on his female devotees and remarked that "saints were designed for the stupid." At the end of the trial, Medrano abjured a light suspicion of heresy. In March 1530, he was extradited to Toledo, where Francisca Hernández, Bernardino de Tovar, and Francisco Ortiz were already on trial.[3] The Toledo prosecutor accused him of false sanctity and errors against the faith; he confessed under torture that his attraction to Hernández was physical.

1. Llorca, *La inquisición española y los alumbrados,* 273–74. Medrano was formally accused by the prosecutor on April 28, 1530. Sometime after his written reply on May 3, 1530, this summary of the prosecutor's main points was drawn up, though Llorca does not specify where it occurs in the trial transcript.

2. Medrano may have been related to Maria de Cazalla, whose inquisition trial is excerpted in Document 12. The best scholarship on Medrano appears in Angela Selke, "El caso del Bachiller Antonio de Medrano: iluminado epicúreo del siglo xvi," *Bulletin hispanique* 58 (1956): 393–420, and the superb transcriptions of his inquisition trials in Javier Pérez Escohotado, *Proceso inquisitorial contra el Bachiller Antonio de Medrano (Logroño 1526–Calahorra 1527)* (Logroño: Gobierno de La Rioja, 1988), and *idem, Antonio Medrano, alumbrado epicúreo: proceso inquisitorial, Toledo 1530* (Madrid: Editorial Verbum, 2003).

3. For Tovar's case, see Homza, *Religious Authority,* chapter 1.

The Toledo inquisitors and their consultadores *disagreed over the verdict,[4] and Medrano's case was submitted to the Suprema, whose members favored a relatively light penalty. In 1532, Medrano abjured a grave* (de vehementi) *suspicion of heresy. The sentence secluded him perpetually in a monastery, suspended him as a priest for two years, commanded him to fast every Friday for seven years, and imposed a fine of thirty thousand* maravedís. *His Toledo prosecution is one of the first that I know of to accuse a male of false sanctity, among other charges.]*

1. On March 30, 1523, Medrano was prohibited by the inquisitors at Valladolid from being within five leagues of Francisca Hernández, under pain of major excommunication and being sentenced to perpetual prison. He himself has confessed that he was thus prohibited. Next, he held the prohibition in contempt; he denied having spoken to Francisca Hernández or having seen her after the 1523 prohibition, [though] it is assured that he spoke to her and saw her in Villa Vaquerín.

2. It is proven by two male witnesses[5] . . . that he said he had revelations from God that told him when someone was receiving the Eucharist or saying Mass in a state of grace or sin, or was preaching with good or evil intent, or was [simply walking around] in a state of sin. He said he knew who came to the Sacrament of the Eucharist unprepared and without devotion, etc. [sic]

3. [Medrano claimed] that after he knew Francisca Hernández, he felt the mercy of God [but] no longer felt the stimulation of the flesh. He could be in a bed with a woman without harm. . . .

4. He said he had divine grace to embrace a woman and get close to her flesh. There are two witnesses.

5. He held Francisca Hernández in as much esteem, or even more, as any of the saints in heaven, except Our Lady. . . .

7. He had an impeccability, and it was not corroborated by God.[6]

8. [Medrano claimed] that to kiss and touch another person was not a sin . . . and it was not a sin to stop observing feast days.

---

4. While the outside *consultadores* maintained that Medrano's statements were not heretical, the three inquisitors argued initially, at least, that he should be relaxed to the secular arm. Such a disagreement among men who had been vetting trials for years suggests perhaps the controversy of Medrano's case, as well as his ability to irritate authority figures.

5. Note the emphasis that the witnesses are doubled and male; see the Introduction.

6. "Impeccability" means an inability to sin. The meaning of the second half of the line is unclear.

9. [He also said that] not observing fasts and the Church's precepts was not a sin.

10. He asked a certain person not to tell the truth about the business with Francisca Hernández if the inquisitors called him to depose, especially if the inquisitors asked who had gone to Villa Vaquerín to speak with Francisca Hernández. . . .

11. Witness number 30 heard Medrano say that Francisca Hernández could not err in anything she said, because she was an *alumbrada*. Witness number 32 said the same, that he heard it said that Francisca Hernández was an *alumbrada*, and for this reason she knew who would go to Heaven or to Hell.

12. Medrano confessed that he believed Francisca knew hidden things and future matters. He believed he said that Francisca Hernández knew who went to Hell or to Heaven, and likewise Purgatory. But he didn't really believe it in the way it came out, namely, that she had such a gift; he was in the middle of saying other things when he said that, and men say lots of things that aren't true.

13. Medrano was heard to say that Francisca Hernández had infinite grace.

14. Medrano was heard to say that Francisca Hernández never sinned mortally. Next, the same witness says that Medrano said he held Francisca Hernández in greater esteem than St. Paul.

15. This witness heard from Medrano that Our Lord revealed the mystery of the Trinity to Francisca Hernández when she was three years old.[7]

16. Medrano confessed that he said he suffered most cruel pains on account of the punishments or pains of his followers and acquaintances.[8] . . .

17. Medrano confessed that he received goods and money from a number of people for himself and Francisca Hernández. . . .

19. [Medrano said] that he could embrace his followers, male and female, when they were nude, as if they were clothed. Cloth did nothing; the will, everything.

20. Medrano was heard to say that it was necessary in the past for him to perform certain penances and abstinences; when he was younger, he was a harsh man from fasts and disciplines and other abstinences. But now he no longer performed such works, because God had accomplished other, greater graces in him . . . and Medrano was heard to say that it was true he used to perform abstinences . . . and he was a fool at that time.

---

7. Meaning that at the age of three, Hernández came to understand how the Christian God could be three-in-one, or Father, Son, and Holy Spirit.

8. Medrano implied that he was taking on penances for the sins of his acquaintances.

21. Medrano was heard to say that men who performed abstinences and penances were low, and the whole business was low; and his life and Francisca Hernández' life exemplified only the highest liberty.

22. Medrano said that he would say Mass with a belt that Francisca Hernández sent him, and the belt was as blessed as if it were a bishop's.[9]

23. It is well known that Medrano said Francisca Hernández was sanctified and could not sin mortally.

---

9. Francisco Ortiz, introduced in Document 9, claimed that one of Hernández' belts helped cure him of masturbation. See Homza, "How to Harass an Inquisitor-General," 312.

DOCUMENT 12

Excerpts from the Trial of María de Cazalla, 1532–1534

[María de Cazalla was born in 1487 in Palma, near Murcia. Her family was related to the Valladolid branch of the Cazallas, which lost most of its members in the Valladolid auto de fe *of May 21, 1559.[1] Like the Valladolid Cazallas, María was a* converso; *she implied that her father was a long-standing convert, but guessed that her mother was tried for judaizing and reconciled. María's brother, Juan de Cazalla (1480–d. before 1532) had a successful ecclesiastical career: a Franciscan friar, he acted as chaplain to Toledo Archbishop Francisco Ximénez de Cisneros, and was assistant bishop* (coadjutor) *to the bishop of Ávila. María frequently and deliberately invoked her brother, "the bishop," during her inquisition trial.*

María was arrested by the Toledo tribunal in 1532 and released in 1534. She had confessed to inquisitors in 1525, during the Edict of Grace aimed at people involved with alumbradismo, *but there is no evidence that anyone contemplated her arrest for the next several years; instead, María came under suspicion after inquisitors seized Francisca Hernández in 1529 and prodded her for the names of accomplices and suspects (see Document 10). María de Cazalla and Francisca Hernández had some followers in common, most notably Bernardino de Tovar, a well-educated and well-connected cleric who had followed Francisca as a spiritual mentor until approximately 1523 and then shifted loyalties to María. Francisca's 1529 arrest provoked Tovar's as well, with María joining them in the prison of the Toledo tribunal three years later.[2] As the reader will see, Tovar and María continued to communicate after their arrests, contrary to prison rules and inquisitorial guidelines.*

María de Cazalla withstood torture in 1534. The inquisitors voted to absolve her for lack of proof on the charges of heresy, but asked her to abjure a light (de

---

1. The Valladolid Cazallas consisted of Pedro de Cazalla, royal auditor; his wife Leonor de Vivero; and their ten children. It used to be presumed that María de Cazalla and Pedro were siblings, but that thesis has been reversed. Both branches of the family were heavily involved in the more avant-garde currents of Spanish Catholicism: Pedro de Cazalla and his wife were great friends of Francisca Hernández and her circle; at the 1559 *autos de fe* in Valladolid, Leonor was burned in effigy for judaizing, while four of her children were burned at the stake for Lutheranism, and two more were sentenced to the *sanbenito* and perpetual prison. See Document 17.

2. Francisca Hernández was also transported to Valladolid in the early 1530s and gave evidence at the inquisition tribunal there as well.

levi) *suspicion of heresy for having conducted correspondence inside the tribunal with other prisoners. The Cazalla case touches on multiple topics in early modern Spanish and inquisition history, such as spiritual networks, the construction of female religious authority, literacy, the rhetoric of a successful defense, and even the vagaries of the Inquisition's prison system. María's trial mitigates any portrait of the Inquisition as a machine that processed helpless victims.]*

María's 1525 confession[3]

March 2, 1525[4]   María de Cazalla was ordered to return tomorrow, Saturday, and Sunday to give evidence about what she knows and what she was asked, notwithstanding that the six-day period of grace had passed.

Very Reverend Lords,

I, María de Cazalla, wife of Lope de Rueda, confess to your lordships that my spirit has done what it could, and I have begged Our Lord to help me, and I find I have nothing to say about such ugly and abominable errors [of the *alumbrados*]. If something else is alleged, I will suffer without being guilty (which is not the case with the other horrible sins for which I do find myself guilty), and I shall suffer whatever penalty Our Lord allows. I declare my guilt formally and from my whole heart, if I had some public or secret pride in speaking or in bidding the faithful to serve Jesus Christ, speaking sometimes with Friar Cristóbal, a lodger in La Sazeda, and with Bishop Cazalla, my brother. As I spoke to those two, so I spoke to others (though I believe it would have been few), speaking about the mercies that Our Lord performs for us in the Most Holy Sacrament of the altar. I said that sometimes my soul moved in a painful desire to finally see God without veils and without my body . . . and not trusting myself, fearing I might be deceived, I said it, and they told me that these were licit movements of my soul. But I did not say that the Sacrament did not have to be adored on the altar, because on the altar, through faith, one saw what one desired in the next life. If there is guilt here or a bad example, I request penance.

Other times, when people complained to me—chiefly friars who were afflicted with wicked thoughts—I told them that all was not lost just because

---

3. Milagros Ortega-Costa, *Proceso de la Inquisición contra María de Cazalla* (Madrid: Fundación Universitaria Española, 1978), 99–101. Topical and summary headings have been added for the assistance of the reader and do not appear in the original trial document.

4. María is confessing in the wake of the *alumbrado* scandal and the arrest of Isabel de la Cruz and Pedro Ruiz de Alcaraz. See Document 8.

such thoughts came to them, because some times God permitted [that sort of test]. In battling wicked thoughts and not giving in to them, there was an opportunity to purge the soul. Sometimes wicked thoughts happened to me, and I became more diligent by shunning them. If I gave people grounds to judge me, I pronounce my guilt.

Because I was speaking with the freedom that God wants His Christians to have (a freedom granted only through Him and not through Christians' own interests)—and because I thought that Christians should not serve Our Lord out of a fear of Hell, but only because He Himself deserves such service—I probably said something that people took the wrong way. Still, in my opinion I did not speak incorrectly, since I [always] first said that Christians who truly obeyed the Catholic Church and its prelates were the ones Our Lord liberated with His precious blood. I pronounce my guilt for my presumption in speaking. I am not guilty of intending to teach anyone. . . .

Witness statements against María de Cazalla, 1525[5]

February 15, 1525   In a sworn statement, Graviel Sánchez, parish priest of Pastrana, said among other things that María de Cazalla, resident of Guadalajara, came to Pastrana and stayed some days in the house of the wife of Çerezeda. This witness saw that María de Cazalla and Alonso López Sebastian spoke several times. This witness did not understand some of the things that they said; María de Cazalla spoke as if she were imparting doctrine in public and quoted certain literary authorities. This witness especially remembers that she expounded the Psalm "Behold how good and how jolly" [*ecce quam bonum et quam jocundum*], and many people went there to confer with her. This witness saw María de Cazalla go to the house of the *beatas* to speak with them, at the insistence of Alonso López Sebastian . . . and she seemed to speak with a great deal of wisdom for being a woman.

February 17, 1525   In a sworn statement, María, wife of García Alvarez Cavallero, resident of Pastrana, said among other things that approximately three years ago, the sister [María de Cazalla] of Bishop Cazalla was staying in the house of the wife of Çerezeda, who lives in Pastrana. María de Cazalla sent for this witness, and said, "They say you cry out in church," and this witness said yes, and María de Cazalla then said, "Be in God and through God, and don't rely upon the appearance of things."[6] . . .

---

5. Ortega-Costa, *Proceso*, 43–45.

6. The term María uses for "appearance" is "accidents" (*accidentes*), a learned concept that medieval theologians adopted from Aristotle to explain, among other things,

February 17, 1525   Catalina Sánchez, resident of Pastrana, wife of Fernando de la Dotora (deceased), said, among other things, that approximately
two years ago, when María de Cazalla was in the house of the wife of
Çerezeda, in the village of Pastrana, this witness went to see her along with
many other widows. María de Cazalla said to them, "I can well believe, sisters, that all of you wish to go to Paradise," and "Love God and keep His
Commandments," and then she took a book in Spanish and read a bit of an
Epistle of St. Paul. . . .

Evidence against María de Cazalla
from other inquisition trials, 1526

Statement of Mari Nuñez, March 13, 1526[7]   During the trial of Pedro
Ruiz de Alcaraz[8]—reconciled, resident of Guadalajara—a woman of mar-
riageable age named Mari Nuñez,[9] a servant of the lady Juana de Valencia,
resident of Guadalajara, appeared in Toledo on March 13, 1526, in the hearing room of the Holy Office, before the lord licentiates and inquisitors
Alonso de Mariana, Anton González Frances, and Baltasar de Castro, to ratify what she had said against Pedro Ruiz de Alcaraz and Isabel de la Cruz before religious and honest people.

Asked about the fourth chapter of her statement, where she said that Pedro Ruiz de Alcaraz said it weighed upon him because he had not sinned
more, she said that since that is written in her statement, she believes she
heard Pedro Ruiz de Alcaraz say it, but she currently has no memory of having heard him say it. As for his saying that he only confessed to comply with
the world, and that he accused his conscience of nothing, she said it is true
that she heard Alcaraz say that many times, and she also heard him say that
he only listened to sermons to comply with the community. When this

---

how the appearances of bread and wine could continue to exist after those substances
had been consecrated and changed into the body and blood of Christ. María was
making the theological point that the other woman should concentrate on substance,
not appearance.

7. Ortega-Costa, *Proceso,* 59–60.

8. Ruiz de Alcaraz was a key *alumbrado,* arrested in 1524.

9. Mari Nuñez appears to have been a spiritual leader in Guadalajara, whose authority was challenged by Isabel de la Cruz. De la Cruz' inquisition trial has been
lost, but we know Nuñez denounced her to the Inquisition in 1519. In this statement, Nuñez may have intended to depose primarily against Ruiz de Alcaraz and de
la Cruz, but she implicated María de Cazalla as well; hence Nuñez' statements were
copied from Ruiz de Alcaraz' trial record and inserted into Cazalla's.

witness praised some sermon that she heard, Pedro Ruiz de Alcaraz reprehended her, saying, "Of course, you would say that," implying that what she
and others said was contrary to what Pedro and his colleagues believed and
felt . . . and Alcaraz and Isabel de la Cruz and María de Cazalla laughed at
the sermons and mocked them. . . .

Likewise, Mari Nuñez appeared in the trial of Pedro Ruiz de Alcaraz on
March 15, 1526, in the city of Toledo, before the lord inquisitors and religious and honest people, to ratify what she had stated against Pedro Ruiz
de Alcaraz and Isabel de la Cruz. She said she asked Alcaraz and María de
Cazalla how they could give so much credit to Isabel de la Cruz and to her
follies. Pedro Ruiz de Alcaraz and María de Cazalla responded that they
would give more authority to Isabel de la Cruz than to St. Paul and all the
saints.

Statement of Mari Nuñez, Toledo, November 3, 1530[10]   Before the
lord inquisitor, licentiate Alonso Mexia, Mari Nuñez de Vargas,[11] who lives
on Santa Isabel in the houses of Juan Dávila de Ribera, swore a legal oath to
tell the truth about what she knew.

She was asked if she remembered having reported that she heard a woman
say that when her husband paid her the marital debt,[12] it was all completely
holy. She said she remembered that about two years before the revolt of the
comuneros[13] [i.e., c. 1518], she was speaking with María de Cazalla, wife of
Pedro de Rueda, resident of Guadalajara, and María told her that when she
was in the carnal act with her husband, she was more united to God than if
they had been in the loftiest prayer in the world.

She was asked if she heard María say that when her husband paid her the
marital debt, it was completely holy. She said she heard her say the aforesaid
words, or ones similar to them.

She was asked how María de Cazalla came to say those words. She said
that she was a great friend of María's before María became an *alumbrada*,
and they lived together in one house; and María [de Cazalla] asked her what

10. Ortega-Costa, *Proceso*, 60–61. The inquisitors are returning to Mari Nuñez for
evidence because she had previously incriminated María de Cazalla; by 1530, Cazalla had been implicated even further in heresy because Francisca Hernández had been
arrested in 1529 and had talked. See below, as well as Document 10.

11. The same Mari Nuñez who testified above.

12. A term in canon law that signifies the mutual obligation of husband and wife to
have sexual intercourse with each other, to prevent sin.

13. The *comunero* rebellion (1520–1521) was an urban revolt against the financial
exactions of Spanish king Charles I, elected Holy Roman Emperor in 1519; when it
began to take on social overtones, the Castilian nobility returned to supporting the
king, and the revolt quickly ended.

she had to do to unite herself to God, and Mari Nuñez told her to be clean in her soul and her body. As for her husband, she should abstain and be clean, except for what pertained to the generation of children. María de Cazalla took to extremes what this witness told her, and denied her husband the marital debt in such a way that her confessors told her it was inappropriate. Afterward María de Cazalla— being then on good terms with her husband and doing everything he wanted—told this witness what happened, reprehended her for what she had advised, and said those aforementioned words to her. . . .

Asked how she knew that María de Cazalla held the opinions of the *alumbrados,* she said she knew because she saw María de Cazalla converse in secret with Isabel de la Cruz and Pedro Ruiz de Alcaraz. She saw them confer night and day, and saw her altered in all her habits and spiritual exercises, so much so that the needleworkers of Orche said María de Cazalla was crazy. . . .

Statement of Francisca Hernández, Toledo, July 27, 1530[14]   Before the lord inquisitor licentiate Vaguer, Francisca Hernández—*beata* and prisoner— came out and swore a legal oath, and deposed the following, among other things:[15]

She knows and has heard that Bishop Cazalla is guilty of what is contained in the thirteenth chapter of [the 1525] edict against the *alumbrados.*[16] . . . the bishop holds that as his opinion, and so does his sister, María de Cazalla, wife of Pedro de Rueda [sic]. This witness saw it in a letter from María de Cazalla, which Bishop Cazalla showed to her; the letter said vocal prayer was not necessary, and taught as much to others. She heard from Bishop Cazalla that María de Cazalla said she conceived her children without carnal pleasure and did not love them as if they were her own, but rather as if they were her neighbors'. And this witness knows that the bishop is a great friend of the *alumbrados* and held their opinions, as she has said.

Statement of Francisca Hernández, Toledo, September 22, 1530   Before the lord inquisitor, licentiate Mexia, Francisca Hernández appeared, and under oath, said she had seen many letters from María de Cazalla . . . carried by a certain cleric whose name and birthplace she does not recall (though she believes he is from Ávila). This cleric carried the letters bound like a book, and María's followers said they wanted to make a book out of them.

14. Ortega-Costa, *Proceso,* 73–75.

15. On Hernández, see Documents 9, 10, and 11.

16. See Document 8: "13. External acts of prayer are irrelevant and unnecessary, and to perform them is imperfection. The *alumbrados* do not humble themselves at the name of Jesus, for humility has to be in the heart. A certain person was reprimanded because he knelt at a cross."

This witness read many of them, and [said] there was not one thing Catholic in them, [but] only things of the *alumbrados*.

Asked if she remembered anything contained in the letters, she said that in one letter, María de Cazalla claimed that she had conceived all her children without pleasure, and that she did not love her own children more than her neighbors'. She also deprecated the state of virginity, and said one earned more merit in the state of marriage, since she felt no pleasure in the carnal act. All the *alumbrados'* opinions were in those letters, but she cannot remember very well what they contained. . . .

Statement of Francisca Hernández, Toledo, October 12, 1530   Before Inquisitor Mexia, Francisca Hernández was asked to declare which people were *alumbrados,* since she had said that Miguel de Eguía[17] praised them. She said that those Miguel de Eguía had praised were Juan López [de Celaín]; Diego López; Bernardino de Tovar; Isabel de la Cruz; Pedro Ruiz de Alcaraz; Francisco Ximénez; *bachiller* Olivares; Gutierrez, chaplain of the Marquis [de Villena]; Marquina [sic]; Pedro de Cazalla; María de Cazalla; Mosen Pascual; Maestro [Juan de] Castillo;[18] and Licentiate [Pedro] Ortiz[19] of Toledo.

Next, this witness said she had heard from Bishop Cazalla that María de Cazalla, his sister, was the teacher of the *alumbrados* of Pastrana and Guadalajara, and that his judgment was nothing in comparison to hers. She also heard him say that exterior works were nothing, and his sister excelled so much and was so wise that she attained perfection in the matter of exterior works. Asked what works the bishop was referring to, the witness said praying, fasting, disciplines, bowing to statues, and other similar things. . . .

The *calificadores'* vote on the case of María de Cazalla[20]

April 16, 1531   In the very noble city of Toledo, being present in the hearing of the Holy Inquisition, the reverend lords Friar Antonio de Picarro and Friar Diego de Alcántara, friars from the Order of St. Dominic, and Franciscan friars Alonso de Ocaña, guardian of the monastery of San Juan de los Reyes, and Juan de Mondragon—all being theologians—saw the

17. Eguía was one of the foremost printers in the university town of Alcalá and ran in both lofty and experimental intellectual and spiritual circles.

18. Castillo was burned at the stake for Lutheranism in 1537.

19. Pedro Ortiz was Francisco Ortiz' brother; see Document 9 for Francisco Ortiz' encounter with the Inquisition.

20. Ortega-Costa, *Proceso,* 31–32. What follows is the deliberation of the theologians who acted as *calificadores;* they assessed the degree of heresy in a case before a formal accusation was launched. Their comments are in italics.

information that exists against María de Cazalla, wife of Pedro de Rueda,[21] resident of the city of Guadalajara, and all four unanimously voted as follows on the propositions against María de Cazalla.

First, that this defendant and Pedro Ruiz de Alcaraz said they would give greater authority to Isabel de la Cruz than to St. Paul and all the saints.

This proposition is injurious to the saints and to evangelical doctrine, and is very scandalous and heretical besides, because this defendant holds the authority of Isabel de la Cruz as greater than the Holy Spirit's, in which the doctrine of St. Paul and the saints is grounded.

The second proposition: this defendant said she was more united to God when she was having sex with her husband than when she was engaged in the loftiest prayer in the world. The defendant also said that when she paid the marital debt to her husband, it was completely holy.

As for the first part, the proposition is horrific, scandalous, heretical, and condemned by this Holy Office. The second part is offensive and scandalous and has the flavor of heresy.

The third proposition: this defendant had a book of letters, and a certain person saw there was not one thing Catholic in them, but only teachings of the *alumbrados.* One of the letters said that this defendant had conceived all her children without pleasure, and that she loved them no more than the children of her neighbors; she also deprecated the state of virginity because she said one gained more merit in the state of matrimony since she felt no pleasure in the carnal act.

The first part is very suspicious; the second is a very arrogant and horrific statement, and it has the flavor of heresy. . . . The third is heretical because it deprecates the excellent state of virginity, which was approved by Christ Our Redeemer as an excellent thing. . . . As far as the reason for preferring matrimony to virginity, the first phrase—which says that marriage is worth more than virginity— is heretical and against the Gospel, which attributes a hundred-fold benefit to the celibate, and a thirty-fold to the married. The [very] idea has also been condemned. As far as the other statement is concerned—that since she felt no physical pleasure, etc.—it is offensive and has the flavor of heresy.

The fourth proposition: this defendant said that people sinned mortally every time they loved something well, whether husbands or children or anything else, according to the love of God. She continued to hold this opinion even after she was challenged over it.

This proposition is very dangerous, very scandalous, and heretical, and is condemned by this Holy Office. It contradicts evangelical law.

---

21. By this point in the transcript, María de Cazalla's husband's name is consistently and mistakenly transcribed as *Pedro* de Rueda (her brother-in-law) instead of *Lope* de Rueda.

Besides these propositions, this defendant has voiced others that are very arro-
gant, offensive, scandalous, and suspicious, on account of this defendant being
so presumptuous as to take on the office of preaching and teaching doctrine,
which is granted only to wise men in holy orders.[22]

Signed by Friar Joanes de Mondragon; Friar Antonius Picarro; Friar Diego
de Alcántara, who was there [sic]; Friar Alonso de Ocaña

Order of imprisonment for María de Cazalla[23]

After the aforesaid, on April 18, 1531, the very reverend lord inquisitors,
Alonso Mexia, Juan Yañes, and Vaguer [sic] said that having seen the opin-
ions of the theologians and the information that exists against María de
Cazalla, their votes and opinion are to seize María de Cazalla, with the se-
questration of her goods. Signed by Licentiate A. Mexia, Licentiate Juan
Yañes, Licentiate Vaguer. I, Francisco Ximénez, notary, was present.

Recommendation from the Suprema[24]

In the city of Medina del Campo, October 26, 1531, the lords licentiate
Aguirre, bishop of Orense and Mondoñedo, and licentiate Hernando Niño,
both from the Suprema, said that after having examined for various days this
information and the things contained in this folder against María de Cazalla, they unanimously voted that before anything else, the judgment of Friar
Juan de Salamanca and Master Quintana should be sought on the following
proposition, to wit, "That she would give more authority to Isabel de la Cruz
than to St. Paul and to all the saints." Salamanca and Quintana gave their
opinion on [the same proposition] when it was voted upon in the trial(s) of
Pedro Ruiz de Alcaraz and Isabel de la Cruz; their judgment should be placed
in the trial record of María de Cazalla. The objections that resulted against
Mari Nuñez, when she was a witness in those two earlier trials, should be inserted too. And Francisca Carrillo, who was a witness against María de Cazalla, should be reexamined so that she might explain her statement, which
was that María de Cazalla had said that every time she loved something
well according to the love of God, whether husband or children or anything
else, she sinned mortally. An explanation is necessary because, given what

22. The same sort of objection was lodged against Francisco Ortiz for treating Francisca Hernández as a spiritual mentor. See Document 9.

23. Ortega-Costa, *Proceso*, 32.

24. *Ibid.*, 35–36. The following paragraph demonstrates the Inquisition's tremendous skill at cross-referencing evidence as officials pulled evidence from one decade
or trial into another.

Francisca Carrillo reported, it looks as if María de Cazalla said something else.[25] Likewise the original confession of María de Cazalla [from 1525] has to be seen so that any marginal notations or information that her confession lacks in this trial, can be filled in if it appears in the original. . . . Once this is done, these inquisitors shall go over this information with learned men, and they shall send it, with their opinions, to the [entire] Suprema. I, Lope Díaz de Carate, secretary of the said Council, was present

Arrest order for María de Cazalla[26]

April 22, 1532. We, the inquisitors against heretical depravity and apostasy in the city and archbishopric of Toledo, etc., order you, the honorable Francisco de Horozco, constable of this Holy Office, to seize María de Cazalla, wife of Lope de Rueda, resident of the city of Guadalajara, wherever you find her, even if she is in a sacred or privileged place. Once she is seized, you shall sequester her goods, furniture, landed property, and semimovable goods, wherever you find them, before the honorable jurist Diego de Ávila, scribe of the sequestrations of this Holy Office, with Juan de Villa, the receiver of this Holy Office, or his deputy, if Juan de Villa cannot be present. You shall place the goods in the care of one or two good people who are honest and creditable, who shall hold the confiscated goods. We order those good people— under penalty of major excommunication and a fine of 50,000 *maravedís* apiece for the extraordinary expenses of this Holy Office—that they accept the said charge and not have recourse to the said goods, nor give any part of them to any person whatsoever without our permission and explicit order.[27] Once María de Cazalla has been seized, bring her to the prison of this Holy Office and hand her over to its prison warden. So executed in Toledo, April 22, 1532. Licentiate A. Mexia; Licentiate J. Yañes; Dr. Vaguer. By order of the lord inquisitors. Juan Ferrandes Obregon, notary.

First interview and genealogy[28]

In the city of Toledo, May 3, 1532, in the hearing room of the Holy Office, the very reverend lords Licentiate Alonso Mexia and Dr. Pedro Vaguer,

25. Francisca Carrillo was reexamined on April 4, 1533, by Inquisitor Alonso Mexia. She noted that a line was missing from her original testimony; in 1525, María de Cazalla had said that every time she loved something well, whether husband or children or anything else, if that love were *not* according to the love of God, she sinned mortally. *Ibid.*, 51

26. Ortega-Costa, *Proceso,* 30.

27. See the instructions about seizures in Document 7.

28. Ortega-Costa, *Proceso,* 101–03.

inquisitors, ordered María de Cazalla—wife of Lope de Rueda, resident of Guadalajara, prisoner in the jail of the Holy Office— brought before them. When she was brought out, their Lordships received the necessary legal oath from her. She swore that she should speak the truth about everything she knew, had done, and said against our Catholic Faith, or had seen others do or say.

Then, because Inquisitor Vaguer left the hearing, Lord Inquisitor Mexia put the following questions to María de Cazalla.

Asked her name, she said she was called María de Cazalla. She is the wife of Lope de Rueda, a resident of Guadalajara, and approximately forty-five years old.

Her parents

Gonzalo Martínez, resident of Palma[29] who worked in farming, and who came from very old converts; she suspects he was reconciled, but she does not know because she was little when he was reconciled, assuming he was. He died more than twenty years ago, more or less.

Isabel de Cazalla, who also was a *conversa*, and she suspects her mother was reconciled, though she does not know it for certain. She died more than seventeen years ago.

Her paternal grandparents

She said she did not know either of her paternal grandfathers or grand-mothers [sic], nor did she know their names.

Her maternal grandparents

She said she believed that her maternal grandfather was called Diego de Cazalla, a native of Cazalla. She did not know her maternal grandmother. She did not know if they were condemned or reconciled.

Her father's siblings

She said she did not know a single one of her father's siblings, because her father was from Ecija, her mother was from Cazalla, and this defendant was born in Palma.

Her mother's siblings

Alonso de Cazalla, resident of Ecija, treasurer of the Count of Palma, deceased. The Inquisition never touched him, so far as she knew.

---

29. This town of Palma is in the area of Murcia.

Francisco de Cazalla, resident of Palma, steward or servant of the Count of Palma, and the Inquisition never touched him, so far as she knew. Deceased.

Rodrigo de Cazalla, resident of Palma, servant of the Count of Palma, deceased, and the Inquisition never touched him, so far as she knew.

Beatriz de Cazalla, wife of Gonzalo de Cabra, resident of Palma, deceased, and she does not know if the Inquisition touched her.

Brothers and sisters of this defendant

Bishop Friar Juan de Cazalla, of the Order of San Francisco, deceased.

Francisca de Carmona, wife of Hernando de Carmona, resident of Ecija, deceased.

Ynés, who died as a maiden.

Bachiller Diego de Cazalla, doctor, who is older than this defendant, and who lives either in Palma or Ecija.

The Inquisition has not touched any of them.

Children of this defendant

Catalina de Rueda, maiden of twenty-one.

Isabel de Cazalla, who is two years younger, maiden.

Juana Bautista, who is younger than Isabel.

Pedro de Rueda, a student who is in Alcalá, younger than the aforesaid girls.

María de Rueda, younger than Pedro de Rueda.

Ana, who is four years old.

When María de Cazalla was asked if she knows why she was brought here as a prisoner, she said she does not know, unless the Inquisition was suspicious of some chatter that this defendant had spoken ignorantly and carelessly. She confessed to those remarks in a document in her own hand, presented before the lord inquisitor Mariana [in 1525]. At the moment she remembers nothing, but if something she said comes back to her, she is ready to confess and to say everything she remembers very clearly . . . and to request mercy, if she has erred in something

The admonitions[30]

First admonition [May 3, 1532]

Inquisitor Mexia admonished her for the sake of God Our Lord and His Blessed Mother, the Virgin Mary, Our Lady, to speak the truth about

---

30. Ortega-Costa, *Proceso,* 103.

everything she knows and has done or said, or knows about someone else, which could be against our Holy Catholic Faith. If she would act in this way, she would do what is appropriate, and would unburden her conscience, and she would be treated mercifully. If she did not comply, they would hear from the chief prosecutor and perform justice.

She said she would think well and completely about everything she might remember and know, whether about herself or others, and she would then disclose it. She was returned to the prison. I, Agustín Yllán, notary, was present.[31]

June 7, 1532: Hearing with Inquisitor Mexia[32]

. . . Asked if this defendant told some people that neither Holy Communion nor confession satisfied her, the defendant said that she remembered . . . that sometimes she did not feel satisfied at the altar [but] it was her own fault, because she was not as well-disposed [to receive the Eucharist] as she wished. . . .

Asked if this defendant said she could hardly restrain herself from laughing when she went to certain feast days at the church and monasteries and saw the care that the clerics, friars, or nuns put into adorning the altars, placing ornaments, and all the other things pertaining to the divine cult . . . this defendant said that when she saw the care that went into preparing the altars and things of the church, she sometimes said that if they were to put as much diligence into cleansing their consciences and abstaining from wicked customs, God would be greatly pleased. . . .

Asked if it was true that she told some people that confession did not sit well with her, and did not hold it as good, she said she never said such a thing.

Asked if this defendant said that a certain confessor was like a stone, she replied that if some confessor were ignorant and an idiot, she might have said he was like a stone, that he sat there like a stone, and that he neither gave good advice nor said worthwhile things. Asked if she had reprehended and made fun of people who went to Mass, calling them "Mass-lovers" or "Pope-massers"[33] and saying "May God preserve me, He must not have

---

31. Inquisitor Mexia issued two more admonitions on May 8 and May 14, 1532. Because María did not confess at any time during the admonitory process, the inquisitors began to describe her as persistently denying the charges (*negativa*).

32. Mexia interrogated María on June 7, 8, 10, and 12, 1532. For the following excerpts from June 7, 1532, see Ortega-Costa, *Proceso,* 105–08.

33. The adjectives in these phrases—*miseras* and *papamisas*—hint at misery in the first instance, "potato" or even "stupidity" in the second. Thanks to Benjamin Ehlers for this insight.

[much of a] place in their houses, and what more did they find in the church than in their houses," she said she never said such a thing. . . .

Asked if she has said that there are loftier things than the Passion of Christ, which the devout contemplate, this defendant believed that she would rather have said "that it was better to contemplate the divinity than the humanity of Our Lord Jesus Christ."[34]

June 8, 1532: Second hearing with Inquisitor Mexia[35]

. . . . Asked if this defendant told people that she held Luther, his works, and his writings as good, she said she never said so. Nevertheless, at the beginning, this defendant heard that Luther's things [sic] had some appearance of good. Hearing it said, this defendant would have said so too. Asked which Lutheran works initially had the appearance of good, she said there were some theses, and at the moment she couldn't remember which ones they were, and if she remembered, she would say so. . . .

Asked if this defendant has cited certain authorities of Sacred Scripture in favor of Luther, she said no.

Asked if she has called St. Thomas an Aristotelian, and Duns Scotus a dreamer and swollen with pride, and if she has criticized scholasticism, she said she has never said so.

Asked if she has praised Erasmus and said that he deserves to be canonized, and that everything he has written was like the Gospel to her. This defendant said that she has frequently praised Erasmus and his works. This defendant has read a *Paternoster* of his in Spanish, as well as the *Enchiridion* and the *Colloquies*. She has considered them good works and will continue to do so until the Church determines something different.[36]

Asked if this defendant has said that she would give more authority to Isabel de la Cruz than to St. Paul and all the saints, the defendant said she never said so, but that she held Isabel as a good woman and a servant of God, until she saw her condemned for being the reverse. . . .

June 10, 1532: Third hearing with Inquisitor Mexia[37]

. . . . Asked if this defendant has written letters, and to whom, regarding the opinions of the *alumbrados,* this defendant said she has written letters to

34. This accusation was also leveled against Pedro Ruiz de Alcaraz: Ortega-Costa, *Proceso,* 108, n. 51.

35. For the session on June 8, 1532, *ibid.,* 108–11.

36. For the circulation of Erasmus' works in Spain, see Bataillon, *Erasmo y España.*

37. The hearing on June 10, 1532 is in Ortega-Costa, *Proceso,* 111–19.

many people, most notably to Isabel de la Cruz, *bachiller* Bernardino de To-var, Mari Nuñez, and a canon of Palencia who is called Francisco (she doesn't remember his surname); and to Pedro de Cazalla, resident of Valladolid. . . . Asked if she wrote to Francisca Hernández . . . and to Miguel de Eguía, she said that though she did not write to Francisca Hernández, she sent letters to her for other people. And she thinks she wrote to Miguel de Eguía. Then she reversed herself and said she had not written to Miguel de Eguía, but be-lieves instead that she wrote to Diego de Eguía, his brother.

Asked on what subjects she wrote to these people, and them to her, she said she does not remember. The principal subject was how to serve God.

Asked if she had conversed at length with the aforesaid people, and if they had visited her, she said that Tovar went to her house many times to see Bishop Cazalla, her brother, and herself. Asked if Dr. Vergara[38] and his sis-ter Isabel de Vergara, and Isabel de la Cruz and Pedro Ruiz de Alcaraz and the others communicated with her, she said that Isabel de Vergara was in this defendant's house for three or four months, recovering from an illness that she had. Isabel de la Cruz also communicated very often with this defen-dant, because she taught this defendant's two daughters how to do needle-work; Isabel de la Cruz came to her house one or two times. Sometimes Pedro Ruiz de Alcaraz came to her house. Dr. Vergara never came to her house, although this defendant believes she wrote to him sometimes. She has also has written many letters to a Friar Cristóbal, and a Friar Alonso de Moya, of the Order of St. Francis, who are in La Sazeda. . . .

Asked if this defendant taught certain people, telling them not to rely upon external things and the exterior works of adoration, prayer, and hu-mility, she said she often said that exterior works had to be treated as a way to progress to interior ones. The defendant remembers that seven and a half or ten years ago (a little more or less), while she was living in Guadalajara, she asked Mari Nuñez if it was enough to adore God in thought when they approached the Eucharist on the altar, without moving the lips of the mouth. Mari Nuñez told this defendant that being preoccupied with thoughts of God was not enough when approaching the Eucharist, because some heretics had risen up who held that opinion. From that moment forward this de-fendant had new vigilance in adoring God with both lips and heart. . . .

---

38. Juan de Vergara was Bernardino de Tovar's half-brother and was even better ed-ucated and more successful, acting as secretary to three archbishops of Toledo. Ver-gara was arrested by the Inquisition in 1533 when his secret correspondence with Tovar—who was being held in the Toledo tribunal—was discovered. On the basis of Vergara's own trial record, we would never have known that he and his sister were personally acquainted with María de Cazalla. The inquisitors in Toledo asked Ver-gara only about *alumbrados* in general and Francisca Hernández (Tovar's former men-tor) in particular; see Homza, *Religious Authority*, chapter 1.

Asked if this defendant said that the Holy Office of the Inquisition was not doing right by the *alumbrados,* that the inquisitors did not understand the *alumbrados,* that the *alumbrados* had good ideas, and that only men with a holy spirit could understand them . . . she said that she remembered having said, "May God give an upright spirit to the people who have to judge the *alumbrados,* so they might know how to determine such subtle matters and how to distinguish among the accused." This is what she said when she held the *alumbrados* as good.

Asked which *alumbrados* this defendant held as good, she said Pedro Ruiz de Alcaraz and Isabel de la Cruz, and she might also say the same about *bachiller* Bernardino de Tovar.

Asked if she knows who has or had Lutheran books that were condemned and suspicious regarding our Holy Faith, she said she does not know who has or had Lutheran books. . . . One day Master Diego Hernández told the defendant that they had treated Tovar badly for having read the works of Luther, and this defendant replied, "If Tovar reads them or has them, it will be with permission of the inquisitors, because Tovar is educated." . . .

Asked if she knows who wrote the book called *Doctrina cristiana,* she said she heard it was by one Valdés[39] who was studying at the University of Alcalá. Asked if anyone had praised this book to her, she said she did not remember. [But] she did remember that *bachiller* Tovar reprehended Valdés for having published the book in such a hurry, without further correction and emendation. This defendant had a copy of the said *Doctrina cristiana,* and one day she heard Pedro de Vitoria, of the Order of St. Francis, preach, and he said wicked things about the book. This defendant consequently threw it into a bottom of a chest until she could see that the book was cleared [of suspicion]; she ordered her daughters not to read any more of it. She did not remember who sent her the book, except that they sent it from Alcalá. . . .

Prosecutor's accusation, June 12, 1532[40]

I, *bachiller* Diego Ortiz de Angulo, chief prosecutor for this Holy Office of the Inquisition of this city and archbishopric of Toledo, and the bishopric

39. Juan de Valdés was born in Cuenca around 1505 and died in Naples in 1541. His name first comes up in the trial record of *alumbrado* Pedro Ruiz de Alcaraz; both men served at the court of the Marquis of Villena in Escalona. Valdés appeared at the University of Alcalá at the end of the 1520s, where he published the *Diálogo de doctrina cristiana* in 1529; the book provoked some interest from the Inquisition. By the early 1530s, Valdés was in Italy, acting as a secretary to Pope Clement VII; upon Clement's death in 1534, he found a circle of friends and supporters in Naples. Valdés' debt to Spanish *alumbradismo* and impact on Italian evangelism is presumed to have been substantial.

40. Ortega-Costa, *Proceso,* 127–34.

of Sigüenza and its district, hereby appear before Your Reverence in order to denounce and accuse, in the best way that I can by law, María de Cazalla, wife of Lope de Rueda, resident of Guadalajara, prisoner in the jail of this Holy Office, who is present. I accuse her of being a heretic, an apostate from our Holy Catholic Faith, an abettor and defender of heretics, and a defamer of the Holy Office and its ministers and officials. . . . she has held and believed Lutheran errors, and those of people called *alumbrados* (who are better called blind), and other kinds of heresy. . . .

The first charge: that María de Cazalla, not believing in confession or that God is in the Eucharist (or that God is not there entirely, like a Lutheran), said that neither the Eucharist nor confession contented her. Sometimes she said she would rather be someplace where two hangmen would whip her than in Mass. And, in fact she attended neither Mass nor confession except to comply with the world, which goes along according to what it sees. . . .

Next, María de Cazalla, not believing Our Lord Jesus Christ was in the Eucharist, said: "O Lord, what blindness is this, and what blindness is in the world, that they decide where You are, when You are infinite; that people look for You in a temple of songs, but neither look for You nor find You in themselves, which are living temples. And to this, laws bind us." . . .

Next, María de Cazalla and other people said that there were other, much loftier things for the devout to contemplate than the Passion of Christ. Like an *alumbrada*, she considered the Passion of Christ and its mysteries as imperfect and defective. . . .

Likewise, María de Cazalla, not having a high opinion of Holy Scripture or the holy doctors of the Church, called St. Thomas an Aristotelian and Duns Scotus a dreamer and swollen with pride. She condemned scholasticism; considering it as nothing, she said, "I believe that the Child Jesus is lost in the sophisms and arguments that you pronounce." And she believes in and quotes Erasmus and holds him like the Gospel, and greatly praises him, saying that he deserved to be canonized, even though he has voiced many errors and scandalous, evil-sounding things against our Holy Catholic Faith in his writings. She greatly praises the book called *Doctrina cristiana,* when it contains errors against the Faith.

Next, María de Cazalla and other people said they would give more authority to Isabel de la Cruz than to St. Paul and all the saints, even though Isabel de la Cruz is and was a heretic and was declared and reconciled as such, as is publicly known and notorious to Your Reverence and to everyone, and on account of her heresy, Isabel de la Cruz is in the perpetual prison [of the Inquisition]. . . .

Next, María de Cazalla, coming from sermons in which [the purchase and value of] papal bulls were preached, considering papal bulls, indulgences, and pardons to be a joke, and believing they benefited no one and achieved nothing, said, "Look, I've bought Christianity and am carrying it around, for one is not a Christian unless you have these bulls; I'd rather throw the money into something else." . . .

Next, María de Cazalla, not having a high opinion of religious orders, said that they were all flesh and ceremonies, which explained why there was evil in the monasteries; and she said there were no Christian men to marry her daughters. She wished her sons-in-law were *alumbrados* or Lutherans, like she was.

Next, María de Cazalla and other people believed that exterior works of adoration achieved nothing and were unnecessary, and to perform them was imperfection. They did not humble themselves physically at the name of Jesus, for they believed humility had to be present in the heart. As for those who said they gained pardon through physical acts of humility and the prayers they performed in the name of Jesus, María de Cazalla and other people said that amounted to business transactions. María de Cazalla and the others taught that vocal prayer was unnecessary. . . .

María de Cazalla and others believed that there was no Mary Magdalene, nor a St. Anne who married three times, nor were there three Marys; they thought the whole thing was a joke. When she was told that the Church held such matters as true, she replied that it was a joke, and some stupid people had so ordered it. . . .

When the clergy raised the Eucharist at the altar, María de Cazalla, kneeling, and holding her body straight up and looking disengaged, held her cloak with her hands. She did not look at the Eucharist, but rather lowered her eyes to the ground and looked toward the door through which people entered. And she did the same when they raised the chalice and the Host, not believing that God and true man were beneath the appearances of bread and wine in the Eucharist.

María de Cazalla, believing that matrimony and sex were worth more than the state of virginity, said that when her husband paid her the marital debt, everything was completely holy. She said that when she was having sex with her husband, she was more united to God than if she had been praying the loftiest prayer in the world.

Next, at other times María de Cazalla said that she conceived her children without carnal pleasure, and that she didn't love them as if they were her own children, but like the children of her neighbors. She reprehended a certain lady who deeply loved her own children, calling that lady a butcher of the flesh who had a piece of her heart in each child.

Likewise, when asked why people didn't come to see her after she had given birth, María de Cazalla said, "May God remove that disgrace from me," as if she considered childbirth disgraceful. She deprecated the state of virginity because she said she gained more merit in the state of matrimony, because she felt no carnal pleasure in sex.

Next, María de Cazalla, with the affection she has for the opinions, errors, and things of the *alumbrados,* wrote many letters to her followers . . . and there was not one thing Catholic in the letters, only the *alumbrados'* errors and opinions.

Next, like a teacher and dogmatist of the *alumbrados,* María de Cazalla preached the *alumbrados'* sayings in public and taught them, quoting authorities and psalms of Holy Scripture, and expounding it all in Spanish, twisting Holy Scripture and the words of its learned commentators for her wicked and hurtful purpose. Many people went to hear her as if she were a preacher, [which caused] great scandal in the community, since she could not and should not have preached. Such preaching is prohibited because she is a woman. And even if she were a man, it would be against the law and evangelical precept to be creating conventicles and holding illicit, forbidden, and suspicious meetings. . . .

As an abettor and defender of heretics, and a defamer of the Holy Office and its ministers and officials, María de Cazalla said that this Holy Office did not do right by the *alumbrados* and did not understand them. She said that the *alumbrados* had good opinions, and to understand them, it was necessary to have men of holy spirit, who were enlightened themselves, as was a certain person whom she named. . . .

Though María de Cazalla knows about people who possess suspicious books against our Holy Catholic Faith, she has not declared or revealed them to Your Reverence, as she is obliged to do. [She has behaved] like someone suspected of heresy and someone who approves of the books' errors.

Next, María de Cazalla has been and is someone who conceals and participates with heretics and people suspect in our Holy Catholic Faith. She was and is obliged to reveal [the names of] those people and their errors.

Likewise, above and beyond the aforesaid, María de Cazalla has been seen by others to have committed many other errors and suspicious, scandalous, and evil-sounding things against the faith. She knows this and maliciously covers it up, thinking it will be a secret between her and the other people, and that it will not come to Your Reverences' attention through another party. I solemnly declare I will state this charge [of concealment] during this prosecution whenever it is my right to do so. I solemnly assure the inquisitors that I add this charge to this accusation.

. . . . I request Your Reverences treat my account as truthful and pronounce and declare that María de Cazalla has been and is a heretic, an apostate from our Holy Catholic Faith, an abettor and defender of heretics, a defamer of the Holy Office and its ministers and officials. May she incur a sentence of major excommunication and lose all her goods and landed property, which shall be confiscated; her property from the day she committed the said crimes up to now shall belong to the Exchequer and Royal Treasury of His

Majesty. May she be relaxed to justice and the secular arm. I request Your Reverences to declare likewise that her descendants—through the masculine and feminine lines up through the first degree,[41] inclusively—shall be deprived of all public offices and benefices, whether ecclesiastical and secular, and of worldly honor. May they be perpetually disqualified and incapable of having, reaching, or holding other offices and benefices henceforth.[42] . . .

I ask that Your Reverences order María de Cazalla to respond truthfully to each chapter of this accusation, without the counsel of any person whatsoever.[43] I beg that justice be completed by the holy and noble office of Your Reverences.

Bachiller Diego Ortiz de Angulo.

María de Cazalla's oral response to the accusation

The accusation being thus presented and read aloud to María de Cazalla, word for word, each chapter individually, an oath was received from her according to the necessary legal form. She was ordered to respond truthfully under charge of the oath to what was contained in the accusation. What she said is as follows:

To the first chapter, she says she has already replied to this, and she is very weak and tired, and at present she could not respond without much effort. She consequently asked that they give her the accusation and she would look at it. She also asked that they give her paper so that when she remembers something, she may say it in writing. And because of her requests and the late hour, the lord inquisitor ordered that she be given the accusation and two folios of paper with four sides. She was returned to her cell.[44]

The written reply to the accusation[45]

In Toledo, June 17, 1532, being in the hearing room of the Holy Office, the very reverend lord licentiate Alonso Mexia, inquisitor, ordered María de

41. "Up through the first degree" meant that María's immediate family (husband and children) would be categorized as infamous, as would her direct blood relations, such as her own siblings and her parents, if they were alive.

42. On the legal category of infamy, see the Introduction.

43. This is a bold request, since inquisition instructions explicitly allowed for a defense lawyer if the defendant asked for one.

44. María's plea—to retire and respond later—violated the Inquisition's procedures.

45. Ortega-Costa, *Proceso,* 134–40. María was allowed to ponder the accusation and her response for five days.

Cazalla brought before him. She presented this reply, which is about three pages long, to the prosecutor's accusation:

Very Reverend Lords,

i. I say to the first that I never expressed doubt in the Eucharist. Sometimes I said that I remained sad and dissatisfied with the preparation I underwent to receive Communion. As for the sacrament of confession [i.e., penance], I said I never was as entirely prepared as I wanted, nor did I do everything that was in me. I also remember saying that I was so sad and heartsick over my bodily pains that it seemed I would have less affliction if hangmen whipped me or other tortures of this sort. . . . I have never lacked faith in the sacraments.

ii. To the second charge, I remember saying many times, "O Lord, what blindness is this, that people look for You in temples of stone, instead of looking for You in living temples; [recall] what Christ says, 'The kingdom of God that you seek is inside you.'" . . . We should look at all times and in all places so that we worthily might find God in the temples and in the Church's sacraments. And my words might well have been erroneous in style, but this is what I intended to say, and what I remember having said. . . .

viii. I never held the memory of the Passion of Christ as spiritual imperfection. I said that the loftiest thing is contemplation of His divinity, not His humanity.

xi. I do not remember ever having said those things about those doctors. I have held Erasmus as good and have praised his works—the ones I have heard [sic] in Spanish— and thus I have said that I would hold him as good until the Catholic Church advised us of something else. I read the *Doctrina cristiana* and praised some things in it that were done well, such as how to know sins and how we violate God's commandments. A friar, Pedro de Vitoria, preached once a long time ago and said that the *Doctrina cristiana* was wicked, and from that moment on I threw it into the bottom of a chest and ordered my daughters not to read it until Your Lordships determined what they would do. I hold nothing as good or well taught except what the Catholic Church says and holds as good. My words might well err, but I cannot be a heretic without wishing to be so.

xii. I never said I would give more authority to Isabel de la Cruz than to the saints. I said I held her as a good Christian and never saw errors in her. I said this before she was a prisoner, when I could not make myself believe the things that were said about her until I saw her condemned. After she was condemned, I then held her as the Church denounced her. . . .

xv. Many times I remember joking or gossiping about the ignorance of the community in this matter of buying papal bulls, as people thought there was nothing more to this business than paying two *reales,* without paying attention to what the Pope says, namely that people have to be truly penitential and contrite, and have fulfilled their penance. And about this I [may] have spoken wildly, but I hold papal bulls as good, and I have bought them and given them. . . .

xvi. Many times I said that I saw vanities in the monasteries, and many unhappy monks and conflicts between them. These things displeased me, and for this reason I did not force my daughters to enter convents against their will, but rather influenced them and told their confessors to guide them to become nuns of their own free will. On the subject of husbands, I said the main thing I looked for was that they should be virtuous and good Christians. . . .

xviii. I never held that opinion. I always held vocal prayer as necessary and very good, and exterior works have to have the intention that I have stated; without such intent, they are imperfect. Performing exterior works for the sole purpose of going after pardons [from God] amounts to a business transaction. . . .

xx. I heard from my brother, Bishop Friar Juan de Cazalla, that there were ancient, holy doctors who had the opinion that St. Anne had not been married more than once; and that María Madala [sic], sister of Lazarus, was not the one whom Our Lord pardoned in Simon's house, but rather there were two Marías. My brother left two books about this, one on St. Ana and the other on the Marías. And I have already said that I simply repeated what I heard my brother say, and I never had, nor do I have, any other opinion except what the Catholic Church has. I also heard my brother say that modern doctors had a different opinion about this. . . .

xxii. Sometimes, when the Host was lifted up [during Mass], I covered my face a little with my cloak, for many reasons: either because I sometimes had the urge to cry, or other times because I was cold. If I turned my head toward the door or lowered my eyes to the ground, that would have been done out of restlessness. I deny doing it to avoid seeing the sacrament of the Eucharist.

xxiii. I have already responded to this.

xxiv. On what pertains to pleasure, I never spoke about it in front of witnesses, except to my confessors, or to a person from whom I intended to get advice. On not loving my children like my own, I don't

remember having said it. I have reprehended myself and others because each child takes away a piece of our heart, and many times I
have noted that we love our children in a disorderly way. . . .

xxv. After I gave birth, some people came to see me, some with good in-
tentions and others jokingly. They said, "What's this, do the devout
give birth?" and I replied, "Well, if [you're implying that] it's evil to
give birth, may God remove this disgrace from me, namely that *you*
think giving birth is evil." I thought it was shameful to offend God
by feeling wickedly about matrimony. I never spoke ill of virginity,
and God knows how much it attracted me from a distance. I say "from
a distance" because I was not a virgin and wished to be.

xxvi. I have written many letters to my relatives and friends. . . . I do not
think the [mere writing of the] letters is so at fault. Show me the letters, and if I recognize them as mine, and if they contain errors, I shall
confess it. Neither in my letters nor my words did I intend to err or
to feel anything contrary to our Catholic Faith. Rather I desired that
we should all grow closer to obeying God.

xxvii. Many times, when my ladies[46] and friends and relatives of Lope de
Rueda visited me, or I visited them, I frequently turned everyone
away from gossiping by saying, "I heard such and such a preacher, and
he said this well, and we shall ponder it for our salvation," or "I read
that a doctor said this in such and such a book," or I took up a book
to read aloud. There were [only a] few people there, and most were
my relatives. Other times I had some hours of Our Lady in my hand,
and reading them, I expounded some verse or psalm or antiphon of
Our Lady, or prayer. From long-standing custom and having prayed
a long time in Spanish, I understand a bit, but I never said more than
the literal meaning.[47]

---

46. María's phrase—*visitándome mis señoras*—is provocative, especially when combined with the testimony that her letters had been made into a book. Though she
insisted she had no intention of practicing *magisterium*—that is, teaching with authority—it seems clear that she acted as a spiritual director for a substantial number
of individuals, both male and female. For an analogous authority on the part of
María's predecessor and spiritual mentor, Isabel de la Cruz, see Ángela Muñoz Fernández, "Madre y mestra, autora de la doctrina. Isabel de la Cruz y el *alumbradismo*
toledano del primer tercio del siglo XVI," in *De leer a escribir, I: La educación de las
mujeres: ¿libertad o subordinación?,* ed. Cristina Segura Graiño (Madrid: A.C. AL-
MUDAYNA, 1996), 99–122.

47. Thus María allegedly concentrated on the first level of scriptural interpretation,
the "literal" or historical meaning of a scriptural text. By the twelfth century, Western theologians had codified four possible levels of scriptural exegesis: the literal

xxix. I have never considered that this Holy Office was acting incorrectly. . . . I hold this Holy Office as very necessary and holy. If I had some misgiving that I uttered verbally, the witnesses' depositions would have relayed it. The people who deposed on this subject were not attending to their consciences; they inflated my remarks, or spoke on a whim, or the Holy Office accepted them without reflection. Sometimes I said that on account of [religious] things being [so] delicate, a person who possessed a holy spirit was needed, someone who combined both fear and love of God, as this is what I mean by a holy spirit. And if I pointed out a person whom I thought had such a holy spirit, I do not remember. If I spoke ignorantly and with too many disordered words, I retract them. I erred in words, not intent.

xxx. To this I say I know nothing about any books, except the ones I've already declared.

xxxi. I do not know suspicious people, except what I have already said.

xxxii. I know nothing more than what I have already said.

The lord inquisitor said that since María de Cazalla was denying the accusation, he would name a lawyer to help defend her. María de Cazalla asked that a transcript of the accusation be given to Lope de Rueda, her husband, or to Pedro de Rueda, her husband's brother, and to the lawyers whom they might name. She said that someone else should name the lawyers, because she did not know any.

Then the lord inquisitor said that what was appropriate would be provided. I was present, Agustín Yllán, notary of secrecy.

The naming of the defense lawyer[48]

In the afternoon of the same day, in the hearing room of the Holy Office, the lord inquisitor ordered Pedro de Rueda . . . to appear before him, and ordered him to name a lawyer in the name of María de Cazalla. He named licentiate Quemada to communicate with her in the court, and if others were needed, he would name them.

(historical and grammatical), metaphorical (allegorical), anagogical (moral), and tropological (prophetic). Of course, María knew a Western theologian—namely her brother, Bishop Friar Juan de Cazalla. There is also evidence that she was versed in Latin. It is possible, then, that María was trying to make her scriptural expositions sound as simple as possible when testifying before the inquisitors. See Henrí du Lubac, *Exégèse médiévale: les quatre sens de l'écriture,* 4 vols. (Paris: Aubier, 1959–1964).

48. Ortega-Costa, *Proceso,* 141.

After the aforesaid, on June 20, 1532, in the hearing room of the Holy Office, Inquisitor Mexia ordered María de Cazalla brought before him, in order to communicate with licentiate Quemada, her lawyer, who was present. María de Cazalla's replies to the prosecutor's accusation were read to licentiate Quemada. Licentiate Quemada asked for a transcript of the replies, in order to respond to the accusation; he likewise asked for a transcript of what she had said and declared before the accusation. He also asked that a time limit not be imposed on their response until he had been given the transcript.

The lord inquisitor said he heard him and would provide what was just. I, Francisco Ximénez, notary, was present.

The defense's first statement[49]

In Toledo, July 30, 1532. The reverend lord licentiate Alonso Mexia, inquisitor, was in his hearing room, and he ordered María de Cazalla brought before him during the morning hearing. Once she was there, she presented him with this written document.

Very Reverend Lords,

[I], María de Cazalla, resident of Guadalajara, wife of Lope de Rueda, prisoner in the Holy Inquisition's prison, appear before Your Lordship in the best way the law allows, to respond to an accusation placed against me by the venerable *bachiller* Diego Ortiz de Angulo, chief prosecutor of the Holy Office. The prosecutor actually accuses me of many different crimes against our Holy Catholic Faith, according to what is contained at greater length in the accusation, whose contents he has alleged repeatedly in this courtroom. Speaking with the necessary respect, I say that the accusation is nothing, and by the power of that accusation Your Lordship cannot proceed against me and must give me my freedom, because of the following. On the one hand, the accusation was not provoked by enough evidence, nor conducted within the proper time limits and in the proper manner.[50] Moreover, the accusation is foolish and badly framed, as it lacks legal substance and the legal formalities that are customary in similar accusations and must be included by law. In particular, the accusation does not declare the day, month, year, place—that is, when and where—the chief prosecutor says I committed the crimes of which he accuses me.[51] If the aforesaid is not declared, I cannot

49. *Ibid.,* 148–50.
50. See Document 20.
51. See Documents 7 and 20 for the omission of details in the publication of witness testimony.

defend myself, and since defense is permitted to me by natural law, Your
Lordship cannot and should not take it away from me. And I solemnly declare that until I am given a copy and transcript of all the aforesaid, and what
I have asked for before now, a time limit should not be imposed on me to
make my case. And not giving up this demand, but rather insisting upon it,
I say that I deny the accusation in general and its particulars, inasmuch as it
is or could be to my detriment; because the truth is that I did not commit
the said crimes, not even one of them. Such crimes did not even pass through
my thoughts, nor can it be proven truthfully that they did.

As I have said and declared, I have been and am a good Christian and
Catholic woman, and as such I am [considered by others]; and I am fearful
of God. I believe and hold everything the Holy Mother Church believes and
holds; and I solemnly declare that I shall live and die in our Holy Catholic
Faith. For these reasons, and for reasons I intend to state more fully during
the prosecution of this case, I ask Your Reverences to give me my freedom.
(I ask also for a copy and transcript of what I have requested, and everything
else appropriate for my defense.) I implore the Holy Office of Your Reverences for my freedom, and above all I beg and request the fulfillment of justice, with costs. And I conclude, denying what is prejudicial and refraining
from innovation.

> Licentiate Quemada.

The document being presented, *bachiller* Diego Ortiz de Angulo, chief prosecutor, who was present, said that he reaffirmed his denunciation; he denied
any prejudice, concluded, and asked to be received for the necessary proof.

Then the lord inquisitor said that since both parties had concluded, he
held the trial as concluded and would receive both parties jointly for proof,
so that each should prove what they were able to prove, with the exception
of things that were irrelevant and must not be admitted into law. He gave
them a time limit of the following nine days to present their proof . . .

Then the chief prosecutor said that he offered the [1525] confession of
María de Cazalla and the statements of the witnesses in this trial,[52] which
were in his favor, as contained above. He asked His Lordship to order the
witnesses' statements ratified, carry out the diligences ordered by the lords
of the Suprema, examine all the deponents, ratify them as to what they said
in his favor, and record the witnesses' statements for the use of the court. . . .
And then the lord inquisitor said the witnesses' statements will be ratified
and all the necessary diligences will be carried out. I was present, Agustín Yllán, notary of secrecy.

---

52. Which meant depositions collected between 1525 and 1532.

• • • •

Petitions of María de Cazalla[53]

Presented by Pedro de Rueda on December 20, 1532, before Lord Inquisitor Vaguer:

Very Reverend Lords,

[I], María de Cazalla, prisoner, say that in order to complete my defense and allow my lawyers to better make my case, it is necessary that Your Reverences tell me the following things:

1. First, tell me in which Guadalajara church the tenth witness says he saw what is contained in his deposition, and in what part of the church the witness was when he says he saw it.
2. Likewise, tell me what place and what church, and at what time, in connection with the twelfth witness, in the second chapter of his deposition.
3. Next, tell me the time and place, and when and where in connection with the fourteenth witness, in the second, third, and fourth chapters of his deposition.
4. Next, I ask that you tell me the time and place, when and where in connection with the fifteenth witness, in all the chapters of his deposition, and I ask the same for the eighteenth witness, in all the chapters of his deposition.

I solemnly declare that until I am given a copy and transcript of all the aforesaid, and every part of it, a time limit to make my case should not be imposed. I beg and implore Your Reverences that you give all of this to me quickly, because with it, I shall respond, and through it, you shall do me a decided mercy, in addition to administering justice.

Rubric of Licentiate Quemada.

January 15, 1533, presented before the lord inquisitors Mexia and Vaguer.

Very Reverend Lords,

[I], María de Cazalla, say that Your Reverences already know that I gave you a petition in addition to the one that I present here, in which I asked you to

---

53. Ortega-Costa, *Proceso,* 183–85. María de Cazalla had received the publication of testimony on October 17, 1532.

tell me the things that I requested. These things are very important to my defense, and they are so important that in no way can I defend myself without your relaying them to me. It is especially important to know the time that the fourteenth witness says the things happened in the second, third, and fourth chapters of his deposition. By the same token, I shall be told the time and place in all the chapters of the fifteenth witness. I beg Your Reverences to provide what I request, because I await nothing else in order for my lawyer or lawyers [sic] to respond. Speaking with the necessary respect, since it is of such importance, I beg Your Reverences that I not be denied [these requests], and I charge your consciences with it. Because I have no other way to respond, Your Reverences shall take charge of the witnesses and ask for their testimony.

Moreover, I say that the seventeenth witness has not been given to me in the publication of testimony. Since it exists, and I have asked for it many times, and Your Reverences have said you would give it to me, I beg Your Reverences that you order it given to me, so that I may allege against him what pertains to my defense.

I [also] beg Your Reverences to order the eighteenth witness to declare at what time he heard what is contained in his deposition from 1523 onward, in such a way that he declares specifically the month or months and the year or years . . . because this is very important for my defense, and otherwise, I will not be able to defend myself.

Rubric of Licentiate Quemada.

Petition enclosed with the one dated January 15, 1533

Very Reverend Lords,

[I], María de Cazalla, prisoner in the prison of the Holy Office, resident of Guadalajara, say that there is a need for Your Reverences to give me a copy and transcript of matters that pertain to my defense, so that my lawyers can make my case. May the transcript be given to my lawyers on the following matters:

First, a copy and transcript of the seventeenth witness' testimony, because it was not placed in the publication. Or it should be stated whether there is a seventeenth witness or not.

Next, whether the witnesses against me have been ratified, or which of them have and which have not; and regarding those who have not, which of them can be ratified.

Next, a copy and transcript of my replies to the admonitions and the published accusation.

Next, a copy and transcript of the petitions that I presented before licentiate Mariana in Guadalajara [in 1525].

Next, since many of the witnesses do not declare the time that they heard what is contained in their depositions, and others do not declare the place, and others do not declare one or the other, I beg Your Reverences that such witnesses be ordered to declare when and where things happened. I solemnly declare that a time limit shall not be imposed to make my case until a copy and transcript of the aforesaid is given to me. . . .

Rubric: Quemada

Interrogatory for the defense witnesses[54]

March 17, 1533, presented before lord inquisitor Vaguer.

The questions that have to be asked of the witnesses who will be presented for the party of María de Cazalla, resident of Guadalajara, prisoner of the Holy Office of the Inquisition of Toledo, in the criminal case undertaken by the venerable *bachiller* Diego Ortiz de Angulo, chief prosecutor of the Holy Office . . . are the following:

i. First, they shall be asked if they know María de Cazalla, resident of Guadalajara, wife of Lope de Rueda, and if they know *bachiller* Diego Ortiz de Angulo, chief prosecutor of the Holy Office.

ii. Next, if they know, believe, have seen, or have heard it said over the last twenty years, and since they have known María de Cazalla, that she has lived as a good, faithful, and Catholic Christian, performing the works of such.

iii. Next, if they know that as a good and faithful and Catholic Christian, María de Cazalla, throughout the time stipulated above, has confessed and received the Eucharist not only once a year, as the Holy Mother Church commands, but frequently throughout the year, and especially on Easter and the principal feast days of the year. The witnesses shall say what they know.

iv. Next, if they know, etc., that when María de Cazalla was sick in bed, she immediately confessed and received the Eucharist before the illness worsened, and if the illness worsened, she then asked for the sacrament of Extreme Unction.

v. Next, if they know that when María de Cazalla confessed during the last twenty years, that she endeavored, with her confessors' help, to

---

54. Ortega-Costa, *Proceso,* 269–73. The calling of character witnesses for the defense was called, in inquisitorial shorthand, *abonos,* from the verb *abonar,* which means "to make good an assertion." María had thirty-six witnesses swear to her Christian character.

become more recollected [*recogida*] and devout, in order to perform her duty to God, rather than to please the community.

vi. Next, if they know whether, over the last fifteen or twenty years (up until María de Cazalla was imprisoned), she had a custom of hearing Mass on Sundays, feast days, and ordinary days, no matter where she was, if she was not sick. And whether she still went even when she was sick, provided the illness did not get much worse.

vii. Next, if they know, etc., that when María de Cazalla was in Mass, she prayed vocally in the style of other women and men who were there, and that she kneeled and rose in the Mass at the customary times: that is, whether she rose at the Gospel and kneeled when they raised the Eucharist, and whether she struck her breast and performed the exterior acts of adoration customarily performed in the Mass by Catholic Christians, and whether she took Holy Water when she entered the Church. The witnesses shall say what they know.

viii. Next, if they know, etc., that María de Cazalla had a custom at that time of praying frequently and vocally from some books of hours that she had. And whether the witnesses would have seen her do so many different times.

ix. Next, if they know, etc., during the last twenty years, whether María de Cazalla was very fond of fasting, discipline, and abstinence. And whether she not only fasted on the days the Church commanded, but also performed other fasts out of devotion, until her illnesses [sic] worsened and took away her ability to do so. And whether she recommended such acts to people who communicated with her, and whether she ordered [them] in her [own] house.

x. Next, if they know that María de Cazalla was and is a very charitable woman who gave many people alms in public and in secret, and whether she was very fond of works of mercy. The witnesses shall say what they know about this. . . .

xii. Next, her confessors shall be asked if they know whether she used the freedom of her free will, blaming and accusing herself of good she could have done, but had neglected to do through her own fault; and whether through that same free will, she accused herself of acting badly. They shall say and declare what they know and saw as it pertains to María de Cazalla. . . .

xv. Next, if they know, etc., that it's a customary thing among Catholic women to read aloud books of Holy Scripture in Spanish to other women who do not know how to read, and that this is a very well-known, public practice.

xvi. Next, if they know, etc., that for a long time it's been the custom in the city of Guadalajara for women to cover their heads with their cloaks, in such a way that hardly any of their facial expressions can be seen. . . .

xviii. Next, if they know, etc., that María de Cazalla was very fond of sermons and went to see and hear them no matter where she was . . . and if they know that many times preachers who preached disagreeably or coldly were gossiped about, just as ones who contented everyone were praised.

xix. Next, if they know, etc., that over the last twenty years María de Cazalla has always purchased the bulls and indulgences that the Roman pontiffs have conceded to Catholic Christians . . . and she has tried to gain the indulgences and pardons conceded in those papal bulls, doing at least as much as she was capable of to gain the indulgences, visiting altars and making sure she received plenary absolution when she bought the bulls. . . .

xxi. Next, if they know that María de Cazalla had some conversation with Isabel de la Cruz, resident of Guadalajara, *beata,* who was later reconciled. And whether this conversation was the cause of Isabel de la Cruz teaching needlework to María de Cazalla's daughters, along with other young girls, daughters of well-off men from Guadalajara. And if Isabel de la Cruz taught María de Cazalla's daughters because María de Cazalla lived in the village of Orche, where her daughters could not learn that skill, and María de Cazalla lived in Orche almost up to the time Isabel de la Cruz was seized. . . .

xxiii. Next, if they know, etc., that at the time María de Cazalla communicated with Isabel de la Cruz and Pedro Ruiz de Alcaraz, those individuals were held as very good and Catholic Christians and as great servants of God, and that this was very public and well known in Guadalajara.

xxiv. Next, if they know that María de Cazalla made canopies in her house for the church of Orche, where she lived for some time . . . and whether she very often washed the altar cloths of the church and the banner of its cross in her house. They shall say what they know and have seen about this. . . .

xxvi. Next, if they know, etc., that María de Cazalla was and is very fond of monks and nuns, for which reason they have visited her. And whether she has visited monasteries of nuns and has communicated with monks and nuns.

xxvii. Next, if they know, etc., that in the year and a half before she was imprisoned . . . they have witnessed her love for her daughters, and have seen her treat them and teach them as any good mother would and should. And if they know whether she and her husband tried to place two daughters in convents, one in the monastery of Lady Brianda de Mendoza, and the other in the monastery of Pedro Gómez, Lord of Pios in Guadalajara. And if they know that the two monasteries have admitted them, though the said monasteries aren't even finished.

xxviii. Next, if they know, etc., that María de Cazalla has tried to marry another of her daughters, and always tried to marry her to a noble, virtuous, Old Christian person, as the witnesses know very well.

xxix. Next, if they know that all of the aforesaid is a matter of public discussion and reputation.

Rubric of Licentiate Quemada.

List of defense witnesses[55]

The list of the defense witnesses, and the questions that each of them shall be asked, for the party of María de Cazalla, resident of Guadalajara.

Lady Duchess Isabel de Aragón. On the first and second, xi, xv, xvi, xvii, xviii, xxvii, xxix.

Lady Brianda de Mendoza. i, ii, vii, xi, xv, xvi, xvii, xviii, xxiii, xxvii, xxix.

Lady Mencia de Mendoza. i, ii, vii, xi, xv, xvi, xvii, xviii, xxiii, xxvii, xxviii, xxix.

Lady Isabel de Mendoza, her daughter. i, ii, vii, viii, xi, xv, xvi, xvii, xviii, xxi, xxiii, xxvii, xxviii, xxix. . . .

María, wife of Francisco Valermo, resident of Orche. i, ii, iii, iv, vi, vii, viii, ix, x, xviii, xix, xx, xxiv, xxvi, xxvii, xxix.

Ynés, slave of Lope de Rueda. i, ii, ix, x, xiii, xiv, xix, xx, xxix. . . .

Alonso Calderón, schoolmaster. i, ii, iii, xi, xxvii, xxix.

Friar Pedro de los Angeles. i, ii, iii, x, xi, xii, xv, xix, xx, xxiii, xxvi, xxvii, xxix.

Gonzalo Paez, cleric. i, ii, iii, iv, v, vi, vii, viii, x, xi, xii, xv, xviii, xix, xx, xxi, xxii, xxiii, xxv, xxvi, xxvii, xxix.

Francisco d'Estrada, cleric. i, ii, iii, iv, v, vi, vii, viii, ix, x, xi, xii, xv, xviii, xix, xx, xxv, xxvi, xxvii, xxix. . . .

Bachiller Yrueste, cleric and master of the sons of the Duke. i, ii, iii, vi, vii, viii, ix, x, xi, xviii, xxvii, xxix. . . .

55. Ortega-Costa, *Proceso*, 273–76. The Roman numerals signify the questions of the *abonos* interrogatory that each witness would be asked.

Martin Hernández, cleric of Orche. i, ii, iii, vi, vii, viii, x, xi, xix, xx, xxiv, xxvi, xxix. . . .

The defense's challenges to witnesses[56]

Presented before Lord Inquisitor Vaguer, March 17, 1533:
Questions that shall be asked of the witnesses presented for the party of María de Cazalla . . . to substantiate her objections to the prosecution witnesses. . . . They shall be asked if they know Mari Nuñez who lived in the city of Guadalajara, and if they knew her in 1526 and 1530. They shall be asked if they know Mari Nuñez to have been and to be still a lying woman, and a violator of the community's peace and a disturber of homes at that time, as well as before and after. They shall state what they know about this, and if they know that she left the city of Guadalajara more than fourteen years ago, and never returned.

Next, they shall be asked if they know that Mari Nuñez was the reason why María de Cazalla's house experienced a very strong quarrel between Cazalla's husband, Lope de Rueda, and certain people, involving offensive and defensive weapons; from that tumult, Sir Alonso de la Cérda emerged with an injured hand . . . on account of this quarrel Lope de Rueda took María de Cazalla to Orche, where he had a house and property, in order to flee from Mari Nuñez. They shall say what they know about this.

Next, if they know that because of this tumult Mari Nuñez lost her reputation among many people in Guadalajara, and María de Cazalla consequently gave her daughters to Isabel de la Cruz, for Isabel to show them how to do needlework. And if they know that Mari Nuñez began to detest María de Cazalla. And if they know that on account of the aforesaid, Mari Nuñez was and is, and has shown herself to be, the capital enemy of María de Cazalla.[57] They shall say what they know about this.

Next, they shall be asked if they know Francisca Hernández, a prisoner in the jail of the Toledo Inquisition. And if they know that Francisca Hernández has been and is a trickster, unchaste, and a great liar; and if they know Francisca Hernández would like to hurt María de Cazalla for saying that Francisca Hernández was not a good person, given how free she was in

---

56. María called fifteen witnesses who attested enmity or verified objections to potential prosecution witnesses through these queries. This strategy and this sort of interrogatory were called *tachas,* from the verb *tachar,* meaning (in a legal situation) "to impeach or to challenge." Ortega-Costa, *Proceso,* 341–45.

57. Capital enmity should have disqualified witnesses automatically; the problem lay in proving it.

conversation with men. And if they know that Francisca Hernández dragged clerics after her as if they were dissolute vagrants.[58]

They shall be asked if they know Master Diego Hernández, resident of Ciudad Real, and if they knew him in March 1532 or before. They shall be asked whether, at that time, or before or after, they knew him as a man of very little judgment, a gossip and evil-sayer, and the kind of person whose statements and testimony were not entirely trustworthy.

Next if they know, etc. [sic] that once, Master Diego Hernández was in María de Cazalla's house and read a letter there; and [if they know] whether, in order to read the letter, he had to put it so close to his eyes that it looked as if it touched his eyelashes. As María de Cazalla knew he was a priest and had to read at the altar, she asked him if he minded his poor vision when he said Mass, as she was pained by it; he said no, because he knew most of it by heart.

Next, if they know, etc., that María de Cazalla remained somewhat vexed about Diego Hernández' manner of reading the letter, on account of which she complained about it to Gonzalo Paez, a cleric, resident of Guadalajara. (Diego Hernández was staying in Gonzalo Paez' house.) Since Diego Hernández had such poor vision, and was Paez' lodger, María de Cazalla told Paez to counsel Hernández to hold the book close when he was at the altar, and to really get close to the passage where the words of the consecration were written, and to place himself in a well-lit spot in order to see that the remains of the Eucharist were consumed, and the cleansing of the chalice was properly carried out.

Next, if they know that Gonzalo Paez repeated these things to Diego Hernández as advice, and that Diego Hernández became angry and fought with Gonzalo Paez to the point that Gonzalo Paez told him it was María de Cazalla who had said such things. And whether they know that Diego Hernández then went to María de Cazalla, and told her that he could cite many learned men who said it was not necessary to read the words of the consecration, but was enough to know them by heart.

Next, they shall be asked if they know that Diego Hernández remained discontent, and sent María de Cazalla many assurances that it was enough to say the said words by heart, even if they weren't read. And whether María de Cazalla wrote to him in return and said that he was up there at the altar with his own conscience, and she was not judging him. And whether Diego Hernández still dared to send messages about the matter to María de Cazalla through García de Vargas, the tailor. . . .

Next, if they know, etc., that García de Vargas, the tailor, demonstrated great hatred and enmity toward anyone who said anything about Diego

58. See Documents 9, 10, and 11.

Hernández, and whether García de Vargas was a great enemy of María de Cazalla because she had said that Diego Hernández was an idiot who knew little, and she would not allow him to enter her house. . . .

Testimony on the prison scandal[59]

May 2, 1533   Mari Fernández appeared before the lord Dr. Vaguer, inquisitor. She said that her mistress, Catalina de Figueredo, told her that the servant of Bernardino de Tovar—called "little Aguilar"[60]—had carried a very large written document to a lady [Cazalla] imprisoned here . . . and that this lady [Cazalla] had wanted to send back another document with Aguilar, which must have been seventeen or twenty folios long. [Cazalla's] servant had walked from cell to cell [with the document], looking for the one that belonged to Tovar; by mistake, she threw the document into the wrong cell, one that contains a prisoner who is squint-eyed. The warden then found the document, took it, and ran through the prison to show it to the inquisitors. Juan Sánchez, the warden's servant, had calmed everyone down.

May 7, 1533   In the afternoon hearing, before the very reverend lord, Inquisitor Juan Yañes, Pedro Luis was ordered to appear. . . . He said that Bernardino de Tovar had written more than twenty folios of paper in his cell; on the back side of those folios, there was a letter that said "lady" at the top and bottom; and this letter was half a folio long. The defendant [Pedro Luis] first read the Tovar letter that was for him; he then saw that the letter that said "lady" at the top and bottom was placed inside. Tovar greatly pestered him to give the letter hidden inside to María de Cazalla, and told [Pedro

59. Ortega-Costa, *Proceso,* 479–88. The inquisitors in Toledo were in the process of discovering multiple secret letters from Juan de Vergara to his half-brother Bernardino de Tovar, imprisoned inside the tribunal, between April 23 and May 17, 1533. The inquisitors' discoveries about Tovar and Vergara led them to turn the tribunal's prison upside down. See Homza, *Religious Authority,* chapter 1.

60. Diego de Aguilar, Tovar's servant, carried messages to other prisoners on his master's command; Diego's involvement in this prison network resulted in his own trial: see Archivo Histórico Nacional, Seccion de Inquisición de Toledo, Legajo 79, n. 1, and Homza, *Religious Authority,* 45. Evidence from the Toledo tribunal as well as numerous others suggests that undermining the rules was routine in the Inquisition's prisons. See Angela Selke, "Vida y muerte de Juan López de Celaín," *Bulletin hispanique* 62 (1960): 136–62; Eugenio Asensio, "El Maestro Pedro de Orellana, minorita luterano: versos y procesos," in *La Inquisición Española: nueva visión, nuevos horizontes,* ed. Joaquín Pérez Villanueva (Madrid: Siglo Veintiuno Editores, 1978), 785–95; and Richard L. Kagan, *Lucrecia's Dreams: Politics and Prophecy in Sixteenth-Century Castile* (Berkeley: University of California Press, 1990), 140–44.

Luis] he could do it through a cat's hole, signaling to Pedro Luis where the cat's hole was. This defendant did not tell him no . . . [but] this defendant did not hand off the letter to María de Cazalla, and instead returned it to Tovar by the same route that Tovar had pointed out. . . . Tovar then wrote to the defendant again . . . and sent another letter inside for María de Cazalla, and the defendant also returned this second letter, since there was no way to get it to her, because the cat's hole was already closed up.

May 9, 1533   Diego de Aguilar appeared before his Reverence [Yañes] and said the following . . . He said he knew what was in Tovar's letters, because he saw most of what went into them. They were messages of consolation and fortitude. He remembers that María de Cazalla gave him a written reply to the prosecutor's publication of witnesses in her case [to carry to Tovar]. He then said he does not know whether Cazalla's reply concerned the publication or the accusation, [but] he took it to Tovar, and he doesn't remember returning it to María de Cazalla.

May 15, 1533   Diego de Aguilar was asked if he remembered having seen or heard any of the female prisoners say that one of them had sent a written document to a prisoner, and that the document was mistakenly given to the wrong prisoner or carried to the wrong cell. He said he would say what he knew about this. At the time the Inquisition gave María de Cazalla the publication of witnesses, her servant girl went out with him one day for water from the well. This defendant went ahead of her, to the right of the well, which was close to the cell that held Diego Hernández and Cristóbal de Atienca. When this defendant stopped to open the well, the girl must have thrown a written document into the cell of Diego Hernández. The girl then took water from the well and returned to the cell of María de Cazalla with this defendant. All this happened in the morning. After a little while, almost immediately, this defendant went to hand out the plates and the wine to the cells as he usually does,[61] and he came to the cell of Diego Hernández. Diego Hernández was holding certain documents in his hand, and said, "Who brought me these writings?" This defendant asked to see them. . . .

May 14, 1533 [sic]   Master Diego Hernández appeared before Dr. Vaguer, inquisitor, and was sworn in the customary way, etc. He was asked if he knows whether certain statements or writings, or letters or messages, have been sent from one cell to another; and whether certain prisoners have

61. Diego regularly left his and Tovar's cell on the pretext of exercise and assistance to the prison warden's servant; he then carried notes from Tovar to other prisoners. Having a prisoner's servant assist the tribunal's staff was a massive violation of procedure. See Homza, *Religious Authority*, 23. It is not explained how Cazalla's servant could have misdelivered a message for Tovar when she was with Tovar's servant.

spoken with each other, sending messages back and forth. . . . He said that on All Saints Day of last year, 1532, this defendant was in his cell, lying on his bed, at 7:30 or 8:00 a.m. Then Ynés, the servant of María de Cazalla, a prisoner in this prison, came to the door of his cell and called out, saying, "Sir!"; she put her hand through the door, and she was carrying a bundle of letters. Cristóbal de Atienca, who shared this defendant's cell, said, "Look, they're calling you over there," and since this defendant wasn't up, the girl threw the letters into the cell and left. This defendant took the letters, which came tied with a cord of white thread, and untied them; he saw how they were four folios altogether, written on all sides in a woman's hand. He began to read the writing, and as it was difficult to read, he didn't even read half a folio. . . . It now seems to him that the letter was about the publication of witnesses. This defendant then called Juan Sánchez, the prison servant, and said, "Did you think I was resting? You've given me something to break my eyes," thinking that Juan Sánchez had thrown the letters into the cell, and even thinking that the lord inquisitor Mexia had sent them to him, so that he might see whether there were others who would say what María de Cazalla was up to.

Juan Sánchez, hearing the above, was astonished and lost all the color in his face, and said he had not brought the letters, and he made the sign of the Cross and asked this defendant when and at what time the letters had arrived. This defendant replied that if Juan Sánchez didn't bring them, the warden must have. Then Juan Sánchez went off to ask the warden, though this defendant doesn't know if he actually spoke with the warden, because Juan Sánchez returned immediately and asked this defendant for the letters. This defendant did not want to give them to him; he told Juan Sánchez to take him out of the cell because he wanted to speak to the warden personally. Juan Sánchez opened the cell, and he [Diego Hernández] went out with him. Then Juan Sánchez called the warden, who crossed over from his underground cell, and Juan Sánchez said to him, "Sir, look, the Master wants to speak to you." Then the warden and this defendant sat down on a bench in the courtyard . . . and this defendant gave the warden the four folios with writing on them, and the warden put on his glasses and began to read them, and said he could read nothing because of the bad handwriting. . . . The warden said, "It's bad handwriting, but I will transcribe it in a legible hand," and he reprimanded Juan Sánchez, who returned this defendant to his cell. The warden remained with the document in his hands, and nothing further happened in this conversation.

Afterward, the same day or the next, Juan Sánchez came to this defendant and said that he and the warden had already read the document, and it was nothing, nor did it contain anything prejudicial against this defendant; and Juan Sánchez told the defendant to say nothing about it to the inquisitors. Juan Sánchez said that he himself wasn't to blame, but the inquisitors could still blame him, saying he had consented to the transfer of letters and had covered it up; and if the inquisitors found out about all this, he would lose the trust that those lords had in him. This defendant promised to say nothing, so long as the warden was on board too, because though they didn't want to incriminate themselves, they might decide to incriminate the defendant. Afterward the warden spoke to the defendant in the patio . . . and said, "Have you spoken to Juan Sánchez?" and this defendant said yes, and the warden begged the defendant to be silent and not say anything about the letters to the inquisitors, lest they blame Juan Sánchez. . . .

[**Afternoon session, same day**]   Asked if the warden and Juan Sánchez had [asked for] an oath from this defendant [Diego Hernández] not to tell the inquisitors about the document, the defendant said he had sworn to Juan Sánchez not to tell, and to keep the secret . . . but this defendant was not satisfied with the arrangement until he knew whether the warden wanted all three to keep the secret. . . . This defendant was happy that he had offered up the letter and writings, because then the warden would treat him better. The defendant had known more love and good treatment from the warden after all this than he had before. Previously, the warden had not wanted to see or hear him, [but now] they brought him two pairs of partridges from his home town. . . . He was also given a dry measure of garbanzo beans, sent from his father's house. . . .

Same day   The lord inquisitor ordered María de Cazalla brought before him. . . . She said she has never spoken with a female prisoner in these cells nor has she seen one, but she knows that *bachiller* Bernardino de Tovar, prisoner, wrote a letter to her a little while before her lawyer responded to the prosecutor's accusation; she does not remember how long ago. Her own servant, Isabel Díaz [sic], received the letter and told her that a male servant of Tovar had given the letter to her, to give to the defendant. As her servant handed over the letter, she said, with great pleasure, "Look here, lady, they've given me a letter from Lope de Rueda." When this defendant saw the letter, she said, "It's not a letter from Lope de Rueda, but from Tovar, who is a prisoner here, because I recognize his handwriting." Afterward she read the letter, which was on one folio of paper, written on only one side (though she does not really remember whether it was longer than a folio). When some days had passed, this defendant then wrote to Tovar on two folios of paper which she sent to him; she sent her letter wrapped in blank paper, along with ink in a small glass container, with a pen. Once she had written the letter, she gave it to her servant to hide in her dress, so that when Tovar's servant came for the reply, her own servant might give it to him. Tovar had said in his letter that he would send for her reply. . . .

May 16, 1533   . . . Asked what was contained in the first letter Tovar wrote to her . . . María de Cazalla said, in effect, he said how he knew her character, life, spiritual exercises, and desires, and he knew she was imprisoned in the tribunal. He had tried to find a way to console her, and asked her to tell him how things looked for her. Tovar also advised her to send her reply with his servant, or to give the reply to her servant, so that one of them might place the letters behind the earthenware jar that was in the corral. And she doesn't remember whether it was in the first letter or the second that he told her to carry out what she had to do with great prudence and vigilance so that no one would know; and if he said anything else in the letter, she doesn't remember it at the moment, and if she does remember anything, she will say so. She was asked if she has the letter in her possession, or all the other letters that Tovar has written to her, or any of them. She said that she has none of the letters that Tovar wrote, because as soon as she received them, she ripped them up, and she kept them no longer than was required to respond to them. . . . She was asked if she told Tovar in her letters that she had responded to the accusation, along with whether she had confessed or denied the charges. She said she doesn't remember, and if she wrote him something, it would have been that she had both confessed and denied, confessing the truth and denying the opposite. Asked what Tovar wrote to her in the second letter, she said she doesn't really remember what he wrote, except that he told her that he could in no way counsel her appropriately until he saw the prosecutor's publication of witnesses, and then he would relay his opinion to her. . . .

May 17, 1533   Before the lord inquisitor Juan Yañes, *bachiller* Bernardino de Tovar was brought into the court and said the following. . . . He said he remembered that María de Cazalla, wife of Lope de Rueda, a prisoner here, wrote to him about ten months ago, a little more or less . . . and told him how she had been questioned by the inquisitors about a little book called *Doctrina cristiana*. She had told the inquisitors the truth, how she had heard this defendant say there were plenty of things in the book that should have been revised before it was printed. It had seemed very good to María de Cazalla that one of the inquisitors had said he would write down what she said, as it would help [Tovar's own] case. Right now he doesn't remember anything else. María de Cazalla wrote the aforesaid to this defendant . . .

The inquisitors and *consultadores* vote on the question of torture[62]

May 8, 1534   Present in the hearing room of the Holy Office were the very reverend lords licenciate Juan Yañes and Dr. Pedro Vaguer, inquisitors.

62. Ortega-Costa, *Proceso*, 433–34. On April 28, 1534, the Suprema and Inquisitor-General Manrique (in the presence of Toledo inquisitors Vaguer and Yañes) ordered

Also present were licenciate Blas Ortiz, canon and *ordinario* [of the arch-bishop of Toledo], Dr. Micer Pastor of the Council of Aragón, and Friar Alonso de Ocaña, guardian of the monastery of San Juan de los Reyes. Having seen the trial of María de Cazalla . . . they voted as follows. (The trial was also seen by licentiate Pedro de la Peña, canon, but because he did not attend this hearing and departed for Alcalá, his vote is not registered. Only the votes of the lords listed above are registered.)

All the inquisitors, the *ordinario,* and the learned men unanimously said that their vote and opinion is that María de Cazalla should be put to the question of moderate torture [sic], in accordance with the quality of her person. Under torture she shall be asked about the heretical or suspicious propositions with which she is charged. The lord guardian Ocaña shall select those propositions from the trial record, with the inquisitors' advice. This was the vote and opinion of all.

[Though the vote *to torture María de Cazalla occurred in May 1534, nothing happened; instead, she was interrogated extensively between August and October 1534. The* order *to torture her was finally issued on October 10, 1534, and she was tortured the same day. She did not confess.]*

The inquisitors and *consultadores* vote on the case[63]

October 14, 1534   The lord inquisitors Yañes, Vaguer, and Diego de Giron de Loaysa; Drs. Blas Ortiz, canon and *ordinario* of Toledo, and Diego Rodríguez, Friar Diego de Alcántara, and Friar Francisco Mexia of the Order of Preachers, were in the hearing room of the Holy Inquisition. Having seen this trial, and what María de Cazalla said under torture, they unanimously said that María de Cazalla should be absolved by order of the court, and a monetary fine of fifty ducats be imposed upon her. They ordered her to be warned with severe penalties not to communicate with those people called *alumbrados,* nor with any other suspicious individuals. She shall perform a public penance in her parish in Guadalajara. Likewise they said that

---

the Toledo tribunal to combine all the charges against María—including the ones involving the prison scandal—to call its *consultadores,* and to vote. The Suprema's attitude seems to have been that the Toledo tribunal should simply finish the case, though the tribunal ignored the Suprema's mandate; see below for events of October and December 1534.

63. Ortega-Costa, *Proceso,* 472.

this sentence shall be read in the church in Guadalajara and she shall be present. So that this sentence may be fully carried out, an official of the Holy Office shall go there to witness it, at the cost of María de Cazalla. Next, the inquisitors said that for the other offenses that resulted against María de Cazalla—from the communication that she had in prison with the prisoners—a penance of another fifty ducats shall be imposed upon her.

[Despite this October 1534 vote to absolve María, she was not released from the Toledo tribunal; there was no necessary correlation between voting on a case and pronouncing sentence. Instead, on December 17, 1534, the chief prosecutor presented new charges against her in connection with the prison scandal. Two days later, on December 19, 1534, the sentence against María was finally read to her in a private ceremony; the verdict listed all the charges brought by the chief prosecutor, whether connected to alumbradismo *or* abetting heretical prisoners, *but it also admitted that the chief prosecutor had not entirely proven his case. The sentence demanded that María perform public penance in her parish in Guadalajara. María accepted the sentence and abjured a light (*de levi*) suspicion of heresy. She was ordered to maintain complete secrecy as to what she had seen and heard in the tribunal, and was forbidden to leave Toledo without the inquisitors' permission, under pain of relapse.*[64]*]*

64. The chief prosecutor presented a petition on December 22, 1534, urging the inquisitors not to release María de Cazalla, and enclosing new evidence against her from Pedro Ruiz de Alcaraz, one of the key *alumbrados* arrested in 1524. There is no evidence that María remained in the inquisitors' custody.

PONDERING WITCHCRAFT

DOCUMENT 13

Deliberations on the Reality and Heresy of Witchcraft, 1526[1]

[In its most intricate form, witchcraft in early modern Europe involved explicit or implicit pacts with demons,[2] and magic that was intended to harm.[3] The pacts were heretical because people making an overt or tacit agreement with the Devil had renounced their baptismal vows. At the same time, intentionally harmful magic or maleficia *(singular* maleficium*)—which could result in the illness or death of people or animals, as well as the destruction of property—fell to the secular courts. Thus the prosecution of witchcraft tended to involve the Spanish Inquisition in conflicts over jurisdiction and debates over process and penalties. These controversies were further complicated by the realization that the witch's imagination could play a role in confessions. The question of fantasy and witchcraft was raised most famously in a text known as the* Canon episcopi, *which forms part of the twelfth-century collection of canon law called the* Decretum, *compiled by the Italian monk Gratian. The* Canon episcopi *reported that certain women believed they could fly with the goddess Diana, but insisted they were mistaken and probably deluded by the Devil; the* Canon episcopi *also adjured bishops and priests to eradicate sorcery from their parishes.[4] The fact that the Spanish consultants below immediately*

1. Archivo Histórico Nacional, Sección de la Inquisición, Libro 1231, ff. 634r–637r.

2. Notions of the implicit demonic pact originated with St. Augustine, who insisted in *City of God* that demons intervened in the performances of ancient magicians. Later Christian theologians, such as Thomas Aquinas (d. 1274) and Jean Gerson (d. 1429), restated the connection between magic and demons, but also expanded the devil's playground to the point that vain works and lies pleased the Devil and might invite his intervention. (Gerson's vernacular and Latin works were of great importance to Spanish writings on witchcraft.) By the sixteenth century, one well-known treatise from Spain insisted, "If [a man's] actions and words have no natural or supernatural power to bring out the [desired] effect, then the operation is vain . . . and if it works, it's because of a secret operation of the Devil." Pedro Ciruelo, *Reprobación de las supersticiones y hechicerías* (1530).

3. Of course, magic could also be intended to *help,* and the Inquisition began to prosecute this sort as well, since it too could involve implicit demonic pacts.

4. The *Canon episcopi* is translated in Alan C. Kors and Edward Peters, eds., *Witchcraft in Europe, 1100–1700: A Documentary History* (Philadelphia: University of

raised the question of delusion, and then mingled it with transvection, or "night-flight," illustrates how well they knew their canon law.

The following text, produced in Granada in 1526, was provoked by something specific, namely, the prosecution and execution of dozens of witches in Navarre by a secular magistrate. But it also should be viewed within the larger context of other inquisition conferences held in the mid-1520s and headed by Inquisitor-General Alonso Manrique to address the thorny issues of alumbradismo *(1525), the baptism of Muslims (1526), and the writings of Desiderius Erasmus (1527).[5] As inquisitors shifted their attention from judaizing to more equivocal matters of belief whose signs were not yet codified, Inquisitor-General Manrique clearly felt it prudent to confer with experts as part of the process of definition.[6] The delegates here evinced both pastoral and legal concerns, as well as a cautionary air; and this approach would be consistently repeated in the Suprema's later rulings on witchcraft cases.[7]*

Doubts that must be resolved
in the present legal case

1. Whether the witches reviewed in this case really and truly commit the crimes they have confessed, or whether they are in fact fooled.

2. For the witches who really commit murders, whether they must be exiled or relaxed [to the secular arm], or handed over to a secular court

---

Pennsylvania Press, 1972), 28–31. The *Canon episcopi* forms *causa* 26, *quaestio* 5, *capitulum* 12 of the *Decretum.* Gratian and his contemporaries believed the *Canon episcopi* was particularly authoritative because it was especially old: they dated it to the Council of Ancyra in 314, though it most probably comes from the ninth century and was part of a collection of Carolingian civil statutes.

5. Some of the consultants on witchcraft listed here also conferred over the forced baptism and conversion of Muslims; see Kamen, *The Spanish Inquisition,* 271. For the 1525 *alumbrado* edict, see Document 8. For the 1527 Valladolid conference on Erasmus, see Homza, "Erasmus as Hero or Heretic?"

6. Manrique thereby took the process of consultation to a more centralized level, whereas *calificadores* typically worked with local tribunals.

7. For the prosecution of witchcraft in the kingdom of Aragón, see Monter, *Frontiers of Heresy,* and María Tausiet, *Ponzoña en los ojos: brujería y superstición en Aragón en el siglo XVI* (Zaragoza: Instituto Fernando el Católico, 2000). For a lengthy and controversial witchcraft case involving demonic pacts, *maleficia,* jurisdictional disputes, conflicts among inquisitors, and sensitive instructions, see Gustav Henningsen, *The Witches' Advocate* (Reno, NV: University of Nevada Press, 1980), and *idem, The Salazar Documents* (Leiden: Brill, 2004).

after their reconciliation [to the Church], so they may be struck with worthy penalties for their actions.[8]

3. Next, whether they should be punished in the same way if they were fooled and did not really commit those deeds.

4. Whether knowledge of those evil deeds [*maleficia*] and their punishment should concern inquisitors of heretical depravity, [or] whether it is [even] appropriate for the inquisitors to know about those deeds.

5. Whether the witches may be sentenced to the greatest ordinary penalty through their own confessions, without other proof or support.[9]

6. Finally, what remedy will destroy the plague of those witches.

First question: Whether the witches reviewed in this case really and truly commit the crimes they have confessed, or whether in fact they are fooled

Those who hold that they really go [sic][10]

Dr. Arcilla

The Bishop of Guadix, who says there's a greater appearance that they go than not.

The Bishop-elect of Granada

Dr. Luis Coronel[11]

Master Arrieta

Dr. May

8. This clause highlights some of the jurisdictional conflicts that could complicate witchcraft cases: the right of secular courts to try a suspect for harm caused by maleficient magic (*maleficium*) while the Inquisition was attempting to try the same suspect for heresy, and the matter of which trial should occur first.

9. The delegates recognized that witchcraft trials might involve exceptions to typical inquisitorial procedure. Given the substantial Christian tradition that the Devil was a liar and that the Devil's human helpers might be consequently deceived (or be liars themselves), a confession without any other evidence might be viewed as less than trustworthy.

10. Though the first question explicitly asks about *maleficia,* the delegates redirected the query to focus on whether the witches flew in fact or in their imagination to the Devil's sabbat. (The sabbat was the orgiastic feast supervised by the Devil, in which witches adored their satanic master and novices entered into demonic pacts.)

11. Coronel studied at the Sorbonne and became a doctor of theology in 1514; he was attached to the royal court of Charles V in 1520 as a preacher and confessor, and worked for the Inquisition in Brussels. A correspondent of Erasmus', a delegate at

Those who hold that they go in their imaginations [sic]

The Bishop of Mondoñedo

Licentiate Polaneo

Dr. Guevara[12]

Licentiate Valdés.[13] His opinion about superstition follows.

Second question: For the witches who really commit murders, whether they must be exiled or relaxed [to the secular arm], or handed over to a secular court after their reconciliation [to the Church], so they may be struck with worthy penalties for their actions

Dr. Arcilla: The matter should be left to the judge's discretion, taking into account the condition and quality of the penitent. He proposes they be relaxed to the secular arm unless the judge sees from the case that something else is warranted.

Bishop of Guadix: They must be completely separated [from other defendants?] and reconverted [to Christianity], but on the question of whether they should be relaxed, he defers to the advice of men skilled in the law.

Bishop of Mondoñedo: They should not be released [to secular judges] [while] they are condemned to the Inquisition's perpetual prison.[14] If they are not condemned to that perpetual prison, they can be prosecuted for other secular crimes.

Master Arrieta: They should be prosecuted as if they were heretics. But if they confess their crimes from their own free will, they should be treated with greater compassion than heretics.

Dr. Coronel: They must be completely destroyed. And for the killing of infants, etc. [sic], with damages, a secular judge may punish them with a suitable penalty. Certainly to the extent that the crime pertains to the offense of the Christian religion, the inquisitors may proceed as they should.

---

the Valladolid conference of 1527, and a noted author on logic, Coronel was both famous and influential. His *Tractatus syllogismorum* was published in 1508; his *Physice perscrutationes* in 1511.

12. Antonio de Guevara, bishop and humanist. See Augustín Redondo, *Fray Antonio de Guevara (1480?–1545) et l'Espagne de son temps* (Geneva: Droz, 1976).

13. Licentiate Valdés was the future Inquisitor-General Fernando de Valdés.

14. Thus an implicit recognition that sentences to perpetual prison were routinely commuted to shorter periods of incarceration.

Dr. May: They must not be released to the secular judges while they are condemned to perpetual prison. A secular judge may prosecute them when an inquisitor has nothing more to put forward.[15]

Licentiate Polanes: They should not be [released to secular judges] after being reconciled.

Dr. Guevara: They should not be released [to secular judges].

Licentiate Valdés: On the first question. In the trials seen so far, the matter is not proven in such a way that one can conclude either that the witches really committed these crimes or only fantasized that they do. As a result, the inquisitors must be ordered to work more diligently to ascertain the truth, inquiring into the preparations the witches made in order to perform their *maleficia* and the circumstances surrounding it all. Such circumstances and preparations can be discovered and proven through witnesses other than the ones who depose that they saw the witches commit the maleficent acts.[16]

On the second question. If the inquisitors find that the witches really do commit these crimes, then the inquisitors must consider the pact made with the Devil, in which the witches deny the Christian Faith or [implicitly] cast aside what they promised in the holy sacrament of baptism by adoring the Devil, offering him prayers for things that depend solely upon the power of God. If it is conclusively proven that they are heretics, then they must be given the ordinary penalty that is usually given, which the laws provide. If the witches deny their guilt, they may be relaxed to the secular arm. If they confess, they shall be given the penalty of jail and the *sanbenito,* more or less, according to the quality of their confession or how quickly they confessed.[17] In such a case, once the witches have completed the penance from the inquisitors, the secular judges can proceed to punish them for the deaths, damages, and other crimes they have committed.

Third question: Next, whether they should be punished in the same way or in some other [sic], if they have been fooled and did not really commit those deeds

Dr. Arcilla says they have to be erased from the earth through a penalty that fits what they actually did. Although they may be fooled in some degree as

15. Most of the delegates voiced a clear hierarchy; the Inquisition's penance should be fulfilled first, and only afterward might convicted witches be turned over to civil authorities.

16. Valdés was looking for witnesses "outside complicity," that is, people who could testify about the witches' actions without having taken part in the same.

17. Meaning, whether the witches appeared during an edict of grace to confess, or confessed during the inquisitors' admonitions, or hesitated or resisted confessing.

to what they actually did, they deserve to be put to death because they firmly consent to what they imagine when they are awake.

Bishop of Guadix: The same penalty should be given when they are fooled as when they truly go to the Devil's assemblies.

Bishop-elect of Granada: They have to be punished the same way when they are fooled and when they really perform *maleficia.*

Bishop of Mondoñedo: They must be punished somewhat more compassionately when they are fooled in their imagination, than when they truly commit *maleficia.* The inquisitors must be attentive to the gravity of the crime and the witches' contrition when they impose the penalty.[18]

Master Arrieta: They should not be punished by the same penalty when they actually commit the *maleficia* as when they are fooled, because the exterior act aggravates the interior crime.

Dr. Coronel: When it is clear that the witches did nothing to become fooled, they must be pardoned rather than punished. But when they performed heinous things that caused them to be fooled, and then subsequently were fooled, they have to be seriously punished for those *maleficia.*

Dr. Micer May: Given a case in which *maleficia* were not really performed, the penalty shall be left to [the inquisitors'] discretion, having considered the frequency [of the *maleficia*] and other circumstances.

Licentiate Valdés: On the third question, an extraordinary penalty should be given to them according to the sort of imagination, passion, or purpose they had for casting aside our Holy Faith and attributing to the Devil the honor that should be owed to God alone. The penalty should be given according to the acts they carried out to achieve their will and wicked purpose, such as making unguents, looking for toads, taking toads and skinning them—or anointing themselves, or other things of this sort—or the methods they used to attract others to their opinion in order to become witches, or the speeches they pronounced to achieve that persuasion.

Fourth question: Whether knowledge of those evil deeds [*maleficia*] and their punishment should concern inquisitors of heretical depravity, [or] whether it is [even] appropriate for the inquisitors to know about those deeds

Dr. Arcilla: Inquisitors should know about these *maleficia,* since the crime is one of infidelity.[19]

---

18. I.e., the degree of contrition which a witch exhibited should affect the penance.

19. Meaning infidelity to God.

Bishop of Guadix: The same.
Bishop-elect of Granada: The same.
Bishop of Mondoñedo: The same.
Dr. Coronel: The same.
Master Arrieta: The same.
Dr. Micer May: The same. . . .

Fifth conclusion [sic]: Whether the witches may be sentenced to the greatest ordinary penalty through their own confessions, without other proof or support

Dr. Arcilla: As far as renouncing the faith, blaspheming our Lord, the pact of serving demons, the unguents they say they make, and the injuries they confess that they caused, the penalty has to rest on their confessions, [assuming those confessions are] made according to the law. [But] as the witches sometimes could be fooled in certain details—such as, being carried bodily from one place or another—diligent investigations should be carried out and witnesses deposed in such matters, so that the inquisitors may construct a whole proof.[20]

Bishop of Guadix: The penalty should rest on their confessions.

Bishop of Granada [sic]: The penalty should rest on their confessions so they can be punished with the ordinary penalty, though a confession made under torture is not valid [without later ratification]. Just as in the crime of heresy, collaborators and the disqualified have to be received as witnesses where *maleficia* are concerned. Yet the witches' confessions are insufficient to prove the *maleficia* they say they committed,[21] and it is necessary that the injury they committed is clear, either through evidence of the deed, or through other supporting evidence and violent presumptions.

Bishop of Mondoñedo: The penalty must not rest on their confessions exclusively, so that their confessions prove they actually performed the said *maleficia*. But the confessions are enough to presume they are fooled, and they must be punished as if they were heretics.

Master Arrieta: The matter should be remitted to senior jurists.

Dr. Coronel: They have to be condemned through confessions made spontaneously, even if there is no other supporting proof.

---

20. As soon as the inquisitors sensed that a witch was deluded, that witch's confession became less weighty as proof.

21. In other words, a witch could confess to a demonic pact, and that confession might suffice as evidence of heresy. But *maleficia* committed with the aid of the Devil required corroboration.

Dr. Micer May: This is a discretionary matter. The judge may decide if the penalty must rest on the confessions or not, given the circumstances.

Licentiate Valdés: Regarding the things they confessed that they did outside of *maleficia*—when they were not anointed, not in the company of the Demon, or not going to the Demon's assembly—for instance, when they were persuading other people to become witches, or making unguents or anointing themselves, chatting with others while not anointed, persuading them or luring them to their evil opinion—then here, what they say against themselves or others should be believed. But what they say they said or did after they were anointed or in the presence or company of the Demon should not be entirely trustworthy, either about themselves or others. And if it cannot be verified through other sufficient proofs, signs, or presumptions, then in such a case they may be punished at least for imagination or intention, if it is clear from their confession that they had such. It seems as if the penalty must be . . . that they are exiled, shamed, and publicly whipped, according to the seriousness of their confessions.

Sixth conclusion [sic]: Finally, what remedy will destroy the plague of those witches

Dr. Arcilla: May they be instructed by teaching and example by good homilists selected to preach the faith to them, who will also perform works worthy of imitation. It would be very useful if the Franciscan and Dominican monasteries of that region reformed themselves, and then the preaching would be easy to do.

Bishop of Guadix: The Inquisition shall proceed against them and Catholic preachers shall be placed in their midst. Some Catholic monasteries shall be set up in those parts, and the clergy (especially ones who have benefices with the care of souls)[22] shall be reformed; and other similar works shall be done.

Bishop-elect of Granada: May preachers excellent in both life and teaching be placed there to instruct the witches so that they will not be so obscenely tricked by the Demon. May the preachers exhort them to confess and frequently receive the body of our Lord [i.e., the Eucharist], attend mass, and perform alms and fasts. May they preach that the female witches shall live and speak with Catholics, and have holy water in their homes, and have the cross and statues [as well]. And under threat of large penalties, order the witches not to speak to one another. Warn the witches about the other things

---

22. Care of souls is expressed through the Latin phrase *cura animarum*, which implies a priest's responsibility for the souls of his parishioners.

relayed in the *Canon episcopi,* [which says] they may not believe in another divinity besides God, and cannot perform transmutations, turning holy things into something else, except through God alone, even if it looks like they do so, which is a demonic illusion. Harshly punish those who perform similar things. The judges who proceed against the witches should be informed that the witches cannot do them any harm whatsoever.

Bishop of Mondoñedo: That they must perform similar remedies. First, preachers should be placed through those parts where this injury exists, who shall declare to the community [*pueblo*] the error of the witches, and how the witches have been tricked by the Demon. The preachers must preach all of this with great insistence, instructing everyone in the Catholic faith. And the preachers shall proceed according to the *Canon episcopi 26 q.5,* where St. Augustine writes down the things they have to preach and teach.[23]

The second remedy is that inquisitors and secular judges must be familiar with the [witchcraft] cases that pertain to them, and should proceed with great diligence and punish the offenders in those cases, imposing more or less serious penalties according to the quality of the offenses. The penalty should be a punishment for the offenders and an example to others. The third remedy is that processions shall be performed from one village to another; all the residents of those places shall go on them, with the clergy and with the crosses of the churches. They shall go sprinkling holy water to drive away evil spirits. All shall gather in some church or hermitage, and there the clergy shall deliver an educational sermon, and teach the people the things relayed by the *Canon episcopi.* And in the field where they say the Demon's assembly occurred, a hermitage shall be built and then once or twice a year they shall go there in procession, in remembrance of past errors. If there should be materials and means to build a monastery there, it would be very beneficial, so that the name of God might be continuously praised where it once was blasphemed and the Demon worshiped.

The fourth remedy is that His Majesty [Charles V] shall be entreated to write to His Holiness the Pope, asking that the pope order the claustral monasteries of that land to be reduced to observance [of their monastic rules], so that there shall be preachers and religious and zealous people who may teach and correct the simple people of those mountains. And for this purpose the [intervention of the] Lord Cardinal who holds the bishopric of Pamplona would be greatly beneficial,[24] since it is his responsibility to

---

23. The bishop is confused as to the provenance of the *Canon episcopi.*

24. The Bishop of Mondoñedo may be implying that the Bishop of Pamplona should supervise the pastoral correction of his diocese, go reside there, or do both; see Dr. Coronel's comment below. Clerical residence was certainly not routine in Spain in the 1520s, and the fact that it was possibly being urged here is significant

provide a remedy; and since his conscience is so aggrieved over the matter, as is well known. In order to discharge his conscience, the Bishop of Pamplona should do everything he can in the matter, being so advised. And if he does not come through, His Majesty shall order preachers and learned people of upright life to be paid from the fruits of that Cardinal's bishopric, in order to preach and teach the simple unlearned people of those parts.

Master Arrieta: The lords have pointed out many remedies; may the best be selected.

Dr. Coronel: Let some witches be punished so that others shall be warned. Next, judges who have a special charge of proceeding against witches shall be put in place. Next, a church shall be built in the place where the witches met with the Demon. Next, the word of God shall be preached frequently in those parts. Next, His Majesty shall see to it that the Bishop of Pamplona takes care of those villages that are under his particular jurisdiction, for this injury has occurred because a prelate has seldom been there.

Dr. Micer May: Has nothing to add to what has been stated. [Though] it would be good to build a church or oratory with the sign of the Cross in the place where they adored the Goat [sic], so that Christ should be adored where they blasphemed Him, as was done in Paris and Salamanca [sic]. The best thing would be to draw the witches [back to] Christ, because the more they removed themselves from God, the more they moved toward the Devil. To achieve this remedy, sermons, good ministers, and a good pastor would be beneficial, whose office would be to teach, scold, correct, and confirm. It would be good if some exemplary penalties or rewards were imposed, so that others would be dissuaded out of fear. He doubted whether they should impose *sanbenitos* on these witches, not because it wasn't appropriate, but because *sanbenitos* are imposed only on Jews, by general custom of the Inquisition; and if Jews saw *sanbenitos* on witches, the Jews could say they had not judaized,[25] but rather had been witches. Next, it would be good to promulgate edicts in the kingdoms of Navarre and Sardinia so that those who came to confess within a certain time limit would be pardoned. Good agents should be commissioned, in the Inquisition's usual manner, for the sequestration of personal property and ordinary penalties; if necessary, more agents should be commissioned in addition to the existing ones. Finally, may

---

in terms of religious values, since no official body of the Church pronounced on the matter until the Council of Trent in 1545–1547. For someone who allegedly resisted clerical residence even in the 1550s, see the descriptions of Inquisitor-General Fernando de Valdés in Document 18.

25. In other words, if witches as well as judaizers were given *sanbenitos,* the judaizers could claim they were convicted for a different heresy.

every petition be carried out so that the Prince of this World [i.e., the Devil] is banished.

Licentiate Valdés: It would be good if the bishop's *ordinario*[26] would send preachers and visitors through those parts of the kingdom affected by witchcraft, along with some bishops [sic] who would perform pontifical acts [sic], especially the administration of the sacrament of confirmation. The people should be ordered to have crosses and holy water in their homes. Everyone reputed to be involved in witchcraft should be obliged to carry around, day and night, a very obvious sign of the Cross, at least for some time; since the Demon is an enemy of the Cross and flees from it. And if one of them should be found without his cross, whether by day or night, he should be seriously punished. It also seems just to oblige these people to confess frequently and to hear Mass every day, at least for some time. It also would be good to build some oratory or hermitage with a great big cross in the location where the witches are said to go [to meet the Devil]. And crosses may be placed along the roads and other places where it is most often reported that these people speak to one another.

26. The *ordinario* was the bishop's representative in legal cases. See the Introduction.

THE INQUISITION AT MID-CENTURY: BLASPHEMERS, HYPOCRITES, PROTESTANTS

Document 14

Trial of Catalina Díaz, Wife of Juan Becervil, for Blasphemy. Penanced May 17, 1543[1]

[Over the last twenty years or so, historians have highlighted the fact that the Spanish Inquisition began to prosecute Old Christians in the second half of the sixteenth century for what we might think of as "moral offenses": bigamy, sodomy, and the belief that heterosexual fornication between consenting adults was not a sin; clerics' solicitation of sexual favors from their female penitents, called solicitación; *statements that being married was more virtuous than being celibate, called* estados; *and blasphemy, which frequently occurred in conjunction with gambling and prostitution.[2] This shift in prosecutorial priorities first occurred in the 1540s with the accession of Fernando de Valdés as Inquisitor-General—Valdés included paragraphs on bigamy and blasphemy in his instructions of 1561, for example—and was reinforced by Inquisitor-General Gaspar de Quiroga after 1573.[3] The latest scholarship stresses that the Inquisition continued to pursue judaizing* conversos *throughout the sixteenth century*

---

1. Archivo Histórico Nacional, Sección de la Inquisición de Toledo, Legajo 34, n. 8.

2. A clear and forceful statement of this shift is in Nalle, *God in La Mancha,* 60–69. The theological justification for prosecuting such cases was that no decent Christian could be a bigamist, blasphemer, sodomite, etc. While prostitution and gambling were not under the Inquisition's jurisdiction, they were viewed as signs of irreligion; the Council of Trent's deliberations, which were widely publicized in Spain beginning in the late 1540s, may have helped energize this new attention to morality. The charges against María de Cazalla hinted at *estados,* given her admittedly confusing comments about celibacy and marital sex; see Document 12.

3. Valdés noted that such offenses might not be formal heresy, but they still rendered people suspect in the faith; he went on to caution against overly severe penances, such as galley service, but also asserted that financial penalties for such errors could be exacted. See the relevant passage in Document 20 and contrast it to the section on blasphemy in Document 7. Historians hesitate to ascribe purely financial motives to this new interest in Old Christians, though tribunals did benefit from an increase in cases and hence confiscations.

and cautions that we may have overstated the Inquisition's attention to the Old Christian population. But there is no doubt that inquisitors saw an increase in their cases as they shifted their attention to blasphemy, bigamy, and the like.[4]

Very Reverend Lords,

I, Catalina Díaz, wife of Juan Becervil, resident of this city, say that on the second day of Pentecost, which has just passed, I went to confront Juan de Acanda in the yard of San Juan de los Caballeros. And a certain person asked me not to go, given how angry I was over the offensive words that Juan de Acanda had spoken to me; and I replied, "Don't speak to me about it, for if God Himself ordered me, I wouldn't listen." I didn't think about what I was saying, and because I spoke those words without thinking, and was so thoroughly angry, I ask Your Reverences to give me a salutary penance for it. And the petition being presented, I legally swear that what the petition contains is true.

Díaz said that an officer of the mint, who lives in the mint, whom she knows by sight but not by his name, was the one who told her not to go.

She said that she is thirty-two years old and lives in San Juan de los Caballeros. . . .

Díaz said she is an Old Christian on both parents' sides. She is the daughter of Damian Montero, resident of Madrid, who is dead. Her mother is named Ana Vizcayna and is a resident of Madrid.

Asked if she has blasphemed at any other time, she said no. She said the Ave Maria, the Pater Noster, the Creed, and the Salve Regina.[5]

The inquisitor asked if she has heard or knows of anything that has been said against the Faith. Then the inquisitor said that he ordered her to complete forty days of penance for having spoken the words contained in her confession. He also ordered her to have a Mass said one day this week, and to hear it with devotion. While the Mass was being said, she should pray for the honor of God, Three in One; and when the Mass was finished, she should give alms to the person who said it. She shall bring back a certificate from the cleric who says the Mass to verify that this occurred within the next six days. The inquisitor orders her henceforth to be more circumspect with her tongue, so as not to say such words or other similar ones. He gives her no other penance, with the resolution that she shall correct herself henceforth.

4. As an example, Nalle, *God in La Mancha* documents just such an increase in inquisition trials.

5. Díaz was asked to say her prayers even before Inquisitor-General Fernando de Valdés mandated it in 1561; the question arises as to whether Valdés was creating a precedent or reflecting one. See Document 20.

Document 15

Trial of Diego de Almodovar, Penanced for Blasphemy, 1545[1]

I, Diego de Almodovar, resident of the village of Aboler—which belongs to the military order of Calatrava, and the diocese and archbishopric of Toledo—appear before your lordships and confess, with the proper respect, that within the last twenty years, a little more or less, I acquired a vice, namely gambling. Sometimes when I practiced the said vice, I said with anger and passion, "I don't believe in so-and-so," or "I deny so-and-so," for which I ask pardon from God and a beneficial penance from your lordships. In all this time I, the said Diego de Almodovar, have confessed every year and received the sacraments, and I have confessed the sin [of swearing], and my confessors have absolved me from it. Now I have heard that your lordships have ordered edicts published and read in which many things are said about such matters, and I have been informed that I cannot be absolved of this sin unless I come to declare it before your lordships, on account of which I beg you to treat me mercifully.

I swear that what is contained in the said petition is true, and I say that what the petition says—"I don't believe in such-and-such," and "I deny such-and-such"—should have said "I don't believe in God" and "I deny God," because in that way this deponent said such blasphemies [sic], and he has said those blasphemies within the last twenty years[2] . . . and he does not remember how many times he said it [sic]. But he remembers that he said it within the last five years, because [people] had falsely told this deponent that a religious superior from Alcalá had something to do with this deponent's wife. When this deponent found the rumor was a lie, he said, "I deny God" three or four times, out of anger over the false allegation.

The deponent was asked if a secular judge had investigated this matter of his wife. He said that an investigation had not been carried out, nor had there been trouble about it, nor had he been punished any other time for any blasphemies.

Asked who was present when this deponent uttered the blasphemies, he said many people from the village were present when he said it, as they were

---

1. Archivo Histórico Nacional, Sección de la Inquisición de Toledo, Legajo 31, n. 21.

2. The narrative voice shifts here: the first is Diego's, as he presents the original petition to the inquisitors at Toledo and then reacts to that petition after it was read back to him; the second is the notary's, as he transcribes what occurred next.

gambling. Those still living, with whom this deponent gambled, are Francisco de Molina and Juan de Molina, and Diego de Espedes, and Antonio de Espedes, his brother, and Hernando de Espedes. These people are all residents of the said village, and he believes they heard it. Next, he said Antonio de Balderas was present during the blasphemies of five years ago . . . Balderas was the one who provoked this deponent [with the story about his wife]. The deponent thinks that a son of the said Balderas was present, though he doesn't remember which of Balderas' two sons it was. Being asked, he said he is an Old Christian. And I, the notary Agustín Yllán, was present.

Having seen the confession of Diego de Almodovar, we find that we condemn him, so that on the forthcoming Sunday, which is March 29, he shall hear the major mass that is said in the church of the village of Alcalá, from the point it begins until it ends, standing upright before the steps of the major altar . . . he shall be barefoot and barelegged, and hold a lit wax candle; he shall not sit nor kneel in the Mass, except that he shall kneel from the time they raise the Holy Sacrament [the Eucharist] until they have consumed it. He shall hand over the candle to the cleric who said the Mass when it ends, and he shall pray five Ave Marias and four Pater Nosters to the Lord, in reverence to God our Lord, whom he offended with his blasphemies. We warn him that henceforth he shall not say similar blasphemies in any way, or he will be punished with all severity. Within fifteen days of completing the said penance, he shall send proof of it with some person who is coming to this city, all of which we order by this sentence.

DOCUMENT 16

Heresy and False Sanctity of Magdalena de la Cruz, 1544–1546¹

[In the early modern period, and especially after 1600, the Spanish and Roman Inquisitions² intermittently but energetically prosecuted "little women" for affecting to be something they were not; namely, mystics who received gifts from God—the wounds of Christ, revelations of Purgatory, the ability to live on the Eucharist—and who were recognized by their local communities as living saints. Inquisitors in both Spain and Italy charged these "aspiring saints" with pretense of holiness, and their questions about simulation and delusion frequently evolved into interrogations about the Devil. Such prosecutions help to illuminate the presumptions and boundaries that early modern people brought to questions of sanctioned and illicit religious behavior, and the way they envisioned demonic forces.

It was not unheard of for professed nuns with a substantial reputation for sanctity to be unmasked as imposters, and the case of Magdalena de la Cruz was one of the most notorious in sixteenth-century Spain.³]

1. Rafael Gracia Boix, *Autos de fe y causas de la inquisición de Córdoba,* Colección de textos para la historia de Córdoba (Córdoba: Publicaciones de la Excma. Diputación Provincial, 1983), 11–14.

2. For the Congregation of the Inquisition founded by Pope Paul III in 1542, see John Tedeschi, *The Prosecution of Heresy: Collected Studies on the Inquisition in Early Modern Italy* (Binghamton, NY: Medieval and Renaissance Texts & Studies, 1991), and Anne Schutte's works cited in note 3 below.

3. The term "aspiring saints" is indebted to Anne Schutte; see below. There has been an explosion of research in this area, with the publication of some fine primary sources as well as secondary studies. See, for example, Gabriella Zarri, *Finzione e santità tra medioevo ed età moderna* (Torino: Rosenberg & Sellier, 1991); Anne Schutte, *Aspiring Saints: Pretense of Holiness, Inquisition, and Gender in the Republic of Venice, 1618–1750* (Baltimore: The Johns Hopkins University Press, 2001); Cecilia Ferrazzi, *Autobiography of an Aspiring Saint,* ed. Anne Schutte (Chicago: University of Chicago Press, 1996); Gillian Ahlgren, ed., *The Inquisition of Francisca.* Readers may also wish to consult other texts in this volume that pertain to false sanctity, namely the documents on Francisca Hernández (10), Francisco Ortiz (9), Antonio de Medrano (11), and Catalina Muñoz (25). Another nun who achieved fame for her holiness in the 1580s but was revealed as an imposter was the prioress of the Convent of the Annunciation in Lisbon, Sor María de la Visitación, the spiritual advisor of the renowned devotional author, Luis de Granada.

Letter dated January 30, 1544[4]

To tell Your Worship what you've commanded about Magdalena de la Cruz, I have to say truthfully that not even a great deal of paper would contain everything I know, but I will say what I saw and heard of her confession, and how Our Lord Jesus wanted the whole matter to be discovered.

We know well, and it's notorious to the whole world, that there is nothing in this life, whether good or evil, that shall not be discovered, even if it exists for a long time; in the end, [secrets] cannot endure long. Your Worship may know, as the whole world knows, that Magdalena de la Cruz has been a nun for forty years, with tremendous fame and exaltation. Among the nuns and monks of her order, there have always been great differences of opinion concerning her manner of living, and for this reason she has been tested frequently and made to suffer great torments; [but] she has always emerged free and with much honor. For this reason, and since she was approved and confirmed by everyone, she was elected abbess of her monastery for nine years. When those nine years were up (as they now are), she worked as hard as she could with the nuns for two years, so that they would again elect her abbess.[5] Yet she never could have achieved this goal, because they were on the verge of discovering her evil conduct, and it served God that such a great evil should be discovered. When Magdalena de la Cruz saw [that she was about to be discovered], she took the alms that great people had given to the convent out of love for her, and frittered them away to whomever she wished; the nuns no longer saw as many alms as they received, and the quantity that Magdalena de la Cruz gave and spent and squandered was so great that the nuns had to accuse her before the Provincial of taking the alms and giving them away. . . . [When this practice was] known to all, her life clearly seemed more indebted to the Devil than to God. . . . And one night all the nuns saw her bed completely encircled by large goats as black as pitch. When they asked who those hideous goats were, she replied that they were souls in Purgatory, who came to beg alms from her.

Another time, when she was in her cell and only one other nun was with her, the nun saw at midnight that Magdalena de la Cruz was with a very ugly and very dreadful black man. The nun was filled with dread and fear, but Magdalena de la Cruz replied, "Don't be afraid, sister, he will not harm us, look, he's a Seraph"; and the other nun ran out screaming and told all the other nuns what she had seen. Because of these things (and countless

4. This letter could have been composed for entertainment as well as didactic purposes.
5. For another tale of conflicts in convents, see Craig Harline, *The Burdens of Sister Margaret* (New York: Doubleday, 1994).

similar ones) that were discovered about her, our Provincial Father made a visitation, and reprehended her very harshly, and ordered her put into [the convent's] prison.

Then, when Magdalena was in prison, she suffered a wound in her hip, from which she was in danger of dying . . . and one night, when the nuns came to sing matins at midnight, they found her on her knees in the choir. Frightened, the convent jailers[6] went to the prison to look for her, and they found her sprawled on her bed; when they asked her how she had managed to get up, she replied that she had done no such thing, that she had not gotten out of bed. Then the nuns told the confessor about it, and the doctor who was taking care of her challenged her, saying that she could not escape from her present illness, that she should confess and put her soul in order. She said she was willing to have them call the confessor. The confessor came and stood by the bed; she began to tremble and ordered them to cover her because she was cold; she said he might come back another day to receive her confession. When the confessor came back, she did the same thing; the confessor returned a third time, and since things were now so out of hand, he returned with an understanding that if she behaved in a similar way, he would exorcise her. She did the same thing the third time, and when the confessor saw this, he ordered all the nuns to leave, and he bound the thumbs of her hands and exorcised her.

Then the demon replied and said he was a Seraph, one of those who had fallen from heaven; he had many legions under his power, and he and another demonic companion had accompanied Magdalena de la Cruz for many years; [he said], "Know that we shall not part from her until we carry her away, for she is ours." Hearing this, the confessor called the nuns to be present, and he said to Magdalena de la Cruz, "What do you think, Mother, about such enormous evils that are in you?" Seeing that she was discovered and could not deny it, she confessed the whole truth verbally: that she had these demonic companions since she was a little girl, and had known them to be evil since she was thirteen. But since she already was viewed as holy, she did not want to part from them. And she said she always had these two in her company, one to be with her, and the other to go throughout the whole world proclaiming her as holy. The latter was the one who took on her shape, and he was the one who went to the choir the night they found her kneeling there.

She said all these things and many more without number, which the confessor wrote down on many sheets of paper. And the confessor sent them to our Provincial Father, but the matter could not be kept so secret that the Inquisition did not learn of it. . . . Magdalena again confessed and affirmed

6. Who would have been nuns as well.

everything before the inquisitors, who told the Provincial to turn her over to them, for this business belonged to them; whoever made a pact with the demon was a heretic.[7] . . .

Then, on New Year's Day, the Provincial, some monks, the inquisitors, and the secretary of the Inquisition came and gathered in a room; all the nuns went in, one by one, to speak with the inquisitors, a process that continued until the next morning. Then a constable of the Inquisition came for Magdalena, on account of which we all were anguished and afflicted. She behaved with great courage and very little shame. They removed the nun's habit from her and dressed her in a black skirt; she left with great resolution and spirit, without any shame at all, saying to the nuns, "Mothers and sisters, do you wish to embrace me?" None of the nuns wanted to embrace her, on account of her shamelessness. Nevertheless, there were great tears among us to see how the demon had spent so much time in our convent, and how we had her as our abbess for so many years. For ten days, she confessed so many serious and horrifying things in the Inquisition that they cannot be written down or said out loud or even heard. I shall not write more because she is a prisoner, and very soon they will take her out [to an *auto de fe*] and her great misfortune shall be known. Written in Córdoba, in this convent of Santa Isabel, January 30, 1544.

May 3, 1546   The sentence that was given to Magdalena de la Cruz and the things about her that were clearly proclaimed, by order of the inquisitors, are as follows:[8]

1. In the confession of Magdalena de la Cruz, she states that since she was five (in her parents' house in the village of Aguilar, of which she is a native), a demon regularly appeared to her in the figure of an angel of light and consoled her in different ways. The demon appeared to her as Christ crucified and moved her to devotion and sanctity; he told her to crucify herself as well, and she crucified herself by putting some nails in the wall; and being thus crucified, he told her to follow him, and in attempting to do so she fell and broke two ribs. The demon constricted her two little fingers as his sign, and they never grew.

2. She said that at age seven, she left her parents' house and went to a cave that was next to the village of Aguilar, in order to create a holy life there. While in the cave, she awoke to find herself in her parents' house, without knowing who had transported her there.

7. On demonic pacts, see Document 13.

8. This sentence was read at the *auto* involving Magdalena. See Gracia Boix, *Autos de fe*, 15–19.

3. She said that when she was twelve and living in that village, she pursued her holiness and was considered holy by all the lords and principal people of the land. As a sign of this, her two little fingers didn't grow, and she showed them off and said it was a miracle; and she made friends with the Devil.

4. She said once, when the Most Holy Sacrament passed through the streets in Aguilar, she was sheltered where she couldn't see it. By chance, the wall had a small chink in it; she scraped at it a great deal in order to see the Holy Sacrament, and when the people passed by, she made some lumps of the wall fall down, and then said it was a miracle, as if the wall had opened up so she could see the Most Holy Sacrament as it passed by.

5. She said that when she was twelve, many demons appeared to her in the shape of gallant men, and one was more gallant than the rest and he was her familiar. Her familiar appeared to her in the shapes of St. Francis and St. Jerome and St. Anthony, and other saints and angels of light to whom she was devoted. Seeing these shapes many times, she became spiritually enraptured; and being thus enraptured, it seemed as if she saw the Most Holy Trinity and other great visions. Many times her familiar appeared to her in the shape of a man and told her to do everything he said, and he would make everyone view her as holy, and would carry her wherever she wished. . . .

6. She said that she went a long time without confessing or receiving the Eucharist; she said she had no need of either, because she was protected from her enemies. She said this many times to many people. Once she took a Host and secretly put in her mouth, then screamed and told the nuns that the Host had come to her when the priest consumed the Eucharist.[9] The nuns prostrated themselves and adored her. After she had received the Eucharist, she was spiritually enraptured for some time, and she remained in that state until the nuns carried her to her cell, and she said she was powerless to stop fainting. . . .

8. Next, she confessed that once when she was enraptured, the demons put some large needles through her feet, and she suffered it with great pain. This was done so that she would be viewed as holy and would not be discovered. She bore these signs on her feet for many days.[10]

9. Next, she said that many times she was crucified in her cell; she had chapped hands and a fissure in her side, and she pointed to them as a

---

9. Catalina Muñoz would confess the same thing in 1588; see Document 25.

10. Magdalena was attempting to recreate some of the wounds of Christ on the Cross, called the *stigmata*.

miracle. She wore an opening in her tunic in order to point out the wound in her side; and she showed it off in order to be viewed as holy. . . .

10. Next, many times she left the convent by order of the demon, and went to the monastery of St. Francis; there, she saw what the monks were doing. She also went to other monasteries. Then she returned to her own convent. . . .

14. Next, she said that it was a lie that she had not eaten in eleven years, because for the first seven, she had eaten bread and water that some nuns brought her . . . and for the other four she had eaten other things. She confessed all this verbally.[11]

15. Next, she said that a certain prelate enclosed her in a certain part of the convent to see if she truly did not eat. He put two monks there as guards. When she felt very weak, she commended herself to her demonic familiar; and that night she saw a light enter through the bars of a little window, and she does not know [sic] if they gave her a hand through the window. She found herself on the street with two monks, one of whom held her hand, and the other accompanied her; she asked who the monk was who held her hand, and he said he was St. Francis and the other St. Anthony; and they put her next to the pond of her convent. . . .

17. Next, once when certain people were receiving the Eucharist, it seemed to her as if some were black and some white. She said the black people were in a state of sin, because she knew certain secret things about them.

18. Next, one day she was carrying a basket of cherries in her hand. Some of the cherries were rotten, but when she washed them in the convent pool, they seemed fresh, and she said it was a miracle, and it was held as such among the nuns. . . .

21. Next, one night the demon abused her because she refused to consent to a certain lascivious act that he wanted her to perform. In anger, he took her by the hair and raised her up very high and then let her fall to the ground. She was greatly wounded and ill for many days. . . .

23. Next, once when she was walking, and desiring to know the pains Our Lady suffered in the death of Her Son, the demon came and gave her a push from behind and made her fall. She was hurt very badly on her chin, which she had to bandage for many days. The demon ordered her to hand out as relics the drops of blood that ran from her chin.[12]

11. The classic historical studies of women, Christianity, and food are Rudolph Bell, *Holy Anorexia* (Chicago: The University of Chicago Press, 1985), and Caroline Walker Bynum, *Holy Feast and Holy Fast: The Religious Significance of Food to Medieval Women* (Berkeley: University of California Press, 1987).

12. Presumably on pieces of cloth.

24. Next, one night the nuns heard a great noise in the convent, and she said it was the soul of a man who had just died, who was in danger of [not] attaining salvation; his soul had come to beg mercy from someone who could give it [namely, Magdalena herself]. In the same way she said that other souls were in Heaven, others in Purgatory, and others in Hell. . . .

26. Next, she said that she spoke many times with her familiar who was called Balvan; the other was called Patonio. She said prayers to them as if she were praying directly to God, in order to give the impression that she spoke with God, though in fact she only spoke with the demon [sic]. Other times she said prayers as if they were directed to Our Lady, to give the impression that she spoke with her, though again she only spoke with the demon. . . .

29. Next, she said she tricked the people by saying that she had gone to Purgatory and had seen many souls doing penance, and that she carried the fire of Purgatory on her feet. And she told the people that she did penance for the souls in Purgatory. When she put her feet into water, a very thick smoke came out of them. She stripped the skin off her feet and wrote on the pieces that she removed, and handed them out as relics.

30. Next, she once said she had seen 30,000 souls condemned and 10,000 saved. . . .

33. Next, speaking with certain people, she said many times that all the abbots and monks had lovers and this was not a sin nor was God offended by it. She said it was commonly done, and she knew very well that this was true, as she said.[13] . . .

35. Next, she made a person eat meat on a forbidden day, and she made others work, saying that it was always better to work than to rest.

36. Next, once she was in the choir and the demon came to her in the shape of a dove, and spoke with her about certain things. She told the nuns it was the Holy Spirit, and the nuns adored her. . . .

All of this was seen and examined by us [the inquisitors], [and] by just people of upright conscience.[14] Although we could proceed against her with many serious penalties for having offended God so abominably, we consider that God Our Lord does not wish the death of a sinner, but rather that he should convert and live and save his soul, for which He suffered. Considering

---

13. See the introduction to Documents 14 and 15 for the Inquisition's prosecution of moral offenses.

14. The latter being the *consultadores*.

the quality of the monastic order in which she professed, and the holy religion of clemency and salvation that she accepted—and other just and holy considerations—we were moved to treat her with customary mercy, being attentive to her dreadful declaration and public confession. Thus we order that she shall always be held as suspect in matters concerning our Holy Catholic Faith. It is our will, that on the day of the publication of this sentence, she shall leave the prisons of our tribunal with a burning candle in her hands, a gag on her tongue, and a rope around her neck, dressed in the habit of St. Francis which she professed. And she shall not wear a black veil. She shall go to the major church of this city of Córdoba, and shall stand on a stage during the Mass and the sermon of the Faith while our sentence is read. We order that she be perpetually enclosed in a convent of the order of St. Francis outside this city, which we shall specify; and we deprive and disqualify her perpetually from voting to elect [convent officers], nor can she be elected. She shall always be last in the choir, chapter, and refectory; and every Friday of the year she shall eat in the refectory as the nuns do when they are performing penance.[15] Next, we order her not to speak with anyone except the nuns or her provincial or vicar, without our permission. Next, we order her not to receive the Eucharist for three years, except out of the greatest necessity and with our permission. Next, we order her not to wear a veil for the rest of her life.

All of which we order her to fulfill, under penalty of being declared relapsed and cut off from the body and union of Our Holy Mother Church, in these writings and through them, etc.

Which sentence was pronounced on the Feast of the Holy Cross of May 1546, in Córdoba. Praise be to God.

15. Compare Magdalena's sentence to the one handed to the Jeronimite friar Juan Bautista de Cubas in 1581, Document 24.

Document 17

Letters from the Suprema, Inquisitor-General Fernando de Valdés, and Philip II on Protestants in the 1550s

[From an inquisitor's point of view, the 1550s demonstrated not only that Spain was being infiltrated by Protestantism, but also that those Reformed views—called luteranismo*—were corrupting members of the highest religious and social order.[1] The sites of infection were Seville and Valladolid; the attack thus looked as if it were being conducted from both north and south.[2] The agents of the contagion were famous preachers (Juan Gil, known as Dr. Egidio; Constantino Ponce de la Fuente), the occasional foreigner (Carlos de Seso was Italian), and men who had left Andalucia to live in Germany (Juan Pérez de Pineda and Julián Hernández). Their success inside Spain apparently depended upon personal zeal, personal contacts, and imported books. The people they converted were priors of monasteries, children of the nobility, members of the royal court, and civil servants of the king. This time, the treason of heresy seemed to menace the state as well as religion—the kind of threat that poor, judaizing women had never embodied—and retired Emperor Charles V,*

1. The latest study argues that cells in Spain somehow managed to import a relatively integral Protestantism without direct contact with leaders such as John Calvin, which was another powerful reason for Spanish authorities' concern. Thomas, *La represión del protestantismo,* 222. The circumstances and theology behind the Seville group are much less clear than in the Valladolid case; *ibid.,* 223. For a detailed narrative of the personalities and events involved in the discovery and prosecution of these Protestant cells, see Lea, *A History of the Inquisition of Spain,* vol. 3, 424–48. For bibliography on Spanish Protestants in the middle of the sixteenth century, see Kinder, *Spanish Protestants and Reformers.*

2. Historians find it easier to explain Seville's reception of Protestantism, since that city was an international center of trade and finance. On the other hand, the location of Protestant heretics in Valladolid—where the royal court tended to reside before 1561, and which was not close to any sea or international border—seems to demonstrate the success of Protestants in infiltrating the country. The Valladolid case also may have been treated as a more startling matter because of the apparent link between heresy and members of the royal court; in contrast, Seville had ready-made, historical precedents for its Protestants, namely the fact that the Inquisition had its first *auto de fe* there in 1481, and Juan Gil [Dr. Egidio] had already come under suspicion of Lutheranism in 1550. See note 13 below.

King Philip II, and Inquisitor-General Fernando de Valdés and the Suprema often alluded to sedition as they reacted to the discoveries.

The group of Protestants in Seville was exposed in 1557, when Juan Ponce de León, eldest son of the Count of Bailén, was arrested with Julián Hernández for distributing literature from Geneva.[3] The discoveries in Seville ultimately resulted in the arrests of approximately 150 people, including the prior and members of the Jeronimite monastery of San Isidro and nuns from the Jeronimite convent of Santa Paula; eleven of the monks successfully fled Spain after Hernández' arrest.[4] In northern Spain, suspected Lutherans were arrested in Zamora in 1558, and the ensuing testimony led inquisitors to investigate heterodox circles in Valladolid itself. The Valladolid tribunal arrested about fifty-five people for Protestantism, including the chief proselytizer, the governor of Toro, Carlos de Seso;[5] Agustín Cazalla,[6] famed preacher and former chaplain to Emperor Charles V; Friar Domingo de Rojas, son of the Marquis of Poza; and Ana Enríques, daughter of the Marquis of Alcañices.

The resulting autos de fe took place over three years. In Seville, they were held on September 24, 1559; December 22, 1560; and April 26 and October 28, 1562. A total of fifty-one men and women were burned in Seville for Protestantism. In Valladolid, the first auto occurred on May 21, 1559, with thirty tried for Protestantism and fourteen burned for the same; the next auto was held on October 8, 1559 in the presence of Philip II, with twenty-six people accused of Protestantism and twelve burned, including four nuns. These were public spectacles of the greatest religious drama: in Valladolid in 1559,

3. For a clear synthesis of Hernández' remarkable career as a smuggler of Protestant literature, see Thomas, *La represión del protestantismo*, 211–14.

4. The monks who successfully fled Spain included Cipriano de Valera, who published original Protestant works in Spanish and a Spanish translation of Calvin's *Institutes*, and Cassiodoro de Reina, who translated the Bible into Spanish and became the head of Protestant churches in London, Antwerp, and Frankfurt.

5. For Seso, see Document 18 as well as Pastore, *Il vangelo e la spada*, 234–40. There was a great irony in Seso turning out to be a Protestant, since he had been sponsored for his job by Philip II's confessor and other highly placed individuals at court.

6. Agustín Cazalla was the son of Pedro de Cazalla and Leonor de Vivero, the couple who befriended *alumbrada* Francisca Hernández and her circle in the early 1520s; see Document 10. Agustín, his brother Francisco, and his sister Beatriz were burned to death at the May 21, 1559 *auto de fe* in Valladolid; his mother, who was dead, was burned in effigy at that *auto* as well. Another brother, Pedro, was burned at the October 1559 *auto de fe*, while sister Constanza and brother Juan were sentenced to the *sanbenito* and perpetual prison. Thus six out of the ten Cazalla children were found guilty of heresy. Leonor's husband Pedro had died in 1543. Unfortunately, Agustín Cazalla's inquisition trial is not extant. The Valladolid Cazalla family was related to María de Cazalla's; see Document 12.

*Agustín Cazalla wept on the scaffolding for his errors and proclaimed the
truth of Catholicism as he was carried to the stake, while Carlos de Seso attested the truth of his Protestantism from a similar platform and was burned
alive without strangulation. The effect of these* autos *on the greater population
is debatable, but the inquisitor-general and the king followed up these legal
proceedings with cultural ones, namely, indices of prohibited books, and a
mandate that Spaniards were allowed to study or teach abroad only at specific
colleges in Bologna, Rome, Naples, and Coimbra. For generations, historians
have wondered what effects this attempt at a* cordon sanitaire *might have had
on Spanish intellectual and religious life. The most recent research emphasizes
the remarkable success of Protestant infiltration into the peninsula, the ineffec-
tiveness of prohibitions on books, and Spaniards' continuing access to the rest
of Western Europe, since the official orders of monarch and Inquisition were
not inherently and inevitably effective.]*

From the Suprema to Philip II, Valladolid, November 17, 1557[7]

To His Holy Catholic Majesty:

We recently entreated Your Majesty to write to the Viceroy of Sicily, Juan de
Vega, to tell him to give the Castle of San Pedro to the Inquisition so that
the Holy Office could operate from there, as [used to be] the case after the
Inquisition was installed in that kingdom. We pointed out the difficulties
that resulted from carrying out the inquisition in the Castle of Castellamar,
on account of not being able to work or receive testimony with the necessary secrecy because of the military guard that was continually at the castle
door; nor were the Castellamar's cells as suitable as the ones in San Pedro.
And though Your Majesty has so commanded the viceroy, we understand
through letters from inquisition officials that this order has not been carried
out. . . . We entreat Your Majesty to take care of this business so that Our
Lord and Your Majesty may be better served, and evils and errors in that
kingdom not take root . . . given that their punishment has been halted. We
also know about the injury committed by Viceroy Juan de Vega when he
arranged that the inquisitor shall not be informed about cases involving
people who marry two or more times. Laying aside the fact that the inquisitor there is able to prosecute such cases according to law (with the usual
limitation that the Holy Office observes in similar prosecutions), it is the
custom in that kingdom—as in the rest of Your Majesty's kingdoms—that

---

7. González Novalín, *El inquisidor general Fernando de Valdés*, vol 2, 180–82.

the inquisitors handle cases of bigamy.[8] We entreat Your Majesty to order it so henceforth.

Inquisition officials have also written to us that Viceroy Juan de Vega has arranged that the Holy Office cannot proceed against any royal official in the usual way according to law, without first giving a warning about it to Your Majesty's deputy who is in that kingdom. Besides being a great novelty, this is a great obstacle to the Holy Office's operating with the appropriate secrecy and freedom. We entreat Your Majesty not to allow such a provision, which is so prejudicial and so obstructs the Holy Office's work.[9]

His Imperial Majesty[10] and Your Highness have ordered that the inquisitors of that kingdom shall take on criminal cases that involve the Inquisition's lay servants [i.e., familiars],[11] [but] it seems that some novelty was almost immediately attempted in this area, from which would result great injury and prejudice as we have declared.[12] We entreat Your Majesty to order that the provisions on this matter be observed, and that inquisitors and their officials be given every consideration so they may carry out their office with complete liberty, so that Our Lord and Your Majesty may be better served, and the rivals of the Holy Office may not be emboldened to put their evil desires into effect. It is understood that the officials of the Holy Office need to be favored by Your Majesty and your ministers in this kingdom of Sicily, more than in any other.

The inquisitors of Seville have written that they have information against some monks of the monastery of St. Isidro, which is close to that city. From the information they have received, they suspect that those monks espouse many Lutheran errors and opinions; they have imprisoned three. Monks who have run away include Friar Francisco de Frías, the monastery's prior; Friar Pablo, the procurator; Friar Antonio del Corro and Friar Pelegrino de Paz, who was prior in Ecija; Friar Casiodoro, Friar Juan de Molina, Friar

8. See the introduction to Documents 14 and 15 for the Inquisition's newfound attention to moral offenses.

9. New research on inquisitors-general demonstrates the importance of jurisdictional conflicts in their daily routines. See the forthcoming dissertation by Kimberly Lynn Hossain, PhD candidate, The Johns Hopkins University, provisionally entitled, "Arbiters of Faith, Agents of Empire: Spanish Inquisitors and Their Careers, 1550–1650."

10. "His Imperial Majesty" refers to Charles V, father of Philip II.

11. Familiars (*familiares*) were lay servants of the Inquisition and were attached to individual tribunals. They ran errands for inquisitors and were not supposed to receive witness testimony.

12. Jurisdiction over the Inquisition's familiars in criminal cases was an inflammatory issue.

Miguel Carpintero, Friar Alonso Baptista, and Friar Lope Cortes. The Inquisition has information that these monks are in Geneva. The inquisitors also have information that there are many people in Seville suspected of the same crimes, against whom information has been received. The tribunal there shall proceed in their cases.

The same inquisitors also report that a great number of books, containing many heresies, have been brought into Seville. These books have been found in the possession of leading people both inside and outside that city. The inquisitors have information that a doctor, Juan Pérez—who fled Seville after the Inquisition seized his great friend Dr. Egidio,[13] and who now lives in Frankfurt—compiled the books and sent them [to Seville] with a Spanish Lutheran [Julián Hernández], who is [now] a prisoner. Dr. Juan Pérez sent some letters for the people who received the books. The tribunal shall proceed in the examination of [Julián Hernández, the Spanish Lutheran who brought the books] and the people who have the books. We shall inform Your Majesty as to what happens. The inquisitors have also written us that they have information that Dr. Juan Pérez also sent many of those books to this court [in Valladolid], though we do not know to whom. We entreat Your Majesty to order the books collected immediately, and those who possess them punished, because the impudence and cunning of these heretics is so great that the ministers of the Holy Office shall remedy the situation only with great difficulty. It is important that Your Majesty order a great demonstration in these matters, so that these heretics shall refrain from committing similar crimes with such boldness.

Licentiate Camino, chaplain of Your Majesty, lawyer for this council, has served for many years and has carried out his duties (and everything else he's been charged with) with great solicitude and fidelity. We entreat Your Majesty

---

13. Juan Gil, known as Dr. Egidio, had been one of Charles V's chaplains and traveled with the emperor to Germany. He was a canon of the Seville cathedral from 1537. Charles V nominated him for the bishopric of Tortosa in 1549, but the appointment disintegrated when Dr. Egidio was accused of heresy in 1550; in 1552, he was ordered to retract ten propositions, secluded for three years in a perpetual prison, and suspended from holy orders for ten years. He probably died in 1555. Dr. Juan Pérez (de Pineda) fled Seville after Dr. Egidio's arrest and lived in Geneva, where he prepared a Spanish translation of the New Testament and became good friends with Julián Hernández after the latter also settled there; the two collaborated on a Spanish edition of a Scriptural translation by Juan de Valdés, and decided together to smuggle Protestant literature into Seville. See Thomas, *La represión del protestantismo*, 212–14; John E. Longhurst, "Julián Hernández, Protestant Martyr," *Bibliothèque d'humanisme et renaissance* 22 (1960): 90–118; Eugénie Droz, "Note sur les impressiones genevoises transportées par Hernández," *Bibliothèque d'humanism et renaissance* 22 (1960): 119–32.

to make him a gift of some pension or some other thing . . . any gift from Your Majesty will be well used by him, and we shall receive it as our own.

Licentiate Calvo, reporter for this council, has served a long time and carries out his job with total solicitude.[14] We entreat Your Majesty to receive him as your chaplain.

May Our Lord guard and prosper the royal person of Your Majesty with the increase of more kingdoms. From Valladolid, November 17, 1557.

[Signed by] Fernando de Valdés [Inquisitor-General], Diego de Córdoba, Licentiate Cobos, Licentiate Valtodano, Dr. Andrés Pérez.

Reply from King Philip II, Brussels, March 4, 1558[15]

I have received the last letter you wrote to us; you have done well to inform me of everything in it. I consequently have ordered measures from here that can be carried out immediately, because I greatly desire substantial vigilance and care in the Inquisition's business. And thus I have ordered the seizure of a cleric whom they say is called Diego de Santa Cruz in those Spanish kingdoms; here, in the Low Countries, he is called Matheo de Santa Cruz. He was in the Spanish infantry, and there is no good account of him. He will be brought here as a prisoner under heavy guard and examined, and we shall see what needs to be done.

I know that you have implemented a good system in all parts of those Spanish kingdoms so that neither books nor writings shall enter which are not healthy doctrine. But agents solicit information and smuggle a number of heretical books into Aragón and Navarre from the lands of Antoine de Bourbon[16]—which are not as firm in the Catholic Faith as they should be—because of their proximity to the [Spanish] border. It's important to take great care in this matter, so it seems appropriate to advise you of it with this letter; we charge you with providing and ordering what you think necessary. If someone has some suspicious books, they should be taken away and the owner told that the books may not enter. And because I shall respond to your

14. Calvo is described as a *relator*, a counselor at law who made known the briefs to be tried; he read them before the court after they were examined and approved by both parties.

15. González Novalín, *El inquisidor general Fernando de Valdés*, vol. 2, 183. See Geoffrey Parker, *The Grand Strategy of Philip II* (New Haven: Yale University Press, 2000), chapter 2, for the time it could take letters to reach their destination.

16. Antoine de Bourbon (1518–1562)—the son of Charles, the duke of Vendôme, head of the house of Bourbon—married Jeanne d'Albret, queen of Navarre, in 1548. The Bourbon dynasty controlled a substantial share of central and southwestern France.

letter once the cleric [Matheo de Santa Cruz] has come and been examined, there is nothing more to say in this one. From Brussels, March 4, 1558.

From Inquisitor-General Valdés to Philip II, Valladolid, May 14, 1558[17]

At the time that Your Majesty left this city, you gave me permission, at my request, to visit my cathedral church, which I held as a great mercy. I was confident that by putting into practice what the Council of Trent mandated about visitation and the correction of churches and cathedral chapters (and given the fervor and favor with which Your Majesty and His Council viewed that Tridentine provision), God would give me grace to produce some fruit in that cathedral, in His service.[18] And so I immediately prepared to go visit that cathedral.

But my hope became lukewarm when I learned that the pope had rescinded the Council of Trent[19] and saw the coolness with which the Royal Council relayed that suspension, not to mention the cathedral chapters' great negligence and insolence in thinking they could defend and continue their abuses, from presuming the papal will was in their favor. Still, I was nevertheless disposed to make my journey, and I left Valladolid and arrived in Salamanca, where I was detained for some days in order to gain advice from certain learned people, and other things relevant to my goal. At that very moment, the cathedral chapters in those Spanish kingdoms began to stop saying the divine office, [because they were angry] over the collection

17. González Novalín, *El inquisidor general Fernando de Valdés*, vol. 2, 187–91. According to Novalín, by the summer of 1557, Valdés was discredited with Philip II for failing to loan the monarch 150,000 ducats for the war with France; Philip intended to confine Valdés to his diocese in Seville (where he had never resided), and to look for an opportunity to name a different inquisitor-general. The discovery of the Protestant cells in Seville and Valladolid was thus a godsend for Valdés, who consequently made himself indispensable; Charles V was in retreat in Yuste, Philip II was in Flanders, and Spain was being governed by Philip's younger sister Juana as regent. See Thomas, *La represión del protestantismo*, 217.

18. For Valdés' biography, see the introduction to Document 20. Valdés was, in sequence, bishop of Elna, Oviedo, and Sigüenza; and then archbishop of Seville. He occasionally visited his dioceses and celebrated synods but habitually resided at the royal court. The Council of Trent hotly debated episcopal residence between 1545 and 1547; rulings requiring it, but not explaining its origins, were first approved in 1547 and again in 1563.

19. The Council of Trent was suspended for the second time in 1552.

of the subsidy, which in Salamanca was implemented with much scandal and some disturbance of the people. Thus it was appropriate for me to deal with the men of the Salamanca cathedral chapter, giving them my opinion, and tempering the matter in such a way that it pleased God that they were among the first to abide by the obligation to pay the subsidy and to celebrate the divine office as before.

While I was in Salamanca, a great many Bibles and other books of sacred Scripture were discovered which were greatly contaminated by the incorporation of Lutheran opinions into their texts. (Similarly tainted works have been found in many other kingdoms, whether in the possession of individuals, or convents and universities.) Furthermore, members of the Suprema sent me a letter that Your Majesty ordered about the *moriscos* in the kingdom of Granada[20] . . . and between the one and the other, the Suprema pressed me urgently to return immediately. Hence I was forced to return to this city of Valladolid, where for many days I held a congregation of many people. Lawyers, theologians, and [faculties at] the universities of Salamanca, Alcalá, and Valladolid were consulted as to what should be done about the said books. A very solemn censure resulted from the congregation that was read and published with great care throughout all these kingdoms.

Afterward, on behalf of the kingdom of Aragón, I was asked with great urgency for some edict of grace for the *moriscos*—in light of their disturbances, and the way they move every day to France or somewhere else—so that they might treat the period of grace as a suitable pact for the quiet and health of their souls. After having looked into it and talked about it, and with the advice of the most serene princess,[21] the edict of grace was carried out in such a way that God and Your Majesty have been much served. And consequently the lords of that kingdom of Aragón, like the *moriscos,* have remained very content and calm, as Your Majesty will understand better when you come to these kingdoms, God willing. As soon as the edict of grace was issued in Aragón, the *moriscos* of Valladolid and their supporters also told me how, a few years ago, entire houses of parents, children, and wives left Valladolid, Ávila, Segovia, and Medina del Campo for France and other places, out of fear of the Inquisition. After pondering the matter, and having consulted with Her Highness, it was agreed that the same treaty should be undertaken with them as with the *moriscos* in Aragón; and so it was done to the contentment of all, as Your Majesty will also understand in more detail when you come to these kingdoms, God willing.

At the same time, it happened that the Law of Moses, which was thought to be extinguished from these kingdoms, began to reappear in the inquisition

---

20. See Document 22 for a description of the Spanish *moriscos.*

21. Juana, Philip II's younger sister, who was acting as regent while he was abroad.

of Murcia, where many guilty people were found.[22] Some of them were punished in a public and solemn *auto de fe* performed in that city, and justice will be done in the future for others who remain suspects, God willing. From this business great complaints resulted, whereby I determined to send one of the Suprema's members to visit Murcia and investigate (though this plan was abandoned because of the indisposition of some of the Suprema's members, among other reasons). Still, I did send an old inquisitor from Granada to investigate these matters, who now is in Murcia with the inquisitors there, and every day I await results, so that the Suprema may see the report and do what is necessary.

The business in Seville—when the Lutherans were discovered—occurred in this same period, and I have already given Your Majesty an account of it. These Lutherans have been of such importance that I would have been unable to resist coming immediately to Valladolid to consult with Her Highness about certain details, even if I [had actually] found myself in Seville. . . .

[Thus] the events that happened after Your Majesty left these kingdoms prevented me from carrying out my good intention to go to my cathedral, as I had wished (and even as certain people wished, who have importuned Your Majesty about it, for purposes which some day will become clear).[23] [Instead], God has been served that in Valladolid, Salamanca, Zamora, Toro, Palencia, and Logroño, among other places, a great number of Lutherans who impudently and boldly taught Lutheran errors have been discovered; and many of those involved were notable in learning, lineage, and the reputation of sanctity. It seems that God was served by my being present to investigate and punish this heresy, for even with my meager talent, my attendance has been very important, given the quality of the cases and the people inculpated in them, and the audacious things that have happened in this court. Not even the royal palace has been exempt.

All possible measures have been carried out to seize the guilty. Friar Domingo de Rojas and Don Carlos de Seso—the latter was a resident of Logroño and the former civil magistrate at Toro—got away from us. At one point they were in Navarre, close to the border of France, in order to pass into Bearne with a safe conduct and letters of recommendation. Among other steps to secure the ports, a particularly good measure was instigated by Pedro de Lamprío—*nuncio* of the Suprema, who had been sent through

22. When Valdés says that the Law of Moses has reappeared, he means that inquisitors in Murcia have discovered judaizing among *conversos*. See the introduction to Document 3.

23. Valdés' refusal to reside in his diocese provoked much criticism; see Document 18.

those territories—which pleased God. [Consequently] Friar Domingo de Rojas, Don Carlos de Seso, and Licentiate Herrera (Mayor of Sacas in Logroño) were seized while wearing laymen's clothes; Herrera was [also] found guilty. All three were brought to the Inquisition's prison in Valladolid, where they are held under close scrutiny, along with the others who have been imprisoned over this business, whose names are contained in the memorial that accompanies this letter. Because the *nuncio* Lamprio carried out a very good and remarkable effort, he deserves some position in the royal household or in this court from Your Majesty, so that others may be inspired by his reward to perform their office; and because the *nuncio* has the ability to undertake anything Your Majesty may wish him to perform. This arrangement may benefit the Holy Office, for everyone will understand that Your Majesty views himself as well served by those who assist the Inquisition.

Although [current] people on the Suprema are very qualified, as Your Majesty knows, I find myself somewhat alone at this moment, because the Suprema no longer has Licentiate Galarza, who is dead; [furthermore,] Licentiate Otarola has been sick for a long time, and Don Diego de Córdoba also has been suffering some indispositions recently, though he does what he can. Given this situation, it seems to me that since these Lutheran cases are so important and involve such respectable people, and in order to satisfy the opinion of the whole kingdom, it is appropriate that Don Diego and Licentiate Valtodano regularly attend the hearings with the prisoners which the inquisitors here must have, so that everything may be carried out with the proper authority and equity. I will remain alone in the Suprema with Diego de los Cobos and Dr. Andrés Pérez. Dr. Pérez is a person of much virtue and learning, but the examination of witnesses, trials, and sentences is not his specialty, though that is what has to be handled right now; Dr. Pérez would be of greater use if he were a lawyer. Thus it is appropriate for Your Majesty to name another person who could be more useful from among those on the Royal Council to replace [the dead] Licentiate Galarza, since Your Majesty knows them all better than I do. Given that I am in such great need of help, I think I will entreat Her Highness to order some of the people on the Council or some prelates with a background in the Inquisition to help me briefly with these matters, which require much prudence and vigilance, as well as authority.

I must consult with Your Majesty about some other matters which I have dared not entrust to a letter, and which I will hold in reserve until your arrival. Your Majesty will know about them when Our Lord sees fit to bring you to these kingdoms, if Our Lord is served for me to still be alive. May He guard your royal person with all prosperity.

In Valladolid, May 14, 1558.

Appendix. People who have been recently
seized and who are in the Inquisition in Valladolid[24]

Friar Domingo de Rojas

Don Pedro Sarmiento, his brother

Doña[25] Mencía de Figueroa, his wife

Don Luis de Rojas, grandson of the Marquis of Poza

Doña Ana Enríquez, daughter of the Marquis de Alcañices

Don Carlos de Seso

Dr. Cazalla and two of his brothers, who are clerics.[26] Two of his sisters.[27]
   Juan de Vivero, brother of the said doctor, married to Doña Juana de
   Silva, daughter of the Marquis of Montemayor[28]

Isabel, servant of one of the doctor's sisters

Doña Francisca de Zuñiga, daughter of Licentiate Baeza

Doña Catalina de Ortega, daughter of Licentiate Hernando Díaz

Joana Velázquez, servant of the Marquesa of Alcañices

Licentiate Herrezuelo, resident of Toro

Juan de Ulloa, commander of the Order of St. John, resident of Toro

Cristóbal de Padilla, resident of Zamora

Licentiate Herrera, mayor of Sacas, of Logroño

Juana Suárez, *beata,* resident of Valladolid

Antón Pasón, servant of Don Luis de Rojas, the cleric

Pedro de Sotelo, resident of Aldea el Palo

A silversmith called Joan García, and others

---

24. González Novalín, *El inquisidor general Fernando de Valdés,* vol. 2, 192.

25. "Don" and "Doña" are Spanish honorifics signifying a gentleman and a lady.
The number of such titles in this list signifies the high social status of the accused.

26. These brothers, who were burned as was Agustín, were Pedro, parish priest of
Pedrosa, and Francisco, parish priest of Hormigos.

27. Beatriz and Constanza. Beatriz was burned at the stake in May 1559; she was
closely associated with the convent of Our Lady of Belén, some of whose nuns were
also arrested by the Inquisition for Lutheranism. Constanza was sentenced to the *sanbenito* and perpetual prison.

28. Juan was sentenced to the *sanbenito* and perpetual prison.

Account of the Lutherans from the Suprema
to Pope Paul IV, September 9, 1558[29]

(Marginal note: This account was sent with the Suprema's letter to His Holiness.)

After the heresies and errors of Luther and his followers had come to light, they extended through much of Christendom. In comparison, by the grace of God the heart of Spain remained untouched by this stain, because of the great care and vigilance of the ministers of the Holy Office of the Inquisition. It is true that some individuals who were barely natives, and others who were outright foreigners, have been convicted and condemned for these Lutheran heresies [in Spain]; when they could be found, the penalties they merited were carried out on their bodies; when they fled, they were tried as rebels and condemned in their absence and contumacy.

A year ago, more or less—because of certain warnings and signs—inquisitors in Seville began to inquire diligently about certain people in that city. The inquisitors' efforts came to the attention of some monks of the monastery of St. Isidro, which was outside the city walls. These monks are members of the Order of Hermits of St. Jerome. Some, understanding themselves to be guilty, immediately fled the monastery, archbishopric, and kingdom; it is understood that they are now in Germany, and their names follow in a memorandum. Out of the monks who remained, eight are imprisoned in the Inquisition in Seville, along with their accomplices.

It was also known at the same time that a Spanish man named Julián [Hernández] had arrived in Seville from Germany;[30] he carried letters from a heretic named Juan Pérez [de Pineda], who was Spanish but was [now] living in Germany. These letters were for certain high-ranking people of Seville. The man named Julián also brought with him many heretical books in Latin as well as in Spanish, and he divided them among certain people who paid him well. This man was alerted, hidden, and persuaded to flee immediately because the inquisitors would know who he was and would burn him. Because of the diligence of the inquisitors, he was seized in the Sierra Morena, thirty leagues from Seville. He was [then] brought to Seville and is [now] imprisoned there. He initially was very obstinate in his heresies and spoke about many other people; he now seems to show repentance and a desire to be under the Catholic Church. From his imprisonment and [the monks'], many more [arrests] have resulted, and they are [all] prisoners. It is hoped that other imprisonments will occur in Seville and its territory.

29. González Novalín, *El inquisidor general Fernando de Valdés,* vol. 2, 215–21.

30. Julián Hernández specialized in the distribution of Protestant literature. See note 13.

It is understood that most of the damage in Seville resulted from some friends and devotees of Dr. Egidio, who was the teaching canon of the cathedral there, and who is now dead. Though in 1553 [sic] Dr. Egidio abjured many errors that he held about these matters, it is now suspected that he abjured falsely and fictitiously, and tricked the inquisitors in such a way that many people remained infected by his poison, including prominent, illustrious, and learned people who are now imprisoned in Seville, not counting the monks from St. Isidro. . . . In addition to the aforesaid, certain signs and warnings were given five or six months ago to the Inquisitor-General, the Suprema, and the inquisitors, that people were very secretly teaching the evil doctrines of Luther in Valladolid, Salamanca, Zaragoza, Toro, Palencia, and Logroño. Although the investigation and inquisition into this was started with all possible dissimulation and secrecy, it nevertheless came to the attention of some of the guilty, among whom were Friar Domingo de Rojas, monk and preacher of the Order of St. Dominic, son of the Marquis de Poza; and Don Carlos de Seso. They fled with precautions, with the monk in layman's clothes, but they were seized in Navarre, where they already had secured a safe conduct to go into France. They would have gone to France if the diligence of the Inquisition—sending word through all the ports and passes of the Spanish borders, maritime as well as land—had not prevented them. They were brought to the Inquisition of Valladolid where the royal court, the Inquisitor-General, and the Suprema reside. Many of their accomplices have been seized and are imprisoned, people who are also prominent, illustrious, and learned. . . .

Inquisitors have been sent to make inquires in Salamanca, Toro, Zamora, Palencia, Logroño, and other places where the principal dogmatizers and the guilty most frequently sent their communications, and from which one presumes they have done much harm. The Bishop of Tarazona, who has been an inquisitor for many years, was sent to Seville, so that as a person of experience and rank, he may accompany the inquisitors and persons who undertake business there, and lend fervor and authority to what is done, beyond what the Inquisitor-General and the Suprema can do at court. . . . His Imperial and Royal Majesty, and the Most Serene Princess, in his name, have thoroughly demonstrated support for the Inquisition, whether with letters or decrees. They have also expended 10,000 ducats to cover the expenses that the Inquisition has incurred and continues to incur. From the work, the Inquisition did not gain one *maravedí;* the Archbishop, the Inquisitor-General, even had to provide monies from his own treasury for the imprisonment of fugitives.

All possible measures have been diligently undertaken so that prohibited books—the principal cause of this evil—are neither sold nor brought into these kingdoms, and censures have been issued against them.[31] Still, the heretics in Germany and elsewhere seem to have corresponded with people here and have found a way to smuggle in such books. In order to provide even more vigilance, and to prevent foreign communication from damned provinces from doing even more harm, inquisitors, with their officials, shall go and reside by the coasts of the sea and in places where people of this quality tend to congregate. . . .

When these matters are pondered, it seems they had their start much further back. . . . The *alumbrados* or *dexados*,[32] natives of Guadalajara and other places in the kingdom of Toledo and elsewhere, were the seeds of these Lutheran heresies. Because the inquisitors of that epoch were not experienced in these Lutheran errors, they did not exercise the appropriate measures. . . . [By] forgoing the appropriate punishment, the inquisitors allowed the *alumbrados* and *dexados* to dare to become obstinate in their errors and to propagate them. It now also seems clear that Dr. Egidio was reconciled in 1553 so that the judges would not have to pursue the difficulties that might have presented themselves down the line . . . and as a result, the damage in Seville has occurred, since the most guilty were the passionate partisans and followers of Dr. Egidio. . . .

These errors and heresies (which Luther and his followers have begun to teach and sow in Spain) amount to a sort of sedition or mutiny among people prominent in lineage, religion, estate, and relatives. There is great suspicion that even greater damage could occur if these people were treated with the kindness that the Holy Office has shown to those converted from the Law of Moses or the sect of Muhammed, who usually have been common people, from whom no one would fear a tumult or scandal in the kingdom. [Conversely, just such a scandal] might be feared or suspected from those guilty of these Lutheran matters, given what has already been said. This is a question of liberty from the Church's obligations and precepts, which the community [*pueblo*] [already] holds as burdensome; the community would happily liberate itself from those obligations and precepts [if it had a role model]. It could be that the apostolic inquisitors, *consultadores*, and even the ecclesiastical judges [i.e., bishops] who have to determine this business . . . at the moment of voting and sentencing those on trial, might have some hesitation about relaxing some of the guilty to the secular arm, since they will be people of quality. And if the guilty are received mercifully, it is suspected

31. See Document 19.

32. See the introduction to Document 8. The noun *dexado* comes from the verb "to abandon"; *alumbrados dexados,* such as Francisca Hernández, were said to have abandoned themselves to the love of God.

that they will not complete the penances or imprisonments imposed upon them with the humility and patience that other people of less luck are accustomed to practice. The quality of such people and their relatives could provoke greater difficulties and scandals, whether in religion or in the question of the kingdom's public peace and tranquillity. Consequently, it is very appropriate that Your Holiness concede and order, through an apostolic brief, that apostolic inquisitors and *consultadores*—without fear or scruple of irregularity—can relax guilty people to the secular arm whom they fear or suspect might be likely to provoke a tumult in the Christian Republic or a perturbation in the peace and quiet of the kingdom, just as inquisitors relax the dogmatists of these heresies and those who are notably guilty.[33] It seems appropriate for the judges to exercise exemplary justice on such people, regardless of their secular, pontifical, or ecclesiastical rank, or their monastic order, habit, religion, and estate. [With that apostolic brief], such judges shall proceed with their trials . . . giving the inquisitors and *consultadores* free power and will to exercise the rigor which is required, given the quality of the business, the times, and the fear of future impediments. They can sentence beyond the boundaries of ordinary law [*etiam ultra terminos juris communis*]. . . .

Inquisitor-General Valdés to Philip II, May 22, 1559[34]

When the dean of the cathedral chapter of Oviedo (who left here on the seventeenth of this month) and I wrote to Your Majesty regarding the status of the current inquisition trials, we noted that an *auto de fe* would be celebrated this month . . . it was celebrated yesterday, Sunday, the Feast of the Most Holy Trinity, in the Plaza of Valladolid. The most serene princess and prince were present, as well as people from all the councils and high court, and nobles and gentlemen. Such a number of people came to see it from all over the kingdom, that no one could remember having seen so many congregated in a single day.[35] Thanks to the favor of God and Your Majesty, the entire community [*pueblo*] and the relatives of the principal prisoners remain satisfied that justice has been done; whether in general or in particular, they

---

33. Against theory and precedent, here the Suprema hints that its inquisitors may relax people to the secular arm even if they confess and repent, rather than reconciling them to the Church. Pope Paul IV gave the Inquisition permission to do exactly that in a brief dated January 4, 1559. Thomas, *La represión del protestantismo*, 225–26.

34. González Novalín, *El inquisidor general Fernando de Valdés*, vol. 2, 231–33.

35. Henry Kamen has insisted that *autos de fe* were highly unusual in most Spaniards' experience—hence the crowds to see them. See *The Spanish Inquisition,* 205–13.

have had no reason to complain about the judges and ministers who have been involved in this business, but rather they understand how much mercy was shown to the prisoners who remain alive. This is a sign that God has favored His cause, even in this instance, with special grace. . . .

I sent Your Majesty an account of some of the confessions and testimony that were read, because to send them all would be too lengthy. Dr. Cazalla was among the people who went to the *auto,* and he was relaxed to the secular arm. The night before the *auto,* he demonstrated a great conversion from his errors to what is Catholic; when his sentence was read and he was degraded from his rank, he declared on the scaffold, in a loud voice, how he had been deceived, [what] false opinions he had held, the mercy that God had shown by allowing him to recognize it, and the obedience he had for our Holy Catholic Faith. He made many solemn declarations about his conversion, namely, that he would die in subjection to the Roman Church and with true belief in the same, giving thanks to God and to the Holy Office of the Inquisition for putting him into this converted state, in which he hoped to be saved through God's mercy. Given the errors and heresies he held, he did not doubt that he could not have been saved before. He said all this with many tears and signs of true repentance, and with many excellent words, he persuaded the others who were relaxed with him to give thanks to God for having removed them from their errors, and for allowing them to die in the Catholic Faith of the Roman Church.

As a result the entire community was very instructed, and the condemned showed signs that they would die as good Christians, except for one who was always very obstinate and who died in his errors. Because of the great number of prisoners and the long sentences . . . it was not possible to celebrate the *auto* in a single day, and it was agreed to divide it up. A large proportion of the prisoners (and not the least guilty) remain in prison awaiting the second *auto,* which will be carried out immediately, God willing. . . . For this second *auto* to occur, we have to wait for your royal reply to the dispatch carried by the dean of [the cathedral chapter of] Oviedo; may there be no delay in sending the reply, because great difficulties would follow, along with the great amount of money that has been expended on the prisoners. In the *auto* yesterday, Friar Melchor Cano[36] preached a sermon of much doctrine, prudence, and great solemnity, as was necessary for such a day and place. Everyone was very satisfied with it, giving thanks to God and to Your

36. Cano (1509–1560) was a Dominican friar and bishop of the Canary Islands (where he never resided). Famous as a theologian and *consultador,* he attended the 1551–1552 sessions of the Council of Trent but sided with Philip II in his battles with Pope Paul IV. Cano played a central role in the Inquisition's vetting of works by Bartolomé Carranza. See Document 18.

Majesty. May your royal person be protected with the prosperity that all your servants desire for you. In Valladolid, May 22, 1559.

Errors of those penanced at the Valladolid
auto de fe of May 21, 1559[37]

The heresies of these people are listed in the twenty chapters below.

1. To say there is no Purgatory, only Heaven and Hell.
2. To say that man remains justified and pardoned through the Passion of Christ.
3. That there are no more than two sacraments, communion and matrimony.
4. That confession had to be a mental process, and that [man should confess] to God alone, with the Spirit; [but] not to monks or clerics, who were idiots.[38] People were saved through this sort of confession and none other.
5. That after such a confession was made, communion had to be performed, with bread and wine, as Our Lord gave on Holy Thursday, eating with His disciples, saying the words that He said. Communion can be done and given from one woman to another, and one man to another, saying those words.
6. That prayers to the saints and taking them as advocates was unnecessary, because most of the people treated as saints were in Hell.
7. Since there was no Purgatory, there was no need for offerings or masses for the dead.
8. They remove words from the Ave Maria, so that nothing is said after the word "Jesus." They also remove the lines, "Holy Mary, Mother of God, remember me, pray for us miserable sinners. Amen."[39] In the Creed, they remove the phrase, "holy church.'"
9. They say that the pope has no power to excommunicate, and that God gave the pope no power except to declare the Gospel. They make this declaration for their own benefit and interest, not the way God commanded and declared it.
10. That the pope is the Antichrist and the cardinals his ministers.

37. González Novalín, *El inquisidor general Fernando de Valdés,* vol. 2, 249–50.

38. *Idiota* in Spanish in this time period can signify stupidity or the inability to read Latin.

39. Thus the invocation of Mary as intercessor was omitted.

11. That clerics, monks, and nuns can be married.

12. It is not necessary to keep the commandments or hold the articles [of the Faith] to save oneself and be justified, and go to glory.

13. That masses did not have to be sold [for the dead and those in Purgatory].

14. That the [papal] indulgence called the *cruzada* was worthless and so were the other jubilees and indulgences, nor was there any reason for them, since there was no Purgatory.

15. To stop the supplicatory processions [*letanías*].

16. To stop fasting.

17. That Martin Luther and his works were very good and that he was another St. Paul, and he had the spirit of prophecy. They call him Luzbel.

18. That God was not alive in the monstrance,[40] that transubstantiation was a joke, and what the Church upholds about it is heresy.

19. Most of those who went to the *auto* had Lutheran books.

20. Others believed that if they were to die while making that mental confession, they would go to Heaven with their clothes and their shoes.[41]

---

40. The monstrance is a vessel that exhibits the Eucharist for the purposes of veneration.

41. For Spanish discussions on death and resurrection, see Carlos M. N. Eire, *From Madrid to Purgatory* (Cambridge: Cambridge University Press, 1995), Part I.

Document 18

Documents Pertaining to the Trial of Archbishop Bartolomé Carranza

[The trial of Archbishop Bartolomé Carranza is the single most famous prose-cution in the history of the Spanish Inquisition. Born in 1503, Carranza en-tered the Dominican monastic order at age sixteen and studied theology at the University of Salamanca, going on to teach that subject at the College of San Gregorio in Valladolid. He was well-connected and well-traveled: he helped Philip II and Mary Tudor reinstate Catholicism in England, accompanied Philip afterward to the Low Countries, and consoled the emperor Charles V on his deathbed in Yuste. He also took a serious approach to pastoral duties; he attended the first sessions of the Council of Trent (1545–1547) and summa-rized the Spanish contingent's outlook on clerical residence in a treatise enti-tled "On the Necessity of Episcopal Residence" [De necessaria residentia episcoporum, *Venice, 1547]. In July 1557, Philip II finally prevailed upon Carranza to accept the archbishopric of Toledo, which made him the Primate of Spain.[1] Within six months of taking up residence there, Carranza had vis-ited every parish and church in the city, reformed the cathedral chapter, and preached innumerable sermons. In April 1559, he left Toledo to conduct a vis-itation of the diocese. In August, he was seized by inquisitors in Torrelaguna.*

The legal basis for Carranza's arrest arose from accusations made by defen-dants charged with Lutheranism in Valladolid, as well as censures of his Com-mentaries on the Christian Catechism *(Antwerp 1558) crafted by fellow Dominican and enemy, Melchor Cano. But the best scholarship on the matter insists there were no substantial theological reasons for Carranza's prosecution; instead, the real motivation lay in the animosity of Inquisitor-General Fer-nando de Valdés.[2] Though Carranza recognized Valdés' enmity and was suc-cessful in having him recused from his case, he had to withstand sixteen formal accusations between 1559 and 1562, followed by a transfer of the case to*

1. Carranza had previously turned down the bishoprics of Cuzco, Peru, and the Ca-nary Islands. The "primate" refers to the principal see of a province, in this case, Spain itself.

2. The latest research demonstrates that Carranza endorsed the private, fraternal, and pastoral correction of doctrinal error, instead of the public, coercive, and legal-istic procedures preferred by Valdés; this difference between the two men probably only heightened their antagonism for one another. See Pastore, *Il vangelo e la spada*, 229–41.

Rome in 1567, which Philip II resisted; Philip continued to resist the resolution of the case until the matter became a diplomatic crisis. Between 1567 and 1576, two popes attempted to issue a verdict while Spain sent new advisors and censures to block Carranza's absolution. Pope Gregory XIII[3] finally pronounced sentence on April 14, 1576. Carranza had to abjure sixteen propositions and a vehement suspicion of heresy; he was also suspended from the administration of his diocese for five years. He died barely three weeks later. His inquisition trial had lasted seventeen years.

All paragraph headings below were added for the ease of the reader and do not occur in the original. The reader should note that Archbishop Carranza was commonly called Friar or Master Miranda, or Archbishop Bartolomé de Miranda, in his lifetime.]

Last declaration of Carlos de Seso, before his death at the *auto de fe,* Valladolid, October 7, 1559[4]

. . . [A]fter having been visited by monks who helped him move toward the discharge of his conscience, Sir Carlos de Seso, prisoner in this Holy Office, said the following at twelve midnight, more or less, the night before the *auto de fe:*

I knew their Lordships had sentenced me to be given up to death, but I never could believe it or be persuaded of it . . . because I never could believe that this tribunal would sentence anyone to death or prohibit them from going free if the indicted person had doubled the number of witnesses,[5] as in

3. Pope Gregory XIII, formerly jurist Ugo Buoncampagni, was Pope Pius IV's legate to Spain between 1559 and 1565, which meant he was in the country during the first half of Carranza's trial and would have known about both the recusation of Inquisitor-General Valdés and Carranza's attempts to get the trial moved to Rome. Buoncampagni was made a cardinal in 1564 and became pope in 1572; he pronounced Carranza's 1576 sentence.

4. Jose Ignacio Tellechea Idígoras, *Fray Bartolomé Carranza: Documentos históricos,* Archivo documental español, vol. XIX, 1 (Madrid: Real Academia de la Historia, 1962), vol. II, 54–59. Seso was an Italian, and a civil governor of the Spanish city of Toro; he had converted to evangelism in Italy, after being affected by the works of Spanish transplant Juan de Valdés; see note 5 in Document 17. Seso was burned alive, without strangulation, in the second Valladolid *auto de fe,* on October 8, 1559, in front of Philip II and his sister Juana. See Inquisitor-General Valdés' description of Seso's and Friar Domingo de Rojas' attempted escape in the letter of May 14, 1558, Document 17.

5. Seso seems to mean that he produced double the number of witnesses as the prosecutor.

fact occurred here. Thus I did not discharge my conscience, because I was hoping to go free and not die, since justice dictated that I go free. And now I see that I must be given up for death. I [thus] present this declaration in order to discharge my conscience and confess the truth. The following is a written record of the reasons that move me to it:

I, Sir Carlos de Seso, now see that God is served to do me this mercy, that I will die for having said that His Son, Jesus Christ Our Lord, has justified his chosen ones with His Passion and Death; and that it was Jesus Christ alone who made peace between us and God; and that *our* works have no role in such a supreme work as this. It is true that I have said this, and I believe it, because the most important thing for our salvation is to believe that Jesus Christ is our salvation, which consists in knowing God and Jesus Christ as sent from the same God; so says St. John. Along with saying and believing that we were justified from God's grace through Jesus Christ, I never stopped saying, and always believed, that though our works are necessary, they are not the cause of our salvation. For Jesus Christ, Our Lord alone, deserves the glory of our salvation, not us; we deserve complete evil. . . .

In my confessions and depositions, I said I believed there is a place of Purgatory after this life. Here I spoke a great falsehood and blasphemy, and offended the love of God and the power of the Passion of Jesus Christ our Lord, and His honor . . . and I beg God's pardon for it, with the confidence that His promises and kindness will pardon me and have pardoned me, which is a work worthy of His infinite love, which I so little deserve. I retract my statement that I believed in Purgatory. I neglected to confess at the time in order not to name the people to whom I communicated my real belief, so as not to harm someone who did not deserve it, since I understood that they would have to be held as heretics and thus dishonored, lost, and perhaps killed. I believed it was Catholic and good to do what I did. . . .

Beyond this, I believe it to be true that no oath before men can oblige me to depose against the honor of Jesus Christ our Lord, or to endanger my neighbor, if I do not believe that what they ask me is evil, and if I know for certain that new cases would result from my deposition. And in this way I always swore, understanding in my soul that I would speak the complete truth so long as it did not dishonor Jesus Christ our Lord or hurt my neighbor. As I say, this is why, from the first moment, I have not said what I felt about justification and Purgatory. I do not want to deny that weakness of the flesh had some part in my wickedness. . . . I know of no others in Spain who hold these opinions, except for some who have testified against me as witnesses in the publication of the charges. I not only pardon them, but thank them for having been the means by which I might achieve such a great mercy, to die like Jesus Christ Our Lord. . . .

Asked where he learned such things and how long ago, Carlos de Seso said, "Lord Inquisitor, I heard justification preached in all the churches in

Italy, although I don't recall in particular by whom." He was in Italy seven or eight years ago, and he heard justification [by Faith] publicly preached there, and from it, he inferred the rest [about the nonexistence of Purgatory].

Asked to whom he has communicated what he said in Italy and Spain . . . and who shared his opinions. He replied that in Spain, the Inquisition should refer to those who say they communicated with him; and he does not recall communicating with anyone in Italy. He once spoke about Purgatory with Pedro de Cazalla,[6] and afterward with the archbishop of Toledo [Carranza], as he has already said. Afterward, he never saw the archbishop again, nor had they communicated before about this matter. . . .

Testimony of Friar Domingo de Rojas, O.P., Valladolid, August 20, 1558[7]

Next, he said that ten or six [sic] years ago, more or less, he was in Alcañizes with Friar Bartolomé de Miranda [Cazalla]. [Miranda] spoke to this defendant about the Passion of Christ, and the confidence that we must have in our salvation through Christ. This defendant said [to Miranda] that he still was afraid, and he believed that first he would have to pass through Purgatory. And Friar Bartolomé de Miranda replied, "A bad year for Purgatory. You're not ready at present for this philosophy." Nothing more was said, and no one else was present. This defendant afterward relayed what had happened to certain people, but he could not recall to whom. Later, when this defendant spoke to Friar Bartolomé de Miranda about justification, Friar Miranda always expounded it in a Catholic way. When Friar Bartolomé de Miranda was in Trent in the Council, he was even noted as going too far in wanting to maintain that the Roman Church had more authority than the Gospel [sic], and that the Gospel was believed because it had its authority from the Roman Church. The greatest Catholics there did not hold this opinion.

Continuation of Domingo de Rojas, O.P., Valladolid, August 23, 1558

. . . [H]e was pained about what he said in the previous session, regarding what the archbishop of Toledo said to him in Alcañizes; he now remembered

6. On the Cazalla family's misfortunes at the Valladolid *auto de fe* of May 1559, see Document 17.

7. Tellechea Idígoras, *Fray Bartolomé de Carranza*, vol. 2, 66–67. Rojas was a noble, the son of the Marquis of Poza; he was burned at the stake at the second Valladolid *auto de fe,* on October 8, 1559. He repented on the pyre and was strangled.

more clearly what had happened. When Friar Bartolomé de Miranda told this defendant that he thought the defendant would go directly to heaven, this defendant replied, "And Purgatory?" And Friar Bartolomé de Miranda replied, "Bad year." The defendant does not recall that Friar Miranda said, "Bad year for Purgatory." Everything else this defendant has said about the matter is true, and he has never understood, suspected, or thought that Master Miranda believed something that wasn't Catholic, and he remembers nothing else.

He was told that he should always consider what he says in these hearings, because variations and contradictions cause many difficulties and obfuscate the truth, and the truth is what this Holy Office particularly desires to know. Thus he must consider what he says, and be measured and circumspect. The defendant said that he had only changed one word. . . .

Testimony of Lady Catalina de Castilla, Valladolid, April 8, 1559[8]

. . . [U]nder oath, Lady Catalina de Castilla, aged twenty-four, declared the following among other things:

She was asked if she knows or suspects the reason why she has been seized by the Holy Office. She said that under charge of the oath she has sworn, that if she had been able, she would not have waited for them to bring her [here], but that she was always sick with fevers after Inquisitor Ybarra was in Logroño. And she said, "Lords, I had a great desire to serve God, and so I asked Sir Carlos de Seso how I could serve Him better. The reason I asked him specifically was because I held him as a very good Christian, and he told me that he would show me how I could serve God better than before. On the feast day of St. John, 1557, he was reading a book; he said that if I promised and swore not to say anything to anyone—not even to my husband, if I were married—that he would read it to me, and would tell me what it meant, and so I promised. He then read me the book, which was written by hand and in the Spanish language. The book concerned the justification of Jesus Christ, and said that because Jesus Christ had paid the penalty for us, we had no more to pay, except that we be cleansed of our sins; with Christ's sacrifice and divine justice, our sins would be paid for. Carlos de Seso gave me the book so that I could read it, and I did read it. In the book there were many quotes from St. Paul, St. Peter, and St. John; all of them implied there was no Purgatory, because with the death of Jesus Christ our sins were pardoned and we satisfied God the Father, and so I believed it.

8. Tellechea Idígoras, *Fray Bartolomé de Carranza*, vol. 2, 189–90.

Continuation of Lady Catalina de Castilla, Valladolid, May 5, 1559[9]

Sir Carlos also told this defendant that he believed Friar Bartolomé de Miranda, Archbishop of Toledo, believed these things too. Sir Carlos said he knew this because Friar Bartolomé de Miranda had called him to Valladolid to speak with him. And Pedro de Cazalla[10] confessed with the Archbishop, and at that point Pedro de Cazalla valued nothing more than justification; and the Archbishop knew that Sir Carlos [likewise] valued justification, and he sent for him, as she has said. The archbishop spoke to Pedro de Cazalla and to Sir Carlos, and told them not to value justification because it would not be tolerated in Spain. Sir Carlos told this defendant that given the way the Archbishop reprimanded him, it seemed as if the Archbishop valued justification as much as he did. It was understood that the justification they discussed involved Purgatory, which ensues from it [sic].[11] The Archbishop of Toledo discussed all of this, and then told them not to discuss it any more. . . .

Information against Carranza presented by prosecutor Camino, May 6, 1559[12]

In Valladolid, Saturday, May 6, 1559, the illustrious lord Fernando de Valdés, Archbishop of Seville, Inquisitor-General, was with the lords of the Suprema, and licentiate Camino appeared, who is the prosecutor of the Suprema. Camino said that he presented the following writings as proof of his intention [to prosecute] in the matter of the Reverend Bartolomé de Miranda, Archbishop of Toledo:

First, a printed book . . . composed by Friar Bartolomé de Miranda, entitled *Commentaries on the Christian Catechism,* printed in Antwerp in the shop of Martín Nucio, 1558.[13] Also the evaluation of the same book made by lords Friar Melchor Cano and Friar Domingo de Cuevas.

9. Tellechea Idígoras, *Fray Bartolomé de Carranza,* vol. 2, 190.

10. Brother of Agustín Cazalla, former chaplain of Emperor Charles V. See Document 17, note 6.

11. She implies that by discussing justification by faith, they naturally and logically began to talk about Purgatory.

12. Tellechea Idígoras, *Fray Bartolomé Carranza,* vol. 2, 302–5.

13. Spanish book titles in the original have been translated into English; Latin titles have been preserved.

Next, another evaluation of the same book by master Friar Domingo de Soto, of the Order of St. Dominic.[14]

Next, an evaluation of the same book by master Friar Pedro de Ibarra, provincial of the Order of St. Francis.

Likewise, Camino presented another book . . . covered in red leather, written by hand, which contains the following works: *Articles of the Faith, Sermon on the Love of God,* an exposition *Quam dilecta tabernacula tua;* another sermon, *Super flumina Babilonis;* another sermon *How to Hear Mass,* another sermon *On the Love of God.*

Another, smaller book written by hand, covered in red leather, which contains the following works: *Sermon on the Lord, On Holy Thursday, Exposition of the Psalm "De profundis," A Work on the Love of God among Us.*

The evaluation of the works contained in these two books by Master Carlos. [sic]

The evaluation of all the works by Master Cano and Friar Domingo de Cuevas, O.P.

Next, the statements and depositions of the following people:

- Pedro de Cazalla, parish priest of Pedrosa[15]
- Lady Ana Enríquez, wife of Sir Juan Alonso de Fonseca[16]
- Lady Catalina de los Ríos, prioress of the monastery of St. Catalina of Valladolid
- Lady Antonia de Mella, wife of Gregorio de Sotelo, resident of Zamora
- Pedro de Sotelo, resident of the village of El Palo
- Lady Francisca de Zuñiga, daughter of Licentiate Vaeza
- Lady Isabel de Quiñones, lady-in-waiting to the Princess
- Ysabel de Estrada, resident of Pedrosa
- Sir Carlos de Seso, resident of Logroño
- García Barbón de Bexega, constable of the Inquisition in Calahorra
- Friar Domingo de Rojas, of the Order of St. Dominic
- Francisco de Coca, peddler of Francisco de Paredes [sic]
- Friar Vicente Paletino, of the Order of St. Dominic
- Licentiate Gálbez, doctor to the Suprema
- Pedro González de Mendoza, prison warden of the Inquisition

14. Prominent theologian who ended up, unwillingly, as a censor of Carranza's works at this stage of the trial.

15. Brother of Agustín de Cazalla. See Document 17, note 6.

16. Doña Ana was also the daughter of the Marquis of Alcañices.

- Fernando de Sotelo, resident of Toro
- Dr. Agustín de Cazalla, preacher of His Majesty the King
- Friar Ambrosio de Salazar, of the Order of St. Dominic
- Juan de Bibero, resident of Valladolid
- Friar Juan Regla, of the Order of St. Jerome
- Lord Luis de Ávila e Zuñiga, Major Commander of the Military Order of Alcántara
- Luis Quixada, formerly majordomo to the Emperor
- Friar Francisco de Villalva, of the Order of St. Jerome
- Friar Marcos de Cardona, of the Order of St. Jerome
- The Count of Buendía
- The Countess of Buendía
- Elbira Xuárez, servant of the Countess of Buendía
- Madalena de Morales, servant of the said Countess
- Pedro de Valdés, chaplain of the said Count
- Juan Baptista Daza, majordomo to the said Count
- Friar Baltasar Pérez, of the Order of St. Dominic
- Juan de Perea, mace-bearer of the King
- Friar Bernardo de Robres, of the Order of St. Dominic
- Friar Antonio de Harze, member of the College of St. Gregory in Valladolid
- Some letters that Juan Sánchez wrote from the port and from Flanders to Lady Catalina de Hortega
- A letter that the Archbishop of Toledo wrote to Dr. Cazalla
- Two letters that the Archbishop of Toledo wrote to Licentiate Herrera
- Two summaries of two sermons that the Archbishop of Toledo wrote to Licenciate Herrera; the Archbishop made the summaries in Valladolid after he returned from Flanders
- Summary of the information that emerged from testimony about the Archbishop
- Next, a note that the lord Bishop of Cuenca wrote to the lord Archbishop of Seville from Pareja, on April 28, 1559[17]

---

17. Inquisitor-General Valdés accepted the prosecutor's evidence. On May 13, 1559, after consulting with other members of the Suprema, Valdés ordered that a letter be sent to Carranza, asking that he appear personally to respond to the prosecutor. I don't know whether the letter was actually sent; Carranza never voluntarily appeared.

Petition from prosecutor Camino
to imprison Carranza, Valladolid, July 15, 1559[18]

Illustrious and Reverend Lord. I, Licentiate Camino, prosecutor for the
Suprema, state that I presented before Your Holy Reverence a papal brief
from our very holy father, Pope Paul IV, by which the Inquisition may proceed against all prelates, bishops, archbishops, patriarchs, or ecclesiastics of
any other rank and condition, who are suspected of heresy. Your Holy Reverence accepted the brief.[19] After which I denounced Friar Bartolomé de Miranda, the current archbishop of Toledo, and said that he was singled out
and testified against in the registers and writings of the Holy Office of the
Inquisition, for having held and believed many serious errors of the repro-
bate sect of Luther, and for having taught and dogmatized these errors to
others. I entreated Your Holy Reverence to order that the said Friar Bartolomé de Miranda be seized, and that the fruits of the Toledo archbishopric
be sequestered; and your Reverence ordered that I give information as to
what was contained in my petition. To substantiate my request, I presented
many witnesses, writings, and the book entitled *Catechism of Christian Doctrine* (which was written by Miranda), along with the evaluations and censures of many eminent theologians and learned men in faculties of theology.
Your Holy Reverence ordered that Friar Miranda appear personally to respond to the prosecutor's accusation. After which arose even more testimony
and proof against Friar Miranda, especially the statement and deposition of
Lady Luisa de Mendoza, wife of secretary Juan Básque de Molina. . . .

Given the quantity of proof that exists against Friar Miranda, and the suspicion that must be held about the great danger that his wicked doctrine
poses in these kingdoms—and to better reach the truth—it seems clear that
seizing the Archbishop must occur. Which seizure must be ordered now, especially in light of the new proof and everything else in this matter. Thus I
entreat, and if necessary require, Your Holy Reverence to order that Friar
Miranda be seized immediately and without delay and put into a secret, secure cell; and may all his income, goods, and estate be sequestered; and his
trial shall conform to law, and to the instructions, custom, and style of this
Holy Office. If it is necessary for this petition to be carried out, I entreat
Your Holy Reverence according to what you yourself have so provided and
ordered, and I allege as offenses what is contained in this petition, and I accuse Friar Bartolomé de Miranda of everything that is currently and subsequently against him in the Holy Office. All of which I will express specifically

18. Tellechea Idígoras, *Fray Bartolomé Carranza,* vol. 2, 320–22.

19. Inquisitor-General Valdés took care to procure this document from the pope in
the middle of the Protestant crisis, before moving in Carranza's direction; his actions
were supported by Philip II. See Document 17.

in the right time and place, after what I have asked in this petition is put into effect. Above all I ask that justice be done. . . .

Imprisonment of the Archbishop of Toledo[20]

I, Juan de Ledesma, public notary by apostolic authority, attest that on Tuesday, August 22, 1559, around five o'clock in the morning, in the village of Torrelaguna, in the diocese of Toledo, by the power of the commission, order, power, and subdelegation dated August 17, 1559, and given to them by the Illustrious Reverend Lord Fernando de Valdés, Inquisitor-General in all the kingdoms of His Majesty, that the very reverend lords Rodrigo de Castro, apostolic inquisitor of Toledo, Valladolid, and their districts, and Diego Ramírez, inquisitor of Toledo. . . . went to the houses of Juan de Salinas Vélez de Guevara, resident of Torrelaguna, where the Archbishop of Toledo, Reverend Lord Bartolomé Carranza de Miranda, was staying. They found him in the room and hall where he slept.

Since he was found there, Juan Cebrían de Ybarra, chief constable . . . seized the person of the Archbishop of Toledo. The capture being achieved, the Archbishop of Toledo asked on what grounds he was seized; I, the notary, by order of the lords, read to him the commission from the Archbishop of Seville, Inquisitor-General, and with it, the papal brief and apostolic letters from Pope Paul IV. . . .

Then Juan Cebrían de Ybarra, chief constable, seized and sequestered a mailbag that was found open, with many papers inside, on top of a table in the room where the Archbishop of Toledo slept. After the mailbag was sequestered, the chief bailiff closed it with its key and gave it to Lord Rodrigo de Castro. Then the Archbishop of Toledo told me, the notary, to take it down as testimony that the Archbishop of Seville, who gave the said commission and order, was not his judge, because Carranza himself was a prelate and the chief ecclesiastic of Spain; and the papal brief was general and said nothing about him. Then the Archbishop said that they must be in conformity with the papal brief if they were going to act on it, and the things required by that brief should precede his capture. Neither the Lord Archbishop of Seville nor the other lord inquisitors were his judges. And Carranza appealed the seizure and everything else to the pope as the judge to whom he was immediately subject; and he asked that the sequestered mailbag be protected, because it contained his defenses and papers of his office, and matters that he was conducting with His Holiness the Pope and His Majesty Philip II. . . .

When this was done, guards were put in front of the apartment and the house. The next day, Wednesday, August 23, an hour before daybreak, more or less, the lord inquisitors and the chief constable took the Archbishop of

20. Tellechea Idígoras, *Fray Bartolomé Carranza,* vol. 2, 327–30.

Toledo from Torrelaguna. . . . In testimony of which I signed my customary signature.

Carranza's attempt to recuse Inquisitor-General Fernando de Valdés, Valladolid, October 17, 1559[21]

Lord Friar Bartolomé Carranza de Miranda, Archbishop of Toledo, Primate of Spain, in the lawsuit with Licentiate Camino, chief prosecutor of the Suprema, regarding the recusation I have placed against the Reverend Lord Archbishop of Seville. I ask your lordships that they decree that the Lord Archbishop of Seville swear an oath and respond clearly and openly to the following interrogatory.

   1. First I propose (and if it is denied, I shall undertake to prove it) that the Lord Archbishop of Seville has known me for more than ten years. Likewise, he knows Lady María de Mendoza, the former wife of the Knight-Commander of León, Francisco de los Cobos, now deceased, whom the Archbishop of Seville also knew; and her son as well, the Marquis de Camarasa.

   2. Next, I propose, etc. . . . [sic] that the Lord Archbishop of Seville has always been the intimate friend of that Knight-Commander, and continues to be such with his son, the Marquis de Camarasa. The Lord Archbishop of Seville favors the son and María de Mendoza as much as he can.

   3. Next, I propose, etc. . . . [sic] that the Archbishop of Seville knows about the lawsuit that the Marquis of Camarasa lodged against me over the governorship [adelantamiento] of Cazorla, which is part of my episcopal prebend, whether that lawsuit was occurring in the Court of Rome or before the members of the Royal Council of His Majesty. The said governorship is of enormous quality and generates much rent.

   4. Next, I propose, etc. . . . [sic] that Our Holy Father, Pope Paul IV, of happy memory, conceded a motion so that the said governorship of Cazorla would be restored to the episcopal prebend and to me in my name, whereby I petitioned the Royal Council that the said restitution be carried out and the papal brief put into effect.

   5. Next I propose that the Lord Archbishop of Seville learned of the papal brief and of what I petitioned in the Royal Council. He immediately went to the house of María de Mendoza to help them, being their intimate friend . . . and next the lawyers of María de Mendoza and her son went to the lodgings of the Archbishop of Seville and put him in charge of the business, and communicated with him about the case against me.

21. Tellechea Idígoras, *Fray Bartolomé Carranza,* vol. 1, 7–13. For Valdés' biography, see the introduction to Document 20.

6. Next, I propose that the Lord Archbishop of Seville knows that I have taught, preached, and maintained that prelates' residence in their dioceses is a matter of natural, divine, and human law; and that prelates are obliged to reside under penalty of mortal sin; and if they do not, then they are in a wicked state. At various times, His Majesty Philip II has ordered the Archbishop of Seville to go reside in his diocese.[22] For this reason, the Archbishop has frequently complained about me with great anger and passion, and has stated that he has great enmity for me on account of my position.

7. Next I propose, etc. . . . [sic] that I have taught and stated that prelates should not become the heads of governmental councils or high courts if they have to reside in them and leave their churches; and those who do otherwise are in a wicked state. The Archbishop of Seville has held and written the contrary; as a result, he has hatred and passion against me.

8. Next I propose that as of a year ago, the Lord Archbishop of Seville, his parents, kinsmen, and servants defamed me as a heretic and said I was suspected as one, because I favored heretics in many places. Thus they demonstrated their hatred for me.[23]

9. Next I propose that once, when I was in the Council of State in 1558, with Juan de Vega, Gutierre [sic] López de Padilla, and Lord Garcia de Toledo, that Juan de Vega said, in front of everyone, that it was a great scandal that the Lord Archbishop of Seville would not go to rule his church, having been ordered to do so by the King; especially since there were so many heretics imprisoned in Seville at that time. He thought that if the royal court left this city of Valladolid, the King should order that the Archbishop not be given lodgings, so that he would have to go to his church; it was unendurable for the Lord Archbishop not to obey royal orders. To which I said, "It's no wonder that whoever does not obey the orders of God, would not obey those of a king." And this remark came to the attention of the Archbishop of Seville, and he has hatred and enmity for me on account of it.

10. Next, I propose that in 1557, the King was in England and in great financial need, as were these kingdoms of Spain. Among other solutions, it was entertained that the King could borrow 100,000 gold ducats from the Lord Archbishop of Seville; if the Archbishop did not want to give the ducats, they could be taken and repaid later, as occurs with those men who bring monies from the Indies. In my vote, I said that though such measures had great inconveniences, it would be better to take the ducats, and so the matter was resolved.[24] When this resolution came to Spain, to the notice of the

22. The implication is that Carranza's well-known position on clerical residence influenced Philip II's actions toward Valdés.

23. Carranza is clearly working to establish a charge of capital enmity.

24. Again, the implication is that Carranza's opinion was decisive for Philip II.

Archbishop's friends and then to the Archbishop himself, he demonstrated great passion and anger toward me and others who shared my opinion.[25]

11. Next I propose, etc. . . . [sic] last year, 1558, I brought an order from His Majesty in Flanders for the Most Serene Princess of Portugal and the Council of State, to devise a remedy for the heresies then arising in Spain, about which His Majesty wished to be informed. Having seen what the Lord Archbishop of Seville had done with the Council on the subject, I said that though matters had been well taken care of in Valladolid, in Seville a greater remedy was needed, because the evil there was long-standing,[26] and the presence of the Bishop of Tarazona[27] would not be enough. So it was concluded in the Council and with the Most Serene Princess. Because I implied that the Lord Archbishop of Seville needed to go to his diocese, he had passion against me.

12. Next, I propose, etc. . . . [sic] that the Archbishop of Seville has had hatred and enmity for me because I tried, against his will, to secure a vacant place in the Suprema for a theologian. Though the said Archbishop resisted this for a long time, in the end he gave in and a theologian was put on the Suprema. The Archbishop was very angry as a result.

13. Next, I propose, etc. . . . [sic] that the Archbishop knew that Master Melchor Cano was my notorious enemy, but nevertheless received Cano's opinion about the Spanish book that I had printed in Flanders.[28] He has favored and continues to favor Master Cano, and takes Cano's business as his own, and favors him with money and letters to go to Rome and other places to pursue that business.

14. Next, I propose, etc. . . . [sic] that not only has the Lord Archbishop of Seville not wanted to receive the opinions of those who approved of my book, but he has even excluded the opinions of those whom he specifically asked to review the book if they ended up viewing it as Catholic. All of this confirms the hatred and enmity that he has for me. He acted in this way with

25. In fact, Valdés refused to hand over the monies, and was shut out of the king's good graces on account of it; Philip II ordered him away from court and to Seville, but the discovery of the Protestant cells prevented Valdés' trip, or so he claimed. See his letter of May 14, 1558, in Document 17.

26. Carranza could be referring to the fifteenth-century actions of the Inquisition against judaizing *conversos,* or to the problem of Dr. Egidio. For the latter, see Document 17.

27. See Document 17, where Inquisitor-General Valdés implies how astute he was to have sent this bishop to Seville.

28. Cano carried out the censure of Carranza's *Commentaries on the Christian Catechism.*

Dr. Delgado, cathedral canon of Toledo; and with the Bishop of Orense, Dr. Francisco Blanco; and he reprehended teacher of divinity Friar Juan de la Peña about it, and reprehended and punished both Master Friar Pedro de Sotomayor and teacher of divinity Friar Ambrosio de Salazar, who are both professors of theology in the University of Salamanca.

15. Next I propose, etc. . . . [sic] that once the Archbishop of Seville understood that the Archbishop of Granada and the Bishop of León—who are such excellent theologians, as everyone knows—were going to approve my book, he did not permit them to give their opinion about it. Thus he ordered and prohibited them, as well as the entire faculty at the University of Alcalá, from giving their opinion.

16. Next I propose that the Lord Archbishop of Seville, in confirmation of the hatred and enmity he has for me, sent his nephew, the Dean of Oviedo,[29] to Rome, to demand a papal brief against me as someone suspected of heresy. The Dean published this brief in Rome and Valladolid, as well as other places, after he returned.

17. Next, I propose that in this city of Valladolid, I spoke to the Lord Archbishop of Seville [Valdés] in the College of San Gregorio (and other times in his lodging), in order to tell him about the book I had printed, and to explain why I had produced it in this particular form. I told him that the book could be emended or revised without any sort of censure. He said nothing to me in return, having already arranged things with Friar Melchor Cano.

18. Next I propose that the Lord Archbishop of Seville offended me personally by telling the Most Serene Princess of Portugal to order me to stop preaching.

19. Next I propose that the Lord Archbishop of Seville took my book away from the Prince, our lord, with personally defamatory remarks. . . . He did the same to the Marquis de Tavara and the Marquesa de Alcañizares.

20. Next I propose that in November 1558 and April 1559, I wrote to the Lord Archbishop of Seville, since he was Inquisitor-General, and offered to make any revisions in my book that seemed appropriate to him, since at that moment revision could have been accomplished without censure. I heard nothing from him. . . .

23. Next, I propose that from September 1558 until the following Easter, the Lord Archbishop of Seville had the two masters, Friar Domingo de Soto and Friar Melchor Cano, say that they were in this city of Valladolid to evaluate my work and my book, which offended me greatly. Furthermore, when they asked permission from the Lord Archbishop to go to their houses, he forced them to stay in this city for the sole purpose of harming me.

29. Meaning that the nephew was head of the cathedral chapter in Oviedo.

24. Next, I propose, etc. . . . [sic] that the Lord Archbishop of Seville ordered an edict read and promulgated in Toledo at the beginning of this year,
1559, which prohibited all books on Christian doctrine in Spanish, printed
outside the kingdom since 1550. He did the same afterward in the city of
Alcalá de Henares.

25. Next I propose, etc. . . . [sic] that I have also taught, stated, published,
and written that no prelate can entail the goods of his church.[30] The Lord
Archbishop has created exactly such entails, for which he hates me, and this
is a certain and credible matter.

Witness Friar Bartolomé de las Casas, Bishop of Chiapas, for Carranza in the recusation of Inquisitor-General Valdés[31]

. . . [sic] he knows the Archbishop of Toledo, and does not know Licentiate
Camino, nor is he related to either party, nor has he been hurt by any of the
major participants.

7. . . . [sic] he knows that Archbishop Carranza has written, preached,
and maintained what the question contains, and it is notorious. He has
heard that His Royal Majesty has ordered the Archbishop of Seville to do
what is contained in the question; he doesn't recall from whom he heard it.
He does not know whether the Archbishop of Seville has complained about
Archbishop Carranza, though he heard that the Archbishop of Seville complained about him after Carranza's imprisonment. And it's notorious, and
this witness holds it as certain, that the Archbishop of Seville has done and
said, by word and deed, the opposite of what the Archbishop of Toledo has
preached; because the Archbishop of Seville has been away from his archbishopric for many years. This witness doubts that such an absence could
occur without very great danger to his conscience, especially when such
painful times of hunger and heresy were occurring in Seville.

8 . . . [sic] He has heard that the Archbishop of Toledo has preached what
the question contains, though the witness hasn't heard it personally; and it
seems correct to him. It is an abuse to make prelates into presidents of a

30. "Entail" allowed an ecclesiastic to pass his office (or lands) to a blood relative,
most often a nephew; the result was the creation of ecclesiastical dynasties. See number 8 below and Barbara McClung Hallman, *Italian Cardinals, Reform, and the
Church as Property* (Berkeley, CA: University of California Press, 1985).

31. Tellechea Idígoras, *Fray Bartolomé Carranza*, vol. 1, 117–21. De las Casas was,
of course, the famous apostle of the Indies who argued for humane treatment of Native Americans. Carranza produced dozens of witnesses who attested the capital enmity of Valdés.

Royal Council or High Court; and he thinks it's true that such prelates are in a dangerous state. He sees that the Archbishop of Seville has done it anyway, as is well known. The witness has heard that the Archbishop of Toledo has written that entails cannot be made from ecclesiastical goods, and he has also heard that the Archbishop of Seville in particular has purchased lands, and it's well known that he bought them to give to one of his nephews, for whom he's making an entail. This witness holds such a practice as very wicked, and it's impossible to do it legally. He did not know that the Archbishop of Seville was impassioned and angry with the Archbishop of Toledo because of entails; but given what the Archbishop of Toledo says, it would be enough for the Archbishop of Seville to feel anger, passion, rancor and perhaps even hatred against the Archbishop of Toledo, unless he were very advanced spiritually. Besides the entail business, the Archbishop of Seville's absence from his archbishopric has been absolutely scandalous to the entire kingdom and a very bad example. . . .

13. . . . [sic] He knows that before the Archbishop of Toledo went to England with the King, he worked and desired for some theologian be put on the Suprema; and one night, when Master Miranda, who is now the Archbishop of Toledo, was coming from a meeting with the Archbishop of Seville about this matter, he arrived in great pain and said to this witness that he was astonished that the Archbishop of Seville would resist and block his efforts, when the presence of a theologian on the Suprema was so necessary and useful for the functioning of the Holy Office. Afterward this witness heard that the Archbishop of Seville had written to the King, resisting the appointment of a theologian to the Suprema. Notwithstanding that the Archbishop of Seville allegedly sent many letters frequently, the King provided for the appointment of the theologian.[32] And hence it seems likely that the Archbishop of Seville would be rude and angry with the Archbishop of Toledo.

14. . . . [sic] this witness knows that Master Friar Domingo de Soto and Melchor Cano were in this court for a long time, and it was said that they were consulting for the Inquisition. Master Soto told this witness that he was lost, because he wanted to leave and the Archbishop of Seville would not let him. This witness doesn't know whether the Archbishop of Seville knew that Master Cano was impassioned against the Archbishop of Toledo or wished him evil. He heard it said by other members of his religious order, as well as by others, that the Archbishop of Seville was favoring Master Cano, having formerly been on very bad terms with him. The witness does not know anything about the rest of the question.

32. The influence of Carranza is again highlighted.

15. . . . [sic] He knows that the book by the Archbishop of Toledo was not examined by learned theologians and religious people who knew how to do it properly and hand out a Catholic censure [if necessary]. This witness heard that the book was given [for evaluation] instead to people who were not as qualified or learned. He doesn't know whether this was done on account of the enmity and hatred that the Archbishop of Seville has for the Archbishop of Toledo. . . .

19. . . . [sic] He has heard from numerous people, whose names he does not recall, that the Archbishop of Seville is a man impassioned against those with whom he's not on good terms. As far as this case is concerned, it seems to this witness as if the Archbishop of Seville has been too rigorous and excessive, specifically in the seizure of the Archbishop of Toledo, in his imprisonment, and in the treatment of his person and household. Because despite being worthy of respect as both Master Miranda and the Archbishop of Toledo, Carranza was seized dishonorably, as if he deserved very little respect and was just one person alone, walking simply through his archbishopric, carrying out the office of a true pastor. . . . As for Carranza's household, the Archbishop of Seville has allowed it to go astray and to be abandoned—its members don't even have anything to eat—though the Archbishop of Seville was entreated many times to support it, as seems just and reasonable. The Archbishop of Seville never gave a response, or at least he did not want to provide for the household, which this witness knows. An enormous scandal has resulted from all this; besides the damage and affront to the Toledo Archbishop himself, the Holy Church of Toledo, the entire Church of Spain—indeed, the whole Christian community—have been damaged through this infamy and demotion. This scandal will only benefit the heretics of England and Germany, enemies of the Cross of Christ and His Roman Church. . . .

Sentence on Carranza's recusation of Valdés, Toledo, February 23, 1560[33]

In the city of Toledo, February 23, 1560. The lord licentiates Juan Sarmiento and Juan de Isunza, members of His Majesty's Council and judge arbitrators, who have seen the lawsuit between the Reverend Lord Friar Bartolomé de Miranda, Archbishop of Toledo, and Licentiate Camino, prosecutor of the Suprema, over the recusation placed by the Archbishop of Toledo against the Archbishop of Seville, Lord Fernando de Valdés, Inquisitor-General of the kingdoms of His Majesty, by commission given and deputized by our very Holy Father, Pope Paul IV.

33. Tellechea Idígoras, *Fray Bartolomé Carranza,* vol. 1, 383–84.

Judges Sarmiento and Isunza said that though prosecu[
fered proof to sustain his objections to some of the wit
this case for the Archbishop of Toledo, they must de/
Archbishop of Seville as recused. They order the Archbisł.
stain from any knowledge of the case while the Reveren. _
Toledo is imprisoned and prosecutor Camino tries to make the case againsι
him. Whether by himself, with the opinion of others, or through an inter-
mediary, the Archbishop of Seville shall not do or provide anything in this
case, nor anything relating to it; nor shall he find himself present with the
judges who undertake the case.

The sentence being thus provided, they ordered and pronounced that I,
the secretary of this case, under pain of sentence of major excommunication,
shall notify the parties and the Archbishop of Seville. And so that His Holiness the Pope may be informed of the current state of this business and the
reason for the recusation, I have signed in such a way that either party may
trust the authenticity of this legal act and sentence. I give the Pope notice,
and reserve to his power, to order the salaries, lawsuit expenses, and outlay
which the Holy Office has incurred in this case of recusation paid from the
sequestered goods of the Archbishop of Toledo, until the judges, notary,
lawyers, procurators, and solicitors are paid, and their names shall be signed.[34]

---

34. On February 24, 1560, Fernando de Valdés was informed of the sentence by
Pedro de Tapia, before Licentiate Valtodano and Dr. Simancas; Valdés in turn immediately notified the prosecutor. The recusation seriously damaged Valdés' career;
Diego de Espinosa was named his assistant inquisitor-general in 1565, and from that
point on, Valdés had little impact on public matters.

DOCUMENT 19

Prohibited Books[1]

[Censorship in Spain appears to have been relatively intermittent and moderate between 1521 and 1550, a period in which Martin Luther's works were condemned in toto and inquisition tribunals were notified through written (but not printed) directives[2] about newly prohibited authors and volumes. Even as late as 1551—when Inquisitor-General Fernando de Valdés issued Spain's first printed index of prohibited books—that document reprinted the index compiled by the University of Louvain in 1550, with only an appendix devoted to Spanish works.

It is generally agreed that the discovery of Protestant cells in Seville and Valladolid between 1557 and 1558 changed everything. In 1559, Inquisitor-General Valdés printed an index that expanded the 1551 catalogue by 253 new book titles, 14 editions of the Bible, and 9 editions of the New Testament.[3] The 1559 Index amplified prohibitions against the works of Desiderius Erasmus, condemned the Commentaries on the Christian Catechism *of Archbishop Bartolomé Carranza, and banned treatises by noted spiritual authors Juan de Ávila, Luis de Granada, and Francis Borja. It severely censured Spanish vernacular literature for the first time.*

The next index produced by Spaniards and printed in Spain was the product of Inquisitor-General Gaspar de Quiroga in 1583–1584, which came in two volumes; the first enumerated books that were prohibited (1583), whereas the second listed books that would be acceptable if they were expurgated (1584).[4] Quantitatively, the 1583 volume was enormous; it prohibited 2,315 items, whereas the 1559 Index had condemned some 700 ones. At the same time, though, the 1583 volume was perhaps less aggressive or innovative than

1. The following description is indebted to Kamen, *The Spanish Inquisition,* 108–22; Bujanda, *Index de l'Inquisition espagnole, 1551, 1554, 1559* (Geneva: Librarie Droz, 1984); *idem, Index de l'Inquisition espagnole: 1583, 1584* (Sherbrooke: Centre d'études de la Renaissance, Université de Sherbrooke, 1993); *idem,* "Índices de libros prohibidos del siglo XVI"; Antonio Márquez, *Literatura e Inquisición en España, 1478–1834* (Madrid: Taurus, 1980); Pinto Crespo, *Inquisición y control ideológico.*

2. These written directives from the Suprema were called *cartas acordadas.*

3. The 1559 Index was also substantially indebted to indices already in print from Louvain, Portugal, Venice, Paris, and Spain itself.

4. Kamen stresses that the Papal Index of 1564 and the Expurgatory Index of 1571 (prepared by Benito Arias Montano in the Low Countries) affected the 1583 Quiroga Index, not least by introducing the notion of expurgation-rather-than-prohibition.

the numbers might suggest, for it absorbed earlier indices from all over Europe without substantially amplifying the prohibited titles that tended to circulate in Spanish; it has been argued that because the 1583 Index condemned titles in Dutch, German, and French, it did not really affect Spaniards' reading habits.[5] The same cautionary outlook could also apply to questions of implementation; when only twelve copies of the 1583 Index were sent to Barcelona, and each of the twelve was supposed to serve an entire bishopric, one might justifiably wonder about the Index's impact.[6] Thus the reader should keep in mind that the interdiction of books—in Spain or elsewhere—was not a clearcut process. Proscriptions in one country could simply duplicate prohibitions from another, a forbidden work could turn into an acceptable one with emendation or excision, mandates could be open to interpretation, and prohibitions could be nearly impossible to enforce.]

Decree of Inquisitor-General Valdés on books, 1558[7]

We, Lord Fernando de Valdés—Archbishop of Seville through divine mercy, general apostolic inquisitor against heretical depravity and apostasy in these kingdoms and lands of his majesty, King Philip II, our lord—to all people of any estate, order, rank, preeminence, and condition, resident in these kingdoms:

Know that our holy father, Pope Paul III of happy memory, was informed of the great difficulties and injuries to the Christian religion which resulted from faithful Catholics owning and reading books that contain errors against our Holy Catholic Faith (books that may be authored by heretical, suspicious, and scandalous men). [Hence Pope Paul III] ordered that a constitution be published which orders that no one—no matter what his estate, rank, order, and quality, not even an archbishop—can read or own forbidden and suspicious books. The constitution revokes any permission that might have been given previously to any person to own and read such books; and the said constitution states this at greater length, and we order placed at the end of it, "Julius, bishop, servant of the servants of God." [i.e., Julius III, 1550–1555].

It has come to our attention that some people are not observing this constitution, and that many people own, read, and transport those books into

---

5. Kamen, *The Spanish Inquisition,* 113–14. The 1583–1584 volumes, Kamen writes, "served more to dissuade Spaniards from reading foreign authors whom none but a few could have read anyway," 117.

6. *Ibid.*

7. González Novalín, *El inquisidor general Fernando de Valdés,* vol. 2, 201–03.

these kingdoms,[8] feigning ignorance as to which ones are suspicious [or were written] by heretical, scandalous, and evil-sounding authors. People must not own, read, or transport these books because to do so is a great offense against our Lord and His Catholic Faith and causes great injury to faithful Christians. The Suprema has discussed the remedy for such a great injury, and has decided that a catalogue should be made of all the books that are heretical, suspicious, and contain errors against our Holy Catholic Faith, or are by heretical authors. . . . This catalogue should be printed and published in all the kingdoms [of Spain], so that each person may know which books he may own and read, and which books and authors he must avoid because of their erroneous and scandalous content (nor is it appropriate for faithful Catholics to handle them and converse about them). Therefore, we order, prohibit, and command that no one, no matter what his estate, order, and rank, may own or read a book contained in the catalogue that is printed by our order; this mandate pertains to any and all residents of the kingdoms and lands of His Majesty. We order that no heretical book or one by a heretical author may be sold without the signature of the Suprema's secretary, Pedro de Tapia. If there is a report of some error, heresy, or suspicion in a book, no printer, bookseller, or merchant can print, transport, or sell any of the forbidden, heretical, or suspicious books under pain of major excommunication and a fine of 200 gold ducats for the expenses of the Holy Office. The inquisition will proceed against such individuals as if they were suspect in matters of our Holy Catholic Faith and disobedient to the Faith's commandments.

So that the aforesaid may be public and known to everyone—and so that no one may feign ignorance of it—we order the apostolic inquisitors in this city of Valladolid, as well as in all the other cities and villages of this kingdom, to immediately publish this mandate in all their districts and jurisdictions, and especially in the cathedral churches, in other churches and monasteries, and in pulpits by preachers. Inquisitors visiting their districts shall read edicts against those who possess prohibited books or know that others have them, or know that such books are in certain libraries of monasteries, universities, colleges, or some other places. The edicts will prompt such people to come and declare what they know before the inquisitors, under pain of the penalties and censures that are appropriate to impose. We grant inquisitors the power, faculty, and plenary authority to proceed against those who are found guilty and to execute the penalties and censures declared here, without any mitigation or remission whatsoever.[9] In testimony of which we order this document signed with our name, sealed with our seal, countersigned by the secretary below. Given in Valladolid on the ____ day of the month of ____ year of the birth of Our Lord Jesus Christ, 1558.

8. For context, see Document 17.

9. This final clause amounted to a "brake" on the inquisitors' discretion.

Decree of the Suprema on books, 1558[10]

All prohibited books contained in the brief shall be collected. Those by heretical authors shall be burned publicly in the *auto de fe;* the rest shall be placed in some well-secured room of the inquisition [tribunal]. A record shall be made of which books were collected and their quantity, and the people from whom they were taken; that record shall be sent here so that, having seen it, we may order what must be done about the books.

As far as books in the humanities are concerned[11]—which may contain glosses, arguments, letters, or annotations by Philip Melanchthon[12] or other heretics—they will be returned to their owners once the heretical annotations have been removed or crossed out. When this cannot be done conveniently, take the books with comments by prohibited authors and do not return them.

As far as Bibles, all printings specified in the catalogue of prohibited books shall be collected. In each Bible, the name of the bookseller or the person who possessed it shall be written down, so that the Bibles can be returned to their owners once the censure is complete and the corrections performed.

And for now, other books are not prohibited and should not be taken if they are not heretical or suspicious, but only if they are contained in the said catalogue. If some other books are offered to the inquisitors, and it is questionable whether they must be prohibited or not, then the inquisitors shall advise the Suprema so that appropriate steps may be taken.

Next, books that do not have a sure author, place of printing, or printer shall be collected and inspected if they were printed in Germany after 1519 or in [other] places outside these kingdoms. They shall be kept if they seem suspicious, but not for any other reason. Books printed in these kingdoms [of Spain] shall not be collected except for ones that are reported to be suspicious. The divine hours in Spanish, scriptural letters and Gospels, sermons, lives of Christ, and lives of the saints shall be returned to their owners. So shall other books by Catholic authors about which the inquisitors have no report that they contain specific heresies or suspicious things.

---

10. González Novalín, *El inquisidor-general Fernando de Valdés,* vol. 2, 203–04.

11. As in, books pertaining to the *studia humanitatis:* the grammar, rhetoric, poetry, moral philosophy, and history of ancient Latin and Greek writers.

12. Philip Melanchthon (1497–1560) was a professor of Greek at the University of Wittenberg, where Martin Luther was a professor of Scripture. The two became acquainted and Melanchthon became a Protestant intellectual who participated in multiple diets and colloquies to hammer out Lutheran doctrine vis-à-vis Swiss Reformers such as Zwingli, as well as Catholics. Melanchthon's biblical translations and commentaries circulated widely.

The books by Theophilactus that were translated by Oecolampadius[13] or some other heretic shall be collected and the owners' names written down; these books shall not be returned until we advise what must be done with them.

Certain books by St. John Chrysostom exist which were translated by the heretic Wolfango Másculo or by Oecolampadius; these must be taken and not returned to their owners until the inquisitors are advised on what to do with them. Other books that do not have a heretical translator must not be taken from their owners except when the inquisitors know that they contain certain errors. If certain Catholic books contain comments from prohibited authors, cross out the comments; afterward, the books may be returned to their owners. If this cannot be conveniently done, take the books that contain comments by prohibited authors and do not return them.

A book of medicine, entitled *Paradoxas de fusión,* printed in Venice in 1547, is said to contain suspicious things even though it is not placed in the catalogue; it must be prohibited. [The same holds true] for all other books reported to contain heretical errors or suspicious things, because a stipulation in the catalogue of prohibited books [forbids] "all books savoring of heresy."

Consultation of Master Sancho about the books, 1558[14]

Very Powerful Lords,

I, Master Francisco Sancho, professor and resident in the University of Salamanca, state that by the commission and command of Your Highness, I have had for many years the charge of looking for and collecting books prohibited by the Holy Office, and ordering them delivered [to the tribunal]. I also have diligently carried out other measures so that such books do not remain in the power of certain people who could easily be deceived, whereby many evils and difficulties would ensue in the Christian community as well as great offense to Our Lord. Consequently, I have in my possession many of the prohibited books, about which . . . many doubts and scruples have occurred which are disturbing the consciences of faithful Christians. I entreat Your Highness to order what should be done about the following matters, so that I may fulfill in Salamanca what Your Lordship has ordered.

---

13. John Oecolampadius (1482–1531) promoted the Protestant Reformation in Switzerland; he defended the Eucharistic doctrine of Zwingli at the Colloquy of Marburg in 1529.

14. González Novalín, *El inquisidor-general Fernando de Valdés,* vol. 2, 205–8.

1. Backed up by the authority of well-respected people, many think that members of the Suprema have no intention of excommunicating, censuring, or penalizing those who do not give up books prohibited by the edicts; they believe instead that people may possess such books if they cross out what seems wicked, or if they intend to cross out the offensive material when it is specified. And so some of the monasteries and other people may retain the said Bibles without giving them up.

The intention of the most reverend lord inquisitor-general and the lords of the Suprema has always been to excommunicate people who have books that are prohibited in the published edicts. Those who possess such books, but have not given them up, have incurred censure. If necessary, such people shall be declared [publicly] and denounced again to compel them to deliver the books.[15]

2. Next, some of the booksellers have copies of the Bibles that were prohibited and have not delivered them [to the tribunal], even though those Bibles were embargoed by the Holy Office. Your Lordship shall decree if this should be overlooked, or if the booksellers should be ordered to give up the books.

Bibles which are hidden away by the booksellers shall be recovered through the booksellers' inventories, and the booksellers shall pledge not to sell or give away any of them. The booksellers shall be ordered not to do this on pain of censures and the appropriate monetary penalty.

3. Next, the edicts from the Holy Office prohibit Hebrew books of Holy Scripture, the Qur'an, and any other book in Arabic. But it is unclear whether men learned in these languages can possess these books, since it seems that professors of such languages must be permitted to use them. It is also unclear whether such books are allowed in public libraries which have not been visited by the Inquisition, such as exist in universities, churches, monasteries, and colleges; some of these libraries have declared that they have the Qur'an in Latin and in Spanish.

People listed in this chapter can have the said books, and so can the libraries of universities, colleges, monasteries, and churches.

4. Next, the edicts order that all books that do not contain the name of the printer, the place of publication, or the name of the author must be relinquished. There is some doubt as to whether the edict means (as it seems to mean) only modern books, not ancient ones; and whether it is applicable to books that lack all three details at once, or only one of the three; and whether it is applicable to books that lack the three details but do not contain anything wicked, or only to books that contain errors.

If books are printed in Germany after 1519 or in another place outside these kingdoms, and if the same books do not contain a specific author, place of

---

15. All comments in italics are from the Suprema.

publication, or printer, they shall be collected and inspected. If the books seem
suspicious they shall be held, [but] not in any other manner. Books printed in
these kingdoms [of Spain] shall not be seized unless there is some report that they
are suspicious. . . .

5. Next, there are many wicked books [sic] that contain only a few errors,
such as: *Evangelical Harmony, Phrases of Sacred Scripture, Method of Law, Pom-*
ponius Mela with Valdiano's commentary, Paradoxes of Leonardo Fuchsi, Eccle-
siastes of Erasmus, and so on. If the few errors were removed, these books
would be held as useful and curious [sic], and thus desirable; and people want
to know if these books are permissible if the errors are removed.
These books shall be seized until further notice.

6. Next, by a general clause in the Inquisition's edicts, all books are prohibited which contain something against the Holy Faith and the Holy
Mother Church and its observances. There are many books by Catholic authors which contain some such errors, such as the *Summa Armacani,* Duran-
dus, Cajetan, Peter Lombard, Origen, Theophilactus, Tertullian, Lactancius,
Lucian's *Dialogue,* Aristotle, Plato, Seneca, and others. These books are commonly used in the schools and elsewhere; it is wondered if they will be permitted if, at their beginning or end, their errors are noted as such.
For now, the books contained in this clause shall not be seized until further notice.

7. Next, since catalogues and memorials of prohibited books currently exist in different formats—one having been done in Louvain, another in Portugal by the Inquisition, others in other places— it seems convenient to combine
them into one large catalogue which would include all the books in all the catalogues, and even all the other [books] which are not in them [yet], which are
numerous, including works in Latin, Spanish, Italian, and French. [People]
have been warned that books in those languages may come with errors; thus
it is necessary to do something about them. May Your Highness also order
that the papal constitution about such wicked books be republished.
It shall be provided. . . .

9. Next, good and permissible books by Cicero, Virgil, Terence, the
Sphere of John Holywood, Chrysostom, and others may contain prologues,
glosses, annotations, or interpretations by heretical authors such as Philip
Melanchthon, Oecolampadius, and so on. Up to now, such books have been
preserved and used, so long as what was evil was erased (if the book contained anything evil), and the name of the heretical author was erased, too.
[Then] the books have been permitted and tolerated. It is unclear if the same
should be done in the future, since all the works of such heretical authors
are prohibited in the edicts. . . .
For books on the humanities which include glosses, arguments, clauses, or anno-
tations by Philip Melanchthon or other heretics: if the annotations by heretical

authors are removed or crossed out, the books can be returned to their owners; if this cannot be easily done, books with comments of forbidden authors shall be taken and not returned.

10. Next, there are some books by heretical authors which do not touch on the faith but pertain to other matters, such as Hebrew and Aramaic grammar, cosmography, the general history and astrology of Sebastian Münster, the Latin and Greek grammar of Melanchthon, and so on. It is unclear whether these books are permitted [even after] erasing the name of the author and their errors, if any; since the edicts prohibit all the works of such authors.

The edicts shall be observed, which provide for this.

11. Next, the inquisition edicts prohibit Bibles and New Testaments in Spanish and any other vernacular language. It is unclear whether the Epistles and Gospels in the vernacular (which are sung and prayed in church) are also prohibited; as well as the vernacular Psalter and divine hours, and other parts of the Bible.

The Gospels, Epistles, and divine hours in the vernacular shall not be seized; everything else contained in this chapter shall be.

12. Next, I have in my possession many prohibited Bibles and other books, as well as diurnals[16] and missals, from which the word "*meritis*" [merits] has been removed or altered in the prayers. May Your Highness order what I should do with them, and [tell me] whether I should return them to their owners so long as they emend what is wicked in the missals and diurnals, and if so, with what sort of pledge [from the owners].

In the diurnals, that phrase "precibus et suffragiis" ["with prayers and suffrages"] shall be emended, and it shall say "meritis" ["merits"] instead; and with this change, the diurnals may be returned, but the missals and other books shall be retained.

13. Next, some people think that they can possess prohibited books by Erasmus if the editions bind together all his works.[17] They also think they can possess his colloquies—which were printed in Portugal with the authority of the Holy Office—once the wicked things in them have been removed and the good things left, in order to practice the Latin language. I entreat Your Highness to order what should be done in this matter, as it is so important for the conservation and well-being of the Holy Faith and the Christian religion, and for the tranquillity and security of conscience of faithful and pious Christians.

16. Diurnals are service books that contain all the traditional canonical hours except Matins.

17. See Bataillon, *Erasmo y España,* 715–24, for the prohibitions on Erasmus in the Spanish indices of prohibited books.

What the catalogue provides should be fulfilled and observed.

14. I, Pedro de Tapia, secretary of the Suprema, pledge that this petition from the reverend lord Master Francisco Sancho, professor of the University of Salamanca, was presented and signed by the same, and it remains in my possession. The lords of the Suprema have consulted over it and communicated its contents to the most illustrious Lord Fernando de Valdés, Archbishop of Seville, Inquisitor-General; and they have ordered and decreed what is at the end of every chapter. All of which occurred before me.

Letter from the inquisitors of Córdoba to the Suprema, regarding the expurgation of books, September 9, 1584[18]

We have received Your Lordships' letter with the order from the Inquisitor-General to collect the books prohibited in the new catalogue. [We have also received] twelve copies of the [new] catalogue and an equal number of expurgatory ones, so that the catalogues may be proclaimed in the most principal places of this district, which has been done. [But] four editors [*calificadores*] who are attached to our inquisition tribunal, and who have been committed to this task [of expurgating books], have said it will never be completed if they undertake it alone, because the books that have to be expurgated are too numerous and require so much work. Once the monasteries heard about this, they pressed for permission to expurgate their books themselves, since many books in their libraries have to be expurgated. We entreat Your Lordships to tell us what we should do, and to send us more catalogues of prohibitions and expurgations for this operation.

One bookseller in this city has more than a thousand copies of a book entitled *Consolation and Spiritual Oratory*. He is claiming that this is not one of the books contained in the new catalogue, [or] at least part of it [sic], for reasons that he gives in a petition that accompanies this letter. May Your Lordships look over it and order what is to be done. May our Lord protect the very illustrious persons of Your Lordships in His service. From Córdoba, September 9, 1584.

> We kiss the hands of Your Lordships.
> Licentiate Montoya. Dr. Vallezillo.

18. Rafael Gracia Boix, *Colección de documentos para la historia de la Inquisición de Córdoba.* (Córdoba: Publicaciones del Monte de Piedad y Caja de Ahorros de Córdoba, 1982), 218–19. This source relates to the promulgation of Inquisitor-General Quiroga's 1583 Index and 1584 Expurgatory Index; see the introduction to Document 19.

STRUCTURE, PROCESS, ROUTINE

Document 20

Gaspar Isidro de Argüello. *Instructions of the Holy Office of the Inquisition, Handled Summarily, Both Old and New,* Part II: The "New Instructions" of 1561[1]

[A large portion of Argüello's 1627 compilation of instructions—see Document 7—was devoted to the instrucciones nuevas *or "new instructions" issued by Inquisitor-General Fernando de Valdés in 1561.[2] Valdés was born in 1483 and died in 1568. Valdés' career, like many other inquisitors', reflected the twin routes of ecclesiastical and royal service, though he went further, faster, than most of his peers: he became bishop of Oviedo in 1533; president of the Royal Chancery of Valladolid, one of the two highest appeals courts in Spain, in 1535; president of the king's Royal Council in 1539; bishop of Sigüenza in 1540; archbishop of Seville in 1546; and inquisitor-general in 1547.*

Valdés is generally recognized as Spain's most important inquisitor-general of the sixteenth century; his tenure in that office was long, running from 1547 to 1566, and his actions were confrontational. He pursued Protestants in Seville and Valladolid, as well as the archbishop of Toledo, Bartolomé Carranza.[3] He issued indices of prohibited books. And his inquisitorial instructions of 1561 laid out in detail a process of arrest and prosecution that every inquisitor was supposed to follow. Though there is no documentation to suggest why Valdés issued the instructions at this particular moment, or under what circumstances they were composed, he may well have thought that inquisitors should benefit from his experience of the Carranza arrest and the Lutheran trials of 1558–1560.[4]]

1. Argüello, *Instruciones del santo oficio de la inquisición.* The material below is excerpted. Topical and summary headings have been added for the reader's convenience and do not occur in the original.

2. Fernando de Valdés' complete *Instructions* of 1561 have been transcribed in Miguel Jiménez Montserín, *Introdución a la inquisición española: documentos básicos para el estudio del Santo Oficio* (Madrid: Editora Nacional, 1980), 198–240.

3. See Documents 17 and 18.

4. See González Novalín, "Las instrucciones de Valdés," in *Historia de la Inquisición,* vol. 1, 637–47.

Compilation of Instructions for the Office
of the Holy Inquisition, Toledo, 1561

Lord Fernando de Valdés, by divine mercy Archbishop of Seville, apostolic Inquisitor-General against heretical depravity and apostasy in all the kingdoms and lordships of His Majesty, etc. We have been informed, reverend apostolic inquisitors against heretical depravity and apostasy in all the said kingdoms and lordships, that although the instructions of the Holy Office of the Inquisition provide and declare that the same procedures shall be kept in all the inquisitions and everyone shall conform, uniformity of procedure has not been observed in some inquisitions. To ensure that henceforth there will be no procedural discrepancies, the matter has been debated various times in the Suprema; and it is agreed that all inquisitions shall observe the following order.

Testimony and consultation   If the inquisitors gather to review the testimony that results from a visitation or from any other cause, and they find that people are sufficiently suspected of something that pertains to the Holy Office of the Inquisition, and the suspicion is such that it requires a ruling, they must consult with theologians of learning and conscience [i.e., *calificadores*]. The theologians shall give their opinion and sign it with their names.

The inquisitors being satisfied that the matter pertains to the faith—whether through the theologians' opinion, known ceremonies of Jews or Moors, clear-cut heresy, or obvious support for the same—the prosecutor shall denounce the suspect or suspects, ask that they be imprisoned, and present the relevant testimony and judgment.

Having jointly seen the information—and one inquisitor should not appear in the hearing without the other, if both [can be] present—the inquisitors shall agree to the suspect's imprisonment. . . .

Imprisonment and sequestration   If the inquisitors agree on the imprisonment, they shall order it done. In a case in which the imprisonment needs to be considered and judged because it concerns a person of quality (or other such circumstances), they shall consult the Suprema before executing their opinion. If there is disagreement in the voting, the case must be remitted to the Suprema, so that the Suprema may decide what to do.[5]

The order of imprisonment has to be signed by the inquisitors and given to the constable of the Holy Office, not to anyone else. . . . The imprisonment has to be accompanied by the sequestration of goods, in conformity with the law and the instructions of the Holy Office. An order of capture

---

5. It is generally recognized that Valdés worked to centralize the Inquisition's operations.

may not include more than one person, so that [impending captures] may remain secret if people outside the Office are put in charge of them. Each order of capture may be placed in the relevant trial record. Goods must be sequestered when the imprisonment is for formal heresy, but not in other cases that may involve imprisonment. The sequestration may only involve goods found in the possession of the person who is ordered imprisoned, not goods that may be in the possession of third parties. The trial record shall contain the act in which the defendant's imprisonment was ordered, the date on which the order was given, and to whom it was given. . . .

Transportation   From the sequestered goods, the constable shall take monies necessary to bring the prisoner to the prison, and six or eight ducats more for the provisioning of the prisoner; no more shall be taken and spent on the prisoner except what he himself eats, what is spent on the beast or beasts on which he is transported, and his bed and clothing. If no money is found in the sequestration, the least valuable goods will be sold until the necessary amount has been raised; the amount received shall be noted at the bottom of the page of the sequestration order. Any money left over from the transport to the prison shall be delivered to the quartermaster[6] of the prisoners before the notary of sequestrations, who will take down in writing the said sequestration. An account of this will be given to the inquisitors. The constable gives the money to the quartermaster in the presence of the inquisitors.

Isolation of the prisoners   Once the defendant is imprisoned, the constable shall put him in such security that no one can see or speak to him, or counsel him through writing or word. The constable will do the same with [multiple] defendants if many are imprisoned, so that they may not communicate with each other, unless the inquisitors have advised that no inconvenience will result from their communication, in which case the warden shall follow the order given to him. The constable will not leave weapons, money, writings or paper, or jewels of gold or silver in the prisoners' possession. . . . [The constable puts the prisoners into the warden's custody.]

The prison warden shall not gather together the said prisoners or leave them to communicate with one another, unless the inquisitors order him to do so. He will faithfully guard the inquisitors' order.

Records of prisoners' belongings   Likewise, the warden will have a book in the prison in which he will write down the bedclothes and clothing that any prisoner brings with him, and he will sign it, and the scribe will sign it too. The warden will follow the same procedure with everything a prisoner receives while imprisoned. Before a prisoner receives anything, the warden will inform both inquisitors about it, even if it only involves food or something

6. The *despensero* distributed food to the prisoners.

similar, and [he must have] their permission. The warden will look at the item and, after examining it to be sure it does not contain some advice, he will give it to the prisoners, assuming it is something they need. . . .

First interview After the prisoner has been placed in the prison, the inquisitors shall order him brought before them and an inquisitorial notary at a time it seems appropriate to them. After the prisoner has taken an oath, they shall ask him his name, age, occupation, and residence, and how long he has been imprisoned. The inquisitors shall treat the prisoners kindly, according to the quality of their person, preserving the appropriate authority, and giving them no reason to become dismayed. The prisoners are usually seated on a bench so that they can handle their cases more attentively, although the prisoners have to be standing at the moment the accusation is placed.

Genealogy Then the prisoner shall be ordered to state his genealogy as extensively as he can, beginning with his parents and grandparents, and all the branches that he remembers. He shall state their occupations and residences, their spouses' names, whether they are alive or dead, and the names of the children of those antecedents and branches. The defendants shall likewise state whom they have married, how many times, and name and ages of the children they have had and currently have. The notary shall write down the genealogy in the trial record, putting each person at the start of a line, and declaring if one of the defendant's ancestors or lineage [sic] has been imprisoned or penanced by the Inquisition.

Admonitions This being done, the defendant shall be asked where and with whom he grew up, and if he has studied at a university, and if he has ever left these kingdoms and if so, in whose company. Once he has declared all these things, he shall be asked in general if he knows the reason for his imprisonment. Depending upon his reply, other questions relevant to his case can be asked. The inquisitors should admonish him to speak and confess the truth, in conformity with the style and instructions of the Holy Office, admonishing him three times on different days, with some intermission. Anything that occurs in the hearing shall be written down by the notary in the trial record. Likewise, the defendant shall be asked about prayers and Christian doctrine, and where and when he [last] confessed, and with which confessors [sic].[7] The inquisitors must always be advised not to importune or

7. These questions about education, travel, and Christian doctrine were an innovation on the part of Valdés and his *instrucciones nuevas* of 1561. A decade later, inquisitors in Cuenca would add queries about literacy and book ownership, and modern scholars have used the ensuing evidence to great effect: see Sara T. Nalle, "Literacy and Culture in Early Modern Castile," *Past and Present* 125 (1989): 65–96. Also see Nalle, *God in La Mancha*, 118.

overly press the defendants, nor, on the other hand, should they be remiss in their questions and fail to ask substantial things. Likewise, they should not ask irrelevant things, unless such matters would prompt the defendant's confession. If the defendant begins to confess, they should let him speak freely, without cutting him off, unless he's saying irrelevant things. . . .

Transcription of the interview   The inquisitors shall not speak to prisoners in the hearing or outside of it, except about what pertains to business. The notary before whom the trial passes shall write down everything that the inquisitor or inquisitors say to the prisoner, and what the prisoner says in return. When the hearing is finished, the inquisitors shall order the notary to read everything he has written during it, so that the defendant, if he wishes, may add or amend something. . . .

The accusation   The prosecutor shall take care to place the accusations within the time limits stipulated by the instructions, generally accusing the defendants of heresy, and accusing them in particular of everything relevant through testimony or confessions. The prosecutor must accuse the defendant of everything attested against him, even if the inquisitors cannot try the crimes that are not manifest heresy (assuming that crimes of another sort were alleged). The defendant must be accused in this way not so that the inquisitors may punish him for everything alleged against him, but because nonheretical crimes aggravate the heresy with which he is charged, and make evident his bad Christianity or manner of living. . . .

The defendant's oath   Because the defendant has sworn an oath to speak the truth from the beginning of his trial, he must be reminded of it every time he enters the hearing. He shall be told that he swore an oath and hence must speak the truth, so that the oath always precedes the deposition. This is greatly effective when he speaks about other people. . . .

The defense lawyer   The inquisitor or inquisitors will advise the defendant on how important it is for him to confess the truth. Once they have done so, they will name a lawyer or lawyers from the tribunal for the defendant's defense, and these lawyers are deputized for this purpose. The defendant will communicate with his lawyer in the presence of either of the inquisitors. With the lawyer's opinion—either in writing or by word—the defendant will respond to the accusation. Before undertaking the defense, the lawyer will swear to defend him well and faithfully, and to keep secret what he sees and knows . . . and the lawyer is obliged (as a Christian) to admonish the defendant to confess the truth; and if the lawyer fails to do this, he shall ask for penance. The prosecutor shall be notified when the reply to the accusation is ready. When both parties are present, along with the defendant's lawyer, the case is concluded and received to proof. . . .

So that the lawyer may better counsel the defendant on what to do, and better defend him, he must read the confessions that the defendant has made in his trial, insofar as they do not pertain to third parties. The lawyer shall read the confessions in the defendant's presence. If the defendant wishes to continue his confession, the defense lawyer shall leave, because he must not be present.

Guardians   If the defendant is under twenty-five, a guardian shall be provided to him before he responds to the accusation. Under this guardian's authority, the defendant will ratify the confessions he has made and will make during the trial. The guardian may not be an official of the Holy Office. He can be a lawyer, or some other person of quality, confidence, and good conscience. . . .

New charges   If new proof surfaces or the defendant commits a new crime at any point in the trial after the parties have been received for proof, the prosecutor must place the accusation again, and the defendant will respond to it in the customary manner. . . .

Requests for hearings   Because there may be some delay between the order for proof and the publication of testimony, every time the prisoner asks for a hearing . . . the inquisitors should take care to give it to him. It is consoling for the prisoners to be heard, and it frequently happens that a prisoner has fixed a day on which he will confess or to say something that would complete the investigation of his case. If hearings are delayed, in such instances prisoners may come to entertain other thoughts and decisions. . . .

Publication of witness testimony   The publication of witnesses is given by one or both of the inquisitors, who read out loud what the notary has to write down. . . . Because the publication of witness testimony is such an important matter, it should not be entrusted to someone else. In the publication, the notary shall indicate the month and year in which the witnesses deposed; but he must not put down the exact day because of the inconvenience that may result from it (as happens frequently with witnesses from prison).[8] The month and year will suffice. Likewise the publication will state the place and time when the crime was committed, because these matters

---

8. Handing a defendant in the tribunal prison a written document that specified the exact day of a prosecution witness' deposition could be dangerous when that prosecution witness *also* resided in the tribunal prison. As is evident from Document 12, it was reasonably easy for prisoners to communicate with one another, despite the inquisitors' efforts; a defendant might be able to deduce which of the other prisoners had testified against him or her, and revenge could follow. See Document 7 for fears about vengeance upon witnesses.

touch upon the defense; but no more specifics have to be given. The witness's full testimony, not just the gist of it, will be given as literally as possible. It should be noted that even if the witness deposes in the first person, saying, "I discussed with the defendant what I [now] testify about him," in the publication the witness' statement has to be turned into the third person, so that it says "he saw and heard the defendant discuss with a certain person."...

The publication of witnesses is given to defendants even if they confess. Thus they may be assured that they were imprisoned only after information against them was received (since prison would not be justified in any other manner), and it can be said that the defendant was convicted and confessed. A sentence can be pronounced against such a person. Moreover, giving the publication of witnesses to defendants who confess may allow the judges to have more liberty with the charges, since a charge cannot be made from witness testimony that is not published.[9] . . .

After the defendant has responded orally to the charges, he will confer with his lawyer over the publication of witnesses that he has received, in the same way they conferred over the accusation. The defendant is never given the opportunity to speak to his lawyer or to any other person except in the presence of the inquisitors and the notary, who shall witness what occurs. . . .

Paper for the defense   If the defendant asks for paper to write down something pertaining to his defense, they must give him numbered sheets of paper which are rubricated by the notary. The sheets that he is given will be noted in the trial record; and when he returns them, they will be counted, so that the prisoner does not keep paper. It should be noted likewise how the prisoner returned the paper, and precautions should be taken about his writing utensil. When the defendant's lawyer has been summoned at his request, the lawyer shall come and communicate what is appropriate to him. Any papers the defendant wrote which pertain to his defense will be delivered to his lawyer. . . .

The prosecutor and the interviews   Throughout the trial the prosecutor must take special care to look over the trial record whenever the prisoner leaves the hearing, in order to see what occurred therein. If the defendant has confessed, the prosecutor should peruse the defendant's confessions, to gauge the degree to which they were in his favor.[10] . . .

Hearing the defense   Then the inquisitors shall diligently occupy themselves in hearing any potentially exonerating defenses that the defendant has

---

9. Theoretically, the prosecutor was not allowed to charge anyone on the basis of unratified testimony, nor could that unratified testimony be entered into publication. But see Document 5 and the objections raised by Marina González' defense lawyer.

10. This phrase is ambiguous; the "favor" could be the prosecutor's *or* the defendant's.

requested. The inquisitors shall receive and examine the character witnesses and those who provide second-hand testimony; as well as the witnesses the defendant presents to prove his objections against prosecution witnesses.[11] The inquisitors will carry out with very great diligence all the things that pertain to settling the defendant's innocence, with the same sort of care they applied to the investigation of his guilt. The inquisitors shall especially note that because of his imprisonment, the defendant cannot do everything necessary to prove his case, as if he were at liberty.

Once the important defenses have been concluded, the inquisitors shall order the defendant and his lawyer to appear before them. The inquisitors shall certify to them that the relevant, requested defenses have been carried out; therefore if they wish to conclude, they may; and if they wish something else, they should state it, so it may be done. If the defendant, his lawyer, and the prosecutor wish nothing else, the case should be concluded, though it is more proper for the prosecutor not to conclude it, since he is not obliged to do so, and so that he can more easily ask for any new investigation that may become appropriate. . . .

The consultation   When the case has reached this stage, the inquisitors shall meet with the *ordinario*[12] and the *consultadores* of the Holy Office, to whom the entire trial record will be communicated, with nothing substantial omitted. Once the trial record has been seen by all, they will vote, each one giving his opinion according to what his conscience dictates. They will vote in this order: first, the *consultadores;* then the *ordinario;* and finally the inquisitors, who vote in the presence of the *consultadores* and the *ordinario,* so that all shall understand the reasons for their votes. If the inquisitors have a different opinion, the *consultadores* may be satisfied that the inquisitors are moved in conformity with the law, not by their free will. The notary will mark each vote in the registry of votes. . . . And the inquisitors must allow the *consultadores* to vote with complete liberty, and not consent to anyone's being obstructed or speaking out of turn. . . .

Reconciliation   If the defendant has confessed, and his confession meets the qualities required by law, the inquisitors, *ordinario,* and *consultadores* shall receive him to reconciliation. His goods shall be confiscated as the law allows; he shall be given a penitential habit, which is [called] a *sanbenito* of yellow linen or cloth, with two red crosses; he shall be sentenced to the prison they call perpetual or merciful. Some parts of the Crown of Aragón have

---

11. These three categories of defense witnesses would fall under *abonos* (character witnesses); *indirectas* (second-hand witnesses); and *tachas* (objections to prosecution testimony).

12. The bishop's representative.

particular *fueros,* privileges, and customs that must be kept in the confiscation of goods and the colors of the *sanbenito;* these conditions stipulate the
time limit for wearing the *sanbenito* and the duration of imprisonment according to the results of the trial. If, for some reason, the inquisitors think
the *sanbenito* should be voluntary, they may mandate as much only by our
will or the will of the inquisitor-general who exists at the time, not according to their own discretion. The imposition of the *sanbenito* is understood
to apply only to people who have not relapsed. It is a matter of law that when
the relapsed are convicted or confess, they must be relaxed to the secular arm.
The inquisitors cannot reconcile them—even if they are not truly relapsed
but only ostensibly so—because of the abjuration *de vehementi* that they
[previously] made.[13] . . .

Persistent denial   When a defendant persistently denies the charges of
heresy—and the heretical crime of which he is accused has been proven by
law—or the defendant is an obstinate heretic, the law clearly states that he
cannot avoid being relaxed to the secular arm. But in such a case the inquisitors must pay great attention to [achieving] his conversion, so that he
will die at least with knowledge of God. In this matter, the inquisitors will
do everything they can as Christians. . . .

Recusation   If any inquisitor should be recused by some prisoner,[14] and
he has a colleague, and that colleague is present, then his colleague shall proceed in the case, while the recused inquisitor must absent himself from that
trial and advise the Suprema [accordingly]. If the recused inquisitor has no
colleague, he should [still] advise the Suprema; he should not proceed in the
case until the reasons for suspicion are heard and the Suprema orders what
is necessary. The same will be done when all the inquisitors [of a particular
tribunal] are recused. . . .

The conduct of the prison warden   The inquisitors shall take great care
to order the warden not to speak to or counsel the prisoners at any time
about their cases. Rather, the prisoners should conduct their cases freely,

13. Thus the category of "relapse" was subject to fine-tuning. A "truly relapsed"
heretic would have confessed a major heresy (such as judaizing or Lutheranism), been
reconciled to the Church, and fallen once again into a major heresy; see the example of Friar Cristóbal de Morales in Document 22. An *ostensibly* relapsed heretic abjured a vehement suspicion of heresy—and had been held as convicted—and then
failed to fulfill a penance, which signified relapse too. For an example of a defendant
who was accused of having relapsed in part because she allegedly violated restrictions
on her dress after her reconciliation, see Document 5.

14. For Inquisitor-General Valdés' intimate knowledge of just such a situation, see
Document 18.

from their own will, without anyone's persuasion. If the inquisitors find that the opposite has been done, they shall punish the warden. So that there will be no cause for suspicion, the warden shall not become the guardian or defender of any minor, nor may he act as a substitute for the prosecutor and exercise that office in the prosecutor's absence. The warden is commanded and permitted to write the prisoner's defense documents when some prisoner does not know how to write; in such an instance, the warden shall note the way the prisoner says things, without speaking to him, or putting anything into his head. . . .

Bigamy and blasphemy   The inquisitors often proceed against people for things that render them suspicious in the faith, [but] because of the quality of the crime and the person involved, they are not judged as heretics; such are people who contract two marriages, or speak well-known blasphemies or evil-sounding words. For such offenses the inquisitors impose various penalties and penances, according to the quality of the crimes, in conformity with the law, and by their lawful discretion. Neither pecuniary nor personal penances and penalties—such as whippings or the galleys, or very shameful penances levied because the defendant could not pay the amount of money he was condemned to pay—shall be imposed in these cases. Such punishments sound bad, and seem like extortion and humiliation of the party involved and his heirs. To avoid all this, the inquisitors shall pronounce their sentences simply, without condition or choices.

Discrepancy in the vote   For all cases in which there is a discrepancy of votes among the inquisitors and the *ordinario* . . . the case must be remitted to the Suprema. But where the aforesaid are in agreement, even if the other *consultadores* disagree and are of a larger number, the vote of the inquisitors and the *ordinario* shall be executed. If very serious cases are involved, though, the votes of the inquisitors, *ordinario,* and *consultadores* should not be executed even if they are in agreement without consulting with the Suprema, as is customarily done.[15] . . .

Perpetual prison   The inquisitors shall visit the perpetual prison during the year to see how the residents are treated, and what sort of life they have. Because there are no perpetual prisons in many inquisitions, and because they are very necessary, houses should be bought for that purpose. Without such prisons, the inquisitors cannot understand how the reconciled fulfill their penances, or observe what needs to be observed.

15. This was one of Valdés' most noteworthy cautions, that tribunals had to send verdicts in difficult cases to the Suprema for approval.

Placement of the *sanbenitos* It's obvious that all the *sanbenitos* condemned, whether dead, alive, or absent, shall be placed in the churches where they were parishioners at the time of their imprisonment, death, or flight. The same should be done with the *sanbenitos* of the reconciled, after they have fulfilled their penances and their *sanbenitos* have been removed, even if they only wore them while they were on the scaffold while their sentences were being read. This procedure should be observed inviolably, and no one has the authority to alter it. Executing this procedure should be charged forever to the inquisitors, who shall place and replace prominently the *sanbenitos* in the places they visit, in order that there may always be memory of the heretics' infamy and their descent. The date of their condemnation, and whether their crime was of Jews or Moors, or the new heresies of Martin Luther and his followers, must be placed on the *sanbenitos*. But inquisitors should not put *sanbenitos* on people reconciled during an edict of grace, because one of the clauses of that grace is that *sanbenitos* shall not be imposed; and if the *sanbenitos* are not worn at the time of reconciliation, then they should not be placed in the churches; doing so would contravene the mercy that was extended at the beginning.

Uniformity mandated We charge and order all the inquisitions to observe and execute the matters presented in these chapters, notwithstanding that some have had a contrary style and customs, because in this way the Inquisition will work toward the service of God, Our Lord, and the good administration of justice. We order it so recognized, being signed with our name and sealed with our seal; and promulgated by the Secretary of the General Inquisition [i.e., the Suprema]. Given in Madrid, September 2, 1561.

DOCUMENT 21

Excerpts from the Visitation Records of the Prison in the Tribunal of Córdoba, 1569[1]

[The Spanish Inquisition imprisoned individuals in a variety of ways. When enough testimony had been collected and a formal accusation was pending, suspects were seized by the constable of a tribunal and put into cells to await trial. While trials were ongoing, defendants were always imprisoned within the inquisition tribunal itself, in a separate part of the building set aside for that purpose: for example, in the middle of the sixteenth century, the Toledo tribunal possessed about twenty-three cells, divided between upper and lower floors, for prisoners whose cases were underway.[2] So long as a defendant's trial was pending or in progress, the tribunal maintained him in food, drink, blankets, and clothing through the sale of the prisoner's own property, which had been sequestered upon his arrest, and which was sold off piece by piece as needed. Once in the tribunal prison, defendants were not supposed to share cells with accomplices or have any access to the outside world, but as the trials often demonstrate, that kind of isolation was difficult to achieve, either because of architecture—such as windows that opened onto the street—or because of the potential corruptibility of the prison warden and his staff.[3]

Incarceration would continue if individuals were sentenced to "perpetual prison" or to seclusion in a monastery or convent. Perpetual prisons were not located in tribunals; instead, the term could refer to the defendant's own house, a whole city, or buildings specially designated for that purpose by the Inquisition.[4] The problem for the inquisitors was how to hold down costs (from having

1. Garcia Boix, *Colección de documentos*, 173–74, 179–80, 189–93.

2. For descriptions and plans of the Granada tribunal, see Bernard Vincent, "Un espacio de exclusión: La cárcel inquisitorial en el siglo XVI," in *Minorías y marginados en la España del siglo XVI*, ed. Bernard Vincent (Granada: Diputación provincial de Granada, 1987); and for the Seville tribunal in the seventeenth century, Francisco Bethencourt, *La inquisición en la época moderna: España, Portugal, Italia, siglos XV–XIX* (Madrid: Akal, 1997), 87.

3. For ways in which defendants foiled theoretical isolation, see the trial of María de Cazalla, Document 12.

4. The *Instructions* of 1488 and 1561 address the difficulties of finding and funding perpetual prisons; see Documents 7 and 20. For more rulings on the creation of perpetual prisons, and the obstacles therein, consult Lea, *A History of the Inquisition of Spain*, vol. 3, 151–57.

to buy prisons), and how to maintain some supervision of the "perpetual prisoners," who were supposed to support themselves. In 1561, Inquisitor-General Valdés commanded tribunals without perpetual prisons to buy houses for that purpose and to inspect them regularly, but uniformity in the matter was not achieved.[5] The fact that penitents could leave their perpetual prison for work may have provoked the inquisitors' constant worry that individuals were taking off their sanbenitos.

The text below concerns the prison inside the inquisition tribunal at Córdoba.]

Excerpts from the visitation to the inquisition prison of the tribunal of Córdoba, 1569

Today, Saturday, January 8, 1569, the lord inquisitor licentiate Alonso Thamaron visited the prisons of this Holy Office and the prisoners therein, who said that they were well-provided for by his representative and the rest [of the employees]. Some asked for things during the visitation; the prisons, and the people in each of them, are as follows:

In the prison of the young girls[6]

Francisco de Córdoba, who requested a hearing

Andrés López, who requested a blanket

Friar Bernardo, who requested another blanket.

Francisco Alfahar

In the prison by the well

Henoc (sic)

Hernando de Aguilar had swollen hands, and requested that he be provided with a bed

In the prison of the young boys

Luis de Mesa, cleric

Luis López de la Rubia

Anton de Molina

5. See Document 20.

6. I have no explanation as to why men were being housed in the part of the prison labeled "young girls," except that perhaps the inquisitors had no young girls under arrest at the time. On January 8, 1569, all the women seem to have been housed in the "prison of the oven"; see below. Such titles—"prison by the wall," etc.—denoted sections of cells or particular cells within the tribunal's area of incarceration.

In the divided prison

Francisco de Ávila

Rodrigo Nicolas

In the prison of the orange trees

Juan Rodríguez

Antonio de Alcocer

Licentiate Villena

In the prison of the oven

Catalina Armijo, who requested some shoes

Magdalena Ruiz

Luisa Martínez

In the prison of the fountain

Hernando Domínguez requested a book of hours

Juan de Ávila requested a shirt and some undershirts and some short
   socks, and said they [sic] may go to his house to get them

Cristóbal de la Guardia

Give the quartermaster a note to go for these things.[7]

. . . . In Córdoba, Saturday, March 19, 1569. The lord inquisitor Alonso
Thamaron visited the prisons of this Holy Office and the prisoners therein,
and all said they were well provided for by his representative and the rest [of
the employees], except for some who asked for the following things:

Prison of the vault

Friar Bernaldo asked that that he be given a shirt, since he is currently
   nude

Florian Rodríguez asked that the food ration be increased, as they have
   reduced it

Henoc asked that they finish his case

Prison of the young boys

Diego de Mesa asked that the inquisitors grant him the city as a jail.[8]

Hernan Domínguez

---

7. Statements in italics are the inquisitor's responses.

8. Making an urban space a defendant's jail was one way to solve overcrowding. The

Prison of the orange trees

Licentiate Antonio de Villena asked for more company.

Andrés López

Prison of fealty

Friar Alonso de Vergara said that he is ill, asked that they give him more company, and asked that the quartermaster take better care of him.

Graviel Carrillo

All of which passed before me, Juan Castellón, Notary.

Saturday, July 16, 1569. The lord inquisitors visited the prisons of this Holy Office and the prisoners therein.

In the prison of the young girls

Juan de Merlo asked that they remove the grille

In the prison of the fig tree

Pedro Joan

In the prison of the well

Andrés de Vaenas asked that they give him company because he is melancholy, and a candle for nighttime

In the prison of the chimney

Juan de Vergara asked that they remove the grille

In the prison of the young boys

Hernan Domínguez, Hernando de Leyva, and Diego de Mesa asked to be given the Córdoban bread at ten. They say the villager comes by at ten, and it's better that the villager give the bread to them. They asked to be given more oil, as stipulated.

In the prison of the orange trees

Licentiate Villena, Juan María, Friar Andrés Cepero, who said the food rations arrive late. . . .

. . . Saturday, July 30, 1569, the lord inquisitors Alonso Thamaron and Antonio de Matos visited the prisons of the Holy Office and the prisoners therein.

Toledo tribunal did this for Juan de Vergara in the 1530s; see Homza, *Religious Authority*, chapter 1.

In the divided prison

Andrés de Vaenas, Francisco de Ávila, Mesegar, Luis de Chincilla

Francisco de Ávila asked that they buy him some shoes

Andrés de Vaenas asked that they give him the handkerchiefs that he requested

Luis de Chincilla asked that they give his daughters and wife the veils and skirts so that they could [go to Mass.]

What Chincilla requests is stipulated by his wife's petition . . . and the rest isn't.

In the prison of the fountain

Alonso Almuedan, Cristóbal de la Guardia, Juan de Ávila. They said they saw the food rations weighed on certain days, but other times not. . . .

In the prison of fealty

Friar Alonso de Vergara, Florian Rodríguez, Pedro Carrero

Friar Alonso said that the quartermaster is late with the food rations, that the shirts are badly washed when they are returned, and that they throw rocks at the quartermaster through the top of the cell

Florian Rodríguez requested that straw be put in the mattress and that the doctor visit him. He also asked for a pigeon because the cow's meat made him sick, and consequently, he had eaten no meat that day. Rodríguez said that the other day, Thursday, at one o'clock, the quartermaster brought him two pies, and he and the other prisoners did not see [the quartermaster and his servant] weigh the food rations. And Rodríguez had asked for seven or eight things and had added them up, and afterward, some were missing, though the quartermaster said he had given them all. In the matter of coal, the quartermaster gives one pound instead of two, and the belt that Florian Rodríguez asked for in the last visit still hasn't been given to him

The straw that Florian Rodríguez asked for in the last visit, which he has not received, shall be purchased; the belt shall be given to him, as stipulated; the doctor shall be called; and the fig tree in their prison shall be removed, so that the boys shall not throw things.

In other matters, the prisoners said they are well taken care of by the warden of the prison and provided for by the inquisitors' employees.

And this passed before me, Juan López de Alegría, Notary.

This same day, in their morning hearing, the lord inquisitors reviewed what had turned up from this visit. [They worried about the plentiful communication the quartermaster has with the prisoners.] . . . . They feared they might get another quartermaster who was worse, given the difficulty there was right now in finding a second one, due to the small salary he was paid. So they resolved that the quartermaster should be informed about the complaints and an investigation launched, and the quartermaster punished for any offense that results.

So that the difficulties shall cease henceforth, the quartermaster should be ordered that every time he has to give the prisoners something that was weighed and measured, the prisoners should see the weighing and measuring. If it seemed that this process would cause a delay, or the possibility of a delay, then the quartermaster should perform the weighing and measuring before the warden, so that the warden could see it. Then the food could be delivered to the prisoners in front of the warden. If the quartermaster did the opposite, he would be punished. The inquisitors so ordered through this act, which occurred before me, Juan López de Alegría, Notary.

Today, while in their afternoon hearing, the lord inquisitors notified the quartermaster, Antón Martínez, of the prisoners' complaints. And Martínez said that regarding the straw, Andrés de Huertas, the warden, had told him that he would stuff the mattress with straw from his house . . . and Martínez did not give the pigeon to Florian Rodríguez because he couldn't find it. The other day at eleven o'clock, Martínez gave Rodríguez two pies, and Rodríguez asked for the pigeon on the same day he received the pies. . . . Today he added one more pound of coal for Florian Rodríguez, in addition to the rationed amount . . . all of which he swore to be the truth through the oath which was received from him in the necessary way.

Afterward, what was contained in this act was communicated to Juan Ortiz, the warden's assistant, because the warden himself was sick; and the assistant said that all his life he has done and shall continue to do what is now ordered through the said act. This occurred before me, Juan López de Alegría, notary.

THE *MORISCOS*

DOCUMENT 22

Auto de Fe Celebrated in Granada, March 18, 1571[1]

[Essential frameworks for the two documents that follow are royal and inquisitorial policies toward the moriscos—*the baptized Muslims of Spain—and the Revolt of the Alpujarras by those* moriscos *from 1568 to 1570 in Granada. The first archbishop of Granada, Hernando de Talavera, initially tried to catechize the Muslims of the kingdom of Granada after the reconquest of 1492; within the decade, other religious authorities—such as Francisco Ximénez de Cisneros, Archbishop of Toledo and Queen Isabella's confessor—argued for a more coercive approach, including mass baptisms. By 1501, it was presumed that most of Granada's population had converted to Christianity, and in 1502, all Muslims in Castile were ordered to convert or emigrate. Similar orders to convert were issued in 1525 for the Muslims of Valencia, and again in 1526 for the Muslims of Aragón.[2] Their baptisms notwithstanding, Spanish* moriscos *generally refused to be assimilated into Christianity, and Spanish clergy and the state fluctuated between missionary efforts and cultural injunctions against the external signs of Islam. Significantly,* moriscos *could be more or less free to practice Islam depending upon where they lived. For example,* morisco *vassals of Valencian seigneurs tended to be relatively safer from inquisitors, because their lords adamantly resisted such interference.[3] In Granada, by contrast,*

1. José María García Fuentes. *La inquisición en Granada en el siglo XVI: fuentes para su estudio* (Granada: Departamento de Historia Moderna, 1981), 95–125.

2. The forced conversion of Muslims in Valencia mostly occurred in 1520–1521, when groups of brotherhoods (*germanías*) rebelled against the local aristocracy and attempted to break the nobles' power over the countryside by baptizing their Muslim vassals. After much discussion, the authorities decided that the Muslims' baptism, however coerced, was valid. It then appeared unreasonable to tolerate unbaptized Muslims in Aragón, and the decrees of Charles V followed.

3. The relative autonomy of Valencian *moriscos*—and the level of their protection—is revealed by the agreements they made with the Inquisition. In 1526, Inquisitor-General Manrique agreed to free them from prosecution for forty years if they submitted to baptism. In 1571, inquisitors in Valencia agreed to stop confiscating property of *moriscos* on trial in return for an annual payment of 2,500 ducats, though small fines could still be exacted. Still, after the Alpujarras revolt, even *moriscos* in Valencia came under increasing fire from the Inquisition, which might not have been able to confiscate their property, but which could sentence them to the galleys.

moriscos *made up a majority of the population and possessed an integral Islamic civilization but lacked intermediaries who could effectively block either the Inquisition or the king for substantial periods of time.*

In 1526, Granada's moriscos *were forbidden to use Arabic, choose Muslim names, or wear Muslim clothing. In 1567, they again were commanded to abandon their language, dress, customs, and religious practices, this time upon pain of imprisonment.* Morisco *leaders and their Old Christian allies attempted to negotiate with Philip II, to no avail, and the Revolt of the Alpujarras—named for the Alpujarras mountain range, southeast of Granada—began in December 1568. Though some 182 rebel villages were recaptured by 1569, it took another year for royal forces to realize they would have to negotiate a surrender with the insurgents, who by now were in rugged territory. The commanders-in-chief of the* morisco *forces finally surrendered in May 1570. It had been an extremely savage conflict: rebel* moriscos *massacred priests; Old Christians sold captured* moriscos *into slavery. The Revolt had serious repercussions for the demographics and inquisition history of early modern Spain. In February 1571, Philip II decreed that all* moriscos *in the kingdom of Granada had to abandon their lands and move into colonies throughout Castile, while Old Christian families in turn were encouraged to resettle in Granadan territory. Hostilities were heightened, and* moriscos *began to appear in increasing numbers in* autos de fe.[4]

The reader will also notice a change in penances in this document, namely, the assignment of galley service. This potentially fatal sentence, which began in Aragón, was designed to provide rowers for Philip II's ships.[5]]

Account of people who appeared at the *auto de fe* celebrated by the Holy Office of the Inquisition of Granada on Sunday, March 18, 1571

People penanced extraordinarily for different things

Ramiro de Palencia, a *mudejar,* a new Christian [sic], descended from Muslims; he is a resident of Granada and native of the city of Burgos. He was

4. See note 3 for the special situation faced by Valencian *moriscos.* Philip II turned down recommendations to expel Spain's *morisco* population in 1582 and 1592. Even as late as 1596, Philip II created a special Committee for the Religious Instruction of the Valencian *moriscos,* whereby each diocese in the kingdom of Valencia would appoint twelve Arabic-speaking missionaries of Christian doctrine, who would be led in turn by friars with experience in the Indies. For the intricacies of the situation in Valencia, and the fluctuation there between missionary impulses and intolerance, see Ehlers, *Between Christians and Moriscos.*

5. Monter, *Frontiers of Heresy,* 32–35.

relaxed to the secular arm before he converted, for having said prayers in which he seemed to name Muhammed. One time, yawning, he said, "May Muhammed close my eyes"; and many times he performed the *zalá*[6] without reason,[7] raising and lowering his head, and bringing his hands over his face. Because the witnesses against him seemed to be unique, and to have other weaknesses, it was not certain that he could be condemned to death. But given the quality of his person and the suspicions that resulted against him, he was condemned to abjure *de vehementi*, and to pay 50,000 *maravedís* for the extraordinary expenses of the Holy Office.[8]

Juan Fernández de Quadros, *morisco,* resident of Málaga. False witness. He made a statement against certain *moriscos* who stoned and broke a cross that was in the road; he said they had put some filth on it; and he claimed to have seen it. Being called afterward to ratify his statement, and being asked certain questions, he eventually confessed that he had committed perjury, and had deposed against those *moriscos* because of the enmity he had for them. The rope, 200 lashes in Granada, 200 lashes in Málaga, 8 years in the galleys.

Sebastian de Alcaráz, *morisco,* pig-keeper, resident of Granada. A book written in Arabic with four Moorish prayers and other things from the Qur'an of Muhammed was found in a certain hole in his house.[9] The hole was plugged up with plaster. He confessed that someone else had put the book there, but he did not know who it was; and he persevered in this confession. Because of the quality of his person and other factors, the rope, 100 lashes, abjuration *de vehementi*, 20 ducats. . . .

Ysabel Xaquiza, *morisca,* resident of Granada. Many books were found hidden in her house which involved the Qur'an of Muhammed, and expositions

---

6. The *zalá* is a ceremonial act of reverence to the Prophet Muhammed, which involves kneeling and bowing the head, and which is performed five times a day in accordance with the five pillars of Islam.

7. *En seco;* literally, without reason or motive.

8. In this instance, the Granada inquisition tribunal seems to have prosecuted an unconverted Muslim—a *mudejar*—for heresy, though the following phrase, "a new Christian," leaves room for doubt; an error in terminology may be to blame, with the scribe writing "*mudejar*" when he meant "*morisco.*" Trying an unconverted Muslim would have violated the Inquisition's theoretical procedures, since non-Christians should not have been under the Inquisition's jurisdiction. Moreover, and again theoretically, there should not have been any unconverted Muslims, native to Spain, who were resident in Granada or in any other locale in Aragón or Castile, since Spanish Muslims had been forced to convert to Christianity in 1502 (Castile), 1525 (Valencia), and 1526 (Aragón).

9. The Inquisition sometimes mistook books in *aljamiado*—Spanish written in Arabic characters—for Arabic itself.

of the Qur'an and the sect of Muhammed. She always denied the charges.[10] Abjuration *de vehementi* and thirty ducats.

Mayor Garcia, *morisca*, resident of Junquera in the territory of Málaga. Discussing the virginity of Our Lady the Virgin Mary with other people, she said, "How could a married woman remain a virgin after giving birth?" Abjuration *de vehementi*. . . .

Lucia de Huete, *morisca*, resident of Nigueles. While living in Nigueles, she rose up with other people and went to the Alpujarras to join the other rebellious Moors. And she went to the rebels at the time they were clashing with Christians, and she invoked Muhammed and prayed to Muhammed to favor the rebels against the Christians. She also performed the *zalá*. She persevered in her denial. Abjuration *de vehementi*, 100 lashes. . . .

People reconciled with the *sanbenito*, perpetual prison, and confiscation of goods for having believed that Mosaic Law was still in effect, that they could be saved by it, that the Messiah had not come, and that they awaited him

Gonzalo Baez, Portuguese student of *converso* lineage, and a native of the village of Cubillan in Portugal,[11] came to confess that a certain person instructed him in the Law of Moses, and told him that he did not have to believe that Our Lord Jesus Christ was the true Messiah as promised in the Law, because the true Messiah still had not come; and when the true Messiah came, he would liberate the Jews. The same person told him that the Law of Moses was the good one and the one to observe, because God had written it with His finger. There was no need to believe the evangelical law, because some fishermen wrote it. Every Saturday had to be observed as a feast day, and no work was to be performed on them at all; and clean shirts had to be worn on that day. One had to fast and keep a great feast on September 10, as well as fast in honor of Queen Esther for three days during the month of September. One also had to observe the Passover, about the flight from Egypt, which falls in the month of March. One has to believe that Mosaic Law is good and better than the law of Christians. . . . Gonzalo Baez in turn taught Mosaic Law to many people, promoting it through citations from the Old Testament; and he taught them many new Jewish prayers. Baez taught one person that Our Lord Jesus Christ had been a whip sent by God to punish men. He also taught that they should not believe in Our Lady or in any other saint, and that Our Lady had not been a Virgin when she gave

10. When defendants persistently denied the charges, inquisitors called them *negativos*.

11. See the Introduction for information on Portuguese *conversos* tried by the Inquisition in Spain.

birth, because it was impossible for a virgin to give birth, and thus what the Christians believed was a complete lie. He taught that the Most Holy Sacrament of the altar was not truly God, and denied that there was Purgatory or Hell, but only a grave that the Jews call Hell [sic]. Baez would teach all this and prove it with scriptural citations. When the prosecutor made a second charge and presented Baez with it, Baez confessed entirely, without any denial. Monastic habit and reclusion in a monastery for one year.

Catalina Méndez, Portuguese, resident of Málaga, native of Martula in the kingdom of Portugal, of *converso* lineage. She told many people that Mosaic Law was holy, good, and just, and that they had to be saved through it, and thus had to observe it. So they henceforth agreed to observe Fridays in the afternoons, and Saturdays as Jewish feast days. On Fridays in the afternoons, they cleaned the oil lamps and put in new wicks of spinning flax, or if that flax were not available, new linen. She told people that the meat should be bled and defatted, and the nerve in the leg removed. She said it was a great Christian blindness to believe that Our Lord Jesus Christ was the Messiah promised in the Law, since he still had not come. Catalina Méndez also said that Our Lord Jesus Christ was merely a man and Our Lady the Virgin a woman just like anyone else. She said the preachers would suffer misfortune and travail if they tried to make her buy papal bulls every day to pardon her sins, and she made fun of the sale of the bulls. Monastic habit and perpetual prison.

Hernando López, Portuguese, resident of Málaga, officer of the Customs Office of Almoxarife in Málaga, native of Dule in Portugal, of *converso* lineage. He told other people in Málaga that the Mosaic Law was the good one, and it had to be believed and observed, and they had to be saved through it. He taught people to observe Friday nights, and light oil lamps with clean wicks of spinning flax or new linen, because it was the night before the Saturday that was observed as a feast day, as was commanded in Jewish law. He taught that meat had to be bled and defatted, because it was a great sin in their Law to consume blood and fat, and they had to remove the nerve from the leg of the meat. He said it was a great blindness[12] to believe that Our Lord Jesus Christ was the true Messiah promised in the Law, since he had not come; and they awaited the Messiah. He said Our Lord Jesus Christ had been a man and Our Lady the Virgin Mary a woman, like anyone else. Monastic habit and perpetual prison.

Ysabel de Ayora, deceased, resident of Málaga, native of Córdoba. She observed Friday afternoons and the following Saturdays as feast days in the city of Málaga, dressing herself in clean clothes and headdresses to observe

---

12. Here López is turning the charge of "blindness," which Christians habitually leveled against Jews, against the Christians themselves.

Mosaic Law along with other people, and they believed it was good for their salvation. She was represented in effigy, in the form of someone reconciled, at the *auto*.

People reconciled with monastic habit, perpetual prison, and the confiscation of goods for having believed the sect of Muhammed was good, and that they would save themselves through it

. . . . Juan Martín Azara, *morisco,* resident of the Albuñuelas, brother of Giron, the captain of the rebels of Albuñuelas. He joined with the rebellious Moors, invoking Muhammed; and he said there was no other law except that of Muhammed, believing that the law of Muhammed was the good one, and that he owed reverence to Muhammed. He performed the *guadoch*[13] and *zalá* to observe the law of the Moors, believing that he could be saved by it. He and his relatives, who were numerous, took up banners and arms in favor of the Moors against the Christians. *Sanbenito* and perpetual prison, 200 lashes, perpetual galleys. . . .

Juan de Velasco el Ducayac, *morisco,* resident of Gabia la Chica. He was inside the territory of Málaga and went with the rebellious Moors to where they could be Moors publicly. He performed the *guadoch* and *zalá* of the Moors, and walked around with weapons. It was voted to relax him to the secular arm for having lied and been defective in his confession . . . and we sent the trial to Your Lordship(s),[14] and you ordered the sentence carried out. But in the midst of carrying out that sentence, he confessed his intention entirely,[15] about himself as well as others. He was admitted to reconciliation in the usual form and sentenced to perpetual galleys.

García de Luna el Guarguali, resident of Orgiva, *morisco,* laborer. He joined with other people of his caste and lineage and they rebelled with other Moors of this kingdom of Granada in order to be Moors publicly. They tried to kill the Christians who were in their village, though the Christians defended themselves. He performed the *guadoch* and *zalá* and the fast of Ramadan, so that Muhammed would favor them. He called himself Ali as a Moorish name. And after he confessed and persevered in that confession for a few days, he [reversed himself] and denied his intention to perform the ceremonies of Moors. It was voted to relax him to the secular arm. After the case was seen by Your Lordship(s), you ordered the sentence carried out. He then confessed entirely about himself as well as others, out of his own free

13. The *guadoch* is a ritual washing ceremony.
14. I.e., the Suprema in Madrid.
15. Meaning that he intended to perform Muslim ceremonies, knowing what they were.

will. He was admitted to reconciliation in the usual form and sentenced to perpetual galleys.

Luis Abenjafar, resident of Alhendin, *morisco*. He went to the Alpujarras with the rebellious Moors and bought weapons in order to go with them. He performed the ceremonies of the Moors, the *guadoch*, the *zalá*, and the fast of Ramadan. Because he denied his intention to practice Islam, he was relaxed to the secular arm. After the case was seen by Your Lordship(s), you ordered us to carry out certain diligences regarding his intention, and after we admonished him about it, he confessed entirely. He was admitted to reconciliation in the usual form and sentenced to perpetual galleys.

Alonso Rufian, *morisco*, resident of Penillos. While in this city of Granada, he planned with others of his caste and lineage to travel to Barbary in order to be Moors there. He actually went to Barbary with these people and had himself circumcised. He performed the *guadoch* and the *zalá*, went to the mosques, and fasted for Ramadan. He performed the prayers of Moors. Learning that the *moriscos* of this kingdom had risen up against the Christian religion and His Majesty the King, he returned to this kingdom with other Moors, bringing gunpowder and weapons with them. And he joined the rebellious Moors and performed the ceremonies of the law of Moors. Because he denied that he intended to help the rebels or practice Islam, it was voted to relax him to the secular arm. After the case was seen by Your Lordship(s), you ordered him admitted to reconciliation in the usual form, with the *sanbenito* and perpetual prison, which he would fulfill in the galleys of His Majesty. But first he was returned to the royal prison of the Chancery and executed. . . .[16]

Juan de Luna, *morisco*, resident of Torrox. He joined the Moors who rebelled in that place, and went to the Alpujarras. He gave himself a Moorish name, performed the *guadoch* and the *zalá*, and bought an arquebus.[17] He came to confess of his own free will, and for this reason he did not enter the prisons. *Sanbenito*, which shall be removed immediately.

Hernan Pérez Alcaraz, *morisco*, resident of Benamaurel, territory of [Baeza]. He joined the Moors who rose up. He was with them in the village of Galera and the river of Almanzora. He gave himself a Moorish name, and acted as a soldier of the Moors and fought against Christians. He performed

16. The Royal Chancery in Granada was one of the two highest appeals courts in Spain, along with the Chancery in Valladolid. This detail reflects competing jurisdictions between the Inquisition and secular justice; this time, the secular court won out, undoubtedly because the charge involved treasonous rebellion.

17. An harquebus or arquebus was a portable but heavy matchlock gun invented in about the middle of the fifteenth century. Originally fired from a support, by the later sixteenth century the gun had been modified and could be fired from the shoulder.

the *guadoch, zalá,* and the fast of Ramadan; he also performed the *zahor* and prayed the prayers of Moors.[18] He came to confess of his own free will, and for this reason he did not enter the prisons. *Sanbenito* which shall be removed immediately.

Beatriz el Tez, slave, resident of Arenas, *morisca.* She went to the Guajaras [sic] with the rebellious Moors. Once she was there, she said, "There is no God except God and Muhammed is His messenger," which are the words by which one becomes a Moor.[19] When someone asked her how she was, she answered that she was bad off, and with any luck she would die and Muhammed would take her away. She said that the law of the Moors was good for salvation and going to heaven. *Sanbenito* which shall be removed immediately. She shall be delivered to her owner, and given 100 lashes.

María García, daughter of Luysa de Baza, *morisca,* resident of Guadix. She joined the rebellious Moors, and performed the *guadoch, zalá,* and the prayers of Moors. She went on a boat for Barbary. She confessed in the first hearing. *Sanbenito* which shall be removed immediately. . . .

María Peón, wife of Agustín Bueno, *morisca,* resident of Paterna. She joined the rebellious Moors, and with them she performed the ceremonies of *guadoch, zalá,* and the fast of Ramadan. She also performed prayers. *Sanbenito* which shall be removed immediately. She shall be delivered to her owner because she is a slave. . . .

Lady Constanca López, wife of Andrés de Córdoba, *morisca,* resident of Valor el Alto, in the Alpujarras. She was extremely happy when the Moors rebelled. In her house, under the floor of the drawing room, she possessed a consecrated, broken altar of a church. She used the wood of that church's *retablo*[20] as firewood in her house. And in front of many Old Christians, she said, "What do you think? That the world is always going to be yours? And because you dress us in a certain way, we have to be Christian? Underneath it all, we have done and will do what we want, because we were Moors, and Moors we shall remain." In that place called Valor, Lady Constanca gave a sermon for Sir Hernando de Valor, the first tyrant [sic], and others, which lasted from morning until midday; and everyone was amazed at what she said in praise of Muhammed and his law. When she was in Jubiles, with others of her caste, she and the others invoked Muhammed and performed prayers . . . and she performed the *guadoch* and *zalá* to observe the law of the Moors, and to save herself and go to heaven. She confessed all of this in

18. The *zahor* is the pre-dawn meal that occurred during Ramadan, when Muslims are supposed to fast between dawn and nightfall.

19. These words are the first of the five pillars of Islam.

20. A *retablo* is a painting on a board that stands behind or next to an altar and is intended as decoration.

the afternoon hearing on the eve of the *auto de fe,* having asked for the hearing. *Sanbenito* and perpetual, irremissible prison. The perpetual prison shall be specifically located in Castile, in an inquisition tribunal there. . . .[21]

Relaxed in person to the secular arm, for having believed the errors of Martin Luther, with confiscation of goods

Friar Cristóbal de Morales, resident of Seville, a Carthusian friar of the village of Cazalla. Relapsed heretic for maintaining that there is no other sacrament except baptism and the Lord's Supper, and that everything else, including the Mass, is a joke. He maintains that there is no Purgatory, but only the [redeeming] blood of Jesus Christ, who died once for everyone. He believes the power of the pope, bishops, and archbishops is . . . a matter of tyranny and ambition. . . . He believes that fasts and other pious works matter little for salvation, and that pious works for the dead are ridiculous and a clerical invention. In this faith he hoped to live and die, though he had been weak in sustaining it. He composed epigrams in praise of Martin Luther. After he was reconciled and thrown into the galleys for the same heresy by the Inquisition in Toledo, he tried to convince other people of these errors once he was there. Relaxed to justice and the secular arm with confiscation of goods.

21. Her prison sentence echoes the forced redistribution of Granada's *morisco* population after the revolt of the Alpujarras had ended. By placing her in perpetual prison "in" an inquisition tribunal, the sentence means such a prison under the supervision of a tribunal.

DOCUMENT 23

Letter from the Granada Tribunal to the Suprema, December 12, 1574[1]

With this letter we send to you the trial of Francisco, a baptized Moor from Barbary, who is the slave of Anton Rodríguez (alive), resident of Antequera. The inquisitor and *consultadores* voted unanimously to relax him to the secular arm.[2] Your Holiness shall order the case reviewed and shall supply what is appropriate to it, because we are on the verge of having enough trials to carry out an *auto de fe*. We are thinking of having the *auto,* God willing, on the second Sunday before Lent, which would be February 6, assuming Your Holiness gives permission for it.

Among the trials that were voted on, some involved people who conceded that they personally, with others, had performed the ceremonies of Moors in the Sierra during the uprising.[3] Some of the trials have witnesses who were also present; and some have no witnesses because they cannot be found. In conformity with Your Holiness' letters which were sent at the time of the uprising, it is ordered that people who describe themselves as having committed these acts in the Sierra, or who confess to such acts, shall be given spiritual penances, not the *sanbenito* or imprisonment. But nothing was [ever] arranged about whether reconciliation to the Church should be public or secret. Hence this tribunal has consistently voted, from the time of the uprising until now, that such people should be reconciled in a public *auto de fe,* where the *sanbenito* would be removed from them, thereby observing the direction from the old instructions of Seville 1484.[4] But we entreat Your Holiness to advise us if it will be allowable to [privately] reconcile one or two people in the tribunal's courtroom; they are young boys who were absolved sacramentally, and it doesn't appear as if they committed the crime of heresy after the uprising.

With all the rest, who seem to have committed a crime [of heresy] after the uprising, direction forty-one of the new instructions [of 1561][5] will be observed. May Our Lord protect your very illustrious and reverend persons, and may you increase even more in His Service, thanks be to God.

December 12, 1574. We kiss the hands of Your Holy Reverence.

1. Archivo Histórico Nacional, Sección de la Inquisición de Granada, Legajo 2604, Caja 1, n. 50.

2. Consult Document 20 for voting procedure during consultations on verdicts.

3. Revolt of the Alpujarras, 1568–1570.

4. For some of the Instructions from 1484, see Document 7.

5. See Document 20.

THE INQUISITION IN THE LAST DECADES OF THE SIXTEENTH CENTURY

Document 24

Scandalous Propositions. Friar Juan Bautista de Cubas, Monastery of San Lorenzo el Real. Penanced, 1581[1]

[Under Gaspar de Quiroga, Inquisitor-General from 1573 to 1594, the Inquisition continued to prosecute moral offenses among Old Christians and to employ the argument that no sound Christian would blaspheme, for instance.[2] The Inquisition grouped most suspicious statements into categories of scandalous words (palabras escandalosas) *or "propositions"* (proposiciones); *the latter was treated more seriously. It was for "propositions" that Juan Bautista de Cubas, a Jeronimite monk, received his penance from the Toledo tribunal in 1581.*

Friar de Cubas lived in Philip II's Escorial, the palace, office, and royal mausoleum which was finished in 1584. He apparently goaded his fellow monks with statements about the Assumption of the Blessed Virgin Mary, the belief that Mary had been "assumed" into heaven, body and soul, once her life on earth was completed. Though the doctrine of the Assumption was unknown in earliest Christianity, it had acquired the papal imprimatur of an octave feast[3] by 863; by the sixteenth century, there should have been nothing to argue about, but Cubas could have been reacting to larger European discussions about relics and Catholic truth.

Meanwhile, the doctrine of the Immaculate Conception—also an item of discussion at the Escorial—stated that the Virgin Mary was free from all stain of original sin from the first moment of her conception. This doctrine was very contentious in the Middle Ages, with Franciscans emerging as its supporters, Dominicans as its detractors. In 1476, Pope Sixtus IV approved the Feast of the Immaculate Conception; some eighty years later, the Council of Trent explicitly declared that its decree on original sin did not *include Mary. The*

1. Archivo Histórico Nacional, Sección de la Inquisición de Toledo, Leg. 218, n. 8.

2. Nalle, *God in La Mancha*, 64–69.

3. An "octave feast" is a commemorative event that occurs eight days after the Church feast itself.

Immaculate Conception was generally accepted in the sixteenth century, and yet the text below illustrates that it was still a matter of some debate, as were the works of Erasmus, many of which had already appeared on indices of prohibited books.]

I, Friar Juan Bautista, monk of San Lorenzo el Real, a cleric (having taken the habit a little more than five years ago), and a boy of little learning and experience, rashly and audaciously made the following propositions before some monks of the monastery:

First, I affirmed that anyone who said that the Virgin Mary's body had not yet been assumed into heaven would not be a heretic or a disseminator of errors detrimental to the Catholic faith, since church councils had not decreed it. . . . And if God has not revealed the body, it's because . . . the Virgin Mary has not been venerated as much as she formerly was, and because . . . we do not merit it.

I said likewise that the reasoning that Friar Bernard [of Clairvaux? d. 1153] used to prove that Our Lady was in Heaven, body and soul, is not as effective as the reasoning I would employ. Friar Bernard's reasoning was that if the body of Our Lady were on earth, God would not permit it to remain hidden this long without being discovered; in the same way, the relics of other saints have been discovered so that they could be venerated. The reasoning I would use instead is that if our Lady has not been discovered, it's because we don't merit that discovery; moreover, her relics have not been discovered so that reverence for her will not diminish. Everyone knows what men are; if they have something at their elbow they end up respecting it less, no matter how esteemed it is. I said likewise that as a result of my reasoning, Alonso de Villegas did not know what he was saying in a *Flos sanctorum quaedam,* namely, that it is Catholic truth that Our Lady is in Heaven, body and soul.

Next, speaking about the conception of Our Lady, I said that I wanted to endorse the opinion that says Our Lady was conceived in original sin, because scriptural authorities attest this, and not the reverse. I said that I would always hold this opinion until the Church determined otherwise. If Our Lady was conceived in original sin, they do her no honor in saying she was not, attributing to her what she does not have.

Next, I often said that they would have to quit chanting in Church, and a council nearly determined that there should be a vote to end it; and if I were the pope, I would end it. If my opinion was solicited over and above this matter, I likewise said that I was disgusted by so much singing. I have called the choir disparaging names.

Next, I have referred to some things that Erasmus said about the monastic orders; he called the Carthusians pigs, and the Benedictines drunks. And speaking of the order of our Father St. Jerome, Erasmus said there was a very good monastic order in Spain but it had one flaw, namely that its members spent the whole day braying like donkeys.

These are the propositions that I remember and confess to having said (as a boy, as I have said, and of little status), which appear to pertain to the Holy Office. I have scandalized and offended certain monks of my monastery with these propositions. The offense that I have committed against them and against Our Lord and his graceful mercy, and the Mother Church, pains me greatly. I beg penance from Your Illustrious Holiness, as a supreme judge; and entreat, for greater satisfaction, that you may hear what I feel about these propositions after I have been repressed and instructed in what I *should* feel about them.

Written in San Lorenzo del Escorial, October 16, 1581.

In Toledo, October 21, 1581   Having seen the confession written above, the Illustrious Lord Gaspar de Quiroga, Cardinal [and Archbishop] of Toledo and Inquisitor-General, said that the inquisitors of this city and kingdom shall hear Friar Juan Bautista as to what he seems to have said and confessed . . . and they shall harshly reprehend him,[4] and impose spiritual penances of fasts and prayers upon him, at their discretion. They shall order him to eat publicly in the refectory of his monastery when the monks come together to eat, on days that suit the inquisitors. They shall especially order that he not be promoted unless he receives a special license from the inquisitors, under threat of penalties that they shall impose. And so the Inquisitor-General ordered that this be communicated on his behalf, before me, Pedro de Valle Villamaran, Secretary

In Toledo, October 21, in the inquisition tribunal   . . . Asked which books of Erasmus he has read, Friar Juan Bautista said he never had any book by Erasmus, except one of his prologues on Cicero and some commentaries on Cicero, which he has read. What he repeated about Erasmus, he had heard from certain monks, that is, from one monk of his own order, who is named Friar Juan de Madrid; Friar Juan said that Erasmus said the Jeronimites brayed all day long. As for calling the Benedictines drunks, Friar Juan Bautista de Cuba heard a Benedictine friar say it, whose name he does not recall. And what he said about the Carthusians (whom Erasmus called pigs), he heard as well from a Jeronimite friar named Friar Gerónimo de Alcalá. Friar Juan Bautista de Cubas repeated these things in conversation with other monks of his order. And the teaching of Erasmus seemed wicked to him, and this is the truth, and he has no more to say. He was ordered to go outside.

---

4. What is nearly comedic is to see the way in which Quiroga's directions and even language were duplicated verbatim by the tribunal's inquisitors.

Then the inquisitors, having seen the declaration and written confession, and what was written at the end of it by the Inquisitor General, and having conferred about it, ordered Friar Juan Bautista de Cubas to come back in. Once he was there, he was harshly reprehended. The inquisitors imposed, as a penance, that he fast for nine Fridays, three on bread and water; and they ordered him to eat on the floor in the refectory, in the way it's usually done. The inquisitors ordered him to pray the seven psalms for all nine Fridays, with the prayer that the Church says on the day of the Assumption of Our Lady. And he cannot be promoted to other ranks without permission from the illustrious Inquisitor-General. Friar Juan Bautista de Cubas promised to comply, and a notice of the penance was given to his companion, who came with him, so that the superior in San Lorenzo el Real would be aware of it. . . .

DOCUMENT 25

Sentence of Catalina Muñoz for False Sanctity, 1588[1]

[Catalina Muñoz, a black former slave, achieved fame in her community for her prophetic visions, miraculous reception of the Eucharist, and manifestation of the wounds of Christ. She lived in Valencia during the lengthy tenure of Archbishop Juan de Ribera, and apparently received his approval at first. Ribera was highly sensitive to local impulses even as he attempted to implement the centralizing Tridentine decrees,[2] and he worked to create a religious environment in which figures who met certain standards of holiness—such as the Franciscan beata Margarita Agullona[3]—could help him communicate with the Valencian people. Yet Ribera's spiritual patronage was not extended to all spiritual figures, and Catalina Muñoz lacked certain crucial attributes, such as membership in a religious order, obedience, and a reliable spiritual director; when questions arose as to her religious practices, Ribera refused to endorse her.[4] Nevertheless, she was part of the wave of prophecy that swept Spain in the 1580s.[5]]

1. Muñoz' sentence is transcribed in Benjamin Ehlers, "La esclava y el patriarca: las visiones de Catalina Muñoz en la Valencia de Juan de Ribera," *Estudis* 23 (1997): 114–16. Muñoz' example can be combined with those of Francisca Hernández and particularly Magdalena de la Cruz; consult Documents 10 and 16. For bibliography on the Inquisition's prosecution of false sanctity, see Document 16, note 3. For a *morisca* visionary several decades later, see Mary Elizabeth Perry, "Contested Identities: The Morisca Visionary, Beatriz de Robles," in *Women in the Inquisition,* ed. Mary E. Giles, 171–88.

2. The decrees of the Council of Trent (1545–1563) explained, in definitive form, the Catholic perspective on salvation, the sacraments, the canonical biblical text, the proper understanding and veneration of saints and their relics, and the obligations of clergy to their parishioners, among other things. See *The Canons and Decrees of the Council of Trent.*

3. *Beatas* were unmarried women who were not members of formal monastic orders, but who quested after holiness by taking vows of chastity and often of poverty.

4. It also looks as if she deliberately imitated the gifts of the "Nun of Lisbon," Sor María de la Visitación, prioress of the Convent of the Annunciation in Lisbon, who was acclaimed for her visions but was condemned as an imposter in 1588. See below.

5. Ehlers, "La esclava," also documents the prophetic activities of a Friar Ruzola, who may have been acting as a sort of spiritual director for Catalina. On prophecy in 1580s Madrid, see Kagan, *Lucrecia's Dreams.*

Account of a public *auto de fe* that was celebrated by the Inquisition of Valencia, Sunday, June 19, 1588[6]

Catalina, slave who belonged to Gerónimo Muñoz, the sculptor; she is black and a resident of Valencia. She was imprisoned through the depositions of five witnesses, four of whom confirmed that they had heard her say many times that she had seen evil visions—including visions of a fish, a dog, and a man with a large face . . . and a child dressed in gold who showed her great treasures of silver and gold— next to a well at her master's house. Other times she saw visions in the form of a snake who was half man, with long horns, a long tail, and hair like a cat. She had good visions as well: the child Jesus, a lady dressed in white, St. Francis, St. Martin, St. Sebastian, the Magdalene and other saints. She also saw the souls of certain important people, who treated her as devoted to the Mother of God. Many people met with Catalina because of these apparitions, and asked her to tell them secret, hidden things that they desired to know. Some of them came forward as witnesses against her.

One witness saw her eating lunch and drinking wine on Good Friday, even though in public she implied that she fasted. Once, two witnesses saw her when she wanted to receive the Eucharist, and the vicar of St. Martin already had a Host in his mouth: she implied to the bystanders that they should kneel and bow in reverence to her, and [then] she held her mouth open and the said Host was in it. Catalina had spoken in secret to another witness and had said that everything she had done in her life was feigned, and she did it so that people would consider her as a saint, and as many people would come to her as possible. And Catalina told this witness that she had put the Eucharist into her [own] mouth in the church of St. Martin, [though she had] implied that God had performed a miracle.

Prior to the prosecutor's accusation, the defendant confessed that she had received the said visions. She said she considered some of them as good, because she experienced them when she pronounced the name of Our Lord and said, "See, that He was made flesh." After the prosecutor's accusation, she was charged likewise over three handkerchiefs that were found in her possession; each of the handkerchiefs bore five drops of blood in the shape of a cross. She saw and recognized these handkerchiefs in a hearing, and said the drops of blood came from applying the handkerchiefs to a pustule that she had. After she was told that [her explanation] did not seem plausible, she confessed in another hearing that she faked the handkerchiefs after hearing the news about the nun at Lisbon.[7] So that people would consider her as a

6. Ehlers, "La esclava," 114–16.

7. Sor María de la Visitación, prioress of the Convent of the Annunciation in Lisbon, who was discredited in 1588.

saint, she said that she had been given the wounds of Our Lord as a special gift, and the wounds were imprinted on the handkerchiefs after she pressed them to her side. She asked for particular forgiveness over this, and for mercy. She confessed nothing else of substance throughout her trial.[8]

The trial having been seen by *consultadores*,[9] it was voted to further investigate the question of dissimulation and a pact with the demon. In the torture room, at the beginning, she confessed that the communion at St. Martin's had been feigned in this way: she had taken a tiny piece of the Host from a child and placed it in her mouth, and when she went to receive the Eucharist and the priest came to give it to her, she implied that our Lord had miraculously given her the Host by thrashing her body about and contorting her face.

Next, she confessed about the crown of thorns that Our Lord had granted to her (fakery with which she likewise was charged.) The proof of this crown lay in some little, lentil-shaped wounds on her head; the wounds made an impression in the hairnet she wore, and her hair fell out around her head in the shape of a crown. She also confessed that at various times in church when the priest was about to consume the Eucharist, she pretended that parts of that Host went to her mouth miraculously. All the above was false and feigned so that she would seem to be a saint and be considered as such by others.

Next, she had said that Our Lord had communicated to her the agonies and afflictions that He had suffered in the garden, with which she likewise was charged. She said this was feigned like everything else; to imply to people that it was true, in the presence of some persons she feigned many anguishes and sweats, in such a way that she seemed to be dying. Another vision that appeared to her was feigned too: this one had a sword of flames, which she said was from the shepherd; and she said Our Lord was enraged against Valencia and intended to punish the city with one of three punishments—plague, fire, or hunger—and she should choose the sword that she wanted.

Next, she said that what she had said was feigned, namely that Mary Magdalene had put into her hand a vessel of ointment from which a fragrance resulted for some days. The fragrance seemed supernatural to those who entered her room, [though] to her, it smelled like something dead.[10] The odor was attested by some who smelled it, and she was charged with it. She also was charged with having said that some nights a vision appeared to her while she was praying; the vision asked her if she wished to go enjoy the Divine Spouse; when she answered yes, she was lifted by the said vision to heaven, where she

8. At least, until she was tortured. See below.

9. The theological and legal consultants, including the *ordinario*—the bishop's representative—who met with inquisitors at the end of a trial to vote upon the verdict. See Document 20.

10. On the olfactory wonders connected with holy women, see Eire, *From Madrid to Purgatory*, 425–46.

saw our Lord, Our Lady, and many saints. Going further, she allegedly saw those who were suffering in Purgatory. She said this vision was feigned.

After the trial was seen by the *consultadores,* it seemed that torture should be continued in order to lessen the suspicion that she had entered into a demonic pact.[11] As they admonished her before taking her down to the torture room, she confessed that she had made an explicit pact with the Demon and had promised him her soul in return for a private agreement that the Demon himself brought her, already written out. The written agreement remained with the Demon; it stipulated that she gave him her soul, and he in turn would tell her the answers to questions put by other people, and all this was arranged so that they would consider her a saint. She said the Demon [first] appeared to her in the shape of a naked man, and afterward he appeared many times to her in terrifying shapes. She did not fear him because she was used to seeing him. Sometimes when she invoked him, he did not come. It was agreed between them that when she called him, she would twice say, "Come, beautiful light."

And she confessed that she had deliberately separated herself from God, for Whom the soul was created; and she had promised and given her soul instead to the Devil [sic], and she had persisted for many days in this resolution. With the passage of time, she left off some [evil] things [when she felt] the stings of conscience in her heart, [but nevertheless] returned to the same determination [to belong to the Demon], and in this she went back and forth. Establishing what happened through demonic art and what was feigned, she said that as for the vessel of ointment, what really happened was that the Demon told her that he wanted to put a bit of fragrance in the palm of her hand so that for a few days the odor would seem supernatural to those who entered and she would be considered a saint. Thus the Demon put a bit of black ointment into her hand, and to all who entered, the ointment and its odor seemed a heavenly thing, [but] to her, it smelled like something dead.

Next, she affirmed that the Communion in St. Martin's was by order of the Demon, who told her that he wanted the people who went to church on a feast day to understand that Our Lord miraculously gave the Eucharist to her. The demon told her to go there and place herself next to the altar, and he would put a tiny piece of the Host, in its usual shape, into her mouth; and when the priest raised the Eucharist, she should say she had already received it, as she in fact had done. Thus when the cleric came to her, he would see the Host in her mouth that the Demon had put there. When she asked the Demon, "How would she be able to do that without being discovered?" the Demon laughed and said that it was very easy. He would also make walls open for her, and she could truly revive the dead.

---

11. False sanctity cases frequently turned into investigations into diabolic influence and demonic pacts. See the introductions to Documents 13 and 16.

Next, she affirmed that as for her claim that Our Lord had communicated the agonies and afflictions He had suffered in the garden [of Gethsemene], the truth was that the Demon occasionally caused her to be taken with fainting spells and afflictions. These afflictions were not feigned, and many times she thought she would die [from them]; people would come to bleed her, and for many days she did not return to her senses.

Next, she affirmed that her vision—of a saint who came to her with a sword of fire in his hands, and brandishing it, said he was the shepherd, and he told her to choose one of three punishments—[was false]. The truth was, the Demon persuaded her to report that [false] vision to the Patriarch [Archbishop Ribera], and told her, "[Then] she would see how she would make them all quake."[12] Afterward, when she was in the presence of Friar Ruzola, the Demon came to her and said, "Look how you have frightened them all." . . .

Next, she affirmed that the wounds of Our Lord and the crown of thorns were feigned, in the way she has confessed; so was her claim that sometimes bits of the Host came to her mouth while the cleric was consuming it; so was having said that she had gone to heaven. Being asked about the demonic pact, she said that she had believed and held it as certain that the Demon had the power to revive the dead and to know things of the future for certain; and she remained in this ignorant error and belief for some time. With tears she asked for pardon and to be restored to the body of the Church, saying with demonstrations of repentance that she wanted to live and die in the Holy Catholic Faith; she ratified her confessions in the presence of her guardian. (We judge the guardian not to have been necessary, given her appearance, since she seems to be forty years old. Not being able to find out her age, the guardian was given to her.)[13] After that ratification, four theologians who were *calificadores*[14] saw her last confessions and gave their opinion after studying them. With the *calficadores'* opinion, and the result of the consultation [among inquisitors, *consultadores,* and the *ordinario*],[15] it was voted that she be reconciled in the usual way: one hundred lashes, reclusion [in a monastery], perpetual prison and confiscation of goods.

[Added in another hand: "This black woman brought deceit and turbulence to this city so that its inhabitants would consider her a saint."][16]

12. This is the evidence that Catalina and Ribera were acquainted.

13. Document 20 addresses the provision of guardians for defendants.

14. *Calificadores* were theologians whom tribunals called upon to gauge the degree of heresy in a suspect's statements. See the Introduction

15. See the Introduction for these individuals and their role in trials.

16. In 1602, Catalina was sentenced again by the Inquisition, this time for "various sorceries"; she received two hundred lashes, the *sanbenito,* and perpetual prison. She died in March 1603. See Ehlers, "La esclava," 113–14.

Document 26

Auto de Fe Celebrated in Granada, May 27, 1593[1]

[Current research suggests that inquisition prosecutions in early modern Spain curved from conversos *to Old Christians to* conversos *again, this time from Portugal. (Which is not to minimize the ample presence of* moriscos *in such trials in the same time period.)[2] Large quantities of Portuguese* conversos *were convicted in Spanish autos de fe between 1570 and 1600, a trend that became even more marked after Spain conquered Portugal in 1580.[3] Portuguese con-versos were often much more informed about their Judaism than their Spanish counterparts; they possessed greater religious knowledge because the Portuguese Inquisition did not conduct trials efficiently and thoroughly until the 1540s. The inaction of the Inquisition allowed Portugal's* conversos *a sort of "breath-ing space" to practice Judaism, Christianity, or a hybrid of the two in relative peace.[4] Meanwhile, the fact that the Spanish Inquisition energetically pursued another population of* conversos *almost a century after it was founded raises questions as to whether this institution ever fundamentally altered its targets.*

The auto de fe, *like torture, is one of the legendary practices of the Spanish Inquisition. Recent scholarship nonetheless indicates that* autos, *like torture, were relatively rare in the early modern period, and that large crowds turned out to see them because they were exceptional events.[5] The* auto de fe *did change over time, becoming an elaborate ceremony that could last for more than a day.[6] Inquisitors valued the* auto *for obvious pedagogical and enter-tainment purposes.*

For the range of punishments handed out at autos de fe—*which the in-quisitors called penances—see the Introduction to this volume.]*

---

1. García Fuentes, *La inquisición en Granada en el siglo XVI,* 421–35.

2. See Documents 22 and 23.

3. Portuguese *conversos* were prosecuted fiercely in the seventeenth century as well; see the Introduction.

4. For the religiosity of Portuguese *conversos* who practiced Judaism in the Nether-lands, see Bodian, *Hebrews of the Portuguese Nation.*

5. Kamen, *The Spanish Inquisition,* 204–7. For an extensive treatment of the struc-tural and ritualistic aspects of the *auto,* see Bethencourt, *La Inquisición en la época moderna,* 281–367.

6. Contrast the *autos* in Documents 5 and 6, for instance, with the one narrated here.

Public *auto de fe* celebrated in the city of Granada on the feast of the Ascension of Our Lord, Jesus Christ, May 27, 1593

This *auto de fe* was announced on May 7, with a great fanfare of trumpets, kettledrums, and flutes. It was ordered that no one should give crucifixes to the penitents. When the day of the *auto de fe* arrived, many people turned out, as shall be detailed below. For the purpose of the *auto,* a very tall scaffold was made in the plaza of Vibarrambla (such scaffolds are usually built in the new plaza), next to Gomeles Street. The scaffold was of such a size that it covered the entire front of the houses next to the cathedral chapter's houses, which are fifty feet long. Three wooden rows of seating were made on top of the scaffold and joined to the houses' balconies. Then a stage was made below the rows of seats; the two secretaries' pulpits, of identical length and eight feet wide, were placed three feet apart on this stage. Then a second stage, the same length as the first and twenty feet wide, was built. Two square seating areas, which faced each other, were built at the end of the second stage; these seating areas were separated by ten feet, and were occupied by the penitents. Other platforms were built along the sides of the second stage; the inquisitors' servants [*familiares*] and others undertook this construction at their own expense in order to see. Between the stage with the rows of seats and the stage with the penitents there was a little narrow passage, two feet wide, which functioned as a privy for bodily necessities. The nobility and other secular friends of the officials sat on the stage with the rows of seats. The inquisitors, members of the Royal Chancery, and the president of the same were seated inside the cathedral chapter house.[7]

The *auto de fe* was set for the day of the Ascension of Our Lord Jesus Christ. Through all the streets of Albira and Zacatín, in all the doors of the houses, and in the entrances of the streets, platforms were constructed so that the people could see, and [still] leave room for the procession to pass by. A fence was built for the same purpose from the entrance of the Zacatín to the scaffold, in order to allow the procession to pass. Many women sat in windows and people sat on the platforms. No one carried weapons because the Holy Office had so ordered it, under threat of serious penalties.

The procession of penitents began at seven in the morning. The lesser servants [*familiares*] of the Inquisition went out first; they made room with rods of justice in their hands, and passed through the more common people who were in the streets. The common people, who came into the city from the kingdom of Granada and its surrounding territory, numbered much more than 20,000. Then the three crosses were carried out, with their arms covered

7. The Royal Chanceries in Valladolid and Granada were the two highest courts of appeals in Spain.

in black flags. Then the penitents themselves began to walk out . . . and most of them were women, and each one carried the sign of her penance. Once the penitents had finished processing, which took half an hour, the lord inquisitors walked out, accompanied by key members of the Royal Chancery and city government. First, officials from the city government, with the town's royal governor and the town council passing by. Then officials from the Royal Chancery, with its primary constable and other constables, then the governors, then the scribes and judges, and then the two most recently appointed inquisitors. The president of the Royal Chancery and the most senior inquisitor appeared last; the president walked holding the senior inquisitor's right hand. The prosecutor of the Holy Office, with the banner of the Church, preceded the lord inquisitors.

Once they all had reached the stage, Father Master[8] Castroverde, of the Augustinian order in Cáceres, preached; he had to say a few things since he was selected for that post. As he condemned the penitents' sect[s], he said— insofar as he could be understood—"Look at the law that guides you! Your apostles amount to one old garbanzo-eater, and the other a tavern-keeper," and other things of this sort. And after the audience agreed, he said, "Look at the preachers of the Catholic Faith and how learned they were, St. Jerome and the other saints." When the sermon was over, the *auto de fe* began.

The hour to eat arrived because the *auto* had so many penitents [to sentence]. They had prepared sideboards and tables and everything necessary inside the houses of the town hall, and one of the lord inquisitors went to eat with four of the Chancery judges. When they came back, they returned to their seats on the scaffold; then another inquisitor went with other judges to do the same thing, and in this way the Chancery's personnel were divided among the three inquisitors until the entire Royal Chancery had eaten. In this way, the scaffolding always had two inquisitors and members of the Chancery on it. . . . Those penanced were the following:

Penanced as blasphemers

Juan Frances, blacksmith [*calderero*], native of San Mauber in France, resident of Ronda. He denied God and His saints. He went to the *auto* shirtless, with a candle, a gag, and a rope.[9] They gave him 200 lashes.

8. The title "Master" (*maestro*) means that Castroverde had a teaching position within the Augustinian order. It is regrettable that the account of his sermon is not more complete.

9. The rope would be placed around the penitent's neck, with knots that signified the number of lashes; one knot meant 100; two, 200; and so forth (though lashings rarely involved more than 200 lashes).

Rodrigo Nuñez, tavern-keeper, resident of Granada. He said, "I vow to God that I don't believe in God."[10] Penalties: he went to the *auto* with a candle, a *sanbenito,* and hatless. Condemned to pay 10,000 *maravedís* for the expenses of the Holy Office.

Penanced over the question of the status of the matrimonial estate

Juan Sánchez, alias Rebeco, resident of Málaga. He said the married state was better and more perfect than the monastic and clerical one. Being warned that his opinion was against the Catholic Church, he confirmed it again. He deprecated monks and nuns, and relayed many infamous stories about them. He went to the *auto* with a candle. Condemned to pay forty ducats, and a year of exile from the city of Málaga and three leagues around it.

Penanced for simple fornication

Master Antonio, a Frenchman, a civilian, native of Salas, resident of the village of Gaucin. He said that asking a woman for her body and having sex with her was not a sin, saying this with lewd words. He went to the *auto* with a candle and a rope, abjured *de levi,* and they carried him to the shaming.[11]

Anton Baquero, native of Alcaudete, resident of the village of Illora. He said that it was not a sin for a man to be with a woman and pay her for it. He went to the *auto* with a candle and a rope. Abjured *de levi* and 100 lashes.

Penanced for various crimes

Juan Tremiño, native of Almagro, resident of Granada. He pretended to be a secretary of the Barcelona Inquisition, and to carry a warrant from the Suprema to collect information on an inquisitorial case. He committed fraud upon Sir Bernardino Manrique and took 600 ducats from him. He went to the *auto* with a candle and a rope. Six years in the galleys, where he once served for ten . . .

Pedro Navarro, shepherd, native of Roncevalles of the bishopric of Pamplona. . . . He said the law of Luther was very good, and it had been revealed that it was the best; he also said that the law of Luther was found in Lutheran preaching, and that Our Lord had ordained that preaching because it belonged to the Old Law; and the Christians [merely] preached what they themselves had ordained. He said that God had commanded no Mass, fasts, or disciplines, and feast days only on Sundays. He said that the world had been

---

10. For similar blasphemous formulas, see Documents 6, 14, and 15.

11. "To take someone to the shaming" means that the culprit would be tied to a column for a certain period, for the purpose of public embarrassment.

lost on account of the condition of the priesthood. He said it was not necessary to confess, but only to ask God for pardon, because only God, not the
pope or the clergy, could pardon sin. He said that Spain was full of wickedness on account of being Catholic. He went to the *auto* in a *sanbenito* with a
red flag, abjured *de vehementi,* and has been shut up for six months in a specially designated place, so he may be instructed in the Catholic Faith. . . .

Penanced for having married twice[12]

María de la Cruz, native of Almenares del Campo, resident of Granada. She
married a second and third time while her first husband was alive. She went
to the *auto* with a candle and a rope and a paper coronet.[13] She abjured *de
levi* and the bond of matrimony was referred to the bishop's representative.

Catalina López, alias Gerónima Pérez and alias Catalina de Tejada, native
of Pozuelo, next to Ciudad Real, resident of Granada. She married a second
time while her first husband was alive. She went to the *auto* with a candle
and a paper coronet. She abjured *de levi* and the bond of matrimony was referred to the bishop's representative.

Brianda de Medina, alias Ysabel de Mendoza, native of Hardales. She married a second time while her first husband was alive. She went to the *auto*
with a candle and a rope. She abjured *de levi,* received 100 lashes, and shall
serve in a specific hospital for two years.

Bartolomé Sánchez Piñero, shepherd, resident of Cohin. He married a
second time while his first wife was alive. He went to the *auto* with a candle,
a paper coronet, and a rope. He abjured *de levi,* was taken to the shaming,
and was sentenced to six years of galleys. The bond of matrimony was referred to the bishop's representative.

Juan Martínez de Pareja, seaman, resident of Almuñecar. For marrying
two times while his first wife was alive. He went to the *auto* with a candle, a
paper coronet, and a rope. He abjured *de levi,* received 100 lashes, and was
sentenced to four years of galleys. The bond of matrimony was referred to
the bishop's representative.

Reconciled for the sect of Muhammed

Beatriz de Herrera, *morisca* of the kingdom of Granada, native of Motril, resident of Málaga. She tried to go to Barbary to observe the sect of Muhammed.

12. See Document 14 for an explanation of the Inquisition's interest in moral offenses. Research into inquisition trials for bigamy in Galicia has demonstrated how
sophisticated female defendants could be when faced with this charge; see Allyson
Poska, "When Bigamy Is the Charge: Gallegan Women and the Holy Office," in
Women in the Inquisition, ed. Mary E. Giles, 189–208.

13. The *coroza* or paper coronet was a sign of infamy.

She went to the *auto* with a candle and a *sanbenito*. She was exiled ten leagues from the sea and the water's edge for the rest of her life, with the confiscation of her goods.

Reconciled for Mosaic Law

Diego Alvarez, Portuguese, silk-weaver, native of Elcaudos in Portugal, resident in Granada, as a judaizer. He went to the *auto* with a candle and a *sanbenito*, which was removed the next day.

Jusarte López, textile merchant, Portuguese, native of [Almandral], bishopric of Lomego in Portugal, resident of Granada, as a judaizer. Having confessed, he reversed himself and retracted what he had confessed, understanding that there was little proof. He went to the *auto* with a candle and a *sanbenito*, and was sentenced to irremissible perpetual prison. And he shall serve five years at the oar in the galleys, and once those five years are completed, he shall return to the Holy Office for his imprisonment.

Beatriz de Olivares, a maiden, daughter of Juan Fernández Marañon, royal scribe, resident and native of Granada, as a judaizer. She went to the *auto* with a candle and a *sanbenito*, which was removed after her sentence was read.

Ysabel Ramírez, daughter of the same Juan Fernández Marañon, resident of Granada, as a judaizer. She went to the *auto* with a candle and a *sanbenito*, which was removed the next day.

María de los Angeles, maiden, daughter of the same Juan Fernández Marañon, as a judaizer. She went to the *auto* with a candle and a *sanbenito*, which was removed the day after the *auto*.

Luisa Ramírez, wife of the same Juan Fernández Marañon and mother to the above. She went to the *auto* with a candle and a *sanbenito*, and was sentenced to prison for one year. . . .

Lady Leonor de Laguna, wife of Diego de Paniza, merchant, resident and native of Granada, judaizer. She went to the *auto* with a candle and a *sanbenito*, and was sentenced to perpetual prison.

Lady Catalina de Laguna, wife of Luis de Valdibia, public scribe of Granada, judaizer. She went to the *auto* with a candle and a *sanbenito*, and was sentenced to perpetual prison.

Catalina Nuñez, daughter of Hernan Gómez, silk-weaver, resident of Granada, judaizer. She went to the *auto* with a candle and a *sanbenito*, which was removed the day after the *auto*.

Ynés Nuñez, wife of Luis de Uzeda, resident of the village Biznar, of Granada, as a judaizer. She went to the *auto* with a candle and a *sanbenito*, which was removed later.

Gracia de Alarcon, wife of Pedro Montero, scribe, extremely beautiful

[sic],[14] native and resident of Granada, as a judaizer, with a candle and a *sanbenito*, and was sentenced to prison for two years.

Lady Mariana de Ávila, maiden, nun, daughter of Gonzalo Fernández de Baena, resident of Granada, judaizer. She went to the *auto* with a candle and a *sanbenito*, which was removed during the *auto*. . . .

Lady María Ramírez Tenerio, daughter of Jorge López, jurist and silk merchant, Portuguese, resident of Granada, as a judaizer. She went to the *auto* with a candle and a *sanbenito*, which was removed later.

Lady Leonor de Olivares, maiden, daughter of Simon López, Portuguese, resident of Granada, as a judaizer. She went to the *auto* with a candle and a *sanbenito*, which was removed later.

Lady Beatriz Enríquez, daughter of Francisco López, Portuguese, merchant, wife of Diego de Mercado, resident of Granada. Judaizer with a candle and a *sanbenito*, which was removed later. . . .

Lady Ynés de Torres, wife of Diego Adame, who died in the prison of the Inquisition. She went to the *auto* in effigy for judaizing, with a *sanbenito* which was removed once her sentence was read, because she confessed and died as a Catholic, with many signs of contrition. . . .

Gaspar de Laguna, a boy, son of Juan de Laguna, silk merchant, resident of Granada, a judaizer since he was seven and he is now fourteen. Candle and *sanbenito*, removing it afterward.

Diego Nuñez, Portuguese maker of sweets, native of Marcalba in Portugual, resident of Granada, for judaizing with the rites and ceremonies of Mosaic Law. He went to the *auto* with a candle and a *sanbenito*, and was sentenced to prison for one year.

Juan de Torres, paymaster for the army of the kingdom of Granada, resident of the same, son of Blas de Torres, for judaizing. Candle and *sanbenito*, which was removed the day after the *auto*.

Fernando de Jaén, royal administrator of former mosques in this city; he had judaized for forty years. A candle and a *sanbenito*, and sentenced to prison for three years.

Licentiate Juan Fernández de Arenas, lawyer, resident of Córdoba, *corregidor* [royal governor] who used to live in Palma; he had judaized for thirty-six years. A candle and a *sanbenito*, which was removed the next day.

Relaxed to the secular arm in effigy[15] for being judaizers who fled

Pedro Alvarez, Portuguese, resident of Antequera. Fugitive, judaizer. Burned in effigy.

14. *Hermosa en extremo.* See García Fuentes, *La inquisición en Granada en el siglo XVI,* 429.

15. These remaining categories feature defendants who were sentenced to the most

Blanca de Sierra, wife of the same, burned in effigy for judaizing.

Relaxed in effigy with the burning of their bones, for judaizing

Ynés Nuñez de Naxera, widow of Hernando Benítez, weaver, resident of Granada, mother of the woman they call "The Patch-Faced." Died in prison, judaizer, bones burned and burned in effigy.

Lady Constancia de Herrera, wife of Alonso Sánchez, administrator of the property which His Majesty the King possesses in this kingdom of Granada. Died in prison, judaizer, bones burned and burned in effigy.

Relaxed in person as judaizers

Marina de Mercado, the woman called "The Patch-Faced," wife of García de Pareja, daughter of Ynés Nuñez de Naxera, resident of Granada. Judaizer who denied the charges, convicted by her witnesses, burned in person. She was a dogmatizer.

María Nuñez, wife of Hernando Gómez, weaver of silks, resident of Granada. Judaizer who denied the charges, convicted, burned in person.

Ysabel Rodríguez, wife of Juan de Quesada, silk merchant, very rich [sic], resident of Granada. Judaizer who denied the charges, convicted on account of rituals, burned in person.

Beatriz Nuñez, widow of Pedro Alvarez, Portuguese, resident of Granada. Relapsed judaizer, burned in person.[16] She was penanced the first time in Lisbon.

Clara Fernández, widow of Jorge de Irsar, Portuguese, resident of Granada. Relapsed judaizer, penanced in Portugal, burned in person.

Lady Ynés Alvarez, wife of Tomás Martínez, constable, judaizer. She went to the *auto* with a paper coronet that signified burning, because she denied the charges. Then she confessed on the scaffolding, and they returned her to the Holy Office without the coronet.[17] She is the sister of Alonso Sánchez' wife; the Inquisition burned her mother.

---

severe punishment available—death by burning at the stake, called "relaxation to the secular arm"—for being unrepentant heretics. Some of those who were relaxed were absent, either through death or flight; they were represented in effigy at the *auto de fe*.

16. Relaxation to the secular arm was the mandatory penalty for individuals who had been reconciled to the Church and then relapsed back into heresy.

17. As the instructions of the Spanish Inquisition make clear, the inquisitors were supposed to listen carefully to any confession made at any time by a suspect, though the same inquisitors could also decide whether to treat that confession as sincere or feigned. See Document 7.

All the people named in this memorial are Jews, descendants of Jewish parents and grandparents who were burned, penanced, and declared as [judaizers] by the Holy Office, by tribunals in Granada, Toledo, and other parts. All this was stated in their sentences.

All the Jews who appeared in this *auto de fe* confessed and observed the following:

First, that there is one all-powerful God, and they deny the plurality and distinction of the three persons, as well as the mystery, of the Trinity.

Second, that they have to observe Mosaic Law; they cannot be saved without it.

Third, they deny the sacraments of evangelical law and [state] that there is no need for vows of chastity, since only matrimony conforms to Mosaic Law. And confessors have no power to pardon sins. For this reason [the Jews] confess only lightweight things, in order to make fun of confession and out of fear of the Inquisition.

Fourth, they deny in general the adoration of statues, saying it is only a matter of gold, silver, or wood.

Fifth, they deny the sacrament of the altar, saying that the bread is only bread. When they appear to adore the Eucharist, they [actually] say "I see a cake of bread, but I believe in and adore God." The same thing occurs with the wine, as they say "I see water and wine, but I believe in and adore Adonai."[18]

Sixth, they deny that the Messiah has come. Thus they say that Jesus Christ is purely a man, a son of Our Lady and St. Joseph. Some say that his father was someone else, that he is the child of adultery. They deny the virginity of the Most Holy Virgin Mary, Our Lady.

Seventh, some say that Jesus Christ did not die for the redemption of men, but he was replaced by someone else when the Passion occurred. Because if Jesus were God, then he must [also] have been a man who could not die; otherwise, God had to die. Thus they say that another man was crucified in the place of [Jesus], who fled.

Eighth, they observed the Sabbath with great care. They fasted Mondays and Thursdays, and all the first days of the moon, without eating until nightfall. Meat was not eaten during these fasts, nor did they eat fish that lacked scales, such as shark, eel, dogfish, striped fish, and cuttlefish;[19] they say that these bottom-feeders are as filthy as a menstruating woman.

18. Aphorisms in Spanish, to wit: "Una torta de pan veo, en Dios adoro y creo," and "Agua y vino veo, en Adonay adoro y creo." See García Fuentes, *La inquisición en Granada en el siglo XVI*, 434.

19. See the introduction to Document 3 for general remarks on Jewish dietary laws.

Ninth, they fasted in honor of Queen Esther in the month of July; the fast lasted three days, and they ate when the moon appeared.

Tenth, they observed the major fast of Ramadan[20] in the month of September, along with the fast of Queen Esther.

Eleventh, they celebrated the Passover of the Lamb on the day of the first moon in March. They ate unleavened bread, following the same ceremonies of Mosaic Law.

Twelfth, they didn't eat the flesh of strangled animals, only decapitated and defatted ones When they decapitate a bird, the person who does it places the bird toward the sun with his knife. They didn't eat partridge, pork, rabbit, or hare, or the flesh of many other animals, nor do they permit anyone to bring them a quarter of an animal . . . because there are nerves in the legs. If they bring legs, they remove the nerves, because they say the nerves make people crazy. They tell this to their servants, and they prohibit long and short sausages.

Thirteenth, they say that when a woman has her menstrual period, she can neither pray nor look at heaven, because it would be a sin. Nor can women sleep with their husbands during the six days of menstruation, and on the seventh day, they wash their entire body in waters . . . [manuscript missing] under the arm, they dress in clean clothing and put clean clothing on the bed, new clothing if they have it. And they pray because God created the world in six days and on the seventh, He rested.

Fourteenth, some say that after a death they have to take down the tapestries that were hanging where the dead lay. They have to wash the extremities and underarms of the dead. They must also shroud the dead with new cloth, and throw all the water out of the house along with the water of the seven surrounding houses. They have to drink water recently brought from the well for seven days. People who were present at the death cannot eat flesh for seven days, nor pray to God.

Fifteenth, they pray all their prayers with Hebrew words, repeating "Adonai." They say some verses from the Psalter in Spanish, and say the penitential psalms without the "Glory be to the Father."

Besides the penalties named above, all the men and women who judaized were condemned to have all their goods confiscated for the King, [amassed] from the time they began to judaize.

---

20. Of course, Ramadan is the major fast of Islam. Attributing that fast to judaizing *conversos* may imply that inquisitors were amalgamating the ceremonies of these two non-Christian religions, or were simply confused.

INDEX